THE GOVERNMENT OF EUROPEAN CITIES

THE MACMILLAN COMPANY
NEW YORK · BOSTON · CHICAGO
ATLANTA · SAN FRANCISCO

MACMILLAN & CO., Limited
LONDON · BOMBAY · CALCUTTA
MELBOURNE

THE MACMILLAN CO. OF CANADA, Ltd.
TORONTO

THE

GOVERNMENT OF EUROPEAN CITIES

BY

WILLIAM BENNETT MUNRO, Ph.D., LL.B.

ASSISTANT PROFESSOR OF GOVERNMENT
IN HARVARD UNIVERSITY

New York

THE MACMILLAN COMPANY

1909

Norwood Press
J. S. Cushing Co. — Berwick & Smith Co.
Norwood, Mass., U.S.A.

To

W. S. M.

Comrade of student days

PREFACE

THE purpose of this volume is to explain, in a general way, the structure and functions of city government in three European countries, and to contrast these, wherever they may be appropriately compared, with the structure and functions of city government in the United States. It has been my aim to describe who the city authorities are, how they are chosen, what they do, and how they do it; but not to examine in detail the physical operation of municipal services or the minutiæ of municipal administration. Considerable attention has been devoted to the relations of the civic and state authorities in each of these countries; for the writer believes that this is one of the most important of all the phases of local administration.

The book is intended to afford an introduction to the study of European city governments, and no attempt has been made to deal in exhaustive fashion with any aspect of the subject. To bring the narrative within reasonable compass it has been necessary to omit many matters of some importance, and to deal in a paragraph with other things which might well have a page. With this in mind an endeavor has been made to indicate in the footnotes convenient sources from which further information may be drawn by readers who may become interested in any part of the general field.

In the task of preparing the volume I have received generous and valued assistance from many quarters. To Professor H. Berthélemy of the University of Paris and

to M. Léon Morgand I am greatly indebted for their kind-
ness in giving careful scrutiny to that portion of the
volume which describes the government of French cities.
Dr. Hugo Preuss of Berlin and Judge Walter Neitzel of
Strassburg have given me much-appreciated assistance in
the revision of the chapter relating to Prussian city government; while that part of the book which deals with the
government of English boroughs owes considerable to the
helpful suggestions made upon its proof sheets by Mr.
Percy W. L. Ashley of the Board of Trade and by Mr.
F. W. Hirst of London.   It is only fair to these gentlemen
to add, however, that they are in no way responsible for
the expressions of opinion which the book contains.   To
my kind friend and senior colleague, Professor A. Lawrence
Lowell, I am extremely grateful for assistance and encouragement at all stages of the work.   In routine matters connected with the publication of the book, Miss
A. F. Rowe of Cambridge and Miss Magdeleine Carret of
Wellesley College have given me much useful aid.

WILLIAM BENNETT MUNRO.

January 5, 1909.

CONTENTS

ix

GOVERNMENT OF EUROPEAN CITIES

CHAPTER I

THE GOVERNMENT OF FRENCH CITIES

THE student of contemporary municipal administration in France finds it hardly necessary to pursue the course of civic development farther back than the period of the Revolution; for this great political upheaval created in the sphere of local government, as in the other domains of French administration, an almost complete break in the continuity of institutional history. Prior to the Revolution France had practically no system of local government; in the various provinces the cities were administered in widely different ways, the centralization of powers in the hands of the royal authorities being much more nearly complete in some places than in others. Even within the bounds of a single province, moreover, the form as well as the spirit of communal administration showed considerable variation. There was, indeed, no approach to uniformity save in the fact that local autonomy was almost everywhere absent, and that in no part of the kingdom was there any security against the captious interference of some higher authority in affairs of purely local concern.[1] The

The Revolution and the reform of local government.

City government during the old régime.

---

[1] Details concerning the administration of the larger communes, or cities, during the century preceding the Revolution may be found in Albert Babeau's

turmoils of the Revolutionary era left the physical boundaries of the communes without any important alterations;
but communal administration carried over into the new
régime scarcely a single heritage of the old.

Work of
the Con-
stituent
Assembly
in 1789.
One of the first undertakings of the Constituent
Assembly, on the threshold of the Revolution, was to
destroy, root and branch, the old methods of local government and to supplant them by a system that should be
democratic, uniform, and symmetrical. In this reorganization, effected in 1789, the 44,000 or more traditional
local units known as the *paroisses,* or *communautés d'habi-
tants,* were utilized as irreducible areas of local self-government, and were provided with a uniform framework of
administration. According to the provisions of the law of
1789, each commune was thenceforth to have a mayor and
council chosen by the citizens upon a basis which came
very close to manhood franchise; for only the very poorest
among the citizens were excluded by the small property
qualification prescribed.[1] It was, indeed, the design of the
law to treat the communes as miniature republics, with
power to select their own local rulers, and with authority
to manage their own affairs free from any interference on
the part of the higher officials. The striking feature of
the law of 1789 was, therefore, the provision which it made
for a system of local government at once democratic and

La ville sous l'ancien régime (Paris, 1880). See also Amédée Gasquet's *Précis
des institutions politiques et sociales de l'ancienne France* (2 vols., Paris, 1885);
Achille Luchaire's *Les communes françaises* (Paris, 1890) ; Adhémar Esmein's
Histoire du droit français (8th ed., Paris, 1908) ; and H. Berthélemy's *Traité de
droit administratif* (5th ed., Paris, 1908), especially pp. 179 ff.

[1] *Décret sur les municipalités* (December 14, 1789). The terms of this decree
may be found in J. B. Duvergier's *Collection complète des lois, décrets, ordonnances, règlements, avis du conseil d'état* (107 vols., Paris, 1834–1907), I. 63–67 ;
and in F. A. Hélie's *Les constitutions de la France* (Paris, 1880), I. 59–72.
An English translation is printed in F. M. Anderson's *Constitutions and other
Select Documents illustrative of the History of France* (Minneapolis, 1904),
24–33.

decentralized.[1] During the years 1789–1790 this plan was applied to all the communes of France, large and small.

Like most of the legislation of the Constituent Assembly, the decree reorganizing the system of municipal government attempted a step too advanced for the actual conditions of French political life at the time. The new plan intrusted too much unsupervised power to a people almost entirely unaccustomed to the art of managing its own local affairs. In obedience to the Revolutionary passion for equality and uniformity, the framers of the decree of 1789 seem to have lost sight of the important differences in needs and problems between urban and rural communities; for they sought to apply to all alike a framework of administration which hardly sufficed for the former and was much too complex for the latter. The most cardinal defect of the system, however, lay in its almost entire abolition of effective central control over the municipalities, a step that deprived the authorities at Paris of the powers necessary to check the local disorders with which France was convulsed during the next four or five years.[2] Indeed, even after the passing of more than a century the French people have not proved themselves fitted either by temperament or by experience to carry out smoothly a plan of local self-government such as that which the Assembly sought to establish in 1789.

The reorganization of 1789 too sweeping.

Its chief faults.

The lapse of a few years served amply to disclose the inherent defects of the new law, for the system which it established proved quite unequal to the strain and stress put upon it during the stormy days of the Terror. Hence,

Changes made by the Directory in 1795.

[1] By the law of 1789 the *communautés*, which had hitherto been in no case more than personal agglomerations, became recognized territorial units, though some of them contained only two or three houses.

[2] On the working of this system during the period 1789–1795, see E. Lavisse and A. Rambaud's *Histoire générale du IVe siècle à nos jours* (12 vols., Paris, 1896–1908), VIII. 79 ff.

when the Directory intrenched itself in control of the national administration in 1795, it lost little time in devising a plan of local government which should endeavor to eliminate much of the spirit of democracy and decentralization that had characterized its immediate predecessor. In its new constitution, therefore, it inserted a number of provisions dealing with the organization of local government.[1] The principle of permitting citizens to elect their own local officials was retained, but the control of the central authorities over these officers was greatly strengthened. Under the new arrangement the canton replaced the commune as the basal unit of local government. Every urban community of any considerable size was made a canton, with its administration vested in the hands of a cantonal directory of from five to nine members elected by the citizens ; and the smaller communes (including all those of less than 5000 population) were grouped into cantons, thus losing their autonomy and becoming mere administrative divisions of the larger areas. The three largest cities of France — Paris, Lyons, and Marseilles — were each divided into three or more municipalities, with a special administration designed to insure the possibility of stricter supervision by the national Directory.

Chief features of the new system.

Although the arrangements of 1795 had their undoubted merits in that they rendered easier the task of maintaining local peace and order, the new system was not generally popular. The canton was a purely arbitrary division, with no historical traditions and no homogeneity of feeling. The commune was the only local unit to which Frenchmen owed any sentimental allegiance; and in failing to utilize it as the basis of local administration the

The new system an improvement.

---

[1] *Constitution du 5 fructidor, de l'an III* (August 22, 1795), in Duvergier's *Collection*, VIII. 223–242 ; printed also in Hélie's *Constitutions*, I. 466–493, and Anderson's *Constitutions and Documents*, 212–254.

national authorities seriously impaired the effectiveness
of the new policy. Although the plan of 1795 affords some
evidence that a spirit of constructive statesmanship was beginning to make itself felt in official circles at Paris, the
whole arrangement is characterized too prominently by
marks of a tendency to experiment. The inauguration of
the new scheme was, however, a tacit confession that communal autonomy could not safely be continued, and that
the decree of 1789 had too greatly weakened the lines
of central control.

The system of municipal government established by the The law of
Directory remained in existence until 1800 only, when the $^{1800.}$
advent of Napoleon Bonaparte to the executive headship
of French affairs as first consul dictated a further change.[1]
In some respects the Napoleonic reorganization may be
looked upon as a development of the system of 1795;
for it elaborated and in some measure strengthened the
lines of national control over local officers, and it went
a step farther than its immediate predecessor by setting
aside entirely the elective principle in local government.
In some other respects, however, it reverted to the arrangements made in 1789, for it made the commune again
the fundamental unit of local administration. The cantonal divisions were retained ; but they became, under the
Napoleonic system, merely judicial districts. It was ar- Characteris-
ranged that every commune, large or small,[2] should thence- Napoleonic
forth intrust the administration of its affairs to a mayor system.
and one or more adjoints, associated with a municipal
council of ten, twenty, or thirty members according to the
population of the municipality; but, since in all cases the

[1] *Constitution du 28 pluviôse, de l'an VIII* (February 17, 1800), printed in
Duvergier's *Collection*, XII. 78–116 ; Hélie's *Constitutions*, I. 611–626 ; and
Anderson's *Constitutions and Documents*, 283–288.

[2] By the elimination of the smallest ones, the number of recognized communes
was now reduced from 44,000 to 36,000.

mayor, adjoints, and councillors were to be appointed
either by the central government or by its departmental
agents, the elimination of local election was about as
nearly complete as it had been under the old régime.

Adminis-
trative cen-
tralization.
The most striking feature of the Bonapartist system of
communal government was the establishment of effective
machinery by means of which the strictest sort of control
and supervision might be exercised from Paris over all the
organs of local administration. To this end the departments (administrative districts into which France had been
divided by the Revolutionary government) were each provided with an executive official directly appointed by the
national authorities and responsible to them alone. These
The pre-
fects.
officers, thenceforth known as prefects, differed but little
either in method of appointment or in the wide scope of
their powers from the much-maligned intendants of the
Bourbon era ; and their elevation to rank as the strongest
link in the chain of Napoleonic administration affords an
interesting illustration of the way in which a violent re-
action against administrative centralization succeeded, in
the long run, only in securing the reëstablishment of an
old office under a new designation. Each department was,
moreover, by the law of 1800, parcelled out into new administrative divisions called arrondissements, each with a
The sub-
prefects.
subprefect, who was vested with jurisdiction substantially
similar to that possessed by the subdelegates of the old
dominion, and who now became local deputy of the prefect. Through the prefects and subprefects the hand of
the central government was able to hold the municipalities with a tight rein : the whole arrangement combined
simplicity and symmetry with extreme centralization.

Permanence
of the
Napoleonic
system.
The Napoleonic system of local administration deserves
more than a passing mention ; for not only have many if
not most of its salient features been retained in France

down to the present time, but its influence upon the local- Its influence outside of France. government policies of other countries — of Italy, Belgium, Spain, Greece, Japan, and the South American republics, for instance — has also been marked. Judged by its qualities of permanence and by its influence abroad, the law of 1800 is one of the best examples of Bonaparte's creative statesmanship, taking rank with the Code and the Concordat among his enduring non-military achievements. If, in the nineteenth century, England has been the mother of parliaments and has exercised a dominant influence upon the evolution of national governments, France has had an equally important rôle in moulding systems of local administration among the nations.

The fall of the Napoleonic Empire did not bring about Changes during the period 1815-1848. any important changes in local government; for, although the restored Bourbons now resumed charge of French national affairs with a sweeping curtailment of the old royal prerogatives, their parliaments authorized no important concessions to the principle of local autonomy. The Napoleonic system of strict prefectoral supervision over the municipalities, and of appointive local officers, was retained intact; it was, indeed, only after the upheaval of 1830, when the Bourbons gave way to the Citizen King of the Orleanists, that the first substantial departure from the imperial policy was effected. By an act passed in 1831, provision was made that the municipal councillors should thenceforth be elected indirectly by such citizens of the commune as possessed certain prescribed property or educational qualifications. The mayors and adjoints were to be appointed, as before, by the national authorities upon recommendation of the prefects; but they were to be chosen only from among the membership of the municipal councils. No lessening in the strictness of central control over municipal affairs was provided for in this enactment; but some six years later a limited amount of independent jurisdiction, especially in the matter of initiating local projects, was intrusted to the councils of communes.

Local government under the Second Republic.

When France again became a republic in 1848, the new republican constitution made explicit provision that in all municipal elections the principle of manhood suffrage should have full recognition.[1] Accordingly, in all the communes councillors were for the time being elected by the adult male citizens; and, as a further step in the direction of decentralization, the municipal councils in communes of not more than 6000 inhabitants were permitted to select their own mayors and adjoints without any interference on the part of the prefects. In the larger municipalities these officials continued to be appointed from above,—always, however, from the ranks of the local councils. By these arrangements municipal government received very substantial concessions in the direction of democracy and autonomy; but its newly-acquired privileges proved of short duration, for in less than five years

The Second Empire.

the Second Republic had become the Second Empire, and the change in the spirit of national administration soon reflected itself in the domain of local government. In 1852 the smaller communes lost the privilege of choosing their

Changes made by Napoleon III.

own mayors; and in the same year the national government abolished the practice of restricting its choice of mayors and adjoints in the larger municipalities to the membership of the councils.[2] It is true that throughout the period of the Second Empire (1852–1870) elections in all the municipalities were conducted upon what was,

---

[1] *Constitution de la République française* (November 4, 1848), § 79, in Duvergier's *Collection*, XLVIII. 560–609; Hélie's *Constitutions*, II. 1102–1129; and Anderson's *Constitutions and Documents*, 522–538.

[2] *Constitution du 14 janvier 1852*, Titre VIII. § 57, in Hélie's *Constitutions*, II. 1171.

in theory at any rate, a basis of manhood suffrage; but the trend of development during this era was, on the whole, very distinctly in the direction of renewed centralization. The powers of the municipal council were, indeed, somewhat extended in 1867, but hand in hand with this expansion went a stiffening of the prefectoral control over this local organ. In fact, throughout the Second Empire the prefectoral system was infused with a new vigor and vitality, and the office of prefect became the real pivotal point of all local administration. The municipal councils did little more during this period than approve the local budgets which were submitted to them each year by the administrative authorities; for, although they were technically entitled to the exercise of a free hand in dealing with municipal funds, they were really subservient to the higher officials, whose constant and effectual interference in the conciliar elections served to make the latter mere travesties, and secured, in the larger cities at least, the selection of councillors who responded readily to the requests of the imperial agents. In the realm of national government the era of the Second Empire witnessed the all but complete extinction of free political life, and the same decadence manifested itself in the areas of local administration. During the late sixties, to be sure, when the empire was tottering to its fall, the baneful effects of a policy which had served utterly to repress the principle of local self-government became so apparent even to the emperor himself that a hastily planned movement along the paths of decentralization marked the closing years of the imperial régime; but in spite of this concession the municipalities of France found themselves in 1870 as completely under the hand of the central authorities as they had been at any time since 1830. The intervening forty years, an epoch of striking economic advance and of

Increased centralization.

Extinction of local autonomy.

the most substantial progress in the modernization of the French cities, had been marked by no important improvements in the system of local administration.

Local government under the Third Republic. The National Assembly that in 1871 assumed charge of the political affairs of France, which had been so badly disorganized by the German invasion and the fall of the empire, found that a revision or a recasting of the whole municipal system was one of the urgent matters demanding its attention. As it was not, however, in a favorable position to proceed with the elaboration of any new and comprehensive municipal code, it decided, as a temporary expedient, to revive, with some few changes, the plan established in 1848.[1] Among the alterations effected **Tentative measures of 1871.** the most important was that which permitted the councils in the smaller communes to select their own mayors and adjoints. In cities of over 20,000 population, and in the chief towns of departments and *arrondissements*, these officials were to hold their appointments, as before, from the higher authorities. Local terms of office were also shortened, both mayors and councillors being restricted to **Centralized features retained.** three-year terms.[2] This plan of 1871 seems to show that, in a large measure, centralization of local government in France had come to stay. To the grant of a large measure of communal autonomy the Assembly was on principle very favorable, but there were those among its leaders who feared to carry the principle into practice.

The temporary arrangements made in 1871 may be said to have served their purpose in compromising matters until the new republican government should have become firmly intrenched. During the decade following the establishment of the Third Republic, however, the central au-

[1] *Cf.* above, p. 8.
[2] *Loi du 14 avril 1871*, in Duvergier's *Collection*, LXXI. 71–79, and Anderson's *Constitutions and Documents*, 612–618.

thorities found their policy of supervising the affairs of the larger cities often difficult to enforce. The spirit of municipal home rule asserted itself, and the national government frequently forestalled trouble only by a tame compliance with its demands.[1] Under the presidency of McMahon the republican ministry showed a disposition to check this drift toward municipal independence effectually; for in 1874 the National Assembly concurred in the passage of a law reviving the right of the president to appoint the mayors and adjoints in the smaller municipalities.[2] The general elections of 1876, however, established in power a national administration more favorable to communal autonomy, and the legislation of 1874 was at once repealed.[3] Eight years later the government followed with the additional concession of permitting every commune, large or small (with the exception of Paris), to select its own administrative officers without interference from outside.[4]

The law of 1874.

Its speedy repeal.

About this time important difficulties in the way of a proper and exact administration of municipal affairs were continually arising from the fact that there had not since 1837 been any thorough revision and codification of local-government law.[5] Every enactment relating to civic administration had been in the nature either of an amendment to the laws immediately preceding, or of a revival of some arrangement belonging to an even earlier period; hence the whole system rested upon a bewildering mass of laws and decrees made and revised by monarchi-

Disorganized condition of the laws relating to municipal administration.

---

[1] On the workings of the system, see Gabriel Hanotaux's *Contemporary France*, I. 235 ff.

[2] *Loi sur les maires* (January 20, 1874), in Duvergier's *Collection*, LXXIV. 2–4.

[3] *Loi relative à la nomination des maires et des adjoints* (August 12, 1876), *Ibid.* LXXVI. 268–271.

[4] *Loi relative à la nomination*, etc. (March 28, 1882), *Ibid.* LXXXII. 116–118.

[5] The codification of 1837 had been somewhat revised in 1867.

cal, imperial, and republican governments. Leading statesmen of the republic recognized clearly enough the need

**Recodifica-
tion of the
laws pro-
posed.**

of a complete revision and codification of the jurisprudence relating to municipal administration; but upon the
fundamental question of the degree to which the principle
of local home rule ought to receive recognition in the proposed code the various factions in the national parliament
were committed to somewhat divergent views. In No-

**The com-
mission of
1883.**

vember, 1883, however, it was decided to appoint a commission of nine members, to which should be intrusted
the whole task of revising and collaborating the various
enactments into a comprehensive municipal code.

**The munici-
pal code
of April 5,
1884.**

This commission completed its work early in the following year; and the measure which it laid before the
French parliament was, with some modifications, passed
by both houses and duly promulgated on April 5, 1884,[1]
shortly after which an elaborate ministerial circular was
issued giving full explanations in regard to the provisions
of the compilation.[2]   The municipal code of 1884 is distinguished by its comparative brevity, its comprehensiveness,

**Its general
features.**

and its simplicity.   It contains in all only one hundred
and fifty-seven sections or articles, most of them very brief,
the whole excellently arranged and furnishing a model of
terse expression.   Since 1884 several amendments to it
have been made; but in all its essentials it is at the

**Not appli-
cable to
Paris.**

present time the basis of all village, town, and city government in France.[3]   The only city excepted from its opera-

---

[1] *Loi sur l'organisation municipale du 5 avril 1884*, in Duvergier's *Collection*, LXXXIV. 99–148.

[2] *Circulaire ministérielle du 15 mai 1884, sur l'application de la loi municipale* (Paris, 1889).

[3] The best commentary on the municipal code of 1884 is Léon Morgand's
La loi municipale (7th ed., 2 vols., Paris, 1907).   A convenient handbook,
which includes the texts of various important ministerial circulars interpret-
ing the law, is Ferdinand Dreyfus's *Manuel populaire du conseiller municipal*
(Paris, 1904).

tions was the capital, which still retains a *régime exceptionnel* based upon legislation prior to that of 1884.[1]

Under the provisions of the code of 1884 the unit of municipal government in France is the commune, a term which is, of course, very comprehensive, for it includes not only small hamlets with a few dozen inhabitants, but large cities like Lyons, Marseilles, and Bordeaux, with populations well above the quarter-million mark. By the last census no less than 36,222 local areas were rated as communes, of which somewhat more than one-half had populations not exceeding 500; and of these 137 had less than fifty inhabitants each.   On the other hand, 250 communes contained more than 10,000 people apiece, and fourteen had populations exceeding 100,000 each.   France, it should be borne in mind, is even at the present day a predominantly rural country ; for only slightly more than one-fourth of her population is massed into the urban communities of above 10,000 population,[2] — a percentage smaller than that of England, Germany, or even of the United States.   The progress of urban concentration, so marked in other countries, has in France been less striking, and for obvious reasons.   For one thing, the total population of the republic has gained very slowly during the last three decades or more, a fact which has in recent years given French statesmen some grounds for apprehension. The country has had no important foreign influx ; on the contrary, there has been some exodus to Algeria and to the other French possessions beyond the seas.   The main cause of tardy urban growth may, however, be found in the fact that industrially and commercially France has scarcely kept pace with her Teutonic sister states, — and

The commune.

Variations in the size of communes.

Proportion of urban to rural population in France.

Causes of slow urban growth.

---

[1] See below, p. 91.

[2] *La situation financière des communes de France en 1906* (published by the Ministère de l'Intérieur, Paris, 1907).

during the nineteenth century, as has frequently been pointed out, industry and commerce have been the handmaids of city expansion.[1]

Uniformity in the French municipal system.
The policy of attempting to provide, by the terms of a single enactment, for the efficient administration of all local units of population, no matter how widely different their people and their problems, is perhaps a logical outcome of that passion for uniformity which has somewhat strongly characterized French administrative methods since the Revolution. Such a policy might reasonably have been expected to encounter serious difficulties, but on the whole it has not done so. The machinery of local government in France is undoubtedly too complex and cumbrous for the thousands of small communes, most of which, like the English parishes, are too diminutive to serve properly as administrative units.[2] On the other hand, it is perhaps not elaborate enough for the largest municipalities;

Disadvantages of a uniform system.
for on more than one occasion the national authorities have made some changes in local administrative machinery, notably in the case of Marseilles, which has very recently been deprived of its control of local police mainly because the communal authorities did not seem, in the eyes of the national government, to be entirely competent in their administration of this service.[3] At the same time, some degree of elasticity has been possible from the fact that, although all municipalities, large and small, have similar organs of government, the membership of the municipal council depends roughly upon the size of the commune. Much is said in the United States about the impossibility of providing, in a general charter law,

[1] The causes of modern city growth are elaborately discussed in Adna F. Weber's *Growth of Cities in the Nineteenth Century* (New York, 1899), ch. iii.

[2] A discussion of this subject may be found in Alfred Porche's *La question des grandes et des petites communes* (Paris, 1900).

[3] See below, p. 73.

for the satisfactory administration of all classes of cities. How, then, would the legislators of an American state regard a proposal to establish a uniform framework of administration applicable not only to all cities of whatever size, but to towns and villages as well? This, nevertheless, is what the French municipal code has done, and with no very evil results. It should be borne in mind, however, that the French system has not been subjected to any severe strain; for the population of the cities has grown very slowly and evenly, and has retained its homogeneity of character.

The municipal code, as has been said, treats all municipal units (with the exception of Paris) as communes, a term for which even Frenchmen have not found it easy to give a concise and comprehensive definition. The commune is, however, the smallest territorial division of the republic, all other sections — cantons, *arrondissements*, and departments — being multiples of it; at the same time, it may cover a whole canton or even several cantons, the canton in that case becoming a division of the commune. Again, the commune has both a territorial and a personal basis. On the one hand, it is a tract of territory the precise limits of which were defined by the law of December 22, 1789, or by some subsequent law or decree; for by the law of 1789 all local units which had a separate identity during the old régime were authoritatively recognized as communes, and since that enactment there have been a number of suppressions, divisions, consolidations, and creations of communal units. On the other hand, the commune is an agglomeration of citizens united by life in a common locality and having a common interest in the communal property. A commune ranks as a legal person : it may sue and be sued, may contract, acquire, or convey property, — it may, in general, exercise all the ordinary rights of a corporation. For the

Definition of the commune.

A territorial and personal unit.

sacredness of communal traditions the provisions of the
code display marked consideration, permitting changes in
boundaries by the higher departmental authorities only after
an elaborate *enquête* has been held and the local feeling
consulted,[1] and providing that even the name of the municipality may not be altered save by a special decree of the
president of the republic.[2]

Framework of communal government. By the terms of the municipal code the organs of administration in all communes consist of a council, a mayor,
and one or more adjoints or assistants to the mayor. In
the laws prior to 1884 the mayor and adjoints were
named before the council as organs of communal administration; and the reversal of this order in the code of 1884
was designed to emphasize the view of the national authorities that the council was thenceforth to be regarded as
the more important branch of local government.[3] Though
it may be doubted whether this intention has been fully
realized, the council, nevertheless, in view of the fact that
it selects the mayor and adjoints, takes rank as the pivotal
organ of the municipality. Its composition and powers
may, therefore, be considered first.

The communal council. The size of the French municipal council depends roughly
upon the population of the municipality, and ranges from
ten to thirty-six members.[4] Communes with populations
Its size. below 500 have ten councillors; in the larger municipalities the number increases according to a graduated scale,
until in cities of 60,000 or over the council has thirty-six
members.[5] All cities above this figure in population

[1] *La loi municipale*, §§ 3–9.
[2] *Ibid.* § 2. See also Albert Ramalho on " Des changements de nom des
communes," in *Revue générale d'administration*, 1896, III. 5 ff.
[3] The *Circulaire ministérielle du 15 mai 1884* makes this clear.
[4] *La loi municipale*, § 10.
[5] By the census of 1901 there were twenty-four cities with populations exceeding 60,000 each.

have uniformly thirty-six councillors, with the single exception of Lyons, which has fifty-four. Save Paris and Lyons, therefore, all the larger cities of France have councils of uniform size, — a size, it may be noted, which is somewhat smaller than that of the municipal council in Germany, England, or the United States.

Members of the council are elected for a four-year term, and there is no provision for a partial renewal. The election usually takes place by *scrutin de liste*, or on a general ticket for the whole municipality ; but in a city of more than 10,000 population a division into electoral districts or wards may be made.[1] Since, however, each ward must elect no less than four councillors, there may not be more than nine wards or electoral districts even in the largest cities. Some of the great cities have been thus divided into wards, but there are still many large municipalities in which no division has been made. Frenchmen have, apparently, not yet reached agreement as to the relative merits of the ward and general-ticket systems. In England, Germany, and the United States the ward method has been adopted almost everywhere in the election of city councillors ; but in at least nine-tenths of the French municipalities the general-ticket plan is maintained. In scores of these cities twenty or more councillors are balloted for by the voters every four years.

It was not the intention of those who framed the municipal code that there should be any gerrymandering of municipal wards in order that the exigencies of some political faction might be served. The division of a municipality into wards can be accomplished only with some difficulty, and never by the city authorities of their own

Term of councillors.

Method of election.

The general-ticket and ward systems.

Redistricting of the municipality.

---

[1] The law also permits a division into districts if a commune, though having less than 10,000 population, is composed of two settlements lacking in identity of interests. See *La loi municipale*, § 11.

C

action. The proposal for a partition may emanate from the municipal council, but the final action upon the project must be taken by the general council of the depart- ment in which the commune is situated. In all cases there must be public hearings upon the question, and from the action of the departmental authorities an appeal may be taken to the appropriate section of the Council of State, which is the highest administrative court of the republic.[1] When wards are once established, moreover, their boundaries are rarely changed. It is not necessary that each ward should be allotted an equal number of councillors ; provided none has less than four, the number may vary. Hence, when wards grow larger or smaller in population there is a redistribution of councillors and not a rearrangement of ward lines. The electoral division is therefore a more or less permanent unit, a fact which enables it to develop a local spirit and local traditions.

The suf-frage.

By the provisions of the code, councillors must be elected by " direct universal suffrage " ;[2] and the voting right is given to all male French citizens who have attained the age of twenty-one years,[3] and who have been actually dom- iciled in the municipality for six months prior to the com- pletion of the voters' list. Besides these, men who pay any of the four chief taxes levied by the municipal au- thorities are entitled to vote at municipal elections even though they may not be resident in the commune. Thus,

Qualifica-tions for voting in French cities.

a man who has his place of business in the city and pays taxes on it is not debarred from voting there because he may reside in some suburban municipality. He may not vote in more than a single commune, but he may choose

---

[1] For the procedure, see *La loi municipale*, § 12 ; also M. Juillet Saint-Lager, *Élections municipales* (6th edition, by C. Vuillemot, Paris, 1904), 15-27.

[2] *La loi municipale*, § 14.

[3] Women do not vote in any French election, national, departmental, or municipal.

to be enrolled either where he pays his taxes or where he resides.[1] This arrangement has proved extremely satisfactory to a considerable class of business men, who are frequently much more interested in the administrative affairs of the large cities where their business is pursued than in the administration of the small suburban communities where they live. In the United States a voter must be enrolled at his "legal residence," wherever this may be; and it very frequently happens to be in a different municipality from that in which his chief financial interests lie. Many large American cities, like New York and Boston, are thus deprived of the votes of thousands of influential business and professional men, who, because they maintain residences in the suburban cities or towns, may neither cast their ballots nor seek to hold office in the metropolis. Yet these are the men who are most directly interested in the efficiency and economy of civic administration.

Non-resident voters.

The municipal franchise in France represents about as close an approximation to manhood suffrage as is to be found in any country. Nowhere in France is there any educational qualification, or any requirement that, in order to secure voting rights, a man must own or occupy any property or pay any taxes or have any income. There are, however, some disqualifications similar to those which commonly exist in other countries. Thus, the right to vote is lost, either for a term of years or perpetually, whenever a voter has been convicted of certain enumerated offences, the list including not only more serious crimes, but many misdemeanors connected particularly with violations of the election laws or of the laws regulating the formation of

Disqualifications.

---

[1] *La loi municipale*, § 14. See also Joseph Dorlhac's *De l'électorat politique: étude sur la capacité électorale et les conditions d'exercice du droit de vote* (Paris, 1890).

clubs and secret political societies.[1] Conviction for illegal
voting, for example, involves perpetual disfranchisement.
When any French court of justice imposes a penalty
which carries with it the deprivation of voting rights,
this action is duly reported by the court official to the
proper administrative authorities; hence a list of disfranchised persons is always at hand when the voters' lists
are being prepared.

The voters' list. In every French commune there is kept at the mairie,
or municipal administrative headquarters, a voters' list
(*liste électorale*), which must be revised annually even
though in some years no election is held. The duty of
compiling and revising this roll is laid upon the mayor
of the commune; but the methods to be pursued are carefully detailed by law,[2] for the same lists are used in both
national and local elections.[3] Ordinarily a single list serves
for the whole commune; but when the municipality has
been divided into wards, or election districts, there is a
separate list for each district. The immediate task of
Method of compiling the list. compiling the list is intrusted to a board of three men,
including the mayor ex officio, a member appointed by the
prefect of the department in which the municipality is
located, and a third member selected by the municipal
council.[4] When the municipality is divided into election
districts there is a board, constituted in the same way, for

[1] Most of the existing disqualifications were provided for in the organic
decree promulgated by Louis Napoleon after his coup d'état (*Décret organique
du 2 février 1852*, in Duvergier's *Collection*, LII. 81–92). A complete table of
present disqualifications may be found in E. Reisser and G. Ridel's *Guide électoral pratique* (Paris, 1901), 11–19.

[2] These methods are set forth comprehensively in Ernest Cénac's *La liste
électorale, sa composition et sa révision annuelle* (Paris, 1890) ; A. de Taillandier's
Manuel formulaire de la révision de la liste électorale (Paris, 1893) ; J. Daure's
Manuel pratique de la révision des listes électorales (Paris, 1898) ; and Robert de
Prevoisin's *Guide pratique d'électeur* (Paris, 1906).

[3] Prior to 1884 different lists were used.

[4] In Paris the system is somewhat different.

each district ; but in this case the mayor is represented
on each board by an adjoint designated for the purpose.
These boards perform their work of compiling the lists
every January, the list of the previous year being used as
a basis in each case.   The procedure is very simple.   The
names of all those who have died, left the commune, or
become disqualified since the last revision are struck off ;
and the names of all those who before the end of March
will have attained the age of twenty-one years, or will
have completed their six months' residence in the municipality, are put on.   All these data can be had from
the records of the *état civil* kept at the mairie.   The work
of preparing the list is not performed publicly ; even representatives of political factions are not permitted to be
present.

When the preliminary work of compiling the list has
been completed, two written copies of the roll are made,
one for the prefect, the other to be retained at the mairie
for public inspection.   Any voter may enter an objection **Protests.**
to names included or omitted, and may file his protest
either orally or in writing.   When all such objections
have been noted, and when the list has remained open to
public inspection for three weeks, it is recommitted to the
board for revision.   For this work two additional members are appointed by the municipal council, so that the **The revis-**
revising board consists of five persons.   During the first **ing board.**
week in February the various objections are considered by
the board in camera, and such changes in the original
list are made as are deemed proper.   From the decisions
of the revising board an appeal may be taken, without
any cost, to the local judge (*juge de paix*) ; and from
the rulings of this official a further appeal, upon points **Appeals**
of law only, may be carried to the Court of Cassation, **from its**
decisions.
which is the highest civil court of the republic.   On the

last day in March the list is declared closed. It is then placed in the archives of the mairie; but copies are posted for inspection, and one copy is transmitted to the prefect to be kept on file at the prefecture. Every voter, also, is upon application to the mayor entitled to make for himself a written copy. After the final posting no changes may be made except as the result of belated judicial decisions. As a matter of fact, appeals from the rulings of the revising board are comparatively few, a circumstance which is the more remarkable in view of the fact that the members of the board are usually laymen, none too well versed in the somewhat intricate jurisprudence relating to the electoral rights of Frenchmen.

Small cost of preparing lists.
An interesting feature of the system of preparing the voters' list is the very small cost which the compilation and revision impose upon a French municipality. The members of the boards that perform the work of compiling and revising serve without any remuneration; and frequently, even in some of the large cities, the lists are not printed but are written by hand. The whole expense is so small that even in the largest cities it is not put into the municipal budget as a separate item, but is lumped in with incidental clerical expenditures. On the other hand, one may venture to criticise the lack of complete publicity which attends the work of revising the lists,

Lack of adequate safeguards.
and to express some doubt whether the safeguards in the way of judicial appeals are an adequate protection against improper inclusions or omissions. It is true that on the whole the revising boards in French cities have been remarkably fair and honest, and that although their sessions are secret their decisions are public; but here and there instances of the scandalous "padding" of the lists have been brought to light. One naturally recalls the famous case of Toulouse of a decade or more ago, when a rigid scrutiny of

the municipal voting lists disclosed the fact that they contained several thousand fictitious names. Although it would be grossly unfair to judge the general workings of the system by this unusual instance, the fact remains that the work of compiling and revising the lists is performed in executive session by men who are more or less directly interested in having certain names added or omitted. The Toulouse incident would, it is true, probably not have occurred had any citizen made it his business to examine the list closely; and it undoubtedly would not have been possible had the French system of compiling the voters' rolls, like that used in English cities, provided for public revision by a semi-judicial body, or indeed if printed copies of the lists had been broadly distributed. At the same time, the French arrangement seems to afford much greater security against fraudulent practices than the American plan of enrolling, usually without any investigation, all who come to the registration bureaus and vouch for right to be put on the lists. *Some results of lack of publicity.*

To be eligible for election to the municipal council one must first be enrolled as a voter, and must in addition be at least twenty-five years of age.[1] It is not required that the candidate should be a resident voter; non-resident taxpayers, if voters, are eligible, but not more than one-fourth of the membership of the council may be drawn from this class.[2] In the larger cities this limitation is hardly necessary; for in France, as in America, the voters endeavor to select councillors from the residents of the municipality. Even in large cities, however, examples of non-resident councilmen are by no means rare; and in the smaller municipalities one frequently finds landowners or retired business *Eligibility to candidature. Non-resident candidates. Non-resident candidacy not common in the larger communes.*

---

[1] *La loi municipale,* § 31. See also, on the qualifications of candidates, Robert de Prevoisin's *Guide pratique d'électeur* (Paris, 1906).

[2] *Ibid.* § 31.

men retaining their membership in the council although they have years since moved away from the commune and taken up residence in Paris or in some provincial city. When a city is divided into election districts a resident of one district is not debarred from candidacy in another; but this privilege seems to be utilized very much less in France than in England. In fact, the feeling that candidates for public office should reside in the constituencies which they seek to represent, though not so strong in France as in the United States, has gained more headway there than in any other European country.

Disqualifi-
cations. Although in general any voter twenty-five years of age is eligible to election as a municipal councillor, there are some important disqualifications from candidacy enumerated in the code, most of them connected with the tenure of various national or departmental offices.[1] A person holding one of these designated posts may be elected to the council, but within ten days after the election he must either resign his previous office or become disqualified to sit at the council-board.[2] All persons directly connected with the providing of public utilities, or acting as direct parties to any contract with the municipality, are similarly disqualified.[3] A somewhat unusual provision makes ineligible to membership in the council all " personal servants," such as coachmen, butlers, and the like; and another stipulates that " in municipalities of five hundred inhabitants or more, ancestors and descendants, brothers, and near relatives by marriage may not be at the same time members of the same municipal council." [4]

---

[1] *La loi municipale*, §§ 32–35.   [2] *Ibid.* § 34.

[3] Decision of the Council of State, December 26, 1896.

[4] *La loi municipale*, § 35. The exact scope of the various disqualifications has been defined by the Council of State in a formidable list of decisions rendered during the last twenty years or more. A convenient summary of these is given in Reisser and Ridel's *Guide électoral pratique* (Paris, 1901), 119–145.

The French municipal code makes no provision what- ever for any system of primaries, caucuses, nomination papers, or, indeed, for any formal method of putting candidates in the field. In fact, the law gives official recognition to no preliminary proceedings on the part of a political organization as an incident of municipal elections. In order to prevent multiple candidatures in national contests, a law was passed in 1889 requiring every aspirant to the Chamber of Deputies to file a declaration of his candidacy with the prefect of the department in which his constituency is located; but this law has no application to the choice of municipal councillors. Indeed, there is perhaps no feature of the French system of municipal elections that commands the attention of the American student of comparative administration so forcibly as the entire absence of any provision for nominating candidates in advance of the actual polling. So far as the election authorities are concerned, they recognize no candidates for municipal office; they set before the voter at the polls no list of aspirants; they restrict his entire freedom of choice in no way whatever. This is not to say, however, that in French cities there is no candidacy for office. Candidates there are in plenty, as in the cities of every other country; but they receive no official recognition as such. In the months preceding a municipal election the various political organizations and partisan clubs reach decisions as to the men upon whom they will concentrate their support; and on the eve of the polling the contest narrows itself down to rival candidates or slates of candidates about as definitely as in American municipalities. To this practice, however, the law lends no inspiration or encouragement; it proceeds upon the theory that the voter shall nominate and elect at one and the same time.

Incidents of the election campaign.

The whole spirit of French legislation relating to election campaigns is in the direction of freedom of action on the part of voters and candidates alike. Hence it is that, although every unofficial poster and placard must bear a government stamp, for which a small fee is exacted, a special exemption from this fee is made in the case of campaign literature, which the candidates and their friends provide in profusion.[1] In the matter of political gatherings, too, there has been a similar exception. Until about a year ago the law required that no public meeting should be held unless, twenty-four hours in advance of such meeting, a declaration had been lodged with the proper police authorities by two responsible citizens, who should become accountable for the proper conduct of the gathering; but in the case of political rallies only two hours' notice was insisted upon.[2] At present no declarations are required for meetings of any sort.[3]

Date of municipal elections.

The exact date of a municipal election is announced by a decree of the prefect, and this decree must be published in the municipality at least fifteen days prior to the date set for the polling. The law requires that the election shall take place on the first Sunday in May in every fourth year.[4]

Sunday elections.

National and municipal elections are never held upon the same date, an arrangement the propriety of which seems never to have been questioned by Frenchmen. In fixing dates for by-elections (that is, elections to fill vacancies in the council) the prefect has entire discretion, provided always that he choose a Sunday. This practice of holding elections, both national and local, upon Sundays rather than upon week-days is characteristic not only of

[1] *Loi du 29 juillet 1881*, in *Bulletin des lois de la république française*, 1881, II. 125–138. See also Alfred Dodanthun's *Des affiches électorales* (Paris, 1903).

[2] *Loi du 30 juin 1881*, in *Bulletin des lois*, 1881, II. 345–347.

[3] *Loi du 28 mars 1907.*

[4] *La loi municipale*, § 41.

France but of the other Catholic countries of Western Europe. It is regarded as an advantageous arrangement, in that it serves in some degree to prevent the operations of polling from interfering with the regular course of daily business, besides affording an unusual opportunity for every voter not only to indicate his choice but to have time to inform himself of the claims of rival candidates. Frenchmen seem to look upon Sunday voting as in thorough accord with their ideas of the entire equality of all citizens at the polls, because the system affords to all voters, of whatever social class, an equal opportunity to exercise their right of suffrage. It is suggested that the large ratio of polled to registered votes which is a characteristic of French elections may be due in some measure to the practice of choosing Sundays for polling-days. Merits claimed for the practice. Its relation to the vote polled.

The places to be used as polling-rooms are designated by the prefect in his decree convoking the electors. In the smaller municipalities one place suffices; but in the cities a number of polling-rooms are provided, and are located where the prefect thinks they will be most convenient for the voters. Whenever practicable, public buildings, particularly schoolhouses, are used for this purpose. When there is but one polling establishment in the municipality, it is in charge of the mayor; when there are several, the various polls are presided over by the mayor and adjoints, and if these are not sufficiently numerous, by the councillors in order of seniority. If there should happen to be more polls than there are members of the municipal government, the mayor may designate voters to take charge of them.[1] Polling-places. Officials in charge of the polls.

Whenever a body of Frenchmen are gathered together The poll-bureau.

[1] An exhaustive treatment of the law and the administrative decisions relating to municipal elections is embodied in Juillet Saint-Lager's *Élections municipales* (5th edition, by C. Vuillemot, Paris, 1900; re-edited under the title *Guide général des élections*, by C. Robany, Paris, 1908). See also Victor Jeanvrot's *Manuel des élections municipales* (Paris, 1892).

for any public or semi-public proceeding, their first care
is not to select a chairman, as is the custom among Americans, but to constitute a bureau, or committee of direction,
to which is intrusted the conduct of the business. The
law requires that, when a polling-place is opened, " the two
oldest and the two youngest voters present " shall be called
upon by the officer in charge to act as " assessors,"
provided they are able to read and write. These four
with the officer himself constitute the polling-bureau, and
by majority vote provisionally decide all questions that
may come up during the day. Three out of the five members must always be present while the polling is going on.[1]
Sometimes there is keen competition for the honor of
serving on the poll-bureau; but more often, perhaps, the
presiding officer has some difficulty in persuading four
voters, whether old or young, to give him their assistance.
It is customary, therefore, to arrange the matter beforehand, lest when the poll opens there may not be present a
sufficient number to constitute the bureau. A poll-clerk
or secretary, chosen by the bureau, completes the personnel of the polling-place. This official is not, however, a
member of the poll-bureau, nor has he any voice in the
decision of mooted questions that may arise during the
day. It is his duty merely to keep the records of the poll,
including written minutes of all matters decided by vote
of the bureau. These items are recorded in proper form,
that they may be available in case appeals from the decisions of the bureau are carried to the administrative
courts after the day of the election. In order that the
decorum and dignity of the polling-place may be conserved, members of the bureau are forbidden to discuss
political questions in the room, and, needless to say, are

Method of constituting it.

Poll regulations.

----

[1] *La loi municipale*, § 19.

prohibited from interesting themselves in the success of any of the candidates. It is, however, somewhat at odds with the method of conducting elections in the United States to put the polls in charge of men who very frequently are themselves candidates for reëlection and who have therefore a direct interest in the various matters that come before them. No official connected with the poll, it may be noted, receives any remuneration for his services, another point in which the French methods are sharply at variance with the American.

The paraphernalia of the French polling-booth are very simple. On a large table in the room is placed the *urne électorale*, which is nothing but a wooden ballot-box with a slit in its lid, a symbol of democracy that sometimes bears rather crude evidence of its local manufacture. Near by stands another open wooden box, in which are deposited such *cartes électorales*, or official notifications of the election, as have not been distributed to voters either because the latter have not been found at home or because they have not called for their cards at the mairie, as the case may be. A written copy of the voters' list completes the brief catalogue of essentials. When the poll is open, each voter as he enters the room presents his election card, which is a printed notice that has been sent to him from the mairie, sometimes by mail, some days prior to the polling. On it are printed the date and place of the election, together with a statement of the hours during which the poll is open, the whole authenticated by the signature of the mayor and the seal of the municipality. In the larger cities it has become customary to require the voter to call at the mairie for this notice; and sometimes, though very rarely, his signature is secured as a receipt for it, and then is used as a means of checking personation at the poll in case any attempt at such imposture should be made. It is not abso-

The ballot-box.

The *carte électorale*.

Identification of voters.

lutely necessary that the voter should present his *carte
électorale* at the poll; in the event of his failing to do so
any other satisfactory identification may be accepted, especially since the missing card will usually be found among
the undistributed notices in the box already mentioned.
The main point is that every voter must either be known
to members of the poll-bureau or must establish his identity in some way wholly satisfactory to them.   That this
regulation has been salutary is evidenced by the almost
entire absence, even in the largest cities, of any accusa-
tions of personating, repeating, or resorting to kindred sinister practices concerning which allegations are so freely
bandied about in American cities.

The ballot.   At French elections no official ballot is provided; each
voter is supposed to furnish his own.   The law requires
only that the ballot which he presents shall be a slip of
white paper, without external mark,[1] upon which there shall
have been printed or written plainly the names of those persons for whom he wishes to have his vote recorded.   The
ballot must be prepared outside the polling-room, never
within; and it must be presented by the voter in person.
Voting by proxy is not permitted, although this concession
has been suggested as a means of increasing the number of
polled votes without opening the doorway for forgery and
fraud; for, it is urged, every ballot tendered by proxy
would be authenticated by its accompanying *carte électorale.*[2]   When the ballot is presented to the officer in charge
of the poll, the latter, having satisfied himself that only
one slip has been handed to him, drops it into the ballot-
box (*urne électorale*).   At the same time he returns the

---

[1] "Le papier du bulletin doit être blanc et sans signe extérieur" (*La loi
municipale*, § 25).

[2] See, for example, A. Guy's *Des moyens de diminuer les abstentions et en
particulier du vote par correspondance* (Paris, 1902).

carte électorale to the voter, first tearing off a corner in order that the card may not by any chance be made to serve again. The torn corner of the card is put into the adjacent box, and the name of the voter is then checked off the list.

Although the law takes it for granted that each voter will prepare his own ballot, this is not usually done. On the days preceding the polling, ballots are made up by candidates or their supporters and distributed by their agents. Not infrequently they are scattered about from house to house, or mailed to all voters before the election; in any case they are to be had from agents of the various candidates who congregate about the entrance of the polling-place on the day of the election. Thus it comes about that a man rarely goes to the trouble of preparing his own voting-paper. He is indeed a fastidious voter who cannot obtain a ballot that fits his own particular taste; for not only are "straight tickets" provided for those who support without any variation the nominees of the political factions, but papers are prepared with almost every possible combination of candidates. In other words, ballots representing what Americans would call "split tickets" are provided by those candidates who are interested in inducing voters to make departure in their behalf from the regular partisan lists. There is, moreover, nothing to prevent a voter from crossing out one or more names on the printed ballot and writing in others; this is, indeed, a very common practice. Nevertheless, the system seems to set a premium on "voting the straight ticket"; for in those municipalities in which the ballot takes place *au scrutin de liste* the slate of the dominant party usually goes through intact.

If a voter so wishes, his choice may be registered with entire secrecy; for, according to the letter of the law, the

Marginal notes:
Ballots prepared by candidates.

Nature of these papers.

"Split tickets."

The ballot is potentially secret.

"slip of plain white paper without external mark" ought to afford no indication of what is written or printed within. The courts, however, have been somewhat liberal in their interpretation of this clause in the code; for they have held ballots on tinted paper and of various shapes to be acceptable. Hence it has come about that the

Ballots are often distinguishable.

ballots provided on behalf of different groups of candidates are sometimes distinguishable by their differences in shape and shade; and it is therefore not always difficult for those within the polling-room to tell how the average elector has voted.[1] The ballot, it may be repeated, is secret only when the voter takes the trouble to make it so; and this he does not commonly do. The French system, indeed, except that it relieves the municipal treasury from the expense of printing official ballots, seems to possess no substantial advantage over the use of the so-called Australian ballot, now generally employed in American cities.

Hours of polling.

The polling in French municipal elections may not extend over more than a single day; but the exact hours during which votes will be received are fixed by the prefect, with the proviso, however, that polls must be open for at least six consecutive hours. Any disobedience of the prefect's orders in any of these matters affords adequate ground for nullifying an election. As a rule, the poll is opened about eight o'clock in the morning and closed late in the afternoon. Immediately after Mass the voters congregate, and in a few hours the larger part of the vote is

Orderly conduct of polling.

cast. Despite the somewhat excitable nature of the French voter, the polling is conducted, almost without exception,

---

[1] Some time ago the French Chamber of Deputies gave assent to a measure designed to make the ballot absolutely secret by directing that no votes should be received except in uniform envelopes provided for the purpose, and that all polling-booths should be equipped with marking compartments (*cabines d'isolement*). This measure did not, however, receive the concurrence of the Senate.

in a dignified and orderly manner. The officer in charge of the room is vested by law with wide powers for the prevention of disorder at elections. To secure this end, he may call upon the regular police officers, or he may even summon the assistance of soldiers to quell any menacing disturbance; but soldiers may not, under any circumstances, be stationed at the polls, a prohibition which harks back to earlier days, when the presence of the military at the polling-places was looked upon as a means of affording "moral support" to those candidates who enjoyed the favor of the national authorities.

When the hour for closing the poll has arrived, the ballot-box is opened by the presiding officer and the total number of ballots ascertained. This total is compared with that of the names checked off on the polling-list, and if the two numbers do not correspond the fact is at once noted on the records. As a further means of verification the torn corners of the *cartes électorales* are also usually counted; but this precaution is not required by law. If more than three hundred ballots have been cast, the officer in charge of the poll selects from among the voters who may happen to be about the room as many assistants as he may deem necessary to expedite the counting of the ballots, any voter who can read and write being eligible. These men take their places at the table, and the ballots are distributed among them. The counting proceeds publicly; all voters who can get into the room are admitted, and are allowed to stand about as the enumeration proceeds. As soon as the results are totalled they are announced by the officer in charge. Then all spoiled or disputed ballots, all records and other papers, are sealed up and transmitted to the prefect or the subprefect,[1] and the ballots

Counting the votes.

Spoiled ballots.

---

[1] The number of spoiled ballots is usually very small, for the law deals generously with ballots which are not prepared in strict accordance with the require-

D

which have been properly marked are burned in the presence of such voters as may have remained to witness this formality.

An absolute majority necessary for election on the first balloting. In order to be elected, a candidate for admission to the council must have secured a clear majority of the votes cast, and in addition must have polled in his favor at least one-fourth of the total enrolled vote. If he satisfies the first condition, he rarely fails to fulfil the second ; for, although the political indifference of the Frenchman has become proverbial, the percentage of the total enrolled vote which is regularly polled at municipal elections does not compare unfavorably with that in other countries. It is an interesting fact that the national elections, which are held in August, draw out a smaller number of voters than do the municipal elections in May. A successful candidate, then, must have received one-half of the polled vote and one-fourth of the enrolled one. If no candidate shall have met both these conditions, none is declared

The supplementary election. elected, and a supplementary election takes place the Sunday following.[1] If the conditions are satisfied by a smaller number of candidates than the quota to be elected, those who have fulfilled the requirements are declared to have been chosen, and the second election is held for the remaining posts only. In these supplementary elections a mere plurality is sufficient to elect.

Differences between the French and Prussian systems of supplementary elections. The procedure in French supplementary elections is, fortunately, different from that in similar elections held in Prussian cities. In the latter, as will be shown later, the contestants in the second election are narrowed down to those candidates who have stood highest at the first

ments. Thus, a ballot is not spoiled if it contains more names than there are posts to be filled ; in such cases the vote is recorded for the names that come first on the paper.

[1] *La loi municipale*, § 30. In the national elections the supplementary polling takes place on the *second* Sunday following a general vote.

general polling: no votes cast for other than these are valid. In France, on the contrary, the voter's choice is as free at the second polling as at the first; indeed, it is possible, although not common, for the voters to select by mere plurality, at the later polling, one who was not a candidate at the regular election.   In the smaller cities, where elections take place by general ticket, supplementary pollings *Frequency* are not often required, for the whole party slate usually *of supplementary* goes through intact; but in the cities that are divided into *elections.* wards second pollings in some of the precincts are almost certain to be necessary.   In Paris, at the elections of 1904, supplementary pollings were required in twenty-five out of the eighty council districts.[1]   The vote at the second election is usually somewhat smaller than that polled at the regular time.[2]

For the commission of electoral frauds, or for any im- *Provisions* proper interference with the conduct of elections, penalties *against corrupt* are provided both by the penal code and by a considerable *practices.* number of special laws.   Personation, repeating, intimidation, bribery, disorders at or near the polling-place, and so on, are all cognizable by the regular criminal courts of the land.   Complaints regarding irregularities in election pro- *Contested* cedure are, however, heard not by these tribunals, but by *elections.* the administrative courts, which alone have power to unseat a councillor by declaring an election void.   Such complaints, if not already made at the poll and duly inscribed on the poll records, may be offered by any qualified voter *Procedure* who chooses to lodge with the prefect or the subprefect, *in contested* within five days after the polling, a written protest with a *elections.* petition for annulment.   On receipt of this protest the prefect must notify the councillor whose election has been

---

[1] *Encyclopédie municipale de la ville de Paris* (Paris, 1904), I. 15–21.

[2] M. de Pindray, *De l'abstentionisme en matière électorale et des moyens propres à y remédier* (Paris, 1902).

impugned, and must require him to file his defence within five days.   An investigation (*enquête*) is thereupon held by the administrative court of the prefecture (*conseil de préfecture*), and upon the evidence presented this body publishes a decree either confirming or annulling the election.   If, however, the issue is not on a question of fact but, as it almost always is, on a point of law, no inquest is necessary. As a rule, elections are not voided except for important and inexcusable irregularities ; they are never annulled for mere technical violations of the law.   From the rulings of the council of the prefecture appeals may be taken by any of the parties concerned to the Council of State ; and such appeals are very numerous, hundreds of them being made after every general election.[1]

No limitation of expenditures for legitimate purposes.

It may be noted here that in France there is not, as in England, any definite limit set upon the amount of money which a candidate for election to a municipal office may expend in the course of his electoral campaign.[2]   Despite the emphasis which the French have laid upon the principle of equality of opportunity at the polls, they have not deemed it necessary to restrict the amount which a candidate may disburse for legitimate expenses.   Still, the sums spent are usually so small that it may be doubted whether the average expenditure in France is any larger than the maximum limit fixed by law in the cities of Great Britain. It is true that during the Second Empire the so-called " official " nominees were so vigorously supported by the higher authorities that candidates who sought successfully to oppose them were forced to spend liberal sums in their preëlection campaigns ; but since 1871 this state of affairs has undergone a decided change.

Elections more economical than formerly.

[1] Charles Uzé, *De la nullité en matière d'élections municipales* (Paris, 1896).

[2] The jurisprudence of the Council of State relating to municipal elections may be studied in Chardenet, Panhard, and Gérard, *Les élections municipales* (Paris, 1896).

This is not to say that under the Third Republic the higher authorities have strictly applied any policy of laissez-faire to local elections. On the contrary, one frequently encounters vigorous complaint that the prefects and subprefects interest themselves entirely too much in the municipal elections within their respective jurisdictions. It would, however, seem out of consonance with the spirit of French local administration if the agents of the central government were to abstain entirely from any part in local politics; for through the prefects and subprefects the state controls an enormous patronage, and the temptation to use it for political purposes in local elections is naturally hard to resist. It is, of course, true that the pressure which the central authorities are now able to exert is less direct than it was in the days when the mayors and adjoints of municipalities were appointed by the national government; but, even though all municipal officials are nowadays chosen locally, they have still, in the exercise of nearly all their more important functions, to reckon with the prefect, a state officer. From his point of view it is of course highly desirable that the municipal authorities should be of the same political allegiance as himself; for such harmony serves to smooth the relations between the prefecture and the mairies. It is not a matter for surprise, therefore, that the prefects, who are to some extent the political organizers as well as the administrative agents of the central government, should frequently seem to show more than a mere academic interest in municipal election campaigns.

With reference to the procedure at elections, something should be said regarding the place and influence of political parties in municipal affairs. The decentralization of the French national party system is well known; and the wide ramifications of this disintegration as shown in the practical workings of national administration have been

[marginal notes:] Relation of higher authorities to local elections.

Use of patronage.

The prefect as a local "boss."

Party politics in municipal elections.

duly emphasized by all writers on matters connected with the politics of the republic.[1]   In general one may say that

Decentralization a feature of all party organization.

this splitting up of voters into groups or factions is as fully characteristic of municipal as of national politics, and that each faction in the nation has its prototype in the municipalities.   It is, of course, true that the appearance of important local issues sometimes serves to obliterate for the time being certain of these dividing lines, and to rearrange the local voters in new groups; but, in the main, political parties poll about the same strength in

National and local parties.

local as in national elections.   In all the larger French cities the elections are conducted on a partisan basis; and with a few important exceptions the national and local party divisions coincide so nearly that the outcome of a general municipal election is closely watched from Paris as affording a good indication of the gain or loss in strength of the various parties in the republic as a whole.   In

Radical element in local politics.

France, as elsewhere, the cities are the strongholds of radicalism; it is from them that the radical groups in the national government derive most of their strength.   So powerful, indeed, is this element in the municipal electorate that practically all the larger cities are controlled by it, till their municipal elections have become little more than contests between two radical factions, one more advanced than the other.   Each faction gathers about itself such strength as it can secure from the smaller political followings, its relative success in this endeavor determining its ultimate victory.

Lack of excitement at elections.

The political psychology of the Frenchman presents more or less of a puzzle to the foreign student of com-

---

[1] For a discussion of this matter, see A. L. Lowell, *Governments and Parties in Continental Europe* (2 vols., Boston, 1897), I. 101 ff. ; J. E. C. Bodley, *France* (2 vols., London, 1900) ; and L. de St. Preuil, *L'impuissance des partis politiques actuels en France* (Paris, 1898).

parative institutions. That a race which possesses such natural impulsiveness, and which, as history abundantly shows, can be so easily stirred to united action, should consistently display such unusual poise and calm in hotly contested elections, is indeed a matter that seems to call for comment. To the casual observer the French voter seems the acme of apathy and indifference; no one who watches a French municipal campaign can fail to get the impression that, save for the stir created by a small group of politicians, the local elections do not even ruffle the surface of everyday life. It may be that this general lack of interest shown by the average voter is due in part to the comparative inefficiency of the local party organizations; for neither in vigor nor in machine-like discipline do these compare with their prototypes in American cities. One might almost say, indeed, that the French do not possess local party organizations in the American sense of the term. French and American party organization.

In the *comités électoraux*, or local political clubs, however, — societies which seek to combine political and social aims, — the adherents, or at least the leading adherents, of each political faction have elementary leagues that enable them in some degree to work together for a common end. These bodies, though alike in their main tendencies, display so great variation in method of organization, in composition, in purpose, and in the nature of their operations that it is difficult to speak of them in general terms.[1] The clubs.

As a rule, the *comités électoraux* do not, like the American local party organizations, include in their membership all the party adherents in the ward or the city, but only Their organization.

[1] The political "clubs," that played so important a rôle during the republic of 1848 (see Alphonse Jouet, *Les clubs, leur histoire et leur rôle*, Paris, 1891), were suppressed during the Second Empire, and in their old form have not been revived since 1871. The present-day *comités* are regulated by the *Loi du Ier juillet 1901* (*Bulletin des lois*, 1901, II. 1273 ff.)

the leaders and the more active and prominent partisans.
Nor do they follow local geographical lines with any strictness ; indeed, their jurisdictions very frequently overlap.
Few of them have any fixed headquarters, some local café
commonly serving as a meeting-place. Each club, however, has its own permanent committee, or bureau of control, the members of which are usually taken from the
ranks of local politicians or government officials. The
clubs of the more conservative factions are drawn largely
from the ranks of the *petits rentiers*, or lower-class business
men, and are often dominated by petty functionaries, the
underlings of the prefect, although such officers are forbidden by law to take any active part in election campaigns.
The radical clubs, on the other hand, find their leaders
among professional men, journalists, and those prominent
in the labor unions. In addition to the *comités* there are
in France many secret organizations — ostensibly of a fra-
ternal nature, like the freemasons — which interest themselves in political matters to a very marked degree.[1]

Their personnel.

The clubs meet at intervals throughout the year in a
social way, frequently listening to political speakers and
almost always discussing current political topics. On
the eve of an election this phase of their activities becomes
more pronounced, general meetings of voters (*réunions
électorales*) are arranged, and in due time certain candidates
are selected, indorsed, or assured of assistance. As a rule,
however, there is no vigorous contest for support or in-
dorsement ; on the contrary, the clubs frequently have difficulty, after selecting their candidates, in persuading them to
accept candidacy. A *comité électoral* has but a lax disci-

*Their ac-
tivities.*

*Their selec-
tion of
candidates.*

---

[1] The very extensive influence exerted by one of these secret organizations
(*La Fédération du Grand-Orient de France*) upon the distribution of patronage
by the national authorities was clearly disclosed by the scandals connected with
the promotion of various army officers some four years ago. See *L'année politique*, 1904, pp. 399 ff.

plinary power over its members and following; and it possesses neither the funds nor the machinery necessary to give its candidates that vigorous and united support which an American party organization usually affords its regular nominees. In the larger French cities, however, the work- Laboring-ingmen's clubs have during recent years developed a unity men's clubs and a discipline somewhat akin to those features of American political parties, and hence have been able to afford their own candidates more effective support. In fact, the increased influence of the labor and socialist elements in the political affairs of the larger French cities has been due in no slight degree to their superior solidity and greater efficiency in organization.

The results of this party decentralization upon the Results of general course of municipal politics are so numerous that party decentralization. they would require too much space to be enumerated in detail. One that cannot be passed over, however, is seen in the considerable number of supplementary elections for Increases which it is largely if not wholly responsible. When a the number of supplementary elections. municipal party is sufficiently strong, it is frequently mentary elections. able, in an election by general ticket, to carry through its full slate on the first ballot. There are, indeed, some cities in France in which the smaller factions find themselves during long periods of years without any representation whatever in the municipal councils, a state of things that has in certain quarters given rise to a demand for the adoption of some plan whereby the minority factions may have assurance of proportional representation.[1] When, however, no political faction is strong enough

---

[1] Ambroise Rendu on "La représentation proportionnelle dans les conseils municipaux," in *Revue municipale*, March 3, 1900; and Severin de La Chapelle, *Le principe proportionnel dans les élections municipales françaises en 1904* (Paris, 1904). A committee of the Chamber of Deputies (*commission du suffrage universel*) and a committee of the Paris municipal council have each recently recommended the adoption of a proportional system.

to command a majority for its candidates, the election usually becomes a scramble for office on the part of too many aspirants, no one of whom has much chance of securing an absolute majority of votes on the first ballot. Each faction, however small in numbers, puts forward its own list, even though it has not the slightest hope of success; then, when the supplementary election is at hand, many of these candidates withdraw and swing their influence to those who are more likely to succeed. The result is that in many cities municipal politics are characterized by all sorts of deals and dickerings between the various factions, the final victory at the polls often going to those who are the most adept at gathering to their support the odds and ends of political organizations. Local politics are thus frequently reduced to an undesirable plane, the attention of the voters being often concentrated more upon men than upon principles, and personal matters of a somewhat petty nature playing a larger rôle than broad questions of municipal policy.

Lowers the plane of local politics.

Although the absence of official nominations, the decentralization of political parties, and the practice of supplementary polling are all wholly foreign to American ideas of procedure at municipal elections, the results, as exemplified in the caliber of the men elected to local office in France, will bear comparison with the results of American methods. It is true that the character of the men chosen to the French municipal councils varies considerably in municipalities of different size; but it may in general be said that even in the larger cities, despite the existence of manhood suffrage, the propertied element of the population has a large representation in the ranks of the council. During the last decade or more, however, the increasing strength of the socialistic propaganda has served, in large centres, to draw into the ranks of the councils

Calibre of men elected.

many representatives of the working classes, as well as Recent growth of the socialist element.
many young professional men, particularly lawyers and
journalists, who have been inclined to identify themselves
with advanced radicalism. Accordingly, the councils in
practically all the large cities are less conservative in
their make-up than they were in the years following the
enactment of the code ; in some cities, indeed, the radical
elements have even obtained a preponderance in the
councils. But radicalism in the ranks of the French municipal council does not, as in England, necessarily mean the
pursuance of a policy of municipal socialism ; for the restraining hand of the prefect must be taken into account,
and the temper of the central government, as exercised
through its prefectoral agents, has consistently aimed to
restrain the municipal authorities from proceeding too
rapidly along the paths of innovation.[1]

It would be presumptuous for an outsider, none too well Character of men elected to the council.
qualified by residence among the French people, to venture
upon any general comparison between the caliber and
standing of French municipal councillors and those of
other countries ; for, of all nations, France is the one in
which sound social and political generalizations seem the
most facile but in the end prove the most difficult. The
opinion expressed by Dr. Albert Shaw, that the councillors Comparison with cities of other countries.
of French cities form a less substantial set of men than
those of Germany or England, may be taken as the conclusion to which any outside student of politics is very
likely to arrive ; for in a matter of this sort one can pursue no scientific method of comparison, but must inevitably
rely upon one's own powers of observation. At any rate,
few who have any familiarity with political conditions in
French and American cities will venture to deny that, city

---

[1] E. Bourdeau on "Le socialisme municipal," in *Revue des deux mondes*,
July, 1900.

for city, the French councillors compare very favorably with the common-councilmen of American municipalities, whether the comparison be made on the ground of substantial interests, business ability, administrative experience, or general reputation for integrity and public spirit.

Organization of the council after the elections. After the supplementary elections have been held, the municipal council meets and is duly organized. A table of seniority is prepared, and the members-elect take precedence according to this list. One of them is selected secretary of the body; and, as the post is largely honorary, one or more assistants are chosen from outside the membership of the council to do the secretarial work. At this organizing session the council likewise elects, in a manner explained later on, a mayor and one or more adjoints, the senior councillor presiding while the mayor **Regular sessions.** is being selected. In addition to the May session, a municipal council must hold at least three regular sessions during the year, — namely, in August, November, and February. The exact date upon which the council convenes is fixed by an *arrêté* of the prefect; or, in the absence of such a decree, it may be convoked by the mayor. Meetings are held at the mairie, or municipal building; business done at any council-meeting convened elsewhere has been held by the Council of State to be **Sessions are public.** illegal. Ordinarily the deliberations of the council are open to the public, but even in the largest cities they seem to attract small audiences.[1]

Special sessions. In addition to the four regular sessions the prefect may at any time authorize special meetings, or the mayor may convoke the council of his own accord; moreover, a

---

[1] Executive sessions may be decided upon at any time by majority vote of the councillors present (*La loi municipale*, § 54). For further details relating to procedure, see D. de Maithol's *Code des conseillers municipaux* (Paris, 1885), and H. Gourgeois's *Code manuel des conseillers municipaux* (Paris, 1890).

special session must be called at the request of a majority
of the councillors. Whenever a meeting is held otherwise
than as a result of the prefect's orders, this official must
forthwith be notified, and must be told the reasons which
dictated the calling of a special session. It should be
emphasized, however, that the prefect cannot prevent the
council from convening. A regular session of the council
may not ordinarily last more than fifteen days; but the
regular session at which the municipal budget is considered
may be prolonged to any period not exceeding six weeks,
and from the prefect or the subprefect an extension of
time may be had for any good reason. For special sessions
the law fixes no limit.

Limits upon the length of sessions.

A feature of French conciliar procedure is the custom
of continuing in session day after day, as legislatures commonly do. In Germany, England, and the United States
the city council meets at frequent intervals, — weekly,
fortnightly, or monthly, — and only for a single afternoon
or evening at a time, a practice which has its advantage
in permitting urgent matters to be brought promptly before the council and thus obviating the necessity of de-
puting its regular functions to any standing committee or
other subordinate body. In France the council meets
much less frequently; hence, when it does convene, it
finds so many matters waiting for consideration that in
the larger cities it usually has to prolong its sessions
over several days. When its work is done, it adjourns
much after the fashion of a parliament or a legislature.
The result of this system of holding council-meetings is
that business, unless it be urgent, must often wait until
the next quarterly sederunt, a delay which is sometimes a
source of great inconvenience. Moreover, the practice has
undoubtedly brought about the transfer to the mayor and
adjoints of many routine functions which, if the council

Council meetings last for several days.

were in the habit of meeting frequently, would probably be dealt with by that body or by one of its committees.

Limitations on the scope of the council's deliberations.   Some of the regulations relating to council procedure seem to indicate that the national authorities have viewed with suspicion the policy of permitting to councillors freedom of deliberation and discussion. In the United States the presiding officer of the municipal council usually has the entire responsibility of keeping discussions within proper and pertinent bounds ; but in France the municipal code makes express provision that the council may not during session discuss any matter which is not clearly within the scope of its powers. Councillors may not concern themselves with any matter of national or departmental politics, and may not engage in criticisms of the policy and actions of the prefect or of any other of the higher authorities.

Penalties for contravention.   Any infraction of this regulation may bring upon the body its suspension by prefectoral decree. Indeed, whenever a prefect deems the discontinuance of a municipal council urgently desirable in the public interest, he is empowered to suspend the councillors from office for any period not exceeding one month ; or, if this discipline be deemed insufficient, he may report the matter to the president of the republic, who is, in turn, vested by the code with authority to dissolve the council altogether and to replace it for the time being with a municipal commission composed of from three to seven members appointed by himself.[1] This commission may, however, deal only with urgent matters ; it may in no case pass the annual budget or make any change in the personnel of municipal administration.[2] Within two months, moreover, an election of a

---

[1] *La loi municipale*, § 43.

[2] *Ibid.* § 44. Some interesting discussions concerning the powers of these interim commissions (*délégations spéciales*) may be found in the *Revue générale d'administration*, especially 1897, II. 65 ; and 1899, I. 183.

new council must take place.[1] Councillors who have been removed from office are eligible to reëlection.

This power of suspension and dissolution gives to the central authorities an effective whiphand over the municipal council, enabling them to hold that body rigorously to the observance of its duties and responsibilities. Naturally, however, such an unusual power has in it many elements of danger. When, for instance, the prefects and the councils represent, as they very frequently do, political interests that are antagonistic, this semi-dictatorial authority may readily be made a weapon of political pressure, a means of visiting upon the representatives of one party faction the wrath of its opponents. On the whole, however, the powers of suspension and dissolution do not appear to have been used arbitrarily or injudiciously; for, it must be remembered, the prefects are responsible to the minister of the interior, who, again, may be at any time interpellated and called to account in the national parliament for any acts of his subordinates. Even the president of the republic, in the exercise of his power of dissolution, acts only upon the advice of his ministers. When, therefore, a municipal council is suspended or dissolved, the action of the higher authorities may be promptly brought before the direct representatives of the people, whose failure to approve it is tantamount to a vote of want of confidence in the ministry.[2] The effectual guarantee against arbitrary action is thus to be found in the responsibility of the central executive to the national legislature. As a matter of fact, municipal councils have since 1884 been suspended or dissolved only on very in-

The power of suspending and dissolving the council.

Checks upon the power of the higher authorities.

---

[1] *La loi municipale,* § 45.

[2] A discussion of the principle of ministerial responsibility as applied in the French national government may be conveniently found in Lowell's *Governments and Parties,* I. 117-134.

frequent occasions, usually not unless they have plainly neglected their functions, — as, for example, when they have failed to hold the required meetings. During the period of the Second Empire, however, the prerogative was grossly abused by the imperial authorities, who used their large powers frequently and arbitrarily. Much of this time Paris, Lyons, and several other cities were administered by commissions, their municipal councils being regularly dissolved on the first sign of hostility to the imperial government. Arbitrary interference from Paris at that time is not to be wondered at; but that it should, even in its restricted form, be continued by the present government is, in view of republican traditions, somewhat surprising.

Restrictions relating to procedure. In addition to the foregoing important limitations, many minor restrictions relating to procedure have been imposed by law upon the French municipal council. It may not proceed with business, for instance, unless a majority of the councillors are present; but if, after two successive meetings called at intervals of three days, this quorum has not been secured, such members as happen to be on hand may proceed.[1] Provision is made that the seat of any councillor who has been absent from three consecutive sessions may be declared vacant by the prefect unless the absentee furnishes satisfactory reasons to the council. Members are permitted to resign from office, but their written resignations must be filed with the prefect. On all questions a majority of the councillors present and voting is decisive, and in the event of a tie the mayor has a casting vote.[2] Three different methods of **Methods of voting.** voting at council-sessions are recognized by law: (1) by

---

[1] *La loi municipale*, § 50.

[2] *Ibid.* § 51. The mayor may not refuse to exercise this prerogative (see *Revue générale d'administration*, 1894, I. 287).

the ordinary standing vote, which does not involve the use of a ballot and which is the usual method of submitting questions; (2) by non-secret ballot (*scrutin public*); and (3) by secret ballot (*scrutin secret*). At the demand of one-fourth of the councillors the non-secret ballot — that is to say, a ballot on which the names of councillors are signed — may be employed; the secret ballot may be called into service by one-third of the members. This latter method must be employed when the council proceeds to the election of the mayor or the adjoints, or of any other official whom it has power to appoint. The open ballot serves only as a means of having the votes of councillors recorded in the council proceedings (*procès-verbal*); it is to all intents equivalent to the American system of vote by roll-call.

Although, as has been said, the deliberations of the council are open to the public, provision is made for secret sessions if such are deemed desirable by a majority of the councillors. Prior to 1871 council-meetings were always private;[1] indeed, this secrecy was regarded as one of the most objectionable features of the system of communal administration during the Second Empire. Even after 1871 the authorities of the Third Republic lent sanction to the practice for the time being, although the desirability of public council-sessions was on more than one occasion debated in the French parliament.[2] The minutes (*compte-rendu*) of every session, whether secret or open, must be posted at the door of the mairie within eight days after the close of the meeting; and a copy of them, or of any other records, must be furnished to any voter who demands them.[3]

Executive sessions.

Publication of records.

---

[1] *Loi sur l'organisation municipale*, May 5, 1885, § 22. This law may be found in Duvergier's *Collection*, LV. 136–144.

[2] *Journal officiel*, Chambre des Députés, 12 mai 1877, 12 février 1883, 6 juillet 1883; Sénat, 8 et 9 février 1884, 28 mars 1884.

[3] *La loi municipale*, §§ 56–58.

E

Powers of the council. The powers and duties of the French municipal council are set forth at length in three or four articles that may fairly be said to constitute the most comprehensive and the most important part of the whole code.[1] This section of the law opens with the broad statement that "the council regulates by its deliberations the affairs of the commune," and then proceeds to limit this general grant of power and to impose restrictions upon the way in which it may be exercised. Those who drew up the law of 1884 fully recognized the importance of this part of it, and gave much consideration to the various provisions that were finally inserted. In regard to the proper division **Division of powers between national and local authorities.** of powers between the council on the one hand and the mayor and his adjoints on the other, there was not much difference of opinion ; but as to what powers should be given to the council to be exercised independently, and what should be given to it to be used subject to the strict control of the prefect, there was a good deal of disagreement. As finally framed, therefore, the article embodied the results of compromises between those members of the drafting commission who favored local autonomy and those who, on the other hand, were partisans of centralization. Only as this fact is clearly borne in mind may the scope of jurisdiction now possessed by the city council in France be properly understood.

Classification of the council's powers. The general powers (*attributions*) granted to the council by the municipal code may be conveniently grouped into three classes. Some are purely advisory, the initiative resting with the higher authorities and the council having nothing but the privilege of tendering its advice, which may or may not be accepted. A larger number of powers may be exercised by the council of its own initiative, but

---

[1] *La loi municipale*, §§ 61, 68–70.

they are effective only when the approval of the higher authorities has been obtained. A third group includes the prerogatives which the council possesses independently, and for the exercise of which it requires no outside concurrence.[1] These three classes of powers are not, it is true, made absolutely distinct; on the contrary, the Council of State has on very many occasions been called upon to define jurisdictions that apparently overlapped. The mass of administrative jurisprudence which has accumulated upon the subject is, indeed, so formidable that the foreign student who essays a thorough mastery of it will find his task a difficult one. No more is attempted here, therefore, than a general survey of the council's more important prerogatives.

Certain powers of the council are, as we have seen, advisory; that is to say, there are some matters upon which full liberty of decision is retained by the higher authorities, but which may not be acted upon till the advice of the council has been requested.[2] The deciding officials are not bound to follow advice when it is tendered, and when a council refuses to give its opinion the authorities may proceed without it; but advice must be asked as a preliminary to valid action.[3] In this class of powers belong various matters relating to the changing of parochial boundaries, to the administration of the system of poor relief, the laying out of main streets and highways, the acceptance of gifts and legacies by charitable institutions situated in the munici-

Advisory powers.

---

[1] An exceedingly clear analysis of the exact scope of the powers committed to the councils by the code may be found in Morgand's *La loi municipale*, I. 397–476. See also Dalloz and Vergé, *Code des lois politiques et administratives* (5 vols., Paris, 1887–1904), Vol. I., under "Commune"; and H. Berthélemy, *Traité de droit administratif* (5th ed., Paris, 1908), 197 ff.

[2] *La loi municipale*, especially § 70.

[3] The Council of State has decided that the higher authorities have no discretionary power as to the desirability of seeking advice from the councils. On this point, see Morgand, *La loi municipale*, I. 465–466.

palities but under state supervision, and some questions pertaining to the system of elementary education. The list used to include, also, a variety of matters connected with the administration of public worship ; but recent national legislation has greatly diminished the share which either the higher or the local civil authorities may assume in the administration of ecclesiastical affairs. Besides being obliged to consult the council on all the matters enumerated, the national government may, at its discretion, instruct the prefects to obtain the advice of the councils upon any other matter with respect to which it deems local counsel of value, — a course which it very frequently pursues, sometimes, it may be, in order to shirk its own responsibility.

Powers that require outside ratification. A more extensive and more important category is that which comprises the prerogatives exercisable by the council subject to higher approval. Thirteen such functions are enumerated in the code.[1] Of these the most important are all powers connected with the purchase, alteration, mortgaging, exchanging, selling, or leasing for long terms of any municipal property. Many of the French cities possess considerable landed property, some of which is by private use made to yield a return ; but, although this property is technically regarded as belonging to the commune and not to the department or the state, the municipality is not permitted to deal with it in entire freedom.[2]

---

[1] *La loi municipale*, § 68.

[2] Communal property in France is usually divided into three categories : (1) lands and buildings devoted wholly to public uses, — the mairie, for example ; (2) property rented to private parties and hence yielding a revenue to the commune ; and (3) the so-termed "commons" (*communaux*), or land in which the inhabitants of the commune have certain rights of pasturage, etc., — a very extensive and valuable property comprising several millions of acres. Strictly speaking, the legal ownership of all three classes of property is vested in the commune as a corporation ; but in respect of its possessions the commune is by French law regarded as a *mineur en tutelle*, or ward, of the national govern-

In this class of provisional powers are also included all The control of streets. matters relating to alterations in municipal highways, to the naming and re-naming of streets and squares, the establishment and closing of parks, gardens, and other public grounds,—everything, in fact, pertaining to the administration and use of municipal thoroughfares for public utilities whether by the municipality itself or by private interests. At this point it may be well to call attention to a distinction which the French make between two classes of streets in the matter of supervision and control. Within the category of *la grande voirie* they include the whole field of affairs pertaining to the construction, repairing, policing, and general regulation of traffic upon all main or major highways of communication. Such highways are, in the first place, the *routes nationales,* or national roads, and in the second place the *routes départementales,* or provincial thoroughfares. Within the category of *la petite voirie,* on the other hand, falls the administration of all matters relating to subsidiary or minor highways, such roads including both *chemins vicinaux* and *chemins ruraux.* All powers relating to *la grande voirie* are exercised by either the national or the departmental authorities ; with this class of matters the government of the municipalities has nothing whatever to do. Powers relating to *la petite voirie,* however, are exercised by the commune over such minor roads as lie within its limits, provided always that these be not sections or continuations of national or departmental thoroughfares. This control of the town streets, squares, passages, and so on is technically known as *la voirie urbaine,* and all expenses connected with the exercise of it are borne in the annual budget of the municipality. The higher

ment, and hence is restricted in the disposition of them. For a further discussion of this topic, see Imbart de La Tour's *Des biens communaux* (Paris, 1899) ; Roger Griffin's *Les biens communaux en France* (Paris, 1899) ; and the article in the *Dictionnaire municipal* on " Biens communaux."

authorities of course decide whether a street shall be put
in one or the other of these two classes; but in general all
the main streets of a city are in the first-named category.
In Paris all the streets, whether main or not, are thus
included.[1]

Divided jurisdiction over streets, and the question of franchises.   This division of jurisdiction over public highways obviously has a direct relation to the whole question of public
utilities in French cities; for the establishment and operation of all the great public services involve the use of the
streets.   Franchises including the use of the main streets
may be given only by the authorities of the department or
the state, and the conditions under which they are granted
are governed by general laws.   When the franchise is designed to carry with it rights in none but the minor streets
of the municipality, it may be given by the municipal council; but before any such grant assumes validity the ratification of the prefect must be secured.[2]   As a matter of fact,
however, no public service of any importance could be effective if restricted to the minor streets.   The use of both
classes of highways is usually necessary, and, in the case of
some utilities, that of the main streets is the more desired.
Since, then, the council can give to no private interests any
serviceable rights in the highways of the municipality, its
power of granting franchises is not of any substantial importance.   Indeed, a municipality may not itself presume
to use main streets for municipal undertakings without permission from the higher authorities.   A French city which

---

[1] For a further discussion of this topic, see H. Berthélemy, *Traité de droit
administratif*, 435 ff.; L. Courcelle, *Traité de la voirie* (Paris, 1900); and
Dalloz and Vergé, *Code des lois politiques et administratives*, under " Voirie "
(III. 1061 ff.).

[2] In some cases this privilege rests with the mayor as an incident of his
" police power "; but, if the public interest seems so to demand, the prefect may
grant privileges which the mayor refuses to allow.   Cf. *La loi municipale*, § 98.
See also below, p. 73.

desires, for example, to establish a system of municipally-operated street-railways must go to the higher powers for leave to use even its own principal streets for this service. Such permits, if granted, are revocable by the granting authorities at any time.

When a private company desires to establish or to ex- *Tramway franchises.* tend a municipal service which it provides, — as, for example, a tramway service, — it must file with the officials of the department an application in due form accompanied by the requisite plans.[1] When these are at hand, the *Procedure in obtaining them.* prefect fixes a convenient date upon which an inquest will be held, and names a commission of seven or nine members drawn from the prominent business men and property-owners of the district concerned. After due notice has been given to all those interested, the commission opens its *enquête* by summoning those persons, whether officials or private citizens, whom it thinks desirable to consult. These are heard, and the gist of what they have to say is framed into a report, which is sent to the prefect. This officer calls upon the local chamber of commerce and other representative bodies for their opinions upon the application, and then forwards the whole *dossier* to the general council to be used by it in determining action upon the application. When the proposal involves the use of streets in more than one department, hearings are held in each department concerned, and the reports are transmitted to the minister of public works at Paris. In such cases the national authorities pass upon the application, as they do also in any case in which the use of a *route nationale* is involved. Those who grant a franchise supervise the con-

---

[1] This regulation and those that follow are prescribed by a decree of May 18, 1881, which may be found in *Bulletin des lois*, 1881, I. 895–899. See also Clément Colson's *Abrégé de la législation des chemins de fer et tramways* (2d ed., Paris, 1904). Various details relating to the subject are given in Léon Thorlet's *Traité des travaux communaux* (Paris, 1894), 310–319.

struction and operation of the utility.[1] When difficulties arise between the city authorities and the holders of the franchise, matters are carried before the council of the prefecture, which is competent to adjust them.[2]

Voting the budget. Another function exercised by the council under strict supervision from the higher authorities is the voting of the municipal budget.[3] This budget is, as will be seen later, prepared by the mayor, and is considered item by item at one of the stated sessions of the council. The *dossier* is prepared in triplicate, and when it has passed the council a copy is sent to the prefect for his approval. **Approval of the higher authorities essential.** If, however, the total revenue of the municipality is estimated in the budget at more than three millions of francs, another copy must be forwarded to the minister of the interior, for approval, on his advice, by the president of the republic. In each case the copy of the document must be accompanied by such data as may be of service to the financial and legal experts who at the prefecture or at the ministry carefully scrutinize the various items. These explanatory data must include a copy of the council minutes, a copy of the mayor's annual report, a copy of the treasurer's annual statement, and various other papers of a similar nature. All papers must, moreover, be prepared in an approved and uniform way in order that the higher officials may do their work with promptness and accuracy.

[1] Elaborate regulations concerning the construction and operation of street railways are prescribed in the decree of August 6, 1881, printed in *Bulletin des lois*, 1881, II. 791–812.

[2] On this point, see the decision of the Council of State in the case of the Compagnie des Tramways de Nice, March 1, 1885.

[3] The regulations relating to municipal budgets are contained in *La loi municipale*, §§ 132, 145–150. See also A. G. Desbats, *Le budget municipal* (Paris, 1895) ; A. Rey, *Théorie du budget communal* (Paris, 1897) ; Paul Dubois, *Essai sur les finances communales* (Paris, 1898) ; and Boucard and Jèze, *Éléments de la science des finances et de la législation financière* (2d ed., Paris, 1902).

The prefect (or the minister) has power to increase or
to reduce any item in that portion of the budget which is
devoted to estimated receipts, and thereby to affect the
annual tax-rate of the municipality ;[1] but in the case of
items relating to estimated expenditure he is, except in
two circumstances which very rarely occur,[2] restricted to the
power of reduction alone.[3] The higher authorities may
introduce no new items into the list of estimated expenditures except those which, though rendered obligatory by
law, the council has declined to pass. After due examination the budget is promulgated by an *arrêté* of the prefect or, in the case of the largest cities, by a decree of the
president. If necessary, a supplementary budget may
be passed by the council later in the year; and this is
submitted to the same procedure as the regular one. If
the council should fail to vote any budget at all, the prefect is empowered to prepare one covering all the necessary
expenses, and to put this into force by prefectoral order.
In such case, however, the number of items may not exceed the average in the budgets of the three preceding
years.[4] In the French municipal budgets the obligatory
items form a very considerable part of the whole, and
intervention on the part of the prefects to secure proper
attention to these has not been at all infrequent. On the
whole, however, the municipalities have been dealt with
fairly, and the close scrutiny which is given to their
accounts and budgets at the prefecture or at the ministry
has been wholesome in its results.

Powers of the prefect with reference to municipal budgets.

[1] See the decision of the Council of State in the case of the commune of
Villeneuve-Saint-Georges, July 3, 1891, in *Revue générale d'administration*,
1891, III. 296 ff.

[2] These are stated in *La loi municipale*, § 145, par. 2, and § 147, par. 2.

[3] *Ibid.* § 148.

[4] *Ibid.* § 149. The procedure in such cases is discussed in Morgand's *La loi
municipale*, II. 464–481.

Municipal
loans.

Closely related to the council's power to make the annual appropriations is its right to authorize borrowing on the credit of the municipality; and this power also it exercises subject to strict supervision and control.[1] Within certain narrow limits, loans to be applied to public improvements may be authorized by the council without the approval of any higher authority; but when sums of any considerable importance are required the concurrence of the prefect must be had, and if the loan involves any special-tax levy during a long period the approval of the government at Paris must be obtained. Indeed, special-tax levies of all sorts (*contributions extraordinaires*) must have the approval either of the prefect or of his superiors; and changes in any of the regular taxes must be similarly approved before going into effect. The

Restrictions
on the
council's
power to
borrow.

borrowing power of the municipality is thus very closely circumscribed. Each loan must be authorized on its merits; and even after the council has indorsed a proposal to borrow it is required, in connection with the application for approval by the higher authorities, to prepare and forward to the prefect an elaborate statement in regard to the financial condition of the commune, with various other informational documents.[2] Apparently, however, the restrictions from above have not prevented most of the larger French cities from becoming involved in heavy indebtedness.

Other
powers in
the second
group.

Other functions exercised by the council subject to the approval of the higher authorities are the establishment and control of markets, and the power to accept or re-

[1] *La loi municipale*, §§ 133, 141–143, modified somewhat by the *Loi du 7 avril 1902* (*Bulletin des lois*, 1902, I. 2239 ff.). See also the article in the *Dictionnaire municipal* on "Emprunts communaux." An older work, which has still some value, is Romain Verdalle's *Traité pratique des emprunts des communes* (Paris, 1881).

[2] A ministerial circular of May 14, 1902, prescribes the list of papers that must be provided.

ject contested gifts and legacies. With reference to such gifts somewhat extended regulations are imposed by the municipal code ;[1] for the practice of bequeathing to local authorities money for public uses is so common in France that, if discrimination in acceptance were not required, some municipalities might become involved in expensive litigation with the relatives of donors or testators. There are several other functions which the council is permitted to exercise only under close supervision ; but those which have been indicated comprise all that are of importance.

Action taken by the council on any of these matters goes to the prefect for validation ; and if the approval of this official be not forthcoming within one month appeal may be made to the minister of the interior for a decision.[2] When, however, the prior assent of competent authorities has been secured, or when the council is merely engaged in carrying into effect the provisions of some mandatory law or decree, such submission of its proposals to the higher powers is of course not necessary.

Procedure in obtaining concurrence.

During the last quarter-century the general tendency in France has been in the direction of strengthening central control over local administration.[3] Undoubtedly this supervision is, in practice, more extensive to-day than it was when the code was framed in 1884,— a result not so much of actual changes in the law as of the continued extension of prefectoral powers through ministerial orders and decisions of the Council of State.[4] The prefect has,

Importance of the prefect's office.

---

[1] *La loi municipale,* §§ 111–113, modified by the *Loi du 4 février 1901* (*Bulletin des lois,* 1901, I. 1469 ff.). See also Th. Ducrocq, *Cours de droit administratif* (7th ed., 6 vols., Paris, 1905), 327–356. [2] *La loi municipale,* § 69.

[3] A discussion of the present scope of central supervision may be found in P. Lavergne's paper on " Du pouvoir central et des conseils municipaux," in *Revue générale d'administration,* 1900.

[4] On the recent growth of prefectoral jurisdiction, see H. Taudière on " Restrictions apportées aux libertés locales depuis un quart de siècle," in *La réforme sociale,* November, 1904.

indeed, become the real pivot of the French administrative system. His part in direct municipal administration has come to be so important that, only as one regards him as a versatile bureaucrat-politician and seeks his hand at every turn, can one get an adequate grasp of the system of city government. It is, therefore, not easy for the American student, whose political system provides for no officer in any way corresponding, to come to a proper appreciation of the dominating rôle which the prefect plays in local French politics and administration.

Share of the council in local administration. In strictly local matters not comprised within the two foregoing categories the civic authorities have independent jurisdiction. Some few powers, notably the control of municipal police, are committed to the mayor;[1] but the larger share in local government is given by the code to the council. Although this share may not seem to be very extensive, it includes some important functions with **Its relation to municipal services.** reference to the management of various municipal services, such as fire protection, the *monts-de-piété* (city loan offices), municipal cemeteries, parks, and so on. When a public service like water, gas, or electricity has been municipalized, the powers of independent management exercised by the local authorities — partly by the council and partly by the mayor and adjoints — appear prominently.[2] The exact relation of the council to the municipal services, and the precise division of powers between the local organs, are, however, matters upon which the administrative jurisprudence has grown so complex as to render impossible, within the limits of the present volume, any attempt at a

---

[1] *Cf.* below, pp. 73–75.

[2] In matters relating to municipalization of services and to the relation of the municipality to public-utility corporations, the French have not made use of the referendum as a restraining agent; but this expedient has sometimes been proposed. See Robert de la Sizeranne's *Le referendum communal* (Paris, 1893).

specific statement.[1]   In general, the council defines the main lines of policy, the mayor and his subordinates assume the responsibilities of detailed management.

Surveying the functions of the French municipal council as a whole, we find that it takes a larger share in direct civic administration than do the councils in German or American cities.   On the other hand, its rôle is quite inferior to that of the borough council in England, partly because the principle of division of powers between local organs, entirely unknown in England, receives recognition in the French republic to some extent, but chiefly because in France the hand of state is heavier upon the local councils than it is in England.   At the same time, the French councils have not, like the common councils of many American cities, become mere organs for the granting of funds; they exercise in many branches of local administrative life an influence which, if not always controlling, is usually very substantial.   This influence has certainly not increased since 1884.   On the contrary, although the French council has not meantime been so ruthlessly shorn of its prerogatives as has its prototype in American municipalities, its power has undergone some diminution; and contemporary indications seem to point to further decline rather than to any increase in its control over local administration.[2]

Powers of the municipal councils in France and England.

In France and America.

---

[1] On the general relation of the French municipality to its public services, those sufficiently interested may be referred to Léon Thorlet's *Traité des travaux communaux* (Paris, 1894) ; Eustache Pilon's *Monopoles communaux* (Paris, 1899) ; Louis Roger's *Le domaine industriel des municipalités* (Paris, 1901) ; L. Stehlin's *Essais de socialisme municipal* (Paris, 1901); A. Sausson's *Des monopoles communaux* (Paris, 1902) ; Pierre Mercier's *Les exploitations municipales, commerciales, et industrielles en France* (Paris, 1905); and Maurice Gaucheron's *Études sur l'œuvre économique des municipalités* (Paris, 1906).   The relation of private interests to the exercise of the council's powers is discussed in Lucien Dalem's *Des voies de recours contre les délibérations des conseils municipaux* (Paris, 1904).

[2] *Cf.* Albert Shaw, *Municipal Government in Continental Europe* (New York, 1897), 175–176.

Much of the council's work is handled by the various standing or special committees which it selects from among its own members. Ordinarily there is a standing committee for each important municipal department; but these committees, it should be clearly understood, merely consider questions relating to the departments without actively participating in the government of them. Actual administration is the prerogative of the mayor and his assistants; the committees are only advisory in their functions, and may not exercise even this privilege except through reports made to the council and tendered by that body to the real administrative authority. Hence the council committees play a much less important part in French cities than they do in the English or German. Not that the deliberations of the French committees are entirely without influence; on the contrary, the adjoint in charge of a department usually gives great weight to any representations which the appropriate committee may make. Unlike the English committee or the Prussian deputation, however, the French committee does not possess any power to order, direct, or control.

Having outlined the composition and powers of the council, one may turn to a consideration of the executive organ, which in all the French communes, large or small, consists of a mayor and one or more adjoints or assistants.

The number of these adjoints varies with the size of the municipality, a city with 2500 inhabitants or fewer having but one, and a city with a population ranging between 2500 and 10,000 having only two. In the larger municipalities there is an additional adjoint for every additional 25,000 people; but the total number must not exceed twelve, except in the city of Lyons, where it is fixed at seventeen. Both mayor and adjoints are elected by the council for a term of four years, — that is, for the lifetime

of the council itself.   All adjoints go out of office together;
there is no system of partial renewal at stated periods.
The election takes place at the first meeting of the new   Methods of
council following the general polling in May, provided that   election.
in the interval the necessary supplementary elections have
been held.   It may not proceed, however, if one-fourth or
more of the seats at the council-board remain unfilled.
The sitting at which the choice is made is presided over
by the senior councillor in attendance; the selection takes
place without any formal nominations and by secret ballot
(*scrutin secret*).[1]   On either of the first two ballots an absolute majority is necessary for election; after this a plurality suffices.   In the event of a tie the elder of two
opposing candidates is declared chosen.

The mayor and adjoints must be selected from within   Eligibility
the membership of the council;[2] but there are no special   to executive
offices.
disqualifications other than the proviso that financial
officers in the employ of the central government who are
eligible to membership in the council shall not be chosen
as executive officials of the municipality.   There are no
requirements as to previous municipal service; indeed, a
councillor may be chosen mayor of the commune immediately after his first election to the council, and this not
infrequently happens.   The adjoints are commonly men
who have served one or more terms at the council-board;
but the selection of those who have had no prior municipal
service is not, especially in the larger cities, regarded as
anything unusual.   Reëlections to both the mayoralty and   Reëlections
are com-
the adjointships are of frequent occurrence, particularly   mon.
in the smaller communes, where one often finds mayors
who have been in office continuously for twelve or even

---

[1] The exact procedure to be followed is set forth at length in Saint-Lager's
Élections municipales, 383–426.
[2] *La loi municipale*, § 73.

for sixteen years. Occasionally a local magnate holds the office during his lifetime and passes it on to his son after him; but such instances are of course very rare. In the larger towns and cities a mayor is frequently chosen for a second term, but third terms are probably not more common than in the cities of the United States. One who has served his term as adjoint satisfactorily may reasonably look for reëlection unless there has been a decided change in the party complexion of the council; and even in this case an adjoint whose administration has been notably successful has sometimes been chosen to succeed himself.

Party politics in mayoralty elections. In electing a mayor and adjoints the municipal council divides along partisan lines, which may be widely divergent; for, when its members have been chosen from different electoral districts or wards, several partisan factions are likely to be represented in it. In such cases the dominant faction may manage to secure the election of its candidates by a plurality on the third ballot; or the selection may be the result of "deals" or coalitions between two or more of the groups. When, on the other hand, the councillors have been elected *au scrutin de liste*, or by general ticket, the whole body is likely to represent a single political faction. In this case there is usually little or no open contest for the offices, the whole matter being arranged by the leaders beforehand, sometimes even before the date of the council elections.[1] Complaint is frequently made that the mayor and adjoints of the French city do not always represent the voters, and that direct election by the latter would result in the choice of a different set of men.

Weakness of the system.

Character of men chosen. Nevertheless, the class of men selected both as mayors and as adjoints in the larger municipalities has been of a satisfactorily high order; for, despite the influence of

---

[1] On this point see Léonard Léonard's *L'élection du maire de la commune par le nouveau conseil municipal* (*farce électorale*), Paris, 1902.

partisanship, the councillors recognize the desirability of having experienced men in the administrative posts.

The results of the election must be posted at the mairie within twenty-four hours, and must within the same period be duly communicated to the prefect or the subprefect, as the case may be. No approval on the part of these officials is necessary to the validity of the choice, and no right of withholding ratification exists; but if the council has proceeded with the election in any irregular fashion, or if it has selected any councillor who is not legally competent for the post, a formal protest may be lodged with the prefect by any voter. Such protests are considered by the council of the prefecture, which acts as an administrative court with original jurisdiction in all matters affecting municipal elections and the qualifications of municipal officers; and in every case appeal may be taken to the highest administrative court, the Council of State.[1]

Contested elections.

Mayors and adjoints, like councillors, give their services without remuneration; in fact, the principle of gratuitous service on the part of all elective municipal officers has been strongly anchored in the minds of the French people ever since the Revolution. Adjoints receive neither salaries nor allowances for expenses; but the mayor, though he has no stipend, may accept from the council such sum as it deems a reasonable compensation for expenses actually incurred by him in the direct discharge of his office. In a large city, where the chief executive is often called upon to uphold the dignity of the municipality on the occasion of fêtes and public ceremonies, as well as in entertaining distinguished visitors, the mayor's personal disbursements are frequently very heavy. The council is not, how-

Mayors and adjoints serve gratuitously.

Allowances for expenses.

---

[1] *La loi municipale*, § 79. A large number of important decisions resulting from these protests are summarized in Saint-Lager's *Élections municipales*, 414–420.

F

ever, permitted to afford him a virtual salary under the
guise of an allowance for expenditures of this nature; for
the sum allotted must be put into the annual budget, and
this budget, as has already been seen, comes under the scrutinizing eye of the prefect, who takes care that there is no
violation of the spirit of the law.[1]   The mayor's allowance,
though scarcely ever adequate, is sometimes substantial;
indeed, were it not for this fact it would be next to
impossible for any citizen, not possessed of private means,
to accept the office of mayor in the larger cities with any
hope of performing properly the social duties which the
tenure of the post entails.

When the council elects a mayor and adjoints from
among its own members it thereby creates no vacancies in
the body, as the English council does when it chooses certain of its members to the mayoralty and aldermanships.
The French mayors and adjoints continue in their seats at
the council-board; hence no by-elections become necessary,
as they do in England under similar circumstances.

Powers of
the mayor.

The powers of the mayor and adjoints cannot easily be
set forth in general terms ; for, although by the provisions
of the law they are substantially alike in all of the 36,000
communes, the enormous difference in local conditions
makes the actual exercise of them vastly different in
a large city like Marseilles or Bordeaux from that in
a rural hamlet of a few hundred inhabitants.   Much depends, furthermore, on the character and abilities of the
persons who for the time being happen to hold the respective posts, — a feature particularly worth emphasis in any

[1] In a decision rendered on April 30, 1896, the Council of State denied the
claim of the prefects to require from the mayors any detailed statements of their
expenses, but upheld their right to assure themselves in each case that the
allotted sum constituted a reimbursement and not a remuneration. See *Revue
générale d'administration*, 1898, III. 34.

attempt to explain the actual exercise of the mayor's prerogatives. A mayor who desires to leave almost everything to his adjoints and the permanent heads of the civic Elasticity
departments may easily do so, thereby becoming as little of some powers.
influential in the guidance of municipal policy as is the
mayor of an English borough. On the other hand, a man
of the requisite individuality and energy, like M. Auga-
gneur, the former mayor of Lyons, may make of the office
almost a municipal dictatorship, and may even match the
executive head of New York City in the scope and importance of the powers which he exercises directly. Usually,
of course, the French mayor represents neither extreme.
The more vital of his powers he commonly exercises himself ; the less important he delegates to his adjoints, who
enjoy a generous degree of freedom, sometimes being permitted to use their discretionary privileges in a manner of
which the mayor may not personally approve.

The mayor of the French municipality, as has often been Dual posi-
pointed out, occupies a dual position, — a fact that must tion of the French
be kept constantly in mind if any proper grasp of his place mayor.
and powers is to be had. On the one hand he is the administrative head of his commune, the apex of the local
framework of government, selected by the elective organ
of the municipality and responsible to it for his acts. In Executive
this capacity he presides at all meetings of the communal head of the com-
council, makes an elaborate annual report to that body, mune.
and represents the municipality in all legal proceedings, as
well as upon all ceremonial occasions.[1] As the administra- His appoint-
tive head of the city he also makes practically all appoint- ing power.
ments of municipal officials from highest to lowest, with

[1] The best convenient source for any special study of the French mayor's
powers is G. Franceschi's *Manuel des maires* (2 vols., Paris, 1903). A less
elaborate but a useful work is Durand de Nancy's *Nouveau guide pratique des
maires, des adjoints, des secrétaires de maires, et des conseillers municipaux*
(Paris, 1905).

the exception of one or two important offices, — such as that of treasurer (*receveur municipal*), — which are filled either by the prefect or by the president of the republic.[1] No confirmation of the mayor's appointments is necessary at the hands of the council; but in the case of police officials, as will be seen later, the approval of the prefect is required.[2]   One may say, in fact, that for almost every important civic appointment the mayor is directly and entirely responsible.   In the larger cities this power puts in his hands a considerable patronage, particularly since there are no important limitations upon his freedom to choose appointees; for the cities of France have no system of competitive civil-service examinations as Americans understand them, and only for the more technical posts is any specific qualification demanded by law.[3]   On the other hand, since removals are rarely made to serve partisan exigencies, the mayor usually finds, during his term, very few gaps to be filled; it is his practice, moreover, to leave to the adjoints and the permanent heads of the various civic departments a generous degree of liberty in nominating persons to fill vacancies on their respective staffs.

Suspension and dismissal of municipal officers.   To the mayor is also given the power of suspending or dismissing any municipal officer, a privilege which he may exercise without the concurrence of the council or the approval of any higher authority.   This power of removal does not, of course, extend to the police officials, who may not in any case be interfered with except with the prefect's

---

[1] The choice is made from a list of three persons presented by the municipal council.   When the annual municipal revenue is less than 300,000 francs the appointment is made by the prefect, and not by the president (*La loi municipale*, § 156).   If the revenue of the municipality is less than 60,000 francs the collector of taxes (*percepteur*) performs the functions of the treasurer.   See *Loi du 25 février 1901*, § 50, in *Bulletin des lois*, 1901, I. 2013–2038.

[2] Below, p. 74.   [3] *Cf.* below, pp. 89 ff.

consent. It is worth noting, moreover, that, when the mayor has the power of suspension or dismissal, his action is not subject to review by any civil court; nor may any compensation be awarded by such a court to a deposed official even when the action of the mayor can be shown to have been arbitrary or without good cause. The only authority that has power to review a mayor's action in this matter is the highest administrative court of the republic, the Council of State.[1] This body may, if it so determines, annul the order by which an officer was removed, or it may award him damages to be paid out of the treasury of the municipality; but the cases in which such action has been taken are not numerous. This well-established legal doctrine in France relieves the mayors of what often becomes a gross evil in American cities, — namely, the reinstatement in office, by the ordinary civil courts, of officials who have been suspended or dismissed by the chief executive of the city. In most American states the statutes make provision that the mayor may remove from municipal office only for cause, and that the courts shall decide whether the cause assigned is or is not sufficiently good. In New York, for instance, it has been held that in order to justify removal there must be some clear incapacity or dereliction of duty; that, in the absence of such definite grounds, a mayor may not remove an official for the good of the service and in order to install an officer admittedly more competent and more adequately qualified for the duties of the post.[2] Not that the aggrieved official is in

Restrictions on the power of dismissal.

Jurisdiction of the administrative courts.

French and American methods of affording redress for wrongful dismissal.

---

[1] The law and practice relating to the appointment, suspension, and removal of French officials, national, departmental, and municipal, are discussed at length in L. F. Métérié-Larrey's *Les emplois publics* (Paris, 1883) ; André Delest's *Nomination et révocation des fonctionnaires* (Paris, 1899) ; J. Drouille's *Le pouvoir disciplinaire sur les fonctionnaires publics* (Toulouse, 1900) ; and E. G. Perrier's *De la révocation des fonctionnaires* (Paris, 1903).

[2] People *vs.* Fire Commissioners, 73 *New York Reports*, 437.

France deprived of all redress; on the contrary, he sometimes obtains from the Council of State monetary compensation which would in all probability never be awarded by any court in the United States. In order to obtain this redress, however, he must show adequate basis for his claim before a tribunal which views the matter in its relation to the good of the service rather than from the viewpoint of a protector of private rights.[1]

Financial powers of the mayor. As administrative head of the municipality, the mayor, under the control of the council, has general charge of the financial affairs of the commune.[2] It is his duty to see that the revenues of the municipality, both ordinary and extraordinary, are properly collected and conserved, and to make a report to the council on the matter before that body proceeds to a consideration of the annual budget. His report is, in fact, a general summary of the financial condition of the commune, showing receipts, expenditures, loans, indebtedness, and so on ; and it must tally with the independent report on the same field presented by the municipal treasurer, who, it will be remembered, is not appointed by the mayor. A copy of both reports goes either to the ministry of the interior or to the prefect, for scrutiny by the council of the prefecture or by the *Cour des Comptes*, according to the size of the annual expenditure. These scrutinizing authorities give special attention to such items as uncollectible taxes, miscellaneous expenses, and other like incidents of local finance in which supervision from a higher power is always wholesome. While the financial statement is being considered by the council, the mayor does not preside ; a chairman pro tempore is chosen

---

[1] An interesting discussion of this whole matter may be found in the decision of the Council of State in the case of M. Cadot, municipal engineer of Marseilles, printed in *Revue générale d'administration*, 1890, I. 451 ff.

[2] *La loi municipale*, §§ 52, 71, 151. See also Paul Dubois's *Essai sur les finances communales* (Paris, 1898).

by the councillors, and the mayor retires until the question of adopting the report has been voted upon.

After this report has been accepted the council is at liberty, at its May session, to proceed to a consideration of the budget for the ensuing fiscal year. This budget is drawn up by the mayor, who, though he is assisted in his work of compilation by the adjoints and the heads of departments, bears the sole responsibility of securing the acceptance of the various items by the council. The document is divided into two sections, one comprising estimated receipts and the other estimated expenditures. The section dealing with receipts is also usually subdivided into two parts, one including ordinary and the other extraordinary revenues.[1] The section dealing with expenditures is, in the case of the larger municipalities, parcelled into several subdivisions comprising such heads as " general expenses of administration," "maintenance of municipal property," "pensions and charity," " police," " fire protection," " education," and so on. With respect to some of the items included the mayor has a discretionary power; but most of them represent expenditures that are rendered obligatory by law. The municipal code enumerates not fewer than twenty appropriations which the budget must make in sums deemed adequate by the higher authorities.[2] This list includes such items as the maintenance of municipal property, the preservation of municipal archives, the salaries of the municipal treasurer and some other officers, the pay and equipment of the police establishment, the pensions of local officials, education, the preparation of voters' lists,

Preparation of the annual budget.

Structure of the budget.

Items in the budget required by law.

----

[1] The lines of demarcation between ordinary and extraordinary revenues are fixed in *La loi municipale*, §§ 132–134. Extraordinary expenditures are those of an accidental or temporary character, which do not occur annually; ordinary expenditures are those which come in the budget year after year. See *La loi municipale*, § 135; also above, pp. 56–57.

[2] *La loi municipale*, § 136.

the repair of local highways, the remuneration of all local officers in posts created by the state, and various other expenditures. In fact, a very large part of the budget is made up of these obligatory items, which greatly restrict the discretionary powers of the mayor.[1] These items must all be put into the budget and must be passed; otherwise they will be inserted by the prefect, and, if necessary, the mayor or the councillors or both may be suspended from office for their recalcitrancy.[2] Such drastic action has, however, never yet been necessary. At the May session of the council the energies of the mayor are devoted very largely to getting through the council those items with regard to which he has discretion.

Powers of the mayor in relation to municipal property.

Again, the mayor, as head of the commune, exercises supervisory jurisdiction over the management of communal property, which in some French cities is of large and growing value.[3] All matters of general policy relating to such property are, however, determined by the council, subject to the approval of the prefect. The mayor is also charged with many functions relating to the carrying out of the various conditions which may have been imposed upon the municipal authorities through their acceptance of gifts or legacies.[4] In the actual oversight of sundry municipal works of construction, too, he finds many duties laid upon him. He selects the engineers or architects who make the plans; he appoints the supervisors who secure conformity to these plans in construction; and he is responsible that the authorized expenditure for the under-

---

[1] This point is very clearly brought out in Professor J. A. Fairlie's paper on "Municipal Accounts and Statistics in Continental Europe," printed in National Municipal League, *Proceedings*, 1901, pp. 282–301.

[2] See above, pp. 56–57; and below, p. 83.

[3] This branch of municipal administration is dealt with at length in Edmond Cléray's *De la mise en valeur des biens communaux* (Paris, 1900).

[4] See above, pp. 58–59.

taking shall not be exceeded.[1] Not a single franc may be paid out of the municipal exchequer without his warrant (*mandat*), save when he refuses to order the payment of an obligatory expense. In such cases the municipal treasurer may be commanded by prefectoral decree to make the payment.[2]

To the mayor is further committed the supervision of all matters relating to minor streets and passages. It is his duty to supervise the construction and the repair of these, to see that private abutters do not encroach upon them, to make rules for the regulation of traffic along them, and in general to see that they are kept reasonably safe and convenient. Over all highways within the municipality, whether main or minor, the mayor has police power in his capacity as chief police authority of the commune.

Powers of the mayor with reference to streets.

One of the most important powers possessed by the mayor as chief executive officer of the municipality is that of organizing and controlling the system of municipal police. Throughout France, with only three exceptions, the organization of city police is vested, in the first instance, with the mayor of the commune;[3] but it cannot be too strongly emphasized that this police jurisdiction is exercised by him subject to the strict supervision of the prefect of his

The mayor's police powers.

---

[1] The exact powers and duties of the mayor in connection with the construction and repair of municipal works have been defined in a large number of decisions rendered by the administrative courts in cases brought before them from time to time. The gist of these decisions may be found in Léon Thorlet's *Traité des travaux communaux* (Paris, 1894). Reference may also be made to J. Lefournier's article on "Les battues communales," in *Revue générale d'administration*, 1888.

[2] *La loi municipale*, § 152.

[3] The three exceptions are Paris, Lyons, and Marseilles. In the first, city police control is vested in the hands of a special national officer called the prefect of police (see below, pp. 100–102); in the second it is given to the regular prefect of the department of the Rhône (*La loi municipale*, § 104); in the third it has recently been committed to the prefect of the department of Bouches-du-Rhône (*Loi du 8 mars 1908*).

department.[1] The situation is the more incongruous in
view of the fact that French municipalities are by law
rendered pecuniarily liable to make good any serious
damage to private property which may result from the
inability of their police systems to cope with riots and
other violent breaches of the peace.[2] The *commissaires
de police*, or professional heads of the municipal police
organizations, are always appointed by decree of the president of the republic, the gendarmes by the minister of war

Scope of
this author-
ity.

at the request of the mayors. The mayor himself appoints
all other police officials, such as clerks, inspectors, *agents de
police, sergents de ville*, and in the rural communes *gardes
champêtres;* but all his appointments to the higher posts
must have the concurrence of the prefect or the subprefect.
Subject to prefectoral approval he likewise regulates the
rates of pay, the duties, and the system of discipline, besides
authorizing promotions and making suspensions or dismis-
sals when such seem desirable. In municipalities that have
populations not exceeding 40,000, the mayor is allowed to
exercise a fairly free hand in the organization and control

Differences
in police ad-
ministration
between
larger and
smaller com-
munes.

of the force, with the result that there is, in the less populous communes, a considerable divergence from uniformity.
In cities of over 40,000, on the other hand, the mayor's
discretionary powers are very much narrowed; for in these

[1] A quarter-century or more ago there was some controversy among authorities upon French administration as to whether the mayor exercised his police
powers as a communal or as a national officer; but it is now more or less
generally agreed that it is as administrative head of the municipality and not as
local agent of the central authorities that he exerts his control over local police
affairs.

[2] For further discussions of this liability, see André Spire's *Étude historique
et juridique de la responsabilité des communes en cas d'attroupements* (Paris,
1895); Jean Perrinjaquet's *De la responsabilité des communes en matière de
police* (Paris, 1905); Maurice Vel-Durand's *De la responsabilité des communes
en cas de dommages par des attroupements ou rassemblements* (Paris, 1902); and
M. Michoud's paper on "La responsabilité des communes," in *Revue du droit
public*, 1897, I. 47 ff.

cases the general lines of organization and administration in regard to the municipal police are prescribed by presidential decree. There are at present forty-five cities whose populations exceed this prescribed limit, and for each of these a special decree has been issued by the president, all of them following similar general lines but in matters of detail showing some important differences. Even within the limits marked off by the decrees, however, the police jurisdiction of the mayor in a large French city is far from being that of a mere figurehead.[1]

The police powers of the mayor are not confined to matters of organization and discipline. Even more important than his authority in this field is his power to issue police ordinances or *arrêtés* designed to regulate an extensive category of matters, many of which would not, in American cities, be left to the discretion of any administrative official. In these municipal police ordinances, for instance, are drawn up and enunciated all regulations necessary for the carrying into effect of principles set forth in the national laws. In this connection it may be well to recall the French practice of enacting and promulgating national statutes which sometimes do little more than declare principles or define general lines of policy, leaving the whole range of detailed provisions to be worked out and applied by the hierarchy of administrative officials.[2] When-

Police ordinances.

Nature and significance of the ordinance power.

---

[1] The nature and scope of the mayor's police powers are dealt with at length in Léon Thorlet's *Traité de police à l'usage des maires* (Paris, 1891) ; M. Lagarde's *La police municipale* (Alençon, 1895) ; Émile Miriel's *Des rapports des municipalités et du pouvoir central au matière de police* (Paris, 1897) ; and M. Peletant's *De l'organisation de la police* (Dijon, 1899). A concise but very informing discussion of the topic may be found in De Croissy's *Dictionnaire municipal*, under " Police."

[2] On the significance of this practice, see A. Esmein's discussion of " La délégation du pouvoir législatif," in *Revue politique et parlementaire*, August, 1894; and H. Berthélemy's article on " Le pouvoir réglementaire du Président de la République," *Ibid.* 1898.

ever, therefore, a national law requires an application of
its principles in the local jurisdictions, the appropriate
ministry, usually the Ministry of the Interior, issues a
circular (*circulaire ministérielle*) to the prefects of the eighty-
seven departments of the republic, setting forth the new
policy and indicating the general lines along which it is to
be applied.   This circular the prefects communicate to the
mayors; whereupon the mayor of each municipality issues an
ordinance making specific regulations in accordance with the
minister's instructions and the prefect's additional orders.[1]
These instructions and orders must, to be sure, hew pretty
closely to the lines laid down in the law; for in France,
as in all other countries which maintain the forms of democratic government, all administrative regulations that
do not have for their purport the more efficient carrying
out of the law are properly regarded as incidents of des-
potism.[2]   In general, therefore, the mayors' *arrêtés* do not
differ materially in the different municipalities, for the
instructions issued to the prefects and by these, in turn, to
the mayors are usually explicit; indeed, the ministry or
the prefecture sometimes sends the ordinance fully drafted
and hence requiring nothing but the mayor's signature.   In
any case, the mayor is apt to follow closely the customary
printed form.[3]   Still, his discretionary power is often important, especially in the larger cities, where the municipal
orders have to provide for very complicated contingencies.

In addition to the power of issuing *arrêtés* applying in
detail the provisions of national laws, the mayor may

---

[1] A serviceable volume on this phase of the mayor's powers is M. Tchernoff's
Du pouvoir réglementaire des maires (Paris, 1899).   See also G. Le Breton's
Du pouvoir réglementaire des préfets (Caen, 1900).

[2] See H. Berthélemy on " De l'exercice de la souveraineté par l'autorité administrative," in *Revue du droit public*, 1904, XXI. 209-227.

[3] These forms are compiled, in convenient order, in G. Franceschi's *Dictionnaire des formules ou mairie pratique* (2 vols., Paris, 1903).

promulgate ordinances to carry out resolutions made by the council within its legal sphere of jurisdiction; and he may also publish on his own initiative such orders as he deems necessary to the public safety, provided that these are not inconsistent with the general laws of the land.[1] He may, for example, prescribe drastic regulations for the prevention of epidemics of disease, for the condemnation of unsanitary buildings within the municipal limits, and for other matters incidental to the general health.[2] Within recent years the scope of his discretionary powers in this particular sphere has been defined and in some degree increased.[3] His authority with respect to measures for protecting property from fire is also broad. It is worth noting, moreover, that even for flagrant errors of judgment in connection with the issue of regulations the mayor cannot be held responsible in the ordinary civil courts.[4] Most of his *règlements* may be annulled by the prefect; but even to this check there are limitations, for the Council of State has frequently supported mayors in their appeals against prefectoral vetoes of their ordinances.[5] The private individual who feels himself wronged by the operation of a mayor's order must

Ordinances issued on the mayor's own initiative.

Discretionary powers in many important branches of local administration.

Methods of redress against the pouvoir réglementaire of the mayor.

[1] In *La loi municipale*, §§ 91–99, may be found a long list of matters included within this sphere of the mayor's activity.

[2] L. Jouarre, *Des pouvoirs de l'autorité municipale en matière d'hygiène et de salubrité* (Paris, 1899); Gustave Jourdain, *Les pouvoirs des maires en matière de salubrité des habitations* (3d ed., Paris, 1900).

[3] Albert Guerlin de Guer, *La protection de la santé publique: les pouvoirs des maires et la loi du 15 février 1902* (Caen, 1903); M. Mosny, *La protection de la santé publique* (Paris, 1904); and G. Arnat, *Pouvoirs et rôles des maires au point de vue de la protection de la santé publique* (Paris, 1905).

[4] See the emphasis with which this is stated in a decision of the Tribunal des Conflits, March 2, 1900, reported in *Revue générale d'administration*, 1900, I. 309–311.

[5] An instance frequently cited is afforded by the decision of the Council of State, June 7, 1902, in the appeal of the mayor of Néris against the action of the prefect of Allier (*Ibid.* 1902, II. 297).

seek annulment of such order from the administrative tribunals, not from the civil courts. The redress afforded by these tribunals is, however, reasonably liberal, — more so, in fact, than foreign students of French administrative organization have usually appreciated;[1] for it is an error to suppose that a division of jurisdiction between ordinary and administrative courts necessarily reduces the remedial rights which an injured private interest is able to assert against the acts of public authority.[2] Furthermore, a petition for the quashing of a mayor's *règlement* is not the only or the most effective means of securing immunity from its operations. An individual who is summoned before the ordinary police court (*tribunal de simple police*) for violating a mayor's order may plead that the order is in excess of the mayor's legal powers, and his plea will be recognized by the courts. An acquittal on this ground is, of course, tantamount to an annulment of the regulation.

Important nature of the mayor's ordinance power.

The ordinance power of the French mayor puts in his hands an authority which, in the cities of the United States or of Great Britain, is very rarely committed to any official or even to an administrative board. It is not a mere administrative power; it is in a sense a delegation of the sovereign law-making prerogative of the state, a power to make laws in accordance with a defined general principle, not simply authority to administer the provisions of laws already made.[3] It is the practice of Anglo-Saxon legislatures so to frame laws as to make them cover every con-

A delegation of real legislative power.

---

[1] Édouard Perrin, *De la compétence réglementaire des maires, et des voies de recours contre leurs arrêtés* (Paris, 1904).

[2] On this point see H. Berthélemy, *Traité élémentaire de droit administratif* (5th ed., Paris, 1908), especially Bk. III. ch. i.; F. J. Goodnow, *Comparative Administrative Law* (2 vols., New York, 1903), especially II. 174–175; and E. M. Parker on " State and Official Liability," in *Harvard Law Review*, March, 1906, pp. 335–350.

[3] *Cf.* A. Esmein on " La délégation du pouvoir législatif," in *Revue politique et parlementaire*, August, 1894.

tingency that may arise ; and if the provisions bear more
heavily upon one community than upon another there is no
legally recognized method of varying the pressure. American and British law-makers have been extremely careful
to avoid anything that might be deemed a delegation of
legislative power to any administrative official or board of
officials. Indeed, it is well settled in the United States
that legislative power as such cannot be legally delegated
to administrative officers unless the constitution under
which the legislature exists has expressly authorized such
delegation.[1] The French, on the other hand, by giving a
limited amount of actual legislative authority to the president of the republic, the prefects, and the mayors, have
secured a certain degree of elasticity and adaptability to
local conditions in the substance of the law as well as in
its administration.

French and American methods of law-making.

Besides being the administrative head of the municipality, the mayor is in his second capacity the local agent
of the central government. In the exercise of powers
incident to this office he is not subject to control by
the council ; his responsibility is to the higher authorities
alone, particularly to the prefect of the department in
which his municipality happens to be situated. In addition to all his regular municipal duties, the French mayor
has from time to time been intrusted by national law
with various special functions which he exercises as local
agent of the central authority. Although the number
of these special powers has become very large, many
of them are of slight intrinsic importance, requiring but
little attention and that at considerable intervals. Others
are of the highest significance in the general machinery of
French administration, involving a heavy share of the

Special functions of the mayor.

[1] See the list of cases cited in Emlin McClain's *Constitutional Law in the
United States* (New York, 1905), 54.

mayor's consideration, and laying upon the staff of the mairie a large amount of routine work, which must be performed with accuracy and thoroughness.

Supervision of the civil register. Among the more important of the special functions thus intrusted to the mayor may be mentioned the local supervision of the *état civil*, of which every mayor is ex-officio registrar,[1] the post devolving in his absence or incapacity upon the senior adjoint.   The system of *état civil* involves the preparation and maintenance of a register of all the births, marriages, and deaths that take place within the municipality, together with much other data concerning the personnel of the commune.   It is the duty of the mayor to supervise the issue of the *actes de naissance*, and to see that such subsequent indorsements are made upon them as may be provided for by law.[2]   Within his jurisdiction comes also the whole complicated procedure preliminary to the contracting of civil marriage, a work which in itself concentrates at the mairie of any large city a great deal of clerical routine ; and closely related is his charge of all the municipal archives and records, and his responsibility for the care of all communal rolls and documents.

Administration of laws relating to military service. Again, legal responsibility for the proper administration, in each commune, of the laws relating to compulsory military service has been imposed upon the mayor, who acts in this matter as the local agent of the Ministry of War.   He prepares each year the list of persons liable to service ;

[1] An account of the system of supervising the *état civil*, with examples of the forms used, may be found in Charles Ragel's *Manuel formulaire des actes de l'état civil à l'usage des maires* (Paris, 1898); in E. Destruels's *Manuel de l'officier d'état civil* (Paris, 1903); and in J. Monfreu's *Manuel pratique des actes de l'état civil* (Paris, 1904).   For a short sketch of the system see *Dictionnaire municipal*, under " État civil."

[2] See §§ 45 and 57 of the *Code civil* as modified by the *Loi du 30 novembre 1906* (*Bulletin des lois*, 1907, I. 793 ff.); also J. Rondelet's *Les règles nouvelles pour la délivrance des actes de naissance* (Paris, 1908).

and this list, after due publication and revision, he transmits through the prefect to the proper military authorities. It is his task to see that those who are subject to military service are duly sent forward to the proper place to begin their training. Until a few years ago it was the duty of the mayor to collect the prescribed imposts from those who were, for any reason, exempted from military service; but these taxes in lieu of service are no longer in force.[1] He is required to compile, and to keep constantly revised and up to date, various rosters showing the number of trained and untrained men within the municipality capable of bearing arms, together with lists of horses, vehicles, arms, carrier-pigeons, and other supplies that may be requisitioned by the national authorities in the event of war. In fact, the efficiency of the French military system depends largely upon the work constantly going on at the mairie of every municipality, a work so extensive that a discussion of it in detail has filled two bulky volumes.[2]

Important as are the military functions of the mayor in years of peace, they are doubly so in time of war or of rumors of war. At such crises the mairie becomes at once the local depot of the war authorities for the collection and transmission of supplies, horses, forage, and so forth, as well as a centre for all the incidents connected with mobilization, such as the securing of transportation for troops and reserves, the providing of rations for bodies of men en route through the municipality, the surveillance of strangers, aliens, and suspicious persons, and the securing of information of all sorts for the use of the military

Special duties in time of war.

---

[1] They were abolished by the *Loi du 21 mars 1905* (*Bulletin des lois*, 1905, I. 1265 ff.).

[2] Léon Bauer's *Les devoirs des maires et des municipalités en ce qui concerne l'armée* (Paris, 1894); and C. Rabany's *La loi sur le recrutement* (Paris, 1906).

G

authorities.[1] The 36,000 mayors of France at once become
so many military agents of the central government.

Minor functions of the mayor. Still other tasks of somewhat less importance have
been put by law upon the shoulders of the mayor. He is
responsible for the proper supervision of all matters connected with the preparation of the voters' lists used in the
national and departmental elections; for the exercise of
various important functions that have to do with the administration of the system of direct taxation; and for a
good deal of the work incidental to the taking of the
national quinquennial census. He is expected to preside
at meetings of the local school-commission, and to perform sundry duties pertaining to the supervision of the
system of primary education. He is president of the commission that manages the poor-relief bureau of the municipality (*bureau de bienfaisance*), and is expected to be a
leader in all local enterprises of a philanthropic nature.[2]
An enumeration of all the minor responsibilities which a
paternal government has laid upon the mayor would,
indeed, make up a rather formidable list.

Tasks of the mayor are numerous and varied. From the foregoing general survey of mayoral functions
it may be concluded that the mayor of a large French city
must be a pretty busy man; and one may be pardoned
for wondering why any citizen should feel disposed to
assume such a heavy load of detailed responsibilities without any remuneration whatever. It has been estimated
that the French mayor has more than five hundred specific official acts to perform in the course of each year,
every one of them to be done at a definite time and in a
prescribed way; and this does not include his general

---

[1] These military duties are explained in Paul Dislère's *Les devoirs des maires
en cas de mobilisation générale* (Paris, 1893).

[2] For an exact statement of the mayor's duties in this sphere, see Derouin,
Gory, and Worms, *Traité de l'assistance publique* (2 vols., Paris, 1901).

duties of issuing ordinances, supervising public property, caring for the public health and safety, and preparing and putting his budget through the council. He is, in the words of one writer, "loaded with innumerable and absorbing functions," and is, "for those whom he governs, an almost absolute master."[1]

But while the legal powers and responsibilities of the mayor are great, there are some significant practical checks upon the free exercise of his authority. In the first place, the municipal council exercises a considerable degree of control over his actions, even when it has no definite legal warrant for so doing. By its command of the municipal purse-strings it is very frequently able to make the mayor's policy conform to its own wishes in various important matters; and even in the sphere of municipal police, a function in which the mayor is supposed to be entirely free from its restraint, it very often makes its influence felt. To be successful in his administration a mayor must have the council's coöperation; and this he can secure, in many cases, only by frequent concessions to the sense of that body. When he expects reëlection it is of course more than ever desirable that he should defer to the wishes of the councillors.

In the second place, it should always be remembered that all of the mayor's acts as agent of the central government are performed under the strictest surveillance and control. He may be suspended from his office by the prefect for a period not exceeding one month, and this suspension may be extended to not more than three months by the minister of the interior.[2] He may, by presidential decree, be removed from office altogether, and in this case may not be reëlected to his post by the council for the

Limitation on his powers.

The council as a controlling influence.

The prefect's surveillance.

Suspension and removal of the mayor from office.

---

[1] Paul Deschanel, *La décentralisation* (Paris, 1895), 7 ff.
[2] *La loi municipale*, § 86.

space of one year. Curiously enough, however, he does not lose his seat in the council by virtue of his suspension or dismissal.[1] Against an order of suspension issued by the prefect he has a right of appeal to the Council of State, on the ground that the prefect has exceeded his legal powers or has violated the forms of law; but the justice or the expediency of the prefect's act he may not call into question before this body.[2] Against a decree of suspension by the minister, or of removal by the president, he may avail himself of the same means of redress.[3]

Securities against the arbitrary use of this power.

It is not to be inferred, however, that the powers of suspension and removal are exercised in any arbitrary fashion; for the accountability of all the higher officers to the elected representatives of the people in the national Chamber of Deputies is complete and direct. If, therefore, the minister of the interior supports or advises any suspension or removal which affords ground for criticism, he can, by means of an interpellation upon the point,[4] be compelled by the deputies from the municipality concerned to justify his action before either Chamber. In this roundabout way the deputies are brought into indirect but none the less influential relation to local administration; and by their attitude the relations between the mairie and the prefecture are to a considerable extent determined. There is, indeed, much complaint that deputies, especially

[1] " Rapport fait à la Chambre des Députés par M. Félix Faure, séance du 29 décembre 1880," cited in Morgand's La loi municipale, I. 546.

[2] Revue générale d'administration, 1898, III. 415.

[3] A very recent enactment (Loi du 8 juillet 1908) has given to the mayors some additional securities against arbitrary suspension or dismissal. No such action may now be taken by the higher authorities until after the mayor has been called upon for an explanation of the matters at issue; and the order of suspension or the decree of removal must in every case state explicitly the grounds upon which it is issued.

[4] On the "interpellation" procedure, see A. L. Lowell, Governments and Parties, I. 117-126; also J. Poudra and E. Pierre, Traité pratique de droit parlementaire (8 vols., Versailles, 1878-1880), VII. ch. iv.

those who happen to be supporters of the administration at Paris, are in the habit of putting undue pressure upon the local prefectures, and this for purely political ends; and it is also said that a mayor who incurs the antagonism of the ministerial deputies from his city is very likely to discover the consequences in the course of his relations with the prefect. Many ministerial deputies appear to look upon the prefect as a partisan agent, and to expect him to use his large jurisdiction over the municipal authorities in ways that will conduce to the advantage of the party in power at the national capital.

Although the mayor is directly responsible for the prompt and efficient performance of all the functions which the law imposes upon him, he may distribute the actual work of the office among his adjoints, who in turn may cast most of the routine upon the permanent civic officials and employees. In the distribution of work among the adjoints the mayor has entire discretion. He may assign an adjoint much or little to do, or may leave him to serve out his term without any duties at all. Though he does not select him and cannot remove him from office, he can thus render him powerless in the administrative affairs of the municipality. As a matter of practice, the adjoints are assigned to the various departments of civic administration according to their respective qualifications and experience, the mayor as a rule retaining the police department as his own share. One adjoint is put in charge of streets, another of fire protection, a third of sanitation, and so on, the number of departments usually corresponding to the number of adjoints available. These officers thus perform functions very similar to those which, in the English boroughs, are assumed by the various standing committees of the council and exercised largely by the chairmen of such committees. The system,

The adjoints, or assistant mayors.

Division of functions among the adjoints.

it will be noted, concentrates all responsibility upon the mayor, but enables him to apportion the work at his discretion.

The permanent heads of the municipal departments.
The adjoints, in their work of administration, are after all only amateurs; hence, though many of them may have long consecutive terms of service in general charge of the same departments, and may thus acquire considerable proficiency, they are forced to lean heavily upon the higher employees of the municipality, — upon the professional heads of the various departments. Chief among these
The *secrétaire de mairie*.
heads is the *secrétaire de mairie*, who has charge of the clerical staff at the civic headquarters, an officer upon whom the mayor is especially dependent for the proper carrying out of his functions. Every commune in France, from smallest to largest, numbers this official among its permanent employees, in the smaller villages the post being regarded as one of the perquisites of the local schoolmaster. In the largest municipalities, however, the secretary is a professional and reasonably-paid officer, who devotes all his time and energies to the numerous duties of his position. Not only has he immediate charge of all the clerical work of the mairie, but to him are intrusted most of the responsibilities which the central authorities have laid upon the mayor. Through his long tenure in
His functions and influence.
office he becomes the custodian of communal traditions, a local authority on all points of municipal law and procedure to whom all may turn for information, and is in every sense the most influential officer on the whole staff of civic employees. " He is, indeed, the modest auxiliary who studies earnestly all local questions, who prepares all reports, and finds solutions for all local problems; the man who is in constant touch with the public, who represents the municipality before other administrations, and who rides fearlessly into the labyrinth of law, decrees, cir-

culars, and instructions; the citizen, in a word, who alone
represents and maintains local traditions in the days when
universal suffrage supplants the erstwhile masters of the
city by the new-elect, to whom sound counsel and guidance
are a necessity." [1]

The secretary is, in fact, to the municipal authorities
of France what the town clerk is to the mayors of England; he is even more, for his duties are much more
numerous, more varied, and more responsible because of
the large measure of dependence which the central government puts upon local administration. To a very large
degree, indeed, the efficiency of municipal administration
hinges upon the ability, accuracy, and tact of this important officer, and upon the discipline and *esprit de corps*
which he is able to maintain among the staff at the city
hall, a staff usually divided into four bureaus, each with
its chief and deputy-chief and its corps of subordinate officers.[2] Without an able secretary the French municipality
would soon find its administrative machinery very badly
clogged and its mayor hopelessly entangled in the duties
of his own office. Nevertheless, although the secretary,
like the English town clerk, does perhaps more than any
other single individual to keep municipal administration
running smoothly, the importance of his position has not
always been fully appreciated by students of local government, and, indeed, the officer himself has rarely received
much credit in his own community.

Another prominent municipal officer is the treasurer
(*receveur municipal*), who in the larger municipalities is

May be compared to the English town clerk.

The municipal treasurer.

---

[1] R. Martineau, *Les secrétaires de mairie* (Paris, 1906), 11. In this volume
may be found a full discussion of the position and powers of the secretary. See
also G. Dubarry, *Le secrétaire de mairie* (Paris, 1892) ; and E. Bourgueil, *Le
vade-mecum de l'instituteur secrétaire de mairie* (Paris, 1892).

[2] These bureaus are, ordinarily, (1) *secrétariat*, (2) *bureau de l'état civil*,
(3) *bureau militaire*, (4) *bureau de police*.

selected by the president of the republic from a list of three names submitted by the municipal council. The treasurer, who must be paid and provided with quarters by the municipality, is the custodian of the communal funds and the general head of the city's department of finance.[1] Since, however, the primary responsibility for municipal payments rests with the mayor, the treasurer may not refuse to make a disbursement in response to a mayor's warrant unless there be no appropriation for the purpose or no funds on hand, or unless the proper vouchers be not attached to the warrant. The treasurer, like the mayor, presents an annual report to the municipal council, which examines the paper thoroughly before taking up the budget the next year. This report must also, in due course, be submitted for audit to the national receiver of finances; and if the income of the municipality exceeds 30,000 francs it must also be laid before the national Court of Accounts (*Cour des Comptes*), which has auditing jurisdiction over almost the whole field of public finances in France. If the income be less than this sum, the scrutiny takes place at the local prefecture.

The chief commissaire of police.
A third officer invested with large discretionary power in the French commune is the chief commissaire of police, who is, however, appointed by the president of the republic, and who, although as regards his functions he corresponds to the chief constable of the English borough and is paid out of municipal funds, is not in France regarded as a municipal official. Every other civic department has likewise its permanent professional chief, usually with one or more deputy heads, nearly all of whom are selected by the mayor.

[1] See *Dictionnaire municipal*, under "Receveurs municipaux"; and, for further details, Adam's *Guide pratique du percepteur-receveur municipal* (Paris, 1897). The *Situation financière des communes*, published annually, contains elaborate statistics of communal expenditures drawn from the treasurers' reports.

The number of employees under these heads depends, of Minor officials.
course, upon the size of the municipality. When there are
only a few, the mayor commonly makes appointments
upon his own personal knowledge; but in the larger cities,
where the employees are numbered by hundreds or even
thousands, he usually intrusts his adjoints or the permanent heads with what virtually amounts to the appointing
power. The exercise of this power is not restricted, more- Methods of appoint-
over, by anything corresponding to what is commonly ment.
known in the United States as "civil service regulations";
appointments to municipal posts in France are not usually
made as the result of any competitive examination.[1] For
many of the technical posts, it is true, only qualified
engineers, or persons of some professional training, are
eligible; but, though many restrictions of this sort are
prescribed by national laws or by ministerial instructions,
the mayor and his adjoints still have wide scope for
the exercise of their own discretion.[2] The French seem
in general to put more reliance upon the plan of appointing an officer for a probationary period (usually a year or
two), in order to test him in the work of his post, than
upon the practice of holding competitive examinations to
determine the relative fitness of candidates, — a policy, it
may be added, which they apply to national, departmental,
and municipal offices alike.

On the whole, the character of the French municipal ser- Character of the French
vice has been satisfactorily high. Partisan considerations municipal
doubtless play some part in appointments; but it is seldom service.
that offices of importance are given as rewards for political

---

[1] Important exceptions are to be found in the case of most of the appointments made within the prefecture of the Seine, in Lyons, and in some of the
other largest cities. It may be added that appointments to posts in the national
service are now almost always made as the result of competitive examinations.

[2] Doisnel and Gaudoin, *Les secrétaires de mairie et employés communaux*
(Elbœuf, 1902).

services to persons who are unequal to the responsibilities imposed. The tenure of almost all the higher municipal posts is virtually during life or efficiency; and at the close of a long term of satisfactory service an official is provided, in most of the larger cities, with an annual pension. This liberal treatment by the municipality, combined with the length of tenure and the practice of requiring probationary service, no doubt has a tendency to secure satisfactory results from the staff of municipal employees.

French cities are administered by expert officials.

It would not be too much to say that the cities of France are administered very largely by corps of permanent municipal officials acting under a broad range of authority committed to them by the mayors. Though apparently vested in the hands of laymen, the administration is in reality, therefore, distinctly professional. The French have scrupulously maintained the forms of an elective, non-bureaucratic municipal government; but they have taken similar care to secure that efficiency which comes from the actual performance of all important administrative functions by skilled and experienced officials, who, secure in the tenure of their posts, go about their work with little or no captious interference from the elected representatives of the people.

Provisions for the syndicating of small communes.

Before leaving the discussion of municipal organization, let us glance at the facilities that have been afforded by a law supplementary to the code permitting the coöperation of adjacent municipalities in the establishment and maintenance of such utilities as are of joint or common interest. When the councils of two or more communes of the same department or of adjoining departments agree that any projected enterprise is of common utility to them, the president of the republic is empowered, on the advice of the minister of the interior, to issue a decree forming such municipalities into an association called a "syndicate of communes."[1] Such a syndicate receives the status of a public corporation, with power to acquire and hold property and to establish and maintain public services under the same restrictions and subject to the same higher supervision as the individual communes comprising the union. The enterprises undertaken by a syndicate of communes are in charge of a committee composed of delegates from the various municipal councils interested, each council naming two; but the proceedings of this committee are subject to the general restrictions imposed by the code upon the councils themselves, and all its deliberations must, like theirs, be confirmed by the prefect. The committee draws up its own budget — the receipts accruing mainly from assessments upon the communes comprised in the syndicate — and arranges its own expenditures. The facilities thus afforded by the law of 1890 have served the interests of economy in some of the smaller municipalities, but have not been employed by many of the larger towns and cities; even for syndicating smaller units, indeed, they have not been used so broadly as the framers of the measure had reason to expect. Only about a score of syndicates have been formed in almost as many years.

Administration of syndicated communal enterprises.

The municipal code of 1884 did not, as we have seen, apply to Paris. The metropolis has for a long period retained its own special form of administration, which differs in many important respects from that arranged for the other cities of France. In thus providing a *régime exceptionnel* for the capital, the action of the French authorities is, however, not unique; for London and Washington

The government of Paris.

---

[1] *Loi du 22 mars 1890*, in *Bulletin des lois*, 1890, I. 789–792. See also the supplementary *Circulaire ministérielle* of August 10, 1890; and Morgand's *La loi municipale*, II. 614–647.

both have municipal administrations which differ very radically from those of other British and American cities, and even Berlin is in some respects governed differently from the ordinary Prussian municipality.[1] The Parisian system, so far as the organization of the municipal council of the city is concerned, rests upon the law of April 14, 1871;[2] but the functions and powers of the prefects, who form the apex of metropolitan administration, are set forth in earlier laws.[3] When the law of 1871 was passed, it was expected that the system then established would be only temporary, and that in course of time Paris would receive additional concessions in the way of local control over her administrative organs; but no important step in this direction has since been taken by the national authorities, and the city is still governed under the somewhat makeshift arrangements made thirty-seven years ago.[4]

The arrangements of 1871.

For placing and maintaining the capital under a special regimen the French government has, of course, very ample justification. Not only is Paris the largest city of the republic, being many times as populous as its nearest rival, but it has always played a part in national politics much more influential than even its towering size has seemed to warrant. Again and again it has determined almost absolutely the trend of national history, and not always to the interest of the French people as a whole. The various French revolutions from 1789 to 1871 all had their origin in the capital; and in the changes of government which followed on the heels of these disturbances the people of the provinces were treated with but meagre consideration.

Reasons for the régime exceptionnel in Paris.

The city's boisterous traditions.

---

[1] See below, p. 208.

[2] *Loi du 14 avril 1871*, §§ 10–17, in *Bulletin des lois*, 1871, I. 97–101.

[3] *Loi du 24 juillet 1837*, modified by *Loi du 24 juillet 1867*.

[4] The changes since 1871 may be studied in Paul Massat's *Manuel de législation administrative spéciale à la ville de Paris et au département de la Seine* (Paris, 1901).

Paris, as has aptly been said, has always been both the
head and the heart of France; hence it is scarcely a matter for surprise that the authorities of the Third Republic
should have deemed it wise to hold a tight rein over a city
whose political fickleness has become traditional, and whose
record for making trouble has hardly been matched by any
other city of Europe.

Again, it is to be remembered that the nation has large The repub-
lic's large
material interests in Paris. The city is, for the most interests in
part, what the funds of the national government have made its capital.
it; for during the Napoleonic era, and especially during
the Second Empire, its public edifices were in the main
built by the lavish expenditure of millions drawn from
the coffers of the state. Furthermore, within the city limits
are located enormous amounts of national property in the
form of monuments, museums, legislative halls, and the
like; hence any lapse in the proper maintenance of law
and order is liable to be fraught with serious consequences
to the interests of the national government. In a word, it
is generally felt that the city must be kept upon its good
behavior, and that to insure this end the national authorities, who represent the people as a whole, are justified in
holding the municipality under more than ordinary restraint.

During the period of the Second Empire the administra- The frame-
tion of Paris was intrusted almost wholly to two prefects Paris gov-
appointed directly by the emperor.[1] These two officers ernment.
were retained by the arrangements made in 1871, and they The two
still continue to divide between them the actual manage- prefects.
ment of all municipal affairs; but the work of local legislation, and to some extent the general direction of municipal policy, have been committed to a large municipal

---

[1] On the earlier municipal history of Paris, see Frederick Lecaron's *Les origines de la municipalité parisienne* (2 vols., Paris, 1881–1882).

council composed of eighty members elected by the voters of the city. This council, with the prefects, who are known respectively as the prefect of the Seine and the prefect of police, constitute the framework of metropolitan administration.[1]

The prefect of the Seine. The prefect of the Seine is a national officer appointed by the president of the republic on recommendation of the ministers, to all of whom the prefect is immediately subordinate. Like the prefects of other French departments, he holds office for no definite term, but is removable at any time by the president. In practice, indeed, the length of term has shown considerable variation; for, although the department has had seven prefects since 1871 (the average term being thus about five years), it has had but two during the last quarter of a century,—the present incumbent, M. J. G. C. de Selves, having held the post since 1896, and his predecessor, M. Poubelle, for thirteen years prior to that date.[2] The office is very remunerative as French public posts go, the prefect of the Seine now receiving fifty thousand francs per year, in addition to princely quarters at the Hôtel de Ville and a liberal allowance for expenses.

Political considerations in his appointment. In one sense the appointment to this prefecture is political; that is to say, when the post becomes vacant the new appointee is likely to be an officer who has been a prominent supporter of the political faction or group of factions that hold the reins of power in the nation. The office is not, however, political in the sense that every change in national administration is liable to bring about a change

[1] The best convenient outline of Parisian government is G. Artigues's *Le régime municipal de la ville de Paris* (Paris, 1898). M. Block's *Administration de la ville de Paris et du département de la Seine* (Paris, 1898) is also useful.

[2] The list of prefects may be found in *Encyclopédie municipale de la ville de Paris* (2 vols., Paris, 1904), I. Introd. cxi. This useful compilation also contains a store of information relating to the personnel and the organization of Parisian local government.

at the prefecture ; on the contrary, a score of administrations
have come and gone during the terms of Messrs. Poubelle
and De Selves without any suggestion that these officers
should be removed. It is, of course, quite true that the
prefect of the Seine, as an immediate agent of the central
government, must be in working sympathy with his superiors for the time being ; but changes in the headship of
the Ministry of the Interior do not usually involve any important changes in the general policy of the office, for the
real work of supervision over all branches of local government is performed by permanent under-officers, who do not
move when ministries come and go. The relations between the ministry and the prefecture are, indeed, so well
defined by law, by decree, or by administrative decisions
and precedents, that the various shiftings in national administration have little influence at the Hôtel de Ville.

The office of prefect in any French department is one Difficult
that requires a rare combination of skill, firmness, integ- nature of
the office.
rity, and tact ; but among all the eighty-seven divisions of
the republic the department of the Seine is the one in which
the possession of these qualities by the prefect is the most
urgently demanded. The office of this prefect is perhaps
the most influential in the whole range of French local administration ; since, therefore, the prestige which its tenure
confers upon the occupant is naturally very great, it is almost imperative that the Seine prefect shall be a man of
tested administrative ability, a demand which has in general been fully met. Since the establishment of the office
by Napoleon I. its roll of occupants has made up a very
distinguished list, comprising such familiar names as those
of Odilon Barrot, Baron Haussmann, Jules Ferry, Léon Say,
Ferdinand Duval, and several others known far beyond the
borders of France. The post has not been held by mere
bureaucrats ; the incumbents have not, like too many of

the German bürgermeisters, been merely efficient administrative machines. On the contrary, most of them have been
men of mark drawn from active public life, who have
brought to the office unusual qualities of initiative and
originality.

Powers of the Seine prefect.   The powers of the prefect of the Seine may be grouped
under two main heads. In the first place, he possesses
in the department of the Seine, — which includes not only
the city of Paris, but the environs for some distance beyond the city walls, — all the powers that appertain to
the office of prefect in any of the other French departments. In the second place, he exercises, in the absence
of a Parisian mayor, all the functions (except those relating to police) that belong to the office of mayor in the
ordinary municipality.[1] His position is, therefore, that
of mayor and prefect combined, and his responsibility is
directly to the minister of the interior.[2] As the virtual
mayor of Paris he is the apex of the local framework of
civic administration ; as prefect he is the immediate local
agent of the central authorities. In the former capacity
he is intrusted with the carrying out of such resolutions
as may be passed by the municipal council of Paris and
by the general council of the department of the Seine, —
for, as will be noticed later on,[3] these bodies are somewhat different in composition. He prepares the municipal
budget (except that portion which has to do with the
police establishment), and lays it before the municipal
council at the proper session, appearing in the council-
chamber to explain and defend the various items contained in it. He has general charge of all civic and

[1] See above, pp. 67 ff.
[2] A detailed analysis of the prefect's powers may be found in Eugène Magné
de la Londe's *Les attributions du préfet de la Seine* (Paris, 1902).
[3] See below, p. 108.

departmental property, supervising its construction and maintenance; and in all legal transactions he acts as the representative of the city or of the department, as the case may be. As all the streets of Paris are included within the category of *la grande voirie*, he exercises supervision over these, except in matters that have to do with the regulation of traffic,— a responsibility which rests with his colleague, the prefect of police. The immediate administration of the great public services of the city — the water supply, the sewer system, and various other civic enterprises of a similar character — is vested in his hands, as well as the general oversight of all poorhouses, hospitals, and like institutions. He has important functions in connection with the system of poor relief and with that of primary and higher education;[1] and on all matters within his jurisdiction he has authority to publish orders or decrees such as are issued by the other prefects or by the mayors.[2] In addition to all this, he is responsible for the exercise of a host of minor functions, — for the supervision of the *état civil*, the preparation and revision of the voters' lists, the oversight of many matters connected with the system of military service, and so on. There is, in fact, a greater concentration of administrative powers in the hands of the prefect of the Seine than in those of any other local official in France, or, indeed, in any other country.[3]

For the efficient and satisfactory performance of his various duties the prefect of the Seine is not directly responsible to either of his councils; he is accountable to

His relations to the municipal council.

---

[1] A full account of the organization and administration of these various services is contained in *Encyclopédie municipale de la ville de Paris*. Statistical data may be had in the *Annuaire statistique de la ville de Paris* (1907).

[2] G. Le Breton, *Du pouvoir réglementaire des préfets* (Caen, 1900).

[3] See A. Lavalée on "Le régime administratif du département de la Seine et de la ville de Paris," in *Revue générale d'administration*, 1900–1901, *passim*.

H

the central authorities alone. He must, however, be able to work in tolerable harmony with his councils, for without their coöperation the necessary funds for conducting a considerable part of the administration would not be forthcoming. Many of the items in the annual Parisian budget must, it is true, be inserted by law, and hence are not subject to the control of the council; but many others are completely within its jurisdiction, and with this factor the prefect's administrative policy must reckon. During the last decade or more the relations between the prefect and the council have sometimes become badly strained; but, with the central authorities behind him, the prefect of the Seine has usually maintained his controlling hand.

The staff of the prefecture.   To the proper performance of his varied functions the prefect brings the assistance of a large staff at headquarters, chief among the members of which is the secretary of the prefecture, who assumes a great share of the prefect's responsibilities with reference to clerical routine. The remaining members of the staff are grouped into " services," and these again into bureaus and sections.[1] Each division has its chief and usually its deputy-chief, together with its corps of clerical and technical employees. All the higher posts are filled by the president of the republic on the recommendation of the minister of the interior, the lower ones by the prefect himself, or even by his chief subordinates. The employees of the department of the Seine are selected almost without exception by a system of competitive examinations, which is most efficiently administered by a *jury d'examen*. The available vacancies average in number only about twenty per year; but more than 150 candidates annually take the examinations, and the president of the examining board — who is

[1] For details, consult the *Encyclopédie municipale de la ville de Paris*, Vol. I.

a professor in the law faculty of the University of Paris —
vouches that the successful competitors are an unusually
promising set of men. Positions in the service of the city
are much sought after; for the municipal staff is well paid,
and liberal pensions are given to employees on retirement
after long terms of service.

In addition to what may be called the headquarters
staff of the prefecture, which is directly in charge of the
great municipal services, there is a local administrative
organization in each of the twenty *arrondissements*, or
wards, into which the city is divided. Each division has
its local headquarters—the mairie of the ward—supervised by a mayor, who is an appointee of the central government and gives his services gratuitously. Each mayor
is assisted by a staff of three or five adjoints, who are
similarly appointed and who likewise receive no remuneration. All these officials are the immediate subordinates of
the prefect of the Seine, intrusted with the duty of carrying out his orders in the local areas. The actual work is,
of course, not performed by the mayors and adjoints themselves, but by the permanent staffs maintained at the local
headquarters.[1] Each of the twenty Parisian mairies has
its secretary, its heads of bureaus, and its clerical staff similar to that of the ordinary communal mairie; and by these
officials the work of maintaining the *état civil*, the preparation of voters' lists, the functions connected with the
military system, and various other tasks are performed.
Connected with each mairie, moreover, are a number of
commissions presided over by the mayor or by an adjoint
and composed of lay citizens appointed either by the prefect
or by the minister of the interior. To these local commis-

*The govern-
ment of the
Paris arron-
dissements.*

---

[1] Many interesting details concerning the work done in the mairies may be
found in H. Lesage's *Souvenirs d'un maire-adjoint de Paris*, 1880–1895 (Paris
[1898]).

sions are given many powers relating to poor relief, education, the sanitary utilities, and a multitude of minor municipal services.

The system permits decentralization. In this way much of the administrative work of the prefect has been decentralized; indeed, a large share of the clerical routine is now performed at the various mairies and not at the Hôtel de Ville. Like the headquarters staff, the personnel of the twenty mairies forms a part of the municipal civil service; it is a permanent professional body, which in its work is not influenced to any considerable extent by changes in the higher ranks of the administration. The *arrondissement* authorities have, to be sure, little or no voice in the shaping of general municipal policy, for their work is mainly to see that the plans made at headquarters are carried out in their respective wards; but the system has brought into the service of the municipality a great many public-spirited citizens, who, serving without remuneration as mayor, adjoints, or members of local commissions, give freely of their time for the city's advantage. Since the number of such persons in Paris must run well into the hundreds, their part in municipal administration undoubtedly lends flexibility to the system of metropolitan government;[1] and, furthermore, since the *arrondissements* have no elective councils, the introduction of this lay element into the personnel of local administration insures a certain amount of responsiveness to popular feeling.

The prefect of police. The other Parisian prefect, called the prefect of police, occupies a post that has been in existence for over a century.[2] He is a colleague, not a subordinate, of the prefect of the Seine, is appointed by the president of the republic

---

[1] This point has been very well emphasized in Albert Shaw's *Municipal Government in Continental Europe*, 32–35.

[2] E. Mouneyrat's *La préfecture de police* (Paris, 1906) presents a full account of the history, organization, and powers of this prefecture.

on the recommendation of the interior ministry, and may
be removed by the chief of state at any time.   Since 1871
there have been eleven prefects of police, the average term
of service being thus but slightly more than three years.
The present incumbent, however, M. Louis Lepine, has been
continuously in office since 1899, besides having held the
post during the years 1893–1897.   There has thus been no
change in the headship of either prefecture for almost a
decade, and the indications seem to point to long tenures
as the rule for the future.   The office of prefect of police is
one of commanding influence; its occupant receives a large
stipend, and the demands made upon him are of such a
nature as to call for unusual administrative skill.

The powers of the prefect of police were originally Powers of
determined by the law of 1800, which established the post; the police
prefect.
but so many modifications have been made by subsequent
laws and decrees that the exact scope of his authority is
not easily defined.   In general he has charge of that branch
of administrative jurisdiction which the French include in
their conception of the term "police."   Police jurisdiction in France, however, comprises not alone the maintenance of law and order, but many other functions only
indirectly related to this one,—as, for example, the supervision of sanitary regulations, the oversight of unhealthy
or dangerous industries, the so-called *police des mœurs*, and
many like functions which in America are not committed
to the charge of local police but to special state authorities.
The prefect of police exercises those police powers which
in the ordinary communes are given to the mayors, together
with the larger police functions which in the ordinary departments go to the regular prefects.   His authority is not,
it may be repeated, subject to any surveillance on the part
of the prefect of the Seine ; he is responsible directly to
the minister of the interior.   Under instructions which he

may receive from the ministry, he frames and promulgates *arrêtés* and ordinances dealing not only with matters pertaining to the protection of life and property, but with the regulation of traffic, the abatement of nuisances, the supervision of aliens and political suspects, and the guardianship of various national interests. Subject also to the general rules laid down for his guidance by law or ministerial decree, he regulates everything connected with the personnel, the pay, the promotions, and the discipline of the Paris police force, and is the executive head of the system in all its branches. He is directly and entirely responsible for every incident of police administration; and from his headquarters opposite the Palais de Justice he controls all the various bureaus into which the service is organized.

Difficult nature of this post.
The position is one of great power and of correspondingly great responsibility, for the efficient policing of Paris is no easy task. Not only must the prefect display qualities of firmness and tact which nature does not frequently combine in one individual, but he must also be a man upon whom the national authorities can depend absolutely; for, in view of the city's turbulent traditions, any failure of the police system to cope with emergencies might well be looked upon with apprehension. The marked success of M. Lepine's police administration has been due in no small degree to his rare personal courage, his untiring energy, his ability as an organizer, and especially to his skill in combining the *suaviter in modo* with the *fortiter in re*, — all qualities upon which the problems of his office make severe demands.

The municipal council of Paris.
Although it is commonly said that Paris is governed by these two prefects, there is also a municipal council which is not without an important share in the direction of administrative policy.[1] This *conseil municipal de Paris* is

[1] H. Chrétien, *De l'organisation du conseil municipal de Paris* (Paris, 1906).

composed of eighty members, who are elected by popular vote under a form of suffrage identical with that which exists in the other cities of the country. The methods of compiling and revising the voters' lists, the machinery of election, the system of supplementary polling, and all the other incidents of an electoral campaign are likewise substantially similar to those in the other cities. The Parisian councillors are not, however, elected on a general ticket. Each of the twenty *arrondissements* is divided into four electoral sections or precincts, and each of these elects one councillor. Since, however, these precincts have remained unchanged for the last forty years, they are at the present time so unequal in population and in number of voters that one councillor may, and frequently does, represent two or three times as many municipal voters as one of his colleagues. This circumstance has given rise to so much criticism that from time to time various schemes have been submitted to the central government looking toward a rearrangement of the precincts;[1] but none of these plans have thus far found favor. It would, indeed, be difficult to effect a satisfactory adjustment without either changing the historic boundaries of the *arrondissements* or giving to some wards a larger number of councillors than to others. Either of these alternatives encounters strong opposition; for the bounds of the precincts are traditional, and the principle of equal representation has likewise obtained a degree of sanctity in the minds of many Parisians.

How organized.

Inequalities of the council districts.

The Paris councillors are elected for a four-year term, and the elections are held upon the same day as those of the provincial cities, with supplementary pollings a week later, if necessary, — and in many of the precincts they are

Term and allowance of councillors.

[1] See D. Pénard's *Le problême du mode d'élection des conseillers municipaux de Paris* (Paris, 1905).

always required. No provision is made by law for the payment of councillors; but the council has adopted the practice of voting an annual sum to cover the actual expenses of its members. In virtue of this custom the councillors receive a fixed sum of six thousand francs apiece; and this remuneration, which is practically a salary, has been tacitly approved by the higher authorities.[1] The electoral campaigns are conducted on a purely partisan basis, and in Paris national and municipal party lines are rather closely identified. At one period it was possible for a Parisian councillor to be at the same time a member of the Chamber of Deputies, and there were many instances of this dual membership; but the practice is no longer permitted. On the whole the council has been anti-ministerial, — that is to say, opposed to the party or group of parties whose leaders controlled the policy of the nation. Occasionally, indeed, it has been so violently anti-ministerial that it has involved itself in open breaches with the higher authorities, notably during the period 1900–1904, when the Nationalists obtained the upper hand in the municipal legislature.[2] The council is, in fact, apt to be somewhat radical in its make-up, the socialist and labor elements usually having a strong footing in its ranks, — a circumstance that has often embarrassed the two prefects, who may be said to reflect the more conservative spirit of the central government.[3]

Partisanship at council elections.

[1] In addition, the councillors have voted themselves an annual allowance of three thousand francs each as members of the council of the department of the Seine. This practice both the *Cour des Comptes* and the *Conseil d'État* have declared to be unauthorized by law; but the Ministry of the Interior has consistently declined, apparently for political reasons, to prevent the annual payments from being made. See *Revue générale d'administration*, 1896, III. 34 ff.; and *Revue de science et de législation financière*, 1904, I. 106 ff.

[2] P. de Touche, *Quatre ans de nationalisme à l'Hôtel de Ville, 1900–1904* (Paris, 1904).

[3] E. Bourdeau on "Le socialisme municipal," in *Revue des Deux-Mondes*, July, 1900.

With reference to its general procedure and the scope The council's procedure. of its deliberations the municipal council of Paris is governed by the rules prescribed for the councils of the other French cities. It meets four times a year in regular session; but special meetings are called whenever they are deemed necessary, and as a matter of fact these extra sessions occupy most of the intervals between the statutory ones. Since 1886 the meetings have all been open to the public.[1] At all sessions, whether regular or special, the two prefects have the right to be present and to be heard; but the prefect of the Seine is not the presiding officer. At the first meeting subsequent to the elections the council chooses, by secret ballot, its own president, its vice-presidents, one or more secretaries, and a syndic, or general director of ceremonies. These officers make up the council's "bureau," and this bureau has general direction of all council proceedings.

On account of its size and unwieldiness the Paris coun- The council's committees. cil finds it advantageous to have much of its preliminary work performed by standing committees, of which there are several, and to which are added from time to time, as occasion demands, an even larger number of special committees. The method of selecting the standing committees is somewhat peculiar, and very different from that ordinarily pursued in the municipal councils of England or the United States. Immediately after the elections the members of the council are divided by lot into four equal sections, each section remaining intact during the four years of the council's existence, and each selecting, by vote of its members, two, three, or four representatives to serve on each standing committee of the council. At the present time there are six of these committees, which divide among themselves the more important departments of

---

[1] *Loi du 5 juillet 1886*, in *Bulletin des lois*, 1886, II. 520.

civic administration.[1] The special committees are chosen in a variety of ways, — sometimes by vote of the whole council, sometimes by the selection of representatives from various standing committees, and often by a combination of two or more of these committees themselves.[2] Each committee, whether standing or special, selects its own chairman. In addition to its committees, the council also has representatives upon a considerable number of mixed commissions made up of lay citizens or officials.

Work of these committees.   Matters may come before the council either by message from one of the prefects — usually the prefect of the Seine — or on proposal of some individual member.[3] In either case the question is referred to the appropriate committee or mixed commission for examination and report, and the result is transmitted in printed form to all members of the council some time before the regular session.[4] Service on these various committees and commissions involves heavy demands upon the time and attention of the councillors;[5] it is this fact especially, indeed, that has moved the higher authorities to give their consent to the liberal allowance voted to councillors each year under color of expenses.

[1] Of these six standing committees the First Committee (12 members) deals with finance, civic contracts, municipal and public monopolies ; the Second Committee (12 members) with police, fire protection, and parks ; the Third Committee (16 members) with highways and works affecting highways ; the Fourth Committee (16 members) with education and fine arts ; the Fifth Committee (12 members) with poor relief and municipal pawnshops ; the Sixth Committee (12 members) with sanitation, sewerage, water supply, and navigation of the Seine.

[2] Among the special committees now in existence are those on tramways, gas, and loans. The budget is dealt with by a committee of the whole council, after the English fashion ; but all the standing committees become sub-committees of this " committee of the whole."

[3] These propositions may be found in *Conseil municipal de Paris; Rapports et documents* (issued annually since 1871).

[4] See, for example, A. Rendu, *Rapport sur le service des eaux; conseil municipal de Paris* (Paris, 1904). All the proceedings of the council are printed in the *Bulletin municipal officiel de la ville de Paris*.

[5] Dr. Chassagne's *Dix-neuf ans du conseil municipal élu de la ville de Paris,* 1871–1890 (3 vols., Paris, 1893), gives some interesting details concerning the composition and actual work of the council.

The influence of the French committee is, however, by no
means so great as that of the standing committee of an
English borough council.   The Paris committee does not,
like its English prototype, deal finally with any matter, however unimportant; and its recommendations have no certainty of acceptance by the council.   From the peculiar
way in which the committees are constituted, some of them
may, and frequently do, contain a majority of councillors
who do not coincide in political views with a majority of
the council as a whole; hence committee recommendations, though usually adopted, are sometimes rejected, a
step which is, however, in no wise construed to be an
expression of want of confidence in the committee.   Unlike the English committees, moreover, these Paris bodies
do not directly control any of the municipal services.   The
heads of departments take their instructions from the prefects, not from the chairmen of council committees; the
latter may at best only make suggestions to the whole council, and the council, again, may only in a roundabout way
bring pressure to bear upon the administration.   The Paris
committees investigate and advise ; they do not control.

Not so im-
portant as
the work of
council com-
mittees in
England.

In a word, the fact that the Paris municipal council does
not elect the administrative officers, and does not directly
control their policy, serves greatly to restrict its powers and
to make it even less influential in municipal affairs than are
the councils of the provincial cities.   Its only important
legal function is that of voting the budget, and even here
its discretion is closely circumscribed by law.   It has, to
be sure, certain powers with respect to the acquisition of
municipal property, the regulation of license fees and market tolls, the acceptance of bequests and gifts, and so on ;
but in every case the concurrence of the prefect of the
Seine is essential to any valid action.   It is true that the
resolutions of the council carry considerable weight even

The coun-
cil's powers.

when they relate to matters affecting interests of the city that lie outside the council's own sphere of jurisdiction, and it is also true that the prefect of the Seine is very frequently obliged to bend to its will as a matter of expediency; yet among the legislatures of the world's great cities the Paris council is perhaps the least influential of all.

General council of the department of the Seine.

The municipal council exists for Paris proper; the department of the Seine, which includes not only the city but the district immediately surrounding, has its own general department council.[1] This council is made up of the members of the Paris municipal council, with the addition of twenty-one councillors from the two *arrondissements* outside the walls. As there are so few of these, however, the two councils are substantially alike as regards their personnel ; but they meet separately, enjoy separate powers, and have somewhat different precedures. The general council of the department of the Seine has about the same powers as are possessed by the *conseils gênêraux* of the other French departments.

Plans of metropolitan reorganization.

During the last thirty years or more a good many Parisian voters have been clamoring for a rearrangement of metropolitan organization. Various schemes have been brought forward, most of them making provision for a central mairie, with a mayor of Paris to be elected by the council and invested with many of the powers now possessed by the two prefects;[2] but the central authorities appear to display no signs of weakening in their fixed belief that the capital should continue to be dealt with as a special unit of local administration.

---

[1] H. Lanfant, *Le conseil général de la Seine, ses origines et attributions* (Paris, 1903).

[2] Some of these schemes may be found in S. Lacroix's *Rapport sur l'organisation municipale de la ville de Paris* (Paris, 1880) ; G. Villain's *Paris et la mairie centrale ; étude de centralisation administrative* (Paris, 1884) ; A. Combarieu's paper on "La mairie centrale de Paris," in *Revue politique et parlementaire*, July 10, 1897 ; and J. Delaitre's *La municipalité parisienne et les projets de réforme* (Paris, 1902).

CHAPTER II

THE GOVERNMENT OF PRUSSIAN CITIES

THE concentration of population in cities, and more par- Growth of
ticularly in the larger cities, has been marked with singular cities.
German
clearness throughout that area of territory which now
forms the German Empire. During the last three or four
decades especially, this drift toward the urban centres has
assumed such unprecedented proportions that it has contributed in no small degree to the difficulty which municipal organs have encountered in dealing with the various
problems of city administration. A century ago the German states comprised within their boundaries populations
that were chiefly agricultural in occupation; indeed, with
the exception of important seaports, like Hamburg, Bre-
men, and Lübeck, and of such inland cities as had grown to
importance simply because they were political capitals,
there were very few urban communities of any considerable size. This fact is to be attributed mainly to the
industrial backwardness and general lack of economic ag-
gressiveness that had thus far characterized the German
people; but the free movement of the population was still
further hampered by the heavy shackles which the governing authorities put upon both industry and trade. In Influence of
1816, despite the extensive reforms of the Stein-Harden- reforms.
the Stein
berg period, less than two per cent of the population
of Prussia was to be found in the cities of over 100,000
inhabitants;[1] and forty years later this percentage had

[1] Elaborate statistics of urban and rural population in Prussia during the
period 1816–1864 may be found in H. Schwabe's paper, "Ueber die Quellen für
das Wachstum der grossen Städte im preussischen Staate," in *Berliner Stadt-
und Gemeinde-Kalender und statistisches Jahrbuch für 1867* (Berlin, 1867).

little more than doubled, an evidence that Prussia was sharing to but slight extent in that great movement which was at this time so completely transforming the economic, social, and political organization of England.[1]

Rapidity of growth since 1871. During this period the German cities and towns suffered somewhat from the exodus of many citizens to the United States; but the main cause of tardy urban growth is explained chiefly by the fact that not until after 1867–1871 did Germany come to her own in the matter of industrial and commercial expansion. The successful wars with Austria and France marked the beginning of an industrial revival which sent these economic interests of the new German Empire forging ahead at a quick pace, and which was accompanied not only by a vigorous increase in national population, but by a decline in the emigration of Germans to other countries. More particularly did the new order of things reflect itself in the rapid growth of German cities, caused largely by a hegira of the rural population into the new industrial and trading centres, a movement which has continued for nearly forty years with no apparent diminution in strength. Of the slightly more than 41,000,000 people with whom the German Empire began its history in 1871, only twenty-six per cent were resident in cities and **Strength of urban population at the present day.** towns of more than 5000 population. In 1890 this percentage had risen to thirty-six; and at the last census (1905) it had reached more than forty-five per cent of the whole.[2] The strength and significance of this movement are not

[1] In 1816 the population of Prussia classified as rural formed about 73 per cent of the whole ; in 1864 it had fallen to only 69 per cent. The rural population of England and Wales in 1811 formed more than 80 per cent of the whole, but in 1861 it had dropped to less than 45 per cent. On this point see A. F. Weber's *Growth of Cities in the Nineteenth Century* (New York, 1899), especially ch. ii.

[2] Statistics of German city growth since 1871 may be conveniently found in the *Statistisches Jahrbuch deutscher Städte* (published annually).

readily overestimated.   The growth of American cities has
been so rapid during the same period that one is apt to
regard the phenomenon of urban expansion as peculiar to
the New World; but a comparison of German and American cities in point of relative swiftness of growth will
show that in almost every case the rate of increase has
been greater in the former than in the latter.[1]   This fact
is significant; for it is not infrequently urged that the
failure of many American cities to cope properly with
their municipal problems has been due in part to their
phenomenal expansion.   German cities, however, have not
found steady increase of size an insuperable obstacle to
efficient municipal administration.

*Compara-
tive city
growth in
Germany
and the
United
States.*

[1] The following table shows in round numbers the increase in population of
some typical German and American cities during the period 1890–1905: —

CITY	1890	1905	PERCENTAGES
Hamburg	569,000	800,000	40 %
Boston	448,000	595,000	32 %
Munich	349,000	538,000	54 %
Baltimore	434,000	546,000	25 %
Leipsic	335,000	502,000	49 %
Buffalo	255,000	376,000	47 %
Dresden	276,000	514,000	80 %
New Orleans	242,000	399,000	65 %
Hanover	163,000	250,000	53 %
Milwaukee	204,000	312,000	52 %
Cologne	281,000	428,000	52 %
Cincinnati	296,000	343,000	15 %
Breslau	335,000	470,000	40 %
Cleveland	261,000	437,000	67 %
Frankfort	180,000	334,000	80 %
Pittsburg	238,000	364,000	53 %

These figures are drawn from the *Statistisches Jahrbuch deutscher Städte*
(1906), and from *Bureau of the Census; Statistics of Cities having a Population
of over 30,000* (1907).

Special nature of the problems created by rapid urban expansion in Germany. Not only have the cities of the German Empire been growing more rapidly during the last ten or twenty years than the cities of the United States, but they have found the problems resulting from rapid growth much more bewildering.   In America suburban development has not, as a rule, involved any rebuilding of the older parts of the city; but in Germany the municipal authorities have usually found it necessary to create a modern city out of a grimy mediæval town.   They have had to transform the narrow streets and byways of the old towns into the main highways of large cities, — an expensive sort of reconstruction too well known to require emphasis.   To the proper solution of their greater problems, moreover, the German cities have been able to bring much more slender resources in the way of annual revenues and general borrowing powers.   The only important advantage which they have had over American cities has lain in the comparative homogeneity of their populations; for, unlike the municipal authorities of the United States, the German city governments have to deal with municipal electorates that are almost wholly drawn from the ranks of the native-born.

The government of German cities not a uniform system. Municipal government in the German Empire lies within the sphere of state jurisdiction; the imperial constitution, like the constitution of the United States, makes no provision regarding the structure of local administration. Each kingdom, dukedom, or principality regulates its own plan of municipal rule in its own way; hence there is no uniform system for the whole of Germany, as there is for the whole of England or for the whole of France.   At the same time there is a much closer approach to a single type of city government in Germany than there is in the United States, a circumstance due partly to the much smaller number of state jurisdictions, but more particularly to the

dominating influence of Prussia among her imperial con-
federates. Out of the twenty-five states in the empire,
Prussia has more than three-fifths of the total population ; The Prus-
and, furthermore, by her example she exerts an influence sian city
upon the smaller states which is more than proportionate a fair type.
to her numerical preponderance. Not only does her municipal policy serve much more than a majority of the total
urban population of the empire, but she has to a marked
degree stamped her principles of local government upon
most of the other German states. The Prussian system
may, therefore, very properly be taken as the German
type ; but it must be borne in mind that in all the other
states there are some important deviations from the model.
Indeed, the system is not absolutely uniform throughout
Prussian territory itself ; but the variations are, in the
main, not of sufficient importance to be mentioned in any
general survey.

In outlining the evolution of the Prussian system of Evolution
city government it is hardly necessary to go farther back of Prussian
than to the early years of the nineteenth century, for it city admin-
was not until the period of the Stein-Hardenberg reforms istration.
that Prussian cities received their first substantial measure
of self-government.[1] Before the famous decree of 1808 was
issued the officials of administration in all the cities of the
kingdom had either been appointed by the central author- City govern-
ities or been selected by some process of coöptation, the ment in the
masses of the citizens having in either case little or no eighteenth
voice in the selection of their own local administrators or century.
in the direction of local policy. During the reign of
Frederick the Great, for example, it was common to

[1] See Ernst Meier, *Die Reform der Verwaltungsorganisation unter Stein
und Hardenberg* (Leipsic, 1881); Max Lehmann, *Freiherr von Stein* (3 vols., Berlin, 1902–1905) ; and J. R. Seeley, *The Life and Times of Stein* (2 vols., Cambridge, 1878), especially II. 223–247.

I

bestow municipal posts upon worn-out military officers in order that the state exchequer might not have to bear the burden of pensioning them. The inevitable consequence of this system was that the ordinary municipal services were badly neglected and the larger part of the local revenues went to the maintenance of sinecure posts.[1] Indeed, the condition of affairs was if anything worse than that disclosed in England by the investigations which preceded the act of 1835.[2]

Decree of 1808. By the reforms of 1808, however, the absolute power of the state in local affairs was broken and the right of citizenship was extended to all who owned land or pursued any trade within the municipal limits, a multitude of local privileges were swept away, and the barriers to local progress were almost entirely broken down. **Reforms effected by it.** The reforms also secured the establishment, in each Prussian city, of a framework of municipal government substantially similar to that which exists at the present day ; and they gave to the new organs of local administration power to raise and expend local taxes, to issue municipal ordinances, to control civic property, and in general to make such provision for local public services as might be found desirable.[3]

The decree of 1808 applied to all the territory which was

[1] There is a plentitude of literature relating to the evolution of the Prussian municipal system both before and after 1808, including G. Waitz's *Deutsche Verfassungsgeschichte* (8 vols., Kiel, 1844–1861), especially II. 374 ff. ; K. D. Hullman's *Das Stadtwesen des Mittelalters* (4 vols., Bonn, 1826–1829) ; A. Heusler's *Der Ursprung der deutschen Stadtverfassung* (Weimar, 1872) ; J. E. Kuntze's *Untersuchungen über den Ursprung der deutschen Stadtverfassung* (Leipsic, 1895); Georg von Below's *Das ältere deutsche Städtewesen* (Bielefeld, 1898) ; and Karl Hegel's *Die Entstehung des deutschen Städtewesens* (Leipsic, 1898). A very serviceable short survey may be found in Hugo Preuss's *Die Entwicklung des deutschen Städtewesens* (Leipsic, 1906), or in G. von Below's article on "Die Entstehung der deutschen Stadtverfassung," in the *Historische Zeitschrift*, Vols. XXII.–XXIII. *passim.*

[2] See below, pp. 215–218.

[3] "Städteordnung vom 19. November 1808," in *Gesetz-Sammlung für 1808*, pp. 324 ff.

at that date comprised within the kingdom of Prussia; Extension of
but to the new tracts received in 1815 as a result of the the system to new
arrangements made at the Congress of Vienna the provi- territories.
sions of the decree were not at once extended. Some of
the cities in this newly added territory retained their old
municipal organization. Others had, even before their
annexation to Prussia, remodelled their systems of municipal administration according to the general plan laid
down for the cities of France by Napoleon in 1800; and
this method they were for the time being allowed to continue. In 1831, however, all these municipalities were
brought more or less into line with the system provided for
the other Prussian cities by the arrangements of 1808; and
some time later the cities of Westphalia, Posen, and the
Rhine Province were dealt with in somewhat the same
way.[1]

By the middle of the nineteenth century there was thus Law of 1850.
throughout Prussia a substantial approach to uniformity
in city administration. The smaller urban and rural
areas (Gemeinden) were still under a different system;
but the opinion seems to have gained ground that all
should be administered alike, for in 1850, immediately
after the establishment of the first Prussian parliament,
an attempt was made to provide, by a comprehensive
enactment, a uniform plan of government for all local
units, urban and rural.[2] The lapse of a few months, Its chief de-
however, served to demonstrate the impracticability of ad- fects.
ministering the affairs of large cities and small villages
in the same way, and the law of 1850 was accordingly
suspended. The Prussian authorities then turned their
attention to the drafting of a new code for the cities

---

[1] Westphalia in 1835, Posen in 1841, and the Rhine Province in 1845. See
H. Preuss, *Die Entwicklung des deutschen Städtewesens*, ch. v.

[2] "Städteordnung vom 11. März 1850," in *Gesetz-Sammlung für 1850*, pp. 9 ff.

alone, and their efforts culminated in the City Government Act (Städte-Ordnung) of May 30, 1853.[1]

City government act of 1853.

The act of 1853 originally applied to only the six eastern provinces of Prussia[2]; but with some variations it has from time to time since then been extended to practically all the other territories comprised within the kingdom.[3]

Relation of the code. of 1853 to the decree of 1808.

Though following in general the lines laid down in 1808, it contained several important new features, notably the "three-class system" of voting and the substitution of open for secret balloting. So far as its legal basis is concerned, the municipal system of Prussia to-day rests upon the code of 1853; but in its broader outlines it goes back

---

[1] The code of 1853 may be found in *Gesetz-Sammlung für 1853*, pp. 261 ff. In its original form it is also published in the appendix to A. W. Jebens's *Die Stadtverordneten* (Berlin, 1905); but the amendments since 1853 have been very numerous. These amendments are given in the various standard commentaries on the code, of which the best and most recent are Walter Ledermann's *Die Städteordnung* . . . *nebst ihren gesetzlichen Ergänzungen* (Berlin, 1902); O. Oertel's *Die Städteordnung für die sechs östlichen Provinzen der preussischen Monarchie* (Liegnitz, 1905); and R. Zelle's *Die Städteordnung von 1853 in ihrer heutigen Gestalt* (3d ed., Berlin, 1893). A convenient small handbook is Bruno Schulze's revision of Plagge's *Die Städteordnung* . . . *zum praktischen Gebrauch ausführlich erläutert* (Berlin, 1901).

[2] These were East and West Prussia, Prussian Saxony, Brandenburg, Pomerania, Silesia, and Posen. New Pomerania and the Island of Rügen were exempted from the provisions of the law, but were dealt with in a separate enactment ("Gesetz betreffend die Verfassung und Verwaltung der Städte in Neupommern und Rügen vom 31. Mai 1853," in *Gesetz-Sammlung für 1853*, pp. 291 ff.).

[3] The system was applied to Westphalia in 1856 (see *Städteordnung der Provinz Westfalen vom 19. März 1856*, Berlin, 1897), and in the same year to the cities of the Rhine Province; but in the latter case there were some important deviations from the general lines of the code (*Städteordnung der Rheinprovinz vom 15. Mai 1856*, Berlin, 1897). To the provinces of Schleswig-Holstein, on the contrary, it was applied without much change (*Städteordnung der Provinz Schleswig-Holstein vom 14. April 1869*, Berlin, 1888). Extensions in much altered form were made to Frankfort-on-the-Main in 1867, to the Duchy of Lauenburg in 1870, and to Hanover in 1858; but in the last case less change was made, for Hanover had already, before it became a part of Prussia, established a system of city government which in its main lines followed to some extent the Prussian model (*Hannoversche Städteordnung vom 24. Juni 1858*, Berlin, 1887).

to the enactments of 1808, its true sponsor being Baron von Stein. Since the code of 1853 was framed Prussian cities have expanded so much that their problems have naturally necessitated numerous amendments to the general law; but these changes have for the most part been concerned with matters of slight importance. The general framework of Prussian city administration has remained almost unaltered for a full century.

The various smaller German states have their own municipal codes, adopted and revised at different times,[1] and naturally varying a good deal in details as well as in some very important features. In general, however, there has been a tendency, in the periodical revisions, to approach more closely to the Prussian type, even though there still exists a difference in nomenclature which is very apt to be confusing. Not one of the smaller states, however, has adopted the Prussian three-class system, and none seems at all likely to do so, though practically all of them have imposed limitations upon the suffrage, usually in the form of a tax-paying qualification. In the imperial territory of Alsace-Lorraine the cities have, with certain modifications effected by territorial statutes, been permitted to retain their French system of administration by a mayor, adjoints, and communal council. *Municipal codes of the other German states.*

The Prussian City Government Act of 1853 applies to those units only which are known as Städte; and the distinction between the city (Stadt) and the rural area (Gemeinde) is not based on differences in population, but on a legal principle which has its roots back in the previous century. Originally, no doubt, the term "Stadt" was *Scope of the Prussian municipal code.*

---

[1] Bavaria's in 1869, Saxony's in 1873, Baden's in 1874. For details concerning the municipal systems of these states, see "Verfassung und Verwaltungsorganisation der Städte: Bayern, Sachsen, Würtemberg und Baden," in *Schriften des Vereins für Socialpolitik* (Leipsic, 1905–1908), Vol. CXX.

applied to those settlements only which had considerable populations, and the term "Landgemeinde" to sparsely settled areas only; but this distinction has been so far lost sight of that one now finds many Städte with only a few hundred inhabitants and many Gemeinden which have grown to be populous centres of from ten to fifty thousand. The Gemeinde, no matter what its population may be, is subject to an entirely different legal regimen from the Stadt, and has its own special framework of administration.[1]

Incorporation of new cities.

The municipal code of 1853 applied to all inhabited places (Ortschaften) to which the laws of 1808 and 1831 had been extended; that is, to all such places as had at any time obtained the right to rank as cities no matter what their importance or populousness. Provision was also made that other places might, by royal decree, be ranked as cities and thus brought within the scope of the code, a thing which has frequently been done. Since, however, there is no fixed rule whereby the royal authorities must be guided, the rank is now, as a matter of practice, accorded to larger urban communities only. At the present time there are over twelve hundred cities in the Prussian monarchy, ranging, like the French communes and the English boroughs, from hamlets of a few hundred people to Berlin with over two millions. All these cities are governed in substantially the same way.

Change in city limits.

Not only has the rapid growth in Prussian population as a whole added largely to the number of cities, but it has also necessitated many changes in the boundaries of existing municipal areas. For such changes the code makes explicit provision by arranging that, after the consent of the municipalities affected has been gained, appli-

[1] The administration of the rural communities is provided for in the "Landgemeindeordnung vom 3. Juli 1891," in *Gesetz-Sammlung für 1891*, pp. 233 ff.

cations may be made by interested parties or officials to the higher local authorities, usually to the administrators of the province. In no case may civic boundaries be altered without the approval of the minister of the interior (Minister des Innern), and in some cases the consent of the king must also be had. The detailed regula- Procedure. tions relating to this matter are elaborate and somewhat perplexing; but in general it may be said that all questions relating to the fixing of city boundaries, the annexation of suburbs, and the division of municipalities are determined in the first instance by the localities concerned, with the concurrence of the district or provincial authorities and with a right of appeal to the royal government at Berlin.[1]

The Prussian city is a public corporation, with all the The city as rights and privileges ordinarily appertaining to such a a corpora-body. It has, for instance, in its corporate name and through its chief executive officials, the right to sue and to be sued, to hold property, to make contracts, and so on; but it has in addition a considerable range of powers not derived from any statutory enactment, for the German states are not accustomed to specify with any attempt at exactness the jurisdiction which a city corporation may exercise. The code of 1853 merely empowers the local Sources of authorities to do whatever they may deem necessary or corporate powers. advisable in the interests of the city, provided always that their action shall not be contrary to any law of the land, and provided usually that the assent of some higher authority shall be obtained. Indeed, this practice of making a general grant of powers to the cities and then curtailing their jurisdiction at various points whenever occasion seems to demand, is one of the most salient characteristics of Prussian municipal policy. One might almost say that,

[1] These rules are summarized in Ledermann's *Die Städteordnung*, 10–17.

whereas in the United States a city may do only what it is expressly or tacitly empowered to do by common law or by statute, in Prussia, on the other hand, a city may do anything which it is not prohibited from doing either by law or by veto of the higher powers.[1]   There is thus an important difference between the two countries in what may be termed the theory of civic powers, — a difference in favor of the Prussian cities, for the plan of making broad grants of authority removes from them the necessity for that too frequent application to the state legislatures which American cities find themselves compelled to make. It is, of course, true that specific jurisdiction of a mandatory sort is sometimes conferred upon the cities by the national authorities, — as, for example, in the matter of education or the protection of the public health ; but the number of powers conferred in this way is not large.

German and American theories of civic authority.

Surveying its powers as a whole, one finds that the Prussian city government is the local educational authority, providing for the establishment and maintenance of elementary schools, as well as for the conduct of such secondary and technical institutions as may be deemed necessary, the cost being borne to some extent by the central government, which rigidly exercises its right of supervision and inspection over the whole educational system.   The Prussian city is also the local poor-relief area, the civic authorities having full charge, through officials whom they appoint, of a very comprehensive plan of municipal alms-giving.   The city government is likewise the local sanitary authority, having wide powers with reference to the provision of a sewerage system, the elaboration

General jurisdiction of the Prussian city.

[1] The point has been very well stated by Dr. Albert Shaw in his *Municipal Government in Continental Europe* (p. 323) : " There are, in the German conception of city government, no limits whatever to municipal functions. It is the business of the municipality to promote in every feasible way its own welfare."

of all measures (other than purely police regulations) necessary for the protection of the public health, the erection and
maintenance of hospitals, and the inspection of foodstuffs.
It is permitted, either directly or through the agency of
private corporations, to provide the usual public services,
such as water, gas, electricity, and tramways; but in the
exercise of these powers it is, as will be seen later, very
closely circumscribed by national laws and by the rights
of supervision possessed by the Ministry of the Interior.
The city government controls the fire-protection system,
but upon its management of the local police there are
everywhere strict limitations. Finally, the Prussian city
has been permitted to undertake many functions which in
American municipalities are jealously reserved to private
enterprise, — the maintenance of municipal savings-banks,
for example, and of municipal pawn-shops, employment-
offices, theatres, and concert-halls; the erection of municipal tenement-houses; the establishment of systems of
municipal fire-insurance. The Prussian cities have, indeed,
a much wider scope for their activities than that given
to most cities in the United States, — a circumstance
due in large measure to the fact that in Prussia civic
authority rests upon a broad grant, whereas in America
it must almost invariably be obtained piecemeal, each
specific power being sought and considered upon its individual merits, and being obtained or refused with
reference, too often, to its bearing upon private interests
concerned.

Broad scope of its activities.

The vesting of comprehensive powers in the hands of
the Prussian municipal corporations is seriously restricted
by the rigid control which the central government exercises
over all the local authorities of the kingdom. This control and supervision are exerted through the medium
of an elaborate administrative system, at the head of which

Restrictions on the free exercise of municipal powers.

The system of state supervision.

is the minister of the interior, a member of the Prussian national cabinet, appointed by and responsible to the king. Unlike the minister of the interior in France, however, or the president of the Local Government Board in England, this officer is not directly amenable to the national parliament. He must, it is true, be able to secure some measure of support from the latter, if he would prevent his usefulness to the national administration from being very seriously impaired ; but he does not, on the other hand, hold himself strictly accountable to the Landtag for all his administrative acts. The minister is ordinarily a trained and quasi-permanent officer, who finds his prototype to some extent in the English under-secretary. From the nature of his position he cannot be so effectually influenced by individual members of the Landtag as the minister of the interior in France may be influenced by the deputy, or the president of the Local Government Board in England by the individual member of the House of Commons. He can thus act with more regard for the general national welfare, and with less direct reference to purely local interests, than can his prototypes in the two countries named.

Work of the central and local supervisory authorities.

The duties of the minister of the interior include the supervision and control of the whole machinery of local government ; his office is the focussing-point of the entire system, for in it all the important lines of local jurisdiction converge. Like the other departments of the Prussian national government, the Ministry of the Interior maintains a large permanent staff of expert officials, — legal, financial, and technical, — who assist the minister in the consideration and decision of all matters which may come before him. The amount of work which the office is called upon to perform is very extensive, despite the fact that it deals with the towns and cities directly in very few cases, its functions being performed, for the most part, through intermediate authorities.[1]

For purposes of local government Prussia is divided into twelve provinces, at the head of each of which is a provincial president (Oberpräsident) appointed by the king. This official corresponds in many respects to the French prefect, for he is not only the administrative head of his division, but the local agent of the central government as well. In his work of supervising local government he is assisted to some extent by a provincial committee (Provinzialausschuss), which is appointed, usually from among its own members, by the provincial assembly (Provinzial-Landtag), a body that corresponds roughly to the general council of the French department. These twelve presidents execute ministerial instructions within their jurisdictions, and exercise a general supervision over the district authorities. *Relation of the city to the province.*

Each province is divided into districts, and each of these districts has its president (Regierungs-Präsident) and its district board (Bezirksausschuss), both appointed by the crown, and the latter composed of permanent trained officials whose powers of control are both comprehensive and direct. It is with these district authorities that the Prussian cities come directly into contact. When the exercise of any municipal function requires, for its validity, the approval of the higher authorities, it is usually the district board which must be approached. It is this body, for example, that decides any questions upon which the two houses of the city legislature may come into conflict. *Relation of the city to the district.*

The districts are, again, divided into circles (Kreise); but with the authorities of these sections only the smallest *Relation of the city to the circle.*

[1] For further details concerning the organization and functions of this ministry, see G. Anschütz, *Die Organisationsgesetze der innern Verwaltung in Preussen* (Berlin, 1897).

cities have anything to do, for any city of more than 25,000 population may by ministerial decree be formed into a separate circle. This has, in fact, been done with nearly one hundred of the larger Prussian cities, in such cases the functions ordinarily performed by the authorities of the circle being given to a committee of the Magistrat, the municipal administrative board. Berlin, like its sister metropolis in France, does not deal with the central government through the authorities of either circle or district; its administration is supervised, on behalf of the national government, by the Oberpräsident of Brandenburg.[1]

The powers which appertain to the Prussian city as a public corporation are exercised, in the first instance, through organs of government chosen directly or indirectly by the civic electorate. This electorate, or political personnel of the municipality, is, in the words of the existing laws,[2] composed of all independent (selbständigen) male German citizens twenty-four years of age or over who have, during the period of one year, fulfilled these three conditions: — (1) resided continuously within the city limits; (2) paid the regular municipal taxes; and (3) owned a dwelling-house within the municipality, or pursued some substantial trade or vocation which yields

Special position of Berlin.

The city electorate.

---

[1] The Prussian system of provincial, district, and circle administration may be studied in Karl Stengel's *Organisation der preussischen Verwaltung* (2 vols., Berlin, 1884); Conrad Bornhak's *Preussisches Staatsrecht* (3 vols., Freiburg-i.-B., 1888–1890); and Hue de Grais's *Handbuch der Verfassung und Verwaltung in Preussen*, etc. (17th ed., Berlin, 1906). The texts of the various local-government laws are printed in Gerhard Anschütz's *Organisations-gesetze der innern Verwaltung in Preussen* (Berlin, 1897). Descriptions of the system in English may be conveniently found in F. J. Goodnow's *Comparative Administrative Law* (2d ed., New York, 1903), I. 295–338; A. L. Lowell's *Government and Parties in Continental Europe*, I. 308–377; and P. W. L. Ashley's *Local and Central Government* (London, 1906), 133–153.

[2] *Städteordnung*, § 5. The amending legislation is summarized in Ledermann's *Die Städteordnung*, 26–34.

an income,[1] or been assessed for taxes.[2] Furthermore, non-residents are allowed to vote if they have within the year paid a certain sum in direct local taxes;[3] and corporations, if they satisfy the same requirement, are enrolled in the ranks of the municipal electorate and permitted to vote through their officers. The only important disqualification is against those who, though otherwise entitled to vote, have been in receipt of public poor-relief during the year. Formerly the right of municipal citizenship (Bürgerrecht) was evidenced by a Bürgerrechtsbrief, or certificate, which was obtained from the Magistrat of the municipality by a process of considerable formality. This certificate is, however, no longer required except in the province of Hanover.[4]

Letters of citizenship.

On the whole, the qualifications for voting in the cities of Prussia are not exacting; they seem to exclude very few who would be admitted to voting rights under a simple system of manhood suffrage. In 1905 there were in Berlin, out of a total population of 2,040,148, no less than 374,751 enrolled voters, or about eighteen per cent; in New York during the same year the enrolled vote was

Ratio of voters to total population.

---

[1] In cities of over 10,000 a trade is not deemed " substantial " unless two or more helpers are employed.

[2] By the Prussian Income Tax Law of 1891 (" Einkommensteuergesetz vom 24. Juni 1891," in *Gesetz-Sammlung für 1891*, pp. 185 ff.), the minimum taxable income in cities was fixed at nine hundred marks ; but sometimes cities are permitted to levy upon incomes below this minimum, and in such cases the suffrage must be given to the smaller contributors. See R. C. Brooks on " Berlin's Tax Problem," in *Political Science Quarterly*, XX. 655 ; J. A. Hill on " The Prussian Income Tax," in *Quarterly Journal of Economics*, VI. 21 ; and R. Maatz's *Das preussische Einkommensteuergesetz systematisch dargestellt* (Berlin, 1902).

[3] This amount must be sufficient to enable the non-resident to rank in the " first class " of taxpayers. See below, p. 131.

[4] On the general question of municipal citizenship, see P. Koslik, *Das Bürgerrecht in den preussischen Provinzen* (Berlin, 1888) ; and M. Bergheim, *Der Wohnsitz im bürgerlichen Recht* (Rostock, 1907). Honorary citizenship (Ehrenbürgerschaft) is nowadays accorded very infrequently.

660,000 in a population of 4,000,403, or only about six-teen per cent.[1] In all the Prussian cities taken together voting rights are extended to about eighteen per cent of the population, an average above that in English cities and not substantially lower than that in the cities of the United States. It seems, therefore, to be entirely erro-neous to regard the German electoral laws as shutting out from any share in the city government a much larger proportion of the people than are excluded in English or American cities.[2] In bestowing the franchise the German system is, indeed, much more democratic than has been popularly supposed; but though it enables one easily to secure enrolment on the voters' list, it does not by any means give those who are enrolled equal shares in the selection of their governing authorities. It is in this par-ticular phase of the electoral system that Prussian and American electorates differ most widely, as will appear a little later on.

Organs of city govern-ment.

The organs of administration in a Prussian city are twofold,— a municipal council (Stadtverordnetenversamm-lung), and an administrative board (Magistrat or Stadt-vorstand), of which the chief member is the presiding officer, or burgomaster (Bürgermeister).[3] This official has,

---

[1] Further data along the same lines may be found in the *Statistisches Jahr-buch deutscher Städte* (1906), and in *Bureau of the Census; Statistics of Cities* (1907).   [2] See also below, p. 230.

[3] The best convenient survey of contemporary Prussian municipal organiza-tion is the comprehensive article on the "Verfassung und Verwaltungs-organi-sation der Städte: Königreich Preussen," in *Schriften des Vereins für Socialpolitik* (Leipsic, 1905–1908), Vols. CXVII–CXIX *passim*. A shorter summary is Paul Schön's article on "Die Organisation der städtischen Verwaltung in Preussen," in *Annalen des deutschen Reiches* (1891), 707–846 ; and the chapters on "Die Städteverfassung" in Conrad Bornhak's *Preussisches Verwaltungsrecht* (3 vols., Freiburg, 1889–1890) are also ser-viceable. More exhaustive treatises are H. Steffenhagen's *Handbuch der städt-ischen Verfassung und Verwaltung in Preussen* (2 vols., Berlin, 1887) ; Eugen Leidig's *Preussisches Stadtrecht* (Berlin, 1891) ; and H. Lindemann's *Die deutsche Städteverwaltung* (Stuttgart, 1906).

of course, some powers distinct from those possessed by
the Magistrat as a body ; but they are scarcely of sufficient
importance (except in the Rhine Province) to warrant
one's ranking him as a separate agent in administration
in the sense in which one accords this status to the mayor
of a French or of an American city. The work of the two
main organs is usually supplemented by the services of a
number of citizen deputies (Bürgerdeputirter), who do not
act as an organized body, but serve as individual members
of the various joint committees (Deputationen) which are
maintained by the two official branches.

Of this general organization the council is the pivotal
point; hence its composition, procedure, powers, and general rôle may be outlined first in order, although in point
of power and prestige the administrative board stands
quite above it. In size the council varies widely in the
different cities, — Berlin, as the largest German city, having 144 councillors, Königsberg 102, Mannheim, Karlsruhe,
and Freiburg-i.-B. each 96, Dresden 78, Leipsic and Charlottenburg 72 each, Munich 60, Hanover 24, and so on
down to the smallest cities, which have in no case fewer
than 12. The number of members is fixed by the municipal code with somewhat direct reference to the population of the municipality, a city of 50,000 population being
entitled to a council of 42 members, and other cities to a
larger or smaller number as their populations warrant.[1]

The city council.

Number of councillors in different cities.

---

[1] The exact number of councillors is arranged by the code as follows ; but
changes may be made by local by-laws : —

POPULATION		COUNCILLORS
Less than	2,500	12
2,500 to	5,000	18
5,000 to	10,000	24
10,000 to	20,000	30
20,000 to	30,000	36
30,000 to	50,000	42

On the whole, the municipal councils throughout Germany
are relatively somewhat larger than those in the United
States, but the discrepancy is not striking. Compared
with those of French cities they are distinctly large ; but
between German and English councils there is, in the
matter of size, no difference worthy of mention.[1] Large
as the Prussian council may be, however, it does not, in
view of the sort of work which it is called upon to perform, appear to be unwieldy or ill-adapted to its place in
the general municipal system.

Term and
method of
election.

Councillors are elected for a six-year term, and one-third
of their number retire biennially.[2] The election is by direct vote of all whose names are enrolled on the voters'
list ; and the choice is made, not on a general ticket, but
by the various election districts (Wahlbezirke) into which

The "three-
class
system."

the city is divided. By far the most unique feature of
the system of election, however, is the plan of grouping
all the voters into three general classes according to their
taxpaying strength, a plan commonly known as the " three-
class system."[3] The origin of this peculiar method of

POPULATION	COUNCILLORS
50,000 to 70,000	48
70,000 to 90,000	54
90,000 to 120,000	60

For each additional unit of 50,000 six more councillors are allowed. To this
general rule there are, however, some local exceptions. See Städteordnung,
§ 12; and Leidig, *Preussisches Stadtrecht*, 70 ff.

[1] Boston has 75 councillors in its larger chamber, Chicago 70, Detroit 34,
Cleveland 33, and St. Louis 28. Philadelphia has a council of 149 members,
more than twice as many as there are in any other American city. A table
showing the comparative sizes of municipal councils in Germany, France,
the United States, and England is printed in A. R. Hatton's *Digest of City
Charters* (Chicago, 1906).

[2] Prior to the passing of the Städteordnung of 1853 the term was three years
only. In all cases a councillor is reëligible. In the cities of Schleswig-Holstein
one-sixth of the council retires annually.

[3] Officially the word " Abtheilung" and not " Klasse " is used ; but the
system is commonly known as the " Dreiklassensystem." For further details

grouping voters is to be found in the cities of the Rhine Province, where it was devised by the local government code of 1845 as a means of affording the larger industrial interests of that territory an adequate share of representation in the municipal councils.[1] The system was incorporated, for use in the national elections, into the Prussian constitution of 1850,[2] and three years later found its way into the city-government code for the six eastern provinces.[3] At the present time it is in vogue in nearly all the Prussian cities,[4] but it has not been adopted in the municipal systems of the other German states.

Its origin.

Under the existing system the preparation of the voters' list in any Prussian city is intrusted to the administrative board, or Magistrat; but the actual work of compilation is ordinarily performed by a municipal election bureau, which performs its function under the supervision of some designated member of the board. This bureau, which is composed of a director (Bureauvorsteher) and several assistants, receives from the municipal police authorities copies of all the registrations (Meldungen) that must, according to the police regulations, be made by all persons who come to the municipality to stay or who leave it permanently.[5] It also receives from the local-tax authorities (Steuerverwaltung) statements of the tax assessments of all persons residing within the civic limits. From these

Procedure in dividing the voters into classes.

regarding it, see R. Grassman, *Das Wahlrecht der Städteordnung* (Stettin, 1876) ; I. Jastrow, *Das Dreiklassensystem* (Berlin, 1894) ; Georg Evert, *Die Dreiklassenwahl in den preussischen Stadt- und Landgemeinden* (Berlin, 1901) ; and R. C. Brooks on "The Three-Class System in Prussian Cities," in *Municipal Affairs*, II. 396.

[1] H. Steffenhagen, *Handbuch der städtischen Verfassung und Verwaltung in Preussen*, Vol. II.   [2] *Preussische Verfassung von 1850*, Title V. 70-72.

[3] Städteordnung, Title I. 5-8.

[4] The exceptions are the cities of the province of Hanover ; of Sigmaringen, Stralsund, and Schleswig ; and the city of Frankfort-on-the-Main.

[5] For details concerning this system of registration, see F. Throl's *Das polizeiliche Meldewesen* (Berlin, 1897).

K

data the bureau compiles its list of voters, the largest tax-payer appearing at the head of the list and the others following in order of the amounts assessed upon them.

Old and new methods of division.

Prior to 1900 the task of making the three groups was very simple. The total amount of taxes was first divided into three equal parts; then, beginning at the top of the list, the officers took off, to form the first class, just as many persons as had contributed one-third of the total taxes; proceeding down the list they next took off, to form the second class, those who had contributed a second third, and then grouped all the remaining taxpayers into the third class. In 1900, however, this procedure was slightly modified, and at the same time rendered much more complicated, by a new enactment of the Prussian parliament, which made somewhat different provisions for larger and smaller cities.[1] In the former class the method of dividing the voters is now about as follows: In the first place, the sum of all direct taxes — state, district, and municipal — paid by citizens is reckoned up by the election bureau of each municipality. From this sum is then deducted the total amount of taxes paid by citizens who are exempted by law from the payment of the national income tax, or who for any other reason do not pay this levy. The balance is divided by the number of taxpayers, and the result gives the average per capita tax payment. All those who pay less than this amount are put into the third class. The total sum paid by these is deducted from the total amount of taxes levied, and the balance is divided into two nearly equal parts. Then, beginning with the largest taxpayer at the head of the whole list, the

---

[1] " Gesetz, betreffend die Bildung der Wähler-Abtheilungen bei den Gemein-dewahlen, vom 39. Juni 1900," in *Gesetz-Sammlung für 1900*, pp. 185 ff. The text of the law, with explanations, may be found in Evert's *Die Dreiklassen-wahl*, 1–82.

officials take off as many names as suffice by their payments to make up one of these halves, and these they call the first class. The remaining taxpayers constitute the second class.[1]

The proportion of voters who fall into the three classes differs very greatly in different cities; but it is extremely uncommon to find the members of the first class forming more than two or three per cent of the total.[2] The first and second classes, taken together, ordinarily form

Numerical strength of the three groups.

[1] The method of procedure may perhaps be rendered somewhat clearer by the subjoined explanation in regard to the dividing of the Berlin electorate in 1905, kindly furnished by Magistrats-Sekretär Otto Busse, Vorsteher des Bureaus für Wahlangelegenheiten : " The total number of voters in Berlin for the year 1905 is 374,751, with a total tax payment of 61,754,611 marks. From these totals are taken 32,443 voters, with a total tax payment of 277,459 marks, because they do not pay the national income tax and hence do not come into account in determining the average tax rate upon which the grouping of voters is based. After these two subtractions are made there remain 342,308 voters, with a total payment of 61,377,152 marks or an average payment of 179 marks, 60 pfgs. each. All those whose annual taxes amount to less than this sum are placed in the third class. In Berlin the third class, constituted in this way, comprises 340,565 voters, with a total tax payment of 11,096,743 marks. This sum, subtracted from the first total (61,754,611 marks) leaves 50,657,868 marks as the total tax contribution of the two upper classes. This latter sum is divided as nearly as may be into two equal halves (25,332,669 and 25,325,199 marks), and the number of heavier taxpayers necessary to make up the former sum constitutes the first class, while the number required to make up the latter sum constitutes the second class (34,186). The three classes are thus formed as follows : —

Class	I.	1829 voters contributing a total of	25,332,669 marks
Class	II.	32,357	25,325,199 marks
Class	III.	340,565	11,096,743 marks
		374,751	61,754,611

" The 32,443 special non-income-tax-paying voters who are taken out of the lists before the first average is determined are put into that class to which their respective other annual payments entitle them. The slight inequality in the total sums contributed by the first and second classes arises from the fact that any persons who pay the same amount of taxes as the last voter in the first class are put into that class. The smallest taxpayer in the first class paid in 1905 the sum of 3961 marks ; the lowest in the second class paid 179 marks ; while the lowest in the third class paid 3 marks."

[2] The appended table, compiled from the *Statistisches Jahrbuch deutscher*

only from ten to twenty per cent of the whole electorate; hence it comes about, as will be seen later, that two-thirds of the councillors are chosen by from one-tenth to one-fifth of the voters. In some instances, indeed, the proportions of the classes become ludicrous, as in the familiar case of Essen, the seat of the Krupp Works. Here there were, at the elections of 1900, only three voters in the first class, 401 in the second, and 18,991 in the third ; but the three voters of the first class elected one-third of the whole municipal council, and 404 voters out of nearly 20,000 elected two-thirds of it.

Importance of the arrangement.
This system of classifying voters in Prussian cities is highly important from several points of view, but especially because it puts the preponderance of influence in the hands of the wealthier citizens, who are usually, it may fairly be said, inclined to conservatism in municipal expenditure.[1] Indeed, the system gives practically absolute control of the municipal outlay to those who have contributed the major part of the municipal income, and who have therefore, very naturally, a strong desire to see their contributions spent as wisely and as economically as possible. The Prussian electoral system is based upon the representation of interests rather than of numbers ;

Städte (1906), will serve to give some idea of the proportions of the three classes in different cities. The figures are for the years 1900–1903 : —

CITY	YEAR	CLASS I	CLASS II	CLASS III	TOTAL
Berlin	1903	1857	29,711	317,537	349,105
Breslau	1902	669	4,358	21,184	26,211
Königsberg	1903	385	2,496	19,391	22,272
Cologne	1903	511	5,659	41,321	47,491
Leipsic	1902	1487	4,430	24,463	30,380
Essen	1900	3	401	18,991	19,395
Stettin	1902	374	2,984	29,235	32,593
Halle a/S.	1903	178	1,727	20,297	22,202

[1] The system, it may be noted, does not apply in Frankfort-on-the-Main or in the cities of Schleswig-Holstein.

and the amount of interest which any citizen possesses in the governance of the city is gauged by the amount of taxes he pays. One may suggest that a good deal of the "thrifty municipal housekeeping" for which the Prussian cities have become favorably known results from the plain fact that the expenditure of public funds is controlled almost absolutely by that small proportion of the voters who have the highest interest in keeping this expenditure down to the lowest possible point.

On the other hand, the three-class system has its ob- Disadvantages of the system. vious drawbacks, and some of its incidents are distinctly objectionable. It tends, for instance, to carry social and economic distinctions into the polling-room, where, according to the fiction that American cities have vigorously attempted to maintain, all citizens are equal. It antagonizes a large number of voters who know that, even though Antagonizes many voters. they may stand together, they can at best control but a minority of the councillors, and that even the united wish of perhaps nine-tenths of the citizens plainly expressed at the polls does not have any assurance of effectiveness. That the system thus discourages many of the third class from taking any part in the elections is shown by the fact that the proportion of polled to qualified votes is much smaller in this class than in either of the other two groups, — a feature particularly noticeable in the industrial and commercial centres, where there is a large laboring population and where the Social Democrats form a strong political element. The grievance of this class of voters is strengthened, moreover, by the fact that in the imperial Is not used in imperial elections. elections manhood suffrage, without any divisions into voting classes, has had recognition since 1871. Why, ask many Germans, should all citizens be intrusted equally with the selection of those representatives who control the larger and more important questions of imperial policy, —

the army, the navy, the tariff, the whole field of criminal and civil law, — and yet be denied an equal voice in the choosing of civic authorities, who have to deal with narrower and less momentous problems ? What justification is there for a policy that gives two neighbors equal shares in the control of hundreds of millions annually expended for imperial purposes, but vastly unequal shares in the control of hundreds of thousands annually disbursed for local purposes ? The answer is, of course, that the principle of manhood suffrage made its way into the imperial constitution, not because it was for its own sake regarded with favor by Bismarck and his friends, but because it was held to be a necessary concession to German popular sentiment at a time when it was extremely desirable that all elements should be welded into sympathy with the new constitutional arrangements. In the eyes of the imperial authorities the system of manhood franchise has not proved itself so satisfactory as to warrant any extension of it to municipal elections. On the contrary, there is a strong element among the German population which would very gladly see a retrenchment of the imperial electorate in order that the strength of the Social Democrats might thereby be impaired.[1]

The three-class system in national Prussian elections.

From time to time various proposals for a radical alteration in the three-class system have been brought forward, but none of them have encountered a favorable reception at the hands of the Prussian national authorities. The three-class system of voting, it may be mentioned, is also used in the state elections, but the procedure followed in dividing the groups differs somewhat from that laid down for the municipalities. In some respects the national

[1] The matter is discussed, from the standpoint of an outsider, in H. Nézard's *L'évolution du suffrage universel en Prusse et dans l'empire allemand* (Paris, 1905).

system of grouping the voters offers broader ground for criticism than the municipal plan ; it is against the former, indeed, that popular outbursts have during the last few years been directed. In this sphere, therefore, reforms in the electoral system may first be expected, though as yet the Prussian authorities have shown no signs of yielding to the demands of those who desire concessions in the direction of manhood suffrage. Still, the system has in operation produced so many anomalies and even absurdities that important changes of some sort can scarcely be very long deferred.[1]

For the election of councillors the Prussian cities are divided into electoral districts, each of the three classes having its own set of these divisions. In Berlin, for example, there are sixteen districts for the voters of the first class, sixteen for the second, and forty-eight for the third.[2] These districts are mapped out by the decisions of the administrative board, or Magistrat ; but any action of this body must be confirmed by the higher authorities.[3] Changes in the boundaries of election districts are not made very frequently ; indeed, the boundaries are too often left unchanged when the shifting of population seems to demand redistricting. In Berlin, for example, where there has been no rearrangement of the election districts since 1897, there are at present such important differences in the

Councillors are elected from districts.

[1] It is said that even Prince von Bülow, the imperial chancellor, found himself at the last Prussian elections enrolled in the third class. Bismarck once denounced the three-class system as " the most miserable and absurd election law that has ever been formulated in any country." The relation of the system to Prussian theories of government is discussed in Rudolph von Gneist's *Die nationale Rechtsidee von den Ständen und das preussische Dreiklassensystem* (Berlin, 1894).

[2] Straube's *Plan von Berlin unter Angabe der Grenzen der Gemeindewahlbezirke nach der Eintheilung vom Jahre 1897* (Berlin, 1898).

[3] " Gesetz betreffend die Abänderung und Engänzung einiger Bestimmungen wegen der Wahl der Stadtverordneten von 1891," in *Gesetz-Sammlung für 1891*, pp. 20 ff.

populations of the various divisions that councillors who are elected by voters of the same class at the same election may have by no means the same number of constituents, a situation which may be explained by the fact that, although the election districts have remained the same for more than a decade, the grouping of the voters is rearranged annually. Even though left thus unaltered for considerable periods, the electoral districts acquire no traditions; they have no local sentiment and no unity of interests. The German Wahlbezirk, unlike the French arrondissement, is a purely arbitrary area. It is not, therefore, for any sentimental reason that there has been no redistricting for a decade; it is merely because the election district is used as a basis by so many of the local administrative departments that any changes in boundaries would compel much rearrangement in administrative work.

Berlin as an example of district apportionment.   Each of the sixteen first-class districts in Berlin elects a councillor every two years, and so does each of the sixteen districts of the second class. Each of the forty-eight districts of the third class, however, elects one councillor every sixth year only; that is to say, sixteen third-class districts elect a councillor biennially, the turn of each district arriving every sixth year. Since, then, a voter in the third class is called upon to state his choice only once in six years, and then only for a single councillor, changes in sentiment among third-class voters reflect themselves in the composition of the council much more slowly than do such changes among the members of the two upper classes. This infrequency of polling also militates against the maintenance of any well-developed party organization among voters of the lowest class; for the long intervals between third-class elections permit political interest to subside.

Ordinarily any one who is qualified to vote is competent to become a candidate for election to the municipal coun-

cil.   No individual property qualification is exacted; but Qualifica-
the code requires that at least one-half of the councillors manded of
elected to represent each of the three classes shall be councillors.
owners of real property.[1]   If, after an election, it is found
that this requirement is not satisfied by the men chosen,
those non-propertied councilmen who obtained the smallest
numbers of votes must retire, and allow their places to be
filled by property-owning candidates elected at a supple- Property
mentary polling.[2]   Upon the voters of the two upper ment.
classes this requirement imposes very little restriction in
the choice of candidates; for the number of property-
owners among them, especially among those in the first
class, is naturally large.   To the voters of the third group,
however, the restraint means a great deal, particularly in
a city like Berlin, where the number of property-owners
among third-class voters is very small.   It sometimes
happens, therefore, that voters of this class support candidates whom they would not uphold if their choice were
not curtailed by this provision; and it occasionally comes
to pass that candidates who are themselves voters in the first
or the second group secure election at the hands of third-
class voters largely because there are so few qualified candidates among the latter.   There is nothing in the laws, it
may be added, which prevents a voter of one class from
being chosen to represent another class; but in practice
such choices are not usual.   The two upper classes almost
invariably choose representatives from their own numbers;
it is only the third-class voters who are likely to go outside
their own ranks for candidates.

At various times and in various ways attempts have Attempted
been made to evade the strict application of the rule which this regula-
requires that one-half of the councillors representing each tion.

---

[1] Städteordnung, § 16.
[2] Entscheidungen des Oberverwaltungsgerichts, XXXII. 6.

class shall be owners of real property. Though not wholly
confined to any one group, such attempts at evasion have
been especially frequent among the third-class voters, upon
whom the restriction bears most heavily. Some years
ago, for instance, non-property-owning candidates from this
group adopted the expedient of acquiring, before the election, small undivided interests in some piece of property
within the municipality, paying therefor only nominal
sums, and a dozen or more of them seeking to qualify upon
the same estate. This move, however, the administrative
courts promptly checkmated by deciding that sole ownership (Alleinbesitz) of some substantial parcel of property
was essential to the fulfilment of the requirement.[1]

Some results
of the prop-
erty require-
ment.
When this property restriction was first adopted it was
in many respects salutary, and in its actual operation did
not bear unreasonably upon any class of voters. A century ago, or even a half-century ago, the percentage of property-owners in the larger German cities was considerable,
and the area over which the choice of candidates could
be spread was correspondingly broad ; but at the present
time the proportion of property-owners in Berlin does not
amount to more than five per cent of the population, and
from this small element seventy-two members of the council must be chosen. In the larger Prussian cities, as in
the larger cities of other countries, the ownership of real
property is becoming concentrated in the hands of a comparatively few men, while wealth in the form of personal
property is perhaps becoming more widely diffused. Since
a modern city may thus contain thousands of wealthy
men who own no real property at all, the emphasis which

[1] *Entscheidungen des Oberverwaltungsgerichts*, XXXVIII. 26 ff. The ownership must exist at the time of the election ; but a subsequent sale of the property does not serve to unseat a councillor. On this and various other points
connected with the interpretation of § 16, see Ledermann, *Die Städteordnung*,
70–71.

the Prussian law lays upon such possessions has seemed to
many to be unfair and at the present time unreasonable.
This aspect of the case has been very clearly set forth by
a recent writer, who urges that the requirement should
now be eliminated from the code as no longer in keeping
with economic conditions.[1] In this connection, however,
it should be noted that the proportion of property-owners
in the Prussian councils has almost invariably been well
over the required half if the councillors be taken as a
body, — a condition of affairs which contrasts very sharply
with the situation in most American cities.   In Berlin
about three-quarters of the present councillors are owners of
real property, and in some other cities the proportion is
even higher.

Proposals
for its aboli-
tion.

Subject to the foregoing requirement, almost any voter
is eligible to candidacy ; but there are a few disqualifications which deserve mention.   In the first place, no government official or member of any higher body through
which state supervision is exercised over cities is eligible
to membership in the municipal council ; and, with certain
exceptions in the case of the smaller cities, no paid civic
employee, high or low, is eligible.   The law also disquali-
fies from candidacy all clergymen and all church officers,
as well as all teachers in the elementary schools, all judges
and court officers, and all officials connected with the police
administration.   A curious and interesting provision is
that which prevents members of the same family from belonging to the council at the same time : when two such
are elected, the younger must retire.[2]

Disqualifi-
cations.

Candidates for election to the city council in Prussia

[1] G. Dryander on "Der § 16 der preussischen Städteordnung und die Hausbesitzer unserer Grosstädte," in *Annalen des deutschen Reiches* (1903), 430–450.

[2] The various exclusions and disqualifications are enumerated in the Städteordnung, § 17.   On their exact scope and interpretation, see A. W. Jebens,
Die Stadtverordneten, 38–48 ; and O. Oertel, *Die Städteordnung*, 96–101.

No formal nomination of candidates for election to the council.

are not nominated by any primary, caucus, or other preliminary proceeding; indeed, they cannot be brought to official notice in any legal way. There is no provision for candidacy by nomination papers, or any other form of authoritative announcement; and no nominations are received by any election officer. In the selection of the councillors there is but one official step, the polling. It is, of course, true in Prussia, as in France, that in the weeks preceding an election the various political clubs and party organizations usually reach somewhat definite understandings as to what candidates their members will support at the polls; but such agreements are not communicated to any electoral authority.[1] As no printed ballots are used in the process of polling, there is no necessity for any of the procedure which Americans and Englishmen connect with the term "nomination." So far as the election authorities are concerned, each voter is left entirely unguided in making his choice.

The polling.

The polling in Prussian city elections takes place in November, upon a day or days fixed by vote of the administrative board, or Magistrat.[2] At least four months prior to this date the list of voters in each election district is prepared in the manner already described, and in due time is publicly posted for examination.[3] Objections are heard and disposed of by a committee of the municipal council; but the decisions of this committee must be indorsed by vote of the whole council, and must also have the concurrence of the Magistrat. In the event of a disagreement between these two bodies the matter goes to the higher local authorities, whose decision is final.[4]

Notices sent to voters.

It is the duty of the Magistrat to see that at least fourteen

---

[1] See below, pp. 39–41.   [2] Städteordnung, §§ 19–20.   [3] See above, pp. 129 ff.
[4] Städteordnung, § 20; and amendments summarized in Ledermann's *Die Städteordnung*, 80–84.

days before the date set for polling every voter is duly notified of the date, the place, and the hours of balloting, a notification which it usually communicates by mailing to the address of each voter a postal card giving the necessary information.[1] In addition, every recognized clergyman in the city is requested by the authorities to announce the polling from his pulpit, and at the same time to emphasize the duties of citizens with reference to the election.[2]

Places of polling are likewise selected by the Magistrat, upon recommendation of that particular member of the body whose duty it is to supervise the election machinery. There must be at least one polling-place in every election district; but for voters of the third class it is customary to provide several such places. Very commonly some public building is used for the purpose; but more often the voting takes place in some conveniently situated Lokal, or beer-hall. As no funds are provided to pay rental for polling-places, the authorities find themselves constrained to accept the use of rooms offered gratuitously because of the business which the coming of a throng of voters promises to bring. No intoxicating liquor may be sold in the room where the polling actually takes place; but it may be, and usually is, sold in the adjoining rooms of the same premises. The poll is kept open from morn-

Location of the polls.

---

[1] A translation of one of these notifications reads as follows: —

Official Notice of Municipal Election
on Wednesday, November 30, 1904
from 10 A.M. to 8 P.M.
Election District No. 30, Precinct 2
III. Class
Polling-room: Public School, 67 August St.
(As a means of identification one may present this card.)

THE MAGISTRAT.

[2] There is, however, no means of forcing clergymen to comply with this request. See *Preussisches Verwaltungsblatt*, XXIV. 807, § 27.

ing till evening, the exact hours being fixed by the election authorities.

The poll is put in charge of a committee of three men, made up of a chairman (Vorsitzender), who is appointed by the Bürgermeister, and two associates (Beisitzer), who are named by the city council. These three decide, by a majority vote, any questions which may arise in connection with the voting.[1] A clerk, some scrutineers or watchers appointed by interested candidates, and the inevitable policeman complete the personnel of the polling-place. One notices in the Prussian polling-booth the absence of any ballot-box, ballots, compartments for marking ballot-papers, — in fact, of all the familiar paraphernalia

of the American poll. On the table before the chairman lies a large book in which are inscribed the names, addresses, and occupations of all those entitled to vote, with a blank space after each name in which the voter's choice is to be written. The voter comes to the table, gives his name, and presents the postal card which has been sent to him some days previously. If this has not been received, or has been lost or mislaid, he must present some other identifying document, such as a tax receipt, a certificate of military service, or even a lease ; for no vote will be received until the voter's identification has been established to the entire satisfaction of the poll-committee. This formality having been satisfied, he is asked to designate his choice ; and this he must do orally and in a loud voice (mündlich und laut). The name which he pronounces is then written in the book immediately after his name. The whole procedure is thus extremely simple,

leaving no room whatever for personation, repeating, ballot-switching, and the various other sinister practices which

---

[1] Städteordnung, § 24.

a close contest in an American city too often brings into operation.[1]

The Prussian city elections are conducted with absolute fairness, and in an orderly, dignified manner. The obvious and grave objection to the system is, however, that the voting is open and not secret, — that the voter's choice is indicated in the presence of those watchers who represent the different candidates.[2] Against this publicity there has been a great deal of protest, especially from voters of the third class, who claim that the system lends itself to the exercise of pressure which amounts virtually to intimidation. The leaders among the Social Democrats insist that open voting tends to destroy any freedom of choice on the part of employees who dislike to antagonize their employers, and that it renders the whole body of state and civic officials mere agents for registering the will of their administrative superiors. The system is, indeed, open to all the objections which were raised in American cities against the practice of open voting when that method was in vogue several decades ago. In the German imperial elections the voting is by secret ballot, and the advantages of this system have strongly impressed themselves upon many of the Prussian municipal voters; but so long as the control of Prussian national government is in the hands of the conservative element the adoption of the secret ballot in city elections is not probable.

A feature of the Prussian electoral system is that the three classes of voters do not vote on the same date. The law requires that the voters of the third class shall elect their quota of councillors before the voters of the second class are called to the polls; and these latter, again,

The three classes vote on different days.

---

[1] Various questions relating to procedure at the polls are discussed in Jebens's *Die Stadtverordneten*, 89–107.

[2] Only in the city of Frankfort-on-the-Main is secret voting in vogue.

must conclude their voting before the voters of the first
class proceed to ballot.[1]   For the two upper classes the
polling lasts but a single day, and the poll is sometimes
kept open for only a few hours; but in the case of the
third group the polling may continue for more than a day,

Duration of
polling.

and it sometimes does last for two or even for three days,
the poll being kept open each day from morning till late
in the evening.   As the different classes vote on different
days, the same polling-places usually serve for all three.

Counting
the votes.

At a Prussian municipal election there can of course be
no disputed or spoiled votes, and there are rarely any
questions for the poll-committee to decide.   The watchers,
or scrutineers, who represent the different candidates in
the polling-room, keep tally of the votes; hence the number polled by each candidate is known definitely at every
stage, and when the poll is closed the result is seen at
once.   The official return (Wahlprotokolle) is, however,
carefully compiled from the polling-book, and after it has
been signed by the members of the poll-committee is
transmitted to the Magistrat, by which formal announcement of the result of the election is made.

An abso-
lute ma-
jority
necessary to
an election.

In order to secure election at the first polling, a candidate must have received a clear majority of all the votes
cast;[2] in no case does a plurality suffice to elect unless it be
also a majority.   Owing to the comparative inefficiency
of party organization, however, together with the well-
known native political independence of the German voter,
it very frequently happens that this requirement is not

Supplemen-
tary polling.

satisfied.   In such cases a supplementary election (engere
Wahl) must be held within the next eight days, the place
of polling, the organization of the poll, and the voting procedure being the same as at the general elections.   Notices
are again sent to the voters, but this time they contain

[1] Städteordnung, § 21.   [2] Städteordnung, § 26.

the names of two candidates, to which the voter's choice is rigidly limited. These candidates are the two who received the highest and second highest number of votes at the previous polling. When two candidates are to be elected, the four highest are eligible at the second polling; when three are to be chosen, the six highest, and so on. This system, though similar in principle to the French ballotage, differs from it in one important detail. In France, as has been noticed, the voter's choice at the supplementary election remains as free from restriction as at the first one, but at this polling a mere plurality is sufficient to elect. In Prussia, on the other hand, the political contest is narrowed down to twice as many candidates as there are posts to be filled. In some cases, indeed, the Prussian system works out in such a way as to make the first election correspond to the primary election in American cities: the two candidates who survive for the supplementary election are the representatives of the two strongest political factions, the first poll serving only to weed out from a considerable number of aspirants the real standard-bearers of two opposing parties. In most cases, however, the system does not operate in just this way; for elections at the first polling are the rule rather than the exception. Nevertheless, in the Prussian cities, as in the French, the policy has its influence in multiplying candidatures at the first polling; for it induces small factions to put forward their representatives on this occasion even though there be no reasonable hope of their success.

French and German procedure at supplementary elections.

The election of a councillor may be protested by any qualified voter of the city, no matter what his district or class.[1] This protest may take the form of complaint re-

Election protests.

---

[1] Städteordnung, § 27. See also *Entscheidungen des Oberverwaltungsgerichts*, XVIII. 39–40.

L

garding irregularities in the electoral procedure, or of allegation of corrupt practices on the part of the candidate elected; but it must be lodged with the appropriate authorities within ten days from the date of the polling. Who these authorities are, whether municipal or provincial, depends upon the grounds of the protest.[1] If important irregularities or any corrupt practices are proved, the reviewing authorities have power to void the election and to order it contested anew.   As a matter of fact, however, the Prussian municipal elections have almost invariably been conducted in such a manner as to afford

Infrequency of protests.

little basis for faultfinding.   There is, to be sure, much complaint that the system of open voting puts a premium upon the exercise of undue influence by employers over employed; but of bribery, personation, repeating, fraud, and kindred electoral abuses there is apparently almost no complaint at all.   The absence of these evils is due partly to the simplification of electoral machinery, partly to the high standing of election officials, partly to the vigorous fashion in which the authorities promptly penalize the slightest sign of wrong-doing, and partly, no doubt, to the general respect for law and regularity which characterizes the whole Prussian people.

Influence of political parties in municipal elections.

Municipal party organization in the cities of Prussia does not, unfortunately, lend itself to description in general terms.   Without accepting unreservedly the remark of Heine that a dozen Germans are likely to represent a dozen political factions for the reason that no two are certain to think alike on matters concerning the body politic, one may, nevertheless, be sure that the spirit of political independence is strongly intrenched in German character, and that this independence has apparently

---

[1] For an elaboration of this point, see Jebens, *Die Stadtverordneten*, 104–125; and Oertel, *Die Städteordnung*, 130–137.

proved an insuperable obstacle to party discipline in imperial, state, and local politics alike.   In none of these three
spheres of political action does one encounter that grouping of voters into the ranks of two preponderating political
parties which one finds in England or the United States.
On the contrary, there are, in imperial politics at least,
four important political factions, with several minor Party decen-
groups; and only by the skilful arrangement of coalitions   tralization.
between two or more of these various factions can the
affairs of the empire be carried on.   In Prussian national
politics the decentralization is perhaps not so marked; for
here the franchise system deprives the more radical element among the voters of any important representation
in the legislative organs.   In the municipal elections the
situation seems to represent a stage between the two foregoing: the multiplication of political groups is not so
great as in imperial politics and somewhat greater than
in national.

Party lines in the three realms of political activity are,   Relation of
therefore, not exactly identified.   The ultra-conservatives   imperial,
national,
or reactionaries, who bulk large in the political affairs of the   and municipal parties.
empire, play but an insignificant rôle in local elections
in most of the large cities; on the other hand, the advanced radicals, or Social Democrats, who form a party
of little or no significance in state politics, have shown
great strength in municipal campaigns.   Indeed, the plat-
forms of the various municipal groups represent different
attitudes on issues which are mainly municipal but incidentally national or imperial.   In many of the larger Prussian cities a decided majority of the voters seem, in imperial
matters, to belong to the Social Democratic party; for
under the system of manhood suffrage a majority of the
members sent by these cities to the imperial Reichstag have
been members of this faction.   In the municipal councils, on

the other hand, a large majority of the councillors have, owing to the operation of the three-class system, represented the various wings or sections of the Liberal party. In fact, one might almost range the membership of a typical Prussian city council into three general groups, — the more conservative Liberals (National Liberalen), the more advanced Liberals (fortschrittliche Partei), and the Social Democrats. The councillors of the first two groups are selected largely by the first and second classes of voters; but advanced Liberals are frequently chosen by the third class as well. Among the representatives of this third class there are usually a good many Social Democrats; but in no important Prussian city have they as yet formed a majority of the councillors.

In their attitude toward general municipal policy the more conservative Liberals do not differ much from the more advanced. Both have shown themselves friendly to the municipalization of public services whenever the advantages of this policy have been made clear by direct reference to some particular service. Without making a shibboleth of municipal socialism, the two factions have usually found a common ground in the pursuance of a progressive municipal policy which neither runs riot along the paths of radicalism nor balks at such interference with vested interests as the welfare of the city may seem to demand. The Social Democrats, on the other hand, are not held together by any common bond in regard to local issues; their activity in local politics represents much the same attitude of irreconcilability toward the current order of things that is taken by them in the imperial legislature. They oppose the existing municipal organization as unrepresentative and undemocratic, and insist that every voter have an equal share in the administration of the city's affairs, to the end that municipal

The three important factions in city politics.

Attitude of parties toward questions of municipal policy.

The Social Democrats.

policy may embody the wishes of a numerical majority of the electorate. This attitude is prompted largely by the fact that, under present arrangements, there is no reasonable probability that their party programme, which goes the whole way in the direction of municipal social- ism and all that this implies, will secure official adoption even though it may command the allegiance of a large majority of the municipal voters.

The machinery of party organization in the Prussian cities, and indeed throughout the German Empire, is on the whole elementary and crude. Each faction has its local society, or Verein, — sometimes one for each election district, but more often one for several; and the work of these various bodies is supervised in somewhat loose fashion by a central committee, which may have juris- diction over all the local organizations of the city or over only a part of them.[1] In these bodies, which are political clubs rather than partisan organizations in the American sense, voters are regularly enrolled and usually pay a small membership fee. Their activities are social and intellectual as well as political; for in the intervals between the electoral campaigns they have their regular meetings, in the programmes of which matters political receive minor attention. Most of these political clubs have no permanent headquarters, the members meeting monthly or oftener in some convenient beer-hall; a few, however, maintain regular club-rooms, with permanent sec- retaries in charge. In any case each club has its chair- man and its secretary, elected annually by the members.[2]

Party machinery.

The political "Vereins."

[1] Groups of these district organizations (Bezirksvereine) are sometimes fed- erated, with a committee of direction, — as, for example, the "Bund der frei- sinnigen Bezirksvereine des Ostens und Nordostens" in Berlin.

[2] Further details regarding the organization and activities of well-known and somewhat typical clubs may be found in *Jahresbericht des fortschrittlichen Vereins " Waldeck "* (Berlin, 1907) ; in *Geschichte des fortschrittlichen Vereins*

Nature of
their
activities. On the approach of an election, whether imperial, national, or municipal, the clubs begin to show an increase in political activity; the members devote their meetings to the discussion of political matters, and the discussions turn to the question of candidates. In the case of a local election a club frequently selects a candidate from among its own members; but sometimes it is deemed more advisable to pledge the club's support to an aspirant whose candidature has been inspired by some other interest or organization. In this particular, as in many other matters connected with the work of the local party organizations, there is no approach to uniformity; in fact, there is in the system itself none of that machine-like symmetry and efficiency which characterize the local party mechanisms of American cities. As the clubs comprise within their membership but a small percentage of the total electorate, they do not necessarily represent the wishes

Their
slender
resources. of their respective parties. They possess no substantial monetary resources for use in the election campaigns, and they have no very effective weapons of party discipline; for the average Prussian voter, though not adverse to advice and suggestions from his political leaders, is at best none too docile, and is apt to resent dictation. The local party organizations seek, therefore, to influence rather than to control candidacy, a feature in which they differentiate themselves most clearly from their prototypes in American cities.

Character
of the men
elected to
the council. As to the general character and standing of the men elected to the Prussian municipal councils under this system there is and can be but one opinion. Among the local elective organs of the various countries of Europe and America none have been more successful than the

---

" *Waldeck* " (ed. Hugo Reinwald, Berlin, 1903); or in *Jahresbericht des freisinnigen Vereins der Halleschen-Thor-Bezirke* (Berlin, 1907).

Prussian city councils in securing as members men of ability, integrity, and general prestige. It is well within the truth to say that in a city like Berlin the councillors are chosen from among the very best citizens of the capital;[1] that they form, for the most part, a well-selected élite drawn from the professional, mercantile, and academic circles of the population; that, in short, they represent, not the hasty and transitory judgments of the masses, but the best business sense of the community.[2] Indeed, from whatever point of view the German and American city councils are compared, they differ in nothing more than in the caliber of the men who make up their membership. So striking is the difference between them in this respect that one is led to ask why it is that men whose private interests are so important should be willing to give to the German municipality so much of their time and thought without any direct remuneration and without the slightest indirect possibility of financial recoupment; for it cannot be doubted that by far the larger number of the councillors accept the duties of their office at a substantial sacrifice of their private interests. Why the experience of German and American cities in this matter has been so different, is in truth a fair question.[3]

Undoubtedly this success of the Prussian city in attracting men of unusual ability and influence into the ranks Reasons for the high standard.

[1] The list of members, with occupations, may be found in *Personal-Nachweisung der Berliner Gemeinde-Verwaltung* (Berlin, 1908). Eighty-five councillors are reported as engaged in business, twenty-eight as " rentiers," seven as lawyers, six as physicians, and two as teachers.

[2] This opinion is based on the writer's own observation. It is fair to add, however, that some of the more progressive councillors complain vigorously of the narrow-mindedness and ultra-conservatism of their colleagues. " Die grosse Mehrheit sind Spiessbürger in Reinkultur," is the opinion that one of the liberal leaders expressed to me concerning his fellow-members of the council.

[3] On this point see Professor F. W. Taussig's interesting and suggestive article on " Love of Wealth and the Public Service," in *Atlantic Monthly* (March, 1906), XCVII. 289–300.

of its council is attributable to several reasons, chief among which may be the fact that in Prussia the social prestige which attaches to public service of any sort is greater than it is in any other country. The national authorities have for many years assiduously fostered the doctrine that those who serve the state in either military or civil offices should take rank in the social scale above the ordinary layman, no matter what the wealth or busi-

Social influences.

ness standing of the latter may be. No one who is at all familiar with the structure of Prussian society need be reminded of the large part which this policy has played in securing both for the army and for the national civil service or bureaucracy the most promising element of the rising population. This general attractiveness of the public service has permeated from the state to the city; and the influence which it has had in leading men of wealth and prominence to welcome the opportunity of a seat at

The three-class system and the property requirements.

the council-board can hardly be overestimated. Again, the three-class system of voting, and the requirement that at least one-half of the council's membership shall be made up of house-owners, have no doubt contributed to the maintenance of the standard. There are probably in every city a good many useful men who will readily seek office at the hands of their own business associates, but who would hesitate to ask the suffrages of the masses. To such the three-class system gives just the opportunity that is desired; for those Prussian councillors who represent the first and second classes of voters are virtually chosen by an electoral élite to which they are attached by much more than a mere political bond. At the same time, it is plain that the three-class system is not the only contributing factor to the high personnel of public service; for in Bavaria, Saxony, and the other German states the readiness of the best citizens to serve the municipality at a personal sacrifice is just as marked as in Prussia, though no one of these states has adopted the three-class system or any scheme of voting akin to it.

Other circumstances that probably combine to eliminate, in the German cities, many of the obstacles which in the United States tend to deter men of high standing from entering the municipal service may be found in the long terms which councillors serve,[1] in the reasonable certainty of reëlection which they enjoy, the absence of any regular system of caucuses or primaries, the decentralization of parties and hence the greater stress upon the personal qualities of candidates, the small expense of an election campaign, and the decorum and entire fairness with which an election is conducted. Such advantages, in addition to the social prestige which attends the tenure of public office, may serve to attract the man of public spirit who is willing to make some sacrifice of his own personal interests for the good of the community; but to the man who seeks office for his own profit and advantage the post of councillor in a German city presents little attraction, for the councilman receives no compensation, has little patronage, and can put no sources of profit in the paths of his friends. There are points of view from which the Prussian system may be criticised as unsatisfactory; and, in its method of grouping voters into classes which are broadly distinguished by differences in wealth as well as in several other particulars, it will probably impress many as violating some of the most elementary canons of democratic government. That the plan has, however, served to bring into the service of the cities a body of men who, for devo-

Other features tending to maintain the standard.

---

[1] In the present Berlin council there are sixteen members who have served for more than twenty years each, and fifty who have each had more than ten years of service.

tion to the public interest and for soundness of business judgment, are not surpassed by the membership of any municipal organ in any other country, is beyond all reasonable question.

Compulsory service not a feature of any importance. The high quality of the men selected as councillors is sometimes attributed to the fact that, when a Prussian citizen is elected to membership in the council, he is legally under obligation to accept the post. The municipal code does, it is true, provide that a councillor-elect shall be mulcted in a heavy fine if he refuses to serve his term;[1] but it may be doubted whether this formal regulation has had much influence. The sanction of public opinion would probably have availed sufficiently without any legal provision; for the doctrine that the opportunity of holding public office is an honor not to be declined by any citizen is very well established in the Prussian mind. It may be noted, moreover, that compulsory civic service is not peculiar to the German states; it exists in some other continental countries, and even in England.

The council at work. Immediately after the elections the new councillors are sworn to the proper performance of their functions and the council proceeds with its organization. It elects, from among its own members, a permanent chairman (Vorsitzender) and a substitute chairman (Stellvertreter), each of whom serves for a single year, but may be reelected and is, indeed, usually chosen for two or more successive years. Internal organization. It also selects its secretary or clerk (Schriftführer), who may or may not be one of its own members;[2] if he is not a member, the choice must be

---

[1] Städteordnung, § 74.

[2] Städteordnung, § 38. These officers, together with such additional members (Beisitzer) as may be chosen in the same manner, form the bureau, or executive committee of the council.

confirmed by the administrative board, or Magistrat. The selection of these council officers is made by means of a secret ballot, and in the first instance an absolute majority of votes is necessary to an election. If this be not had by any candidate, a second vote is taken upon the four names which stood highest on the first ballot; and if no one of these four receives a clear majority, a third vote is taken upon the two names ranking highest on the second ballot.[1] All officers of the council other than the three foregoing — such as clerks, messengers, and so on — are appointed by the Magistrat, and hence rank as regular municipal employees.[2]

The council frames its own rules of procedure (Geschäftsordnung); but such rules must be approved by the Magistrat, and, in the event of any disagreement between the two bodies, the point must be decided by the higher local authorities. Every council has its code of procedure, with rules that fix the place, date, and hours of regular meetings, set forth the order in which business is to be taken up, and define the powers and duties of the chairman, vice-chairman, secretary, and other officials.[3] Substantially the same general rules are followed in all the larger cities, but on many minor points the procedure differs. The rules usually followed by public bodies in Germany are on the whole somewhat simpler than those commonly observed in the United States, and in general lend themselves more readily to the prompt despatch of business. A useful practice, which obtains in both France and Germany, is that of referring complicated and

Rules of procedure.

---

[1] Städteordnung, §§ 36, 38.   [2] Städteordnung, § 48.

[3] A typical code of these rules, the "Geschäftsordnung für die Stadtverordneten-Versammlung zu Charlottenburg," may be found in Jebens's *Die Stadtverordneten*, 347–360. The "Geschäftsordnung für die Stadtverordneten-Versammlung zu Berlin" (adopted December 8, 1895) is published in pamphlet form.

difficult problems, especially those connected with jurisdiction, to individual members of the council for investigation and report. Such designated reporters (rappor-
teurs) perform much of the work of examining the law,
the precedents, and the facts relating to intricate questions, thereby greatly relieving the pressure that would
ordinarily fall upon the various standing committees, and
at the same time facilitating prompt action.

Meetings.   In the larger cities the council ordinarily meets once a
week, except during the summer months. Additional
meetings are summoned by the chairman whenever they
are needed; and in the period of the year during which
the annual budget is under consideration they are sometimes needed often. The Berlin council meets every Thurs-
day afternoon (except during the months of July and
August), and the sessions ordinarily continue from five till
eight o'clock; but not infrequently the pressure of business
Frequent prolongs the sitting till midnight. In the practice of hold-
short ing short meetings at frequent intervals the Germans pur-
sessions. sue the system in vogue in England and the United States
as distinguished from that followed by the city councils of
France and the other Latin countries, where sessions are
held at considerable intervals and are sometimes prolonged
No strict over several weeks. The central authorities in Prussia
limitations have set no limits to the frequency and duration of council
on the scope deliberations, and have not thought it necessary, as have
of its delib-
erations. the authorities in France, to make any hard and fast rules
as to the topics which may be discussed. The Prussian
council itself, through its rules and its chairman, controls
the scope of its own discussions without interference by
the higher powers. Unlike the French council, also, it is
not subject to suspension or dissolution by decree of any
subordinate administrative authority, although in the last resort a Prussian city council may be dissolved by royal decree.

The council usually meets at the city hall (Rathaus); Members of the Magistrat present at council sessions. and in the council-room are also provided accommodations for the members of the administrative board, or Magistrat, who have a right to attend all council-meetings and to speak upon any question under consideration, but not to vote. At every session there are some members of the Magistrat; and these may be interpellated or called upon by any councillor present for information upon any matter within his departmental jurisdiction. In fact, almost every important proposal which comes to the council from the Magistrat is supported at the council-meeting by one or more of those members of the Magistrat who may happen to be most directly concerned. The meetings are ordi- Meetings are public. narily open to the public; but secret or executive sessions may be held if necessary, and in some cities they are not at all uncommon.[1] In the larger cities considerable public interest is manifested in the proceedings of the council; and, when questions of importance are under discussion at open meetings, this interest is shown by the attendance of many spectators.

Before every council-meeting in a large city a printed The docket. statement of the business which is to come before the councillors is sent to each member. This statement (Vorlage) is made up for the most part of proposals which are to be laid before the council by the Magistrat, and is accompanied by such statistical and other informational data as are likely to prove of service to the councillors. An examination of these dockets shows that most of the business which comes up in the council is prepared by the Magistrat, and that the latter takes unusual pains to lay before the council, and through it before the public, full details

[1] During 1905 the Berlin council held sixty-seven sessions, from no less than twenty-nine of which the public were excluded. These executive sessions were for the most part very short, however, and dealt chiefly with matters of a personal nature.

regarding all the propositions submitted.[1]   When a project
has been approved by the Magistrat, it is transmitted to
the chairman of the council, who, before presenting it to
the latter body, submits it to the appropriate council committee.   If the matter be of minor consequence, it is sometimes referred to some individual councillor instead, who
prepares himself to discuss the proposal when it comes up.
The items of business on the council docket are taken up
and disposed of in regular order, and more slowly than they
would be dealt with by an American municipal body; for
in Prussia, and especially in the larger cities, the proceedings of the council are conducted with a good deal of formality.   The speeches are frequently of considerable length
and often give evidence of careful preparation; indeed, the
meetings of the Berlin council have at times assumed all

the dignity and seriousness of a parliamentary body.   The
municipal council, it should be remembered, is essentially a deliberative rather than an administrative body,
a fact which its members seem consistently to recognize.
Its main business is to discuss proposals from every point
of view, and to offer suggestions and criticisms rather than
to hurry matters to any definite conclusion.   In fact, the
somewhat leisurely way in which it proceeds with its business has sometimes given rise to unfavorable comment on
the part of the administrative officials; but, so long as the
Prussian cities possess a powerful, efficient, and prompt administrative body in the Magistrat, the plodding methods
of the council need scarcely give rise to any serious misgivings.

The Prussian city council ordinarily has a small number of standing committees, chief among which is one

---

[1] The " Vorlagen für die Stadtverordneten-Versammlung zu Berlin" for the
meeting of June 26, 1906, which I have selected at random from the files in the
Berlin city hall, contains forty items of business, which, with the accompanying
data, cover twenty-seven printed pages.

made up of the chairman, the vice-chairman, and three or four selected councillors, who together constitute a sort of executive committee to which any matter may be referred.[1] All the committees are appointed by the council itself; but their work, which consists mainly in considering and reporting upon matters before they come up at the regular council-meetings, is not relatively important, for the council has so few executive powers that it is loath to refer its duty of deliberation to small committees. It is true that much of the city's administrative work is performed by committees; but it is by joint committees (Deputationen) composed of selected members of the council and the Magistrat.[2] The committees of the council itself do not, as in English cities, deal with the details of civic administration; this field is monopolized by the joint committees of the two bodies.

After each meeting of the council the record of the proceedings (Protokoll) is signed by the chairman and by at least three of the members present. All the resolutions are transmitted to the Magistrat, unless they happen to relate to matters wholly within the jurisdiction of the council, — and of this kind there are very few. It is also customary in the larger cities to issue in printed form after each meeting a stenographic report of the council's proceedings, a copy of which is given to any citizen who applies for it.[3] *Minutes and records.*

The powers of the municipal council are not defined with any exactness by the provisions of the City Government Act of 1853. On the contrary, after explicitly com- *Powers of the council.*

---

[1] This practice is not followed by the Berlin council. It was abolished by that body many years ago.   [2] See below, pp. 197 ff.

[3] In Berlin this report is entitled "Amtlicher stenographischer Bericht für die Sitzung der Stadtverordneten-Versammlung, hgbn. vom Magistrat zu Berlin." All official announcements are also printed in the *Gemeinde-Blatt*, or municipal gazette.

mitting to the administrative board all important powers of initiative in matters of local policy, as well as all important executive functions, the enactment somewhat vaguely declares that the council shall exercise the residuum of municipal power.[1] The council's work, in short, is to deliberate and decide (zu beschliessen), but not to carry out (ausführen) its decisions.[2] This separation between the organ of deliberation and the organ of execution is one of the salient characteristics of the Prussian municipal system; and in composition and procedure the two bodies are adapted to their respective tasks.[3]

As exercised in actual practice, the powers of the municipal council may be summarized under four main heads : —

1. Advice. 1. The council gives its advice to the Magistrat, or to the higher authorities of the district or the province, in all cases in which it is required by law so to do, and on such other occasions as its counsel may be requested in the proper way. The higher authorities are not under obligation to accept the advice so tendered; but in some cases they are required to consult the council before taking action.[4]

2. Appointments. 2. It selects, subject to confirmation by the royal government, one or more Bürgermeisters; it also chooses the members of the administrative board, or Magistrat, and appoints the citizen deputies (Bürgerdeputirter) who serve on the various joint committees (Deputationen).[5] These, however, are the only officials or administrative authorities that it may select; all the regular municipal

---

[1] "Die Stadtverordneten-Versammlung hat über alle Gemeinde-Angelegenheiten zu beschliessen, soweit dieselben nicht ausschliesslich dem Magistrate überwiesen sind " (Städteordnung, § 35).

[2] "Die Stadtverordneten-Versammlung darf ihre Beschlüsse in keinem Falle selbst zur Ausführung bringen " (Städteordnung, § 36).

[3] This idea is clearly brought out in Kapplemann's essay on "Die Verfassung und Verwaltungsorganisation der preussischen Städte," in *Schriften des Vereins für Socialpolitik*, CXVII. i. 1–92.

[4] Städteordnung, § 35.   [5] Städteordnung, § 31.

employees, from the heads of departments downward, are appointed by the Bürgermeister, the Magistrat, or the higher state authorities.

3. It considers and passes upon all matters submitted to it by the administrative board. All proposals, large and small, which affect general municipal policy must be laid before it; indeed, as its records show, in a large city like Berlin hundreds of matters which one might almost regard as of very minor consequence are submitted to it every year.[1] The most important proposal that comes down from the Magistrat is, of course, the annual civic budget, which, after its arrival, engages the attention of the council for several sessions. Upon this budget it deliberates item by item, with full power to strike out, amend, or insert, — a power, it may be added, which the councillors exercise with considerable freedom. The annual budget does not, however, become effective until it has been agreed to by the Magistrat, which is very conservative in giving its assent to any increases made by the council in the list of appropriations. When the two bodies fail to agree on matters connected with the budget, or, indeed, upon any point in which they have concurrent powers, the solution of the deadlock is sought by the appointment of a joint committee of conference; and if this committee fails to effect a compromise the matter goes to the appropriate higher authorities.[2]

4. Within a considerable field the council is permitted to take the initiative and make recommendations to the Magistrat.[3] If a recommendation should meet with favor-

3. Legislation.

The budget.

4. Initiation of projects.

---

[1] In Berlin the number of these " Magistratsvorlagen " sent down during the year 1903 was 807 ; during 1904, 799 ; and during 1905, 841. See *Bericht über die Gemeinde-Verwaltung der Stadt Berlin, 1901 bis 1905* (Berlin, 1907), I. 11.

[2] Ordinarily this authority is the district council (Bezirks-Ausschuss), but in the case of Berlin it is the provincial Oberpräsident. See Ledermann, *Die Städteordnung*, 134–136.   [3] Städteordnung, § 36.

M

able consideration in the latter body it may be adopted and put into force directly, or it may be elaborated and sent back to the council.

The council's influence on civic policy. These powers, though important, are not sufficient to give the council rank with the Magistrat in point of actual jurisdiction. Through its scrutiny of the budget, its power of appointing the chief administrative officials, its representation on the various joint committees, and its concurrent jurisdiction in matters of general policy, it exercises what the City Government Act intended it to exercise, — a " general control over local administration " ;[1] but this control is not very strict or very effectual, for the reason that the Bürgermeister and members of the Magistrat, being appointed for long terms, rarely fail to assert a considerable degree of independence.[2] Moreover, when the council and the Magistrat come into disagreement, the higher authorities are apt to decide in favor of the latter.

Disagreements between council and Magistrat. During a half-century so many appeals have, of course, been made to these authorities that their decisions, rendered from time to time, now form a comprehensive collection of precedents which, taken together, serve to weaken the council not a little in its relations with the administrative board. Notwithstanding all these limitations, however, it is not to be supposed that the Prussian city council is a negligible factor in local government ; on the contrary, its resolutions and opinions are never without weight, and are very often decisive in dictating the course to be pursued by the administrative authorities.[3]

Powers of the higher authorities in this event.

---

[1] " Die Stadtverordneten-Versammlung kontrolirt die Verwaltung " (Städteordnung, § 37).

[2] The council cannot remove the Bürgermeister and members of the Magistrat from office ; but it may prefer charges of malfeasance or non-feasance against any of them, and the higher authorities may, after hearings, remove the offenders (Städteordnung, § 44).

[3] The influence and powers of the council are further discussed in Jebens's *Die Stadtverordneten*, and in A. Reimann's *Der preussische Stadtverordnete*,

The other organ of government in the Prussian city is, as we have seen, the administrative board, or Magistrat.[1] This body consists of a Bürgermeister (in the larger cities of two Bürgermeisters[2]) and a number of members (Stadträthe or Schöffen), some of whom are paid and some unpaid. In the smaller cities most of the members belong in the latter category, but in the larger ones the paid members are sometimes as numerous as their unsalaried colleagues.[3] The number of unpaid magistrates which any city may have is fixed by law according to the population of the municipality;[4] the number of paid members is determined by the city council subject to the approval of the higher authorities. In general, the total membership of the administrative board is from about one-quarter to one-third that of the council. Berlin, for example, with a council of one hundred and forty-four members, has thirty-four members in its administrative board, including the two Bürgermeisters.[5]

The Magistrat.

Its composition.

seine *Rechte und Pflichten* (Danzig, 1900). An older work which still possesses value is L. Ebert's *Der Stadtverordnete im Geltungsbereiche der Städteordnung vom 30. Mai 1853* (Berlin, 1883).

[1] The organization of this body is provided for in §§ 29–34 of the Städteordnung, and its powers in § 56. Some details were considered in *Die Instruktion für die Stadt-Magisträte vom 25. Mai 1835*, issued by the Prussian government. In their present amended form, these may be found in Jebens's *Die Instruktion für die Stadt-Magistrate vom 25. Mai 1835 nach neustem Recht* (Berlin, 1901).

[2] In the larger cities these officers are called "Oberbürgermeister" and "Bürgermeister," if the royal permission for these designations has been obtained.

[3] Magdeburg, for example, has twelve paid and fifteen unpaid members in its administrative board ; Breslau has fourteen paid and fifteen unpaid ; Berlin has seventeen of each class. The figures for all important cities may be found in the annual volumes of the *Statistisches Jahrbuch deutscher Städte*.

[4] Cities of 10,000 to 30,000 population have six unpaid magistrates ; those of 30,000 to 60,000 have eight ; those of 60,000 to 100,000 have ten ; and those of more than 100,000 have two additional unpaid magistrates for every additional 50,000 (Städteordnung, § 29). Exceptions to the general rule have, however, been made in the case of some municipalities.

[5] For further information concerning the personnel of the administration, see the *Statistisches Jahrbuch der Stadt Berlin* (published annually).

Term of members and method of selection.

All the members of the Magistrat are named by the city council. The paid members are chosen for a twelve-year term, except in a few cities where the tenure is for life; the unpaid members are selected for a six-year term only, and one-half retire triennially. Both paid and unpaid magistrates are reëligible, and under ordinary circumstances reëlection follows as a matter of course.[1] The choice is made at the council-meeting by secret ballot, and for election on the first vote the successful candidate must obtain a clear majority. If this be not had, the procedure already detailed is followed.[2] In the case of paid magistrates, the choice of the council must be confirmed by the higher authorities before it becomes valid.[3] If confirmation (Bestätigung) is refused, the council proceeds to make a new selection; if it should decline to do so, the higher authorities may temporarily fill the post on their own initiative.[4] As a matter of practice, however, the council has been allowed to exercise almost entire freedom in the matter of choosing its paid magistrates, and the assent of the higher authorities has rarely been withheld.

Confirmation.

Qualifications of members.

Members of the administrative board are not necessarily, or even usually, chosen by the council from within its own membership. Unsalaried magistrates must be residents of the municipality in which they are chosen; but the paid officials are not subject to this requirement, and hence are very frequently taken from the service of some other city. No one may, of course, be a member of the council and the

[1] There are in Berlin at the present time three members of the Magistrat who have each been continuously in office for over thirty-five years. The average term of the present board is slightly over thirteen years. See *Bericht über die Gemeinde-Verwaltung der Stadt Berlin, 1901 bis 1905* (Berlin, 1907), I. 3–4.

[2] Above, p. 155.

[3] Ledermann, *Die Städteordnung*, 119–122.

[4] An interesting outline of the development of this right of confirmation, with a vigorous criticism of it, may be found in Hugo Preuss's *Das städtische Amtsrecht in Preussen* (Berlin, 1902), ch. vii.

administrative board at the same time, and no persons who are immediate relatives may be members of the respective bodies. There are some other disqualifications provided for in the law, mainly against state officials, clergymen, and persons connected with the police administration; but on the whole the council exercises a free hand in its selection of magistrates.[1]

The paid magistrates are professional administrators chosen for their special skill, who give their whole time and energies to the service of the city and are recompensed with generous stipends. Their salaries vary in amount according to the size of the city and the importance of the work which they are required to perform; but in Berlin the paid magistrates get from twenty-one hundred and fifty to three thousand dollars per year. Moreover, in all the larger cities they receive pensions when they retire from the service of the municipality: after a single twelve-year term a magistrate may retire on half pay, or at the close of his second term he may retire on full salary. It is, therefore, not so much the actual salary paid as it is the security of tenure and the liberal pension on retirement which serve to make the post of paid magistrate in a Prussian city attractive to men of administrative skill and experience.

Paid magistrates.

Every paid member of the administrative board is selected because of his special aptitude in some department of civic administration; and each is, upon election, assigned to this particular branch. In every large city, for example, one paid member of the Magistrat fills the post of Kammerer, or head of the city's financial affairs; another acts as Syndikus, or head of the legal department; a third as Schulrat, or chief of the local system of primary education; a fourth as Baurat, or superintendent of the city's public

Work of the paid members.

[1] Städteordnung, § 30.

works; and so on.   One has the system of poor relief in special charge, another the city's sanitary system, another the hospital service.   Every paid member is assigned to some important department, the minor branches being usually looked after by the unpaid members, who are, however, sometimes put in the more responsible positions as well.

How paid magistrates are secured.

When any large city desires to add to the number of its paid magistrates, or to fill some paid post in the administrative board which may have become vacant, the city council has to find some one who possesses the particular qualifications required.   The usual course is to authorize the Magistrat to advertise the fact that applications for appointment to the office will be received and considered, the advertisement usually stating the amount of salary offered, the provisions in regard to pension, the duties to be performed, and the qualifications expected.[1]   These qualifications differ, of course, according to the character of the post to be filled.   Candidates for the office of Syndikus must have had a legal training; those for the post of Schulrat must be university graduates ; those for the office of Baurat must have been trained in general engineering ; and no one

Technical qualifications demanded.

[1] The appended advertisement, translated from the *Gemeinde-Zeitung* of July 28, 1906, is typical : —

"NOTICE

" The post of Syndikus in the Magistrat of this city has become vacant.   The stipend is 6000 marks per year with an increase of 600 marks every three years until the maximum of 9000 marks is reached.   The appointment is for life ; and provision is made for a pension on retirement after long service, as well as for the granting of an annuity to the widow or orphans of a deceased incumbent of the post.   The Syndikus is expected to preside in the Industrial and Mercantile Court (Gewerbe- und Kaufmannsgericht) and is intrusted with a general supervision over the legal affairs of the city.   Candidates who have passed their second legal examination and who have had successful administrative experience are requested to submit applications accompanied by testimonials and other suitable documents to the city clerk before August 20.

" Frankfort-on-the-Main,

"THE MAGISTRAT."

" July 17, 1906.

may hope for appointment to the office of Sanitätsrat who has not a special knowledge of sanitary science. Applications are received by the Magistrat and are transmitted by it to the council, usually with recommendations. Sometimes they come from unpaid magistrates, occasionally from persons in civilian life, and frequently, in a large city, from men who have filled similar posts in smaller municipalities and who think that their work entitles them to promotion. In any case all the applications are carefully considered, the records and qualifications of candidates are examined, and the list is narrowed down to two or three names before the council as a whole is called upon to make its selection. The Prussian city, in short, selects its highest officials by substantially the same procedure that is followed by any well-organized business corporation. The council aims to obtain the highest skill which the stipend will command, and in making its choice it disregards almost every consideration except the actual capabilities of the candidates as shown by their attainments and records. Partisan interests play practically no part in the selection, — except, perhaps, that an applicant who is known to be an active Social Democrat would in all probability find this fact very much against him, for even were he selected by the council the higher authorities would almost certainly refuse to confirm the choice. On the other hand, though offensive partisanship may bar a man from appointment, partisan services, no matter how valuable, will never of themselves suffice to dictate his selection. *Absence of partisan motives in the selection.*

The unpaid magistrates are not chosen for special aptitude in particular branches of municipal administration, but for their general administrative interest and capabilities. The law prescribes no qualification for their selection save that they shall be residents of the city; but the council usually chooses them from the ranks of its own *Unpaid magistrates.*

members.   Not infrequently, however, it goes outside and
selects successful business men who may have had very
little administrative experience.   As the standard set is
very high, and as acceptance of the post usually entails a
personal sacrifice, the councils have not always found it
easy to secure the men they want ; still, their success has
been remarkable in view of the fact that the office demands most of the incumbent's time without affording
him any remuneration whatever.   In a large city like
Berlin it takes almost the entire time of the men selected ;
hence only men of means and leisure can afford to serve.
It is true that, according to the provisions of the Prussian
law, any citizen who is chosen as an unpaid member of
the administrative board must accept the appointment
and serve at least three years or else pay a considerable
fine.   This provision is, however, of little advantage to
the council ; for the average appointee would find it more
economical to pay this fine over and over again than to
give up to the city the time which the duties of the office
require.   The truth of the situation is that the post is
highly attractive to prominent citizens who possess the
leisure, the means, and the taste for administration.   The
same considerations which render it easy to secure a high
class of men in the city councils operate with perhaps still
greater effect in the case of the unpaid magistracy.

Duties of the Magis-trat.   The duties of the Magistrat are set forth partly in
the code of 1853[1] and partly in the detailed instructions
which were issued by the Prussian government at an
earlier date ; but from time to time during the last half-
century alterations in the scope of magisterial functions have been made by the higher authorities.[2]   At

[1] Städteordnung, § 56.
[2] These may be found in Jebens's *Die Instruktion für die Stadt-Magisträte
vom 25. Mai 1835 nach neustem Recht* (Berlin, 1901).

present the duties of the administrative board cover a wide range, and they do not fall naturally into convenient groups. It may simplify matters somewhat, however, if a distinction be made, first of all, between those powers and duties that belong to the Magistrat as a body, and those which appertain to the individual members as heads of the various commissions that control the civic departments.

As an organ of government, the upper house of the municipal legislature, the Magistrat has powers which may be classified under nine main heads : — As an organ of city government.

1. It is intrusted with the promulgation and enforcement of the national laws within the limits of the city, a function in the exercise of which it is, like the French mayor, the agent of the central government, and hence may act without concurrence on the part of the city council.[1] During recent years its work in this field has been greatly increased : one need only mention the administration of the national laws relating to the establishment of industrial courts in the cities, and of those relating to the various forms of state insurance, to make it clear that the Magistrat of every large city has to create and supervise a large amount of new administrative machinery.[2] Moreover, by the extensive and steadily widening collectivist policy of the national government the routine work of the board has been greatly augmented. Finally, besides thus acting for the state in matters of civil policy, the Magistrat is the recognized local agent of the government in religious matters as well. It has, for example, immediate supervision of all church property within the civic limits ; it appoints the clergymen 1. An agent of the national government. Scope of powers in this sphere.

[1] Städteordnung, § 56, No. 1.

[2] The so-termed "Sozialpolitischen Versicherungsgesetze," which include the laws relating to state insurance against accident, sickness, and old age. For a list of these laws, see Ledermann, *Die Städteordnung*, 219–220.

and church officials ; and it is responsible for the general
administration of the laws by which the relations of the
church and state in Prussia are determined.[1]

German and
American
methods of
administer-
ing state
functions.

In the exercise of these functions the Prussian Magistrat
differs very distinctly from the upper house of an American municipal legislature. In the United States the
laws and policy of a state are carried out, in the main,
by authorities appointed directly by the state government
and responsible to it alone ; the American municipalities are not, as a rule, intrusted with the administration of new functions which the state from time to
time assumes. When the legislature of Massachusetts
recently made provision for the establishment of employment bureaus in the larger cities of the commonwealth, it did not commit the execution of this law
to the mayors or to the aldermen or to any other
municipal authority ; on the contrary, it intrusted the
work to a state officer. In Prussia this duty would,
in all probability, have been given to the administrative boards of the various cities concerned ; indeed, the
idea of committing the administration of laws to some
authority not directly controlled by the law-making
body runs through the whole German governmental system.
In the United States federal laws are executed by
federal officers, and violations are penalized by federal
courts ; in Germany imperial laws are in the main
administered by state officials and enforced by state
courts. The imperial government, for example, frames
the German tariff ; but the duties are collected by an
official who owes his appointment to a state government. So, too, the German imperial parliament makes
provision for a system of industrial courts ; but the

[1] The " Kirchengemeinde- und Synodalordnung " of September 10, 1873, especially §§ 6, 23, 34, and 35.

organization of such tribunals and the appointment of the judges, instead of being undertaken by the imperial authorities themselves, are thrown upon the states, to be by these in turn thrust upon the administrative boards of the cities concerned.[1]

Although this system naturally lessens in some degree the effectiveness of the state's control over the carrying out of its own laws and policy, it has at the same time some distinct advantages, not the least important of which lies in the fact that, by obviating the necessity of creating a new official or board for the administration of every new state function, it prevents the multiplication of state machinery. In Massachusetts, where the opposite policy has been pursued, there are now more than a score of state commissions, most of them performing administrative functions which would in Prussia be committed to the local authorities. This delegation of state functions to the German municipal governments serves, moreover, to enhance the dignity and prestige of the latter. Indeed, not a little of the honor which attaches to membership in the Magistrat comes from the fact that this body is not merely a local organ, but an important agent in the administration of state and imperial policy as well. *Merits and defects of the German system.*

2. In the second place, the Magistrat prepares the business which is to come before the city council at its meetings; and, after this business has passed the council, it has the responsibility of carrying the arrangements into effect. Not that the council has itself no initiative; on the contrary, in many matters the two bodies have equal right of originating measures. In actual practice, however, the council rarely does more than ask the Magistrat to present proposals in certain directions; not infrequently, indeed, it *2. Prepares business for the council and executes joint resolves.*

[1] "Gewerbe-Gerichts-Gesetz vom 29. Juli 1890" (in *Reichs-Gesetz-Blatt*, 1890, p. 141), and amending laws.

asks the administrative board to lay before it measures which it has itself fully elaborated in all their details. With all such requests the Magistrat usually complies. When a matter thus duly submitted has passed the council, it must be passed again by the Magistrat before it becomes effective; and the latter body, it may be added, is entirely free to withhold assent if it deems the proposal to be "in opposition to the welfare of the city or the civic interests."[1]

Relations between the two bodies on matters of concurrent jurisdiction. When the administrative board refuses its concurrence, the council may bring the question to the attention of the higher authorities, who, if they deem the disagreement to be inimical to the general interests of the city, may give the matter validity despite the opposition of the Magistrat. This, however, they have not often done. Though disagreements on important matters have not been rare, yet as a rule the Magistrat has been disposed to regard the council as being in a better position to reflect the wishes of the citizens, and hence has usually accepted its decisions whenever the question has been one of general policy. On the other hand, the council, recognizing that with matters and methods of detailed administration it has nothing to do, has not often ventured to intrude upon the domain of the Magistrat.

3. Supervises municipal enterprises. 3. To the Magistrat, again, belongs the actual supervision of all municipal undertakings (Gemeinde-Anstalten) and departments of civic activity, a function in the exercise of which it is not required to consult the council except on points that involve expenditure of money.[2] Among the various civic affairs under its care are such matters as the maintenance and repair of streets, the systems of water supply, sewage disposal, public lighting and transit, fire protection, and markets, the establishment and regulation of municipal savings-banks and loan-offices, the school

---

[1] Städteordnung, § 56, No. 2.   [2] Städteordnung, § 56, No. 3.

system of the city, and the whole list of enterprises commonly known as municipal services or civic utilities.   In some cases — as, for example, in its supervision of the educational system — the Magistrat is rather closely circumscribed in its actions by the hand of the state authorities; but usually it enjoys a wide range of freedom.

Of all enterprises that have been municipalized the administrative board has entire charge.   Subject to the general rules relating to appointments, it names the permanent officials in charge, and is responsible for the selection of all the subordinate employees.   In this sphere the jurisdiction of the Magistrat is complete, the council having no voice whatever.   The actual work of administering the enterprises is committed to the appropriate joint commissions (Deputationen), but the task of coördinating the work of these bodies rests upon the board as a whole.   The Magistrat is thus the focus of departmental administration.   In the case of services provided by enfranchised private corporations, it is supposed to see that the terms of the franchises are strictly observed.   If a new franchise is to be drawn, it prepares the proposal and gives it full consideration before sending it to the council.   All negotiations with the corporations are carried on through the Magistrat; if, for instance, any utility is to be taken over on the city's behalf, it is the Magistrat that arranges all the plans.

Nature of its supervision.

Relations with public-service corporations.

4. The Magistrat has charge of the municipal revenues, so far, at least, as their collection and custody are concerned.[1]   It does not determine the incidence or the methods of taxation, for in these matters the Prussian tax laws leave little or no discretion to any local authority; but when the passage of the annual budget has enabled the rate of taxes to be fixed the administrative board has su-

4. Has the custody of revenues.

[1] Städteordnung, § 56, No. 4.

pervision over the collection of them. It also has immediate charge of expenditures: no moneys may be paid out of the municipal treasury except upon the authority of the Magistrat. This authority it may use directly by its own vote, or may delegate it to one or more of its members; but as a body it retains the entire responsibility. The Magistrat

Audits. is also answerable for the proper auditing of all municipal accounts, and to this end must arrange for a monthly "revision" of them, as well as for a special audit to be made at least once a year. Of this yearly examination the council must, by the terms of the municipal code, be notified in advance in order that it may, if it so desires, depute one or more of its members to be present while the audit of the books is being carried on. The accounts of Prussian cities, unlike those of French, are not regularly audited by any higher state authority; but certain financial statements must be sent annually to the district or the provincial board, as the case may be, and these authorities may draw attention to any discrepancies.

5. Cares for civic property. 5. To the Magistrat is further intrusted the care and maintenance of all municipal property, including not only lands and other real estate belonging to the city, but all memorials, monuments, and so on.[1] No municipal property may be sold or hypothecated by the administrative board except with the consent of the higher authorities; but, save for this restriction, it may be managed as the local officials think best. For the acquisition of new property, or for any improvements which involve expenditure, the concurrence of the council is of course essential; but the actual administration of all minor business affecting civic property rests with the Magistrat alone.

Closely related to the foregoing powers is that of granting the use of streets and public places to public-service

---

[1] Städteordnung, § 56, No. 5.

corporations. When any such permission is desired, the application, accompanied by the requisite data, is ordinarily carried directly to the administrative board, by which it is at once referred to the proper joint commission for examination and report; if favorably received by this body, the request is then voted upon by the Magistrat as a whole. After the general plan has been approved, the matter is referred to some member of the board in order that the precise terms of the franchise may be arranged; and when these have been satisfactorily determined, the application goes to the council for its approval of the whole detailed plan. The latter may accept, amend, or reject the proposal; or it may refer the whole matter back to the Magistrat for further consideration. When the two bodies agree, their power to grant franchises is comprehensive: in no case is it necessary that the proposal shall go before the voters at the polls in order to become operative. When, however, the two bodies fail to agree, the question must be determined by the authorities of the district or the province.

Although the Prussian cities have been allowed to exercise a liberal degree of freedom in the matter of granting or withholding rights in their own streets, the experience of recent years has served to show that the higher powers sometimes have to be reckoned with at unexpected points. The imperial and state governments, for example, own and operate all the railway, telegraph, and telephone lines within the kingdom, and in connection with any of these public services assume the right to make use of the streets of any city without the permission of the local authorities. Moreover, by leaving in the hands of private corporations many of the smaller steam railways which serve only local traffic, the state continues to regulate these lines by the law relating to light railways

(Kleinbahngesetz). This class of railways, however, it has commonly been assumed, does not include the electric tramways of a city. At any rate, the cities of Prussia have in general been left with a free hand in the matter of enfranchising companies to undertake this service, the authorities of the state merely ratifying any arrangements which the municipalities see fit to make. That the state claims much more extensive and direct powers, however, was shown a few years ago, when the Prussian state authorities, acting under their own interpretation of the scope of the law relating to light railways, issued a decree prolonging until 1949 the franchise of the Greater Berlin Street Railway Company, which had originally been granted for twenty years only by the Berlin city government. This action on the part of the national ministry was taken in direct opposition to the vigorously expressed desires of the municipal authorities, and the issue of the decree evoked loud protests from the citizens in general. The incident serves to show that the respective powers of state and city in regard to enfranchising and regulating the terms of franchises are not easy to define with precision. In this particular case there is every probability that, when the original franchise of the street railway company expires in 1919, the Berlin authorities will strongly contest the legal power of the ministry to decree any prolongation of the term; meantime they have made provisions for the building of municipal lines in those parts of the city which are not served by the company.[1] On the other hand, the national government, if it sees fit to insist upon its rights, will

Case of the Berlin street railways.

---

[1] For a statement of the city's side of this controversy, see the *Berichte aus Anlass des Besuches der englischen Kommission zum Zweck des Studiums städtischer Einrichtungen im Auslande* (published in pamphlet form by the Berlin authorities in 1905), especially pp. 70–74.

undoubtedly be able to make good its claim to final control. Perhaps, however, it is hardly fair to lay too much stress upon this incident; for at the time it occurred there was a good deal of friction between the civic and the national authorities. On the whole, the cities enjoy a generous degree of freedom in making arrangements with public-service corporations and in settling for themselves all matters relating to length of term, rates, payments, and other incidents of a franchise.

6. In the cities of France and of the United States the power to appoint municipal officers rests in general with the mayor,[1] and in the cities of Great Britain with the council.[2] In the Prussian cities it is vested in neither of these organs, but is given to the administrative board, or Magistrat.[3] To this general statement there are, however, some exceptions. In the first place, the appointing power of the Magistrat appertains to paid offices only, the unpaid officials of the municipality being chosen by the city council; but, although the latter class includes such important officials as the citizen deputies (Bürgerdeputirter), the district-poor officers (Armenpfleger), and many others, it may fairly be said that nearly all the more responsible posts in the civic service are filled by paid officers. In the second place, although the Magistrat has the right to appoint all paid officials, it is required by law, before any such appointment is definitely made, to submit the name of the proposed appointee to the council in order that this body may enter its protest if it sees fit to do so. Not that the council can actually prevent an appointment which the Magistrat desires to make; its part in the matter is consultative only.[4] The Magistrat submits the

6. Appoints paid employees.

Consultative powers of the council.

---

[1] Above, p. 68.   [2] Below, p. 294.   [3] Städteordnung, § 56, No. 6.

[4] On the scope and importance of these limitations, see Ledermann's *Die Städteordnung*, 263–282, and his *Anstellung und Versorgung der Kommunalbeamten* (Berlin, 1899).

N

name to the council; and the latter, if it has any objection to the candidate, enters such objection on its records and transmits it in due course to the administrative board, which is supposed to weigh the soundness of the criticism before definitively ratifying the appointment.   If the Magistrat regards the objection as important and reasonable, it usually withdraws its proposal; but it is not bound to do so, nor does the council possess in any sense a right to dictate appointments.[1]   In the third place, the appointing power of the administrative board is in some cases subject to the supervision of the higher authorities, — that is, some of its appointments do not become effective until they have received the approval of some district or provincial officer or board.[2]   This is true, for example, of all officials of the police service, and of many officers connected with the educational system.   Finally, a large number of the minor municipal employees (Unterbeamten) are, as a matter of practice, not appointed by the administrative board itself, but by the various joint commissions (Deputationen) which have charge of the civic departments.   True, the Magistrat is responsible for all such appointments, and it may at any time and for any reason withhold the power from the commissions; but it ordinarily allows them entire liberty.   Subject to these four limitations, the Magistrat ranks as the appointing authority in the Prussian city.

In making appointments the administrative board is not closely restricted by any system of civil service rules, but in most instances is left with a wide latitude of choice.   In the case of a higher post, the national laws frequently provide that the appointee shall have certain professional qualifications, a requirement which may be said to apply

Certain appointments require confirmation.

Minor appointments made by joint commissions.

Absence of special civil service regulations.

---

[1] Jebens, *Die Stadtverordneten*, 189–191.
[2] O. Oertel, *Die Städteordnung*, 320 ff.

to practically all the officers whose duties are of a technical
nature ; but the cities do not themselves hold qualifying
examinations for such positions. It is merely demanded
that the appointees shall have satisfied certain requirements
imposed by the national government for appointment to
the national service, — demands that may be met, in most
cases, by taking certain examinations before a state board
which the Prussian authorities maintain for the purpose.[1]
These examinations are qualifying and not competitive ; in
Prussian cities no appointments are made as the result of
competitive tests, as they sometimes are in America. The
state examinations merely determine eligibility; and
within the large lists of eligibles the Magistrat has full
discretion.[2]

With very few exceptions all important appointments in
the regular municipal service are made for life. Certain
powers of disciplining officials by suspension, fine, and even
imprisonment are, it is true, given to the Bürgermeister ;[3]
but only the Magistrat may remove an officer from his
post, and even in this power it is subject to the right of
the removed official to carry his case before the higher administrative authorities and to secure reinstatement in
case good cause for his removal be not shown. In most
instances the Magistrat determines the salaries or remu-
nerations of the city employees ; but sometimes the minimum remuneration is fixed by national law or by decree
of the higher local authorities. Within the lines laid down

Tenure and removals.

---

[1] The best convenient treatise on the rules of law relating to the municipal
service is Hugo Preuss's *Das städtische Amtsrecht in Preussen* (Berlin, 1902).
Other serviceable works on the same subject are F. Kremski's *Preussische
Kommunalbeamtengesetzgebung* (Berlin, 1901), and Kautz and Appelius's
Preussisches Kommunalbeamtenrecht (Berlin, 1900).

[2] An important limitation in the nature of what we commonly term "veter-
ans' preference" has been imposed by the national laws. The provisions of
these enactments are summarized in Ledermann's *Die Städteordnung*, 295 ff.

[3] See below, p. 193.

by the national government the Magistrat also determines the rules relating to retirement and pensions.[1]

7. Has the custody of documents. 7. To the Magistrat is committed the responsibility of caring properly for all the records, deeds, contracts, and other important official documents belonging to the municipality.[2] This duty it may discharge by transferring the documents to the provincial or national archives, as in some cases it is permitted to do; or it may provide and maintain a safe depository for them in the city itself. The immediate task of caring for the records is usually committed to some individual member of the administrative board, who performs the duties of municipal archivist.

8. Represents the municipality as a corporation. 8. In all official relations with the higher authorities, or with other municipalities, or with private corporations and individuals, the Magistrat acts as the representative of the city.[3] Through it, therefore, all the official correspondence is carried on. The Bürgermeister, it is true, usually signs the papers in the name of the Magistrat; but the city is actually bound only when the signature of some other member is also appended as evidence that the board has assumed responsibility. Except as agent of the administrative body, the Bürgermeister has no right to represent the city in any official transaction; nor may the council undertake direct relations with any authority, national or local, other than the Magistrat.

9. Residual powers. 9. Finally, the administrative board is charged with the distribution of work among civic authorities and officials, with the enforcement of all national laws within the municipal limits, and with the proper performance of all duties, whether permanent or transitory, which may be intrusted to it by any higher authority.[4] It must see that all the fields of local administration are properly covered,

---

[1] See also below, p. 190.   [2] Städteordnung, § 56, No. 7.
[3] Städteordnung, § 56, No. 8.   [4] Städteordnung, § 56, No. 9.

that there is no overlapping of minor jurisdictions, and that there is no friction between subordinate officials. In a word, it is the organ which is expected to keep all the wheels of the local executive machine working smoothly. It is the apex of the local system of administration, and the connecting link between the municipal and the national authorities.

From the foregoing classification of powers and functions it will be seen that the administrative board is a very influential organ. Its jurisdiction includes almost all the powers that are in American cities intrusted to the mayor, the heads of departments, the various civic boards, and, in such of the cities as have the bicameral system, to the board of aldermen. It is not only the upper house of the municipal legislature, but, contrary to the principle of separation of powers which has obtained careful recognition in the framework of the American city, it is also the sole important executive organ. Being technically the creature of the city council by virtue of its appointment by that body, it might be expected to permit the council to dictate the course of executive policy; but by reason of the long terms of office for which its members are elected, and especially of the exclusive powers which it exercises, it has been able to maintain an attitude of vigorous independence. It is, in fact, at once the most indigenous, the most striking, and the most successful organ in the whole range of German local government; for it concentrates enough power to be effective in action, and at the same time its members are held sufficiently amenable to popular control. *General influence of the Magistrat.*

But while a large and important share in the actual administration of the city's affairs is assumed by the Magistrat as a body, service at its meetings does not by any means constitute all the work which its members are called upon to perform. On the contrary, the duties *Powers and duties of the Magistrates as individuals.*

which the individual members of the administrative board undertake as chairmen of the various joint commissions (Deputationen) make by far the larger demands upon their time and attention.[1] Final powers in all the matters just enumerated rest, it is true, with the board as a whole; but in actual practice a large portion of them are virtually delegated to the several joint commissions, and in these bodies individual members of the Magistrat exercise a large influence. This influence is particularly strong on the part of the chairmen of the commissions, who are almost invariably members of the administrative board.

Procedure. The system of procedure in the Magistrat does not present any noteworthy features. Its meetings are held more frequently than those of the council, and they are not open to the public. An attendance of half the members is usually sufficient to constitute a quorum, but in the largest cities a third only is required. Any question may be decided by a simple majority of those present; in cases of appointment the successful candidate must secure this majority, and not merely a plurality over his competitors for the post. If no one obtains it on the first vote, all the candidates except the two who stood highest drop out, and the second ballot decides between these two. Secret ballots are very rarely used; on most matters the members of the Magistrat vote openly. On important questions there is, no doubt, much difference of opinion

Meetings are not open to the public. among them; but, since the meetings are private, little information regarding such contentions ever reaches the ears of the councillors or the general public. All decisions of the board come into public view as unanimous resolutions, a fact which has obviously had great influence in strengthening the popular impression concerning its clear-cut and businesslike methods. Indeed, in all prob-

[1] See below, pp. 199 ff.

ability this deliberation behind closed doors enables the Magistrat to reach its conclusions more readily than it could do if every proposal were discussed concurrently in the newspapers and on the street corners. It is able to keep its plans to itself until it has fully elaborated them, and then to bring them forward in its own time and way, with all the weight and prestige which naturally attach to a unanimous report.

The Magistrat conducts its business somewhat infor- Publication mally; for not only is it in general a comparatively small of its decisions. body, but its business is almost wholly of a strictly executive nature, and at every meeting there is a great deal to do. Though it keeps a record of each session, it publishes nothing but the final resolutions, which are printed in the official organ of the municipality.[1] Such of them as may need the concurrence of the council are also put on the docket of that body before its next meeting.

All meetings of the Magistrat are presided over by the Chairman-Bürgermeister, who, besides having the usual powers of a ship of the Magistrat. chairman, is empowered by law to declare out of order any proposal which may seem to him "to be contrary to the public interest."[2] This comprehensive and important prerogative, however, which might easily be abused were it not that any ruling of the Bürgermeister under this provision may be set aside by the higher authorities on the complaint of the Magistrat, the Bürgermeisters have used very sparingly.

The Bürgermeister of a German city does not, like the The Bürger-meister. mayor of a French or of an American municipality, constitute a separate organ of city government. Like the English mayor, he is the presiding officer of that body

---

[1] In Berlin this publication is entitled *Gemeinde-Blatt der Haupt- und Residenzstadt Berlin, herausgegeben vom Magistrat.*

[2] Städteordnung, § 57.

which exercises the administrative powers of the city; in relation to his fellow-members he is *primus inter pares*, their colleague, not their superior. He does, to be sure, possess some important special prerogatives; but these are, on the whole, scarcely sufficient to give him rank as an

Nature of his office. independent official. He is the chief magistrate of the city, the titular head of the municipal government, and his office is the pivotal point in the machinery of civic administration; but he is not the dominating or controlling agent in directing administrative policy. He may, indeed, fairly be said to occupy a post which, in point of actual influence, is about midway between the positions held by the English mayor on the one hand and the

History of the post. American mayor on the other.[1]

The office of Bürgermeister is a very old one, for the German free cities had such officials as early as the thirteenth century at least. During the later mediæval period the Bürgermeister exercised a general oversight in civic affairs, especially in those connected with taxation and expenditure,[2] and continued to do so down into the nineteenth century, when in the Stein reorganization of 1808 the office was put upon a somewhat different footing. The code of 1853 defined the place and powers of the Bürgermeister in terms that were not altogether explicit; but during the last half-century a large number of decrees of the higher authorities and decisions of the administrative courts have served to give the jurisdiction of the office a fair degree of definiteness. During this period the powers of the Bürg-

[1] Some interesting facts relating to the position and powers of this official may be found in an article on "The Bürgermeister, Germany's Chief Municipal Magistrate," recently published by one of my students, Mr. Joseph Torrey Bishop, in the *American Political Science Review*, II. 396–410 (May, 1908).

[2] Further details relating to the earlier history of the office may be found in G. L. von Maurer's *Geschichte der Städteverfassung in Deutschland* (4 vols., Erlangen, 1869–1871), I. 631 ff.

ermeister have been slightly increased, but only slightly; for it has apparently not been the aim of the higher authorities to use this official rather than the Magistrat as the local agent of central administration, nor has it been their policy, as it has been that of American cities, to seek greater administrative efficiency by localizing greater responsibility in a single hand.[1]

Every Prussian city has its Bürgermeister, and the larger cities have two. When there are two, they are sometimes known as the first and second Bürgermeister respectively, but more often as the Oberbürgermeister and the Bürgermeister, the former designation being employed, however, only when it has been given by special patent from the crown.[2] The second Bürgermeister (when there are two) acts as the representative of his senior colleague whenever the latter is absent or incapacitated, or whenever special functions pertaining to the office are delegated to him; otherwise he ranks as a paid member of the administrative board. Like the other members of the Magistrat, the Bürgermeister is selected by the city council, which, in making its selection, follows the procedure already detailed.[3] The range of choice is not confined to residents of the municipality; as a matter of practice, indeed, the post is, in the larger cities, almost always filled by the election of some one who has already demonstrated his administrative capabilities as Bürgermeister in a smaller municipality. Sometimes the choice is made from among the paid members of the local Magistrat, and occasionally the appointee has been taken from the state service; but in any case the man selected for the post in any important city is an expert who has already had successful adminis-

Number of Bürgermeisters.

Bürgermeisters are elected by the city council.

Previous administrative experience is essential.

---

[1] On this point see Edwin A. Greenlaw's essay on " The Office of Mayor in the United States," in *Municipal Affairs*, III. 33 ff. (March, 1899).

[2] Oertel, *Die Städteordnung*, 140.   [3] Above, pp. 166–167.

trative experience, and who owes his appointment largely if not wholly to his individual abilities and achievements in that field. In this respect the Prussian Bürgermeister may be clearly differentiated from the administrative heads of French, English, and American cities. In all these places the mayor is almost invariably some private citizen who leaves his ordinary vocation for a year or a few years, and during this period devotes a part or the whole of his time to the service of the municipality, expecting not to make a life-work of local administration, but, when his term is ended, to return to private life and to his private business. He may or may not have had some experience in municipal affairs. In France the mayor, as has been seen, is almost sure to have had at least four years' experience as a member of the communal council, and has usually served a term as adjoint.[1] In the United States, however, the citizen who is elected to the office of mayor is more commonly one who has had little or no municipal experience at all; for lengthy service in the civic legislature is likely to identify a man with various measures and movements which, whatever their nature, are liable to make him as many enemies as friends and thus to render him at an actual disadvantage in a voting contest with a candidate who has no local record at all. The aspirant for the mayoralty in an American city must above all things be a good candidate, — that is to say, he must be a good vote-getter in a direct election under a system of manhood suffrage; his capabilities and experience as an administrator are matters which are, too frequently and very unfortunately, regarded as of secondary consequence. The Bürgermeister, on the other hand, is an expert, a professional administrator, who looks upon his

[1] Above, p. 63.

Side notes:

Contrast between German methods and requirements and those of other countries.

German Bürgermeister is an expert.

office as a career, who seeks the post on his public record, and who expects promotion upon this alone.

The Prussian city council selects the Bürgermeister in very much the same way as a business corporation selects its general manager or other executive head. It casts about among the smaller corporations engaged in the same sort of business, and proceeds to rob one of these of its chief official by offering him a post which is more attractive. The smaller cities sometimes advertise for applicants, but the larger ones usually find a field of choice all ready for them. If a certain city like Berlin or Frankfort or Breslau desires to fill its chief magisterial post, it naturally looks to those men who have been commanding attention by their success as Bürgermeisters or paid magistrates in cities of smaller size. It examines the records and qualifications of such officials, and soon eliminates all but a few names, the choice usually lying between no more than three or four candidates by the time the question comes before the council. In making the selection the members may of course be influenced to some slight extent by partisan prejudices; but even at the worst this evil would not be attended by seriously detrimental results, for all the candidates are men who possess undoubted claims to consideration upon their administrative records.

Procedure in selecting a Bürgermeister.

When the council has made its selection, its choice must receive the approval of the higher powers in order to become valid. In the smaller cities this approval is had from the authorities of the province; but in all cities of over one hundred thousand population it must be obtained from the king,[1] who usually gives or withholds concurrence on the advice of the minister of the interior. This royal right to confirm the council's choice has not

Royal approval necessary.

[1] Städteordnung, § 33.

in general been used in any unreasonable manner or made to serve either personal or partisan animosities; indeed, the royal assent has commonly been looked upon as a mere formality. A few years ago, however, the German emperor, in his capacity as king of Prussia, showed that the royal prerogative was something more than a bare theory by flatly declining to confirm the choice of a Bürgermeister selected by the municipal council of Berlin. The council, taken aback by this somewhat unexpected move, promptly chose the same candidate a second time and submitted his name again for the royal approval; but the minister refused to present the matter to his Majesty on the ground that the same name could not legally be returned. After a long deadlock between the royal and the municipal authorities, during which the office remained vacant, the council receded from its stand by selecting a new aspirant whose appointment was finally, after a year's delay, indorsed by the emperor. Too much stress ought not, however, to be laid upon this incident as showing the strict control exercised by the higher authorities of Prussia over the administrative affairs of the cities; for the episode occurred in the capital, where the personal interest of the monarch in local administration is naturally great, and, furthermore, it happened at a time when there were several other matters of friction between his Majesty and the city council.[1] Ordinarily it is rare for either the provincial or the royal authorities to refuse to sanction any reasonable selections which the councils may make; but it may be that the councils refrain from pre-

This approval is sometimes withheld,

but is ordinarily given freely.

[1] Further details relating to this episode may be found in a communication from Professor R. C. Brooks, published under the title "Berlin without an Oberbürgermeister," in *Annals of the American Academy of Political and Social Science*, XIV. 94–98 (July, 1899).

senting objectionable nominations. There have been one
or two cases in smaller municipalities in which confirmation has been refused because the local councils
sought to appoint to office men who were avowed Social
Democrats in politics; but such incidents are of greater
interest as showing the national government's intolerance
of this political party than as evidencing its interference with the principle of municipal home rule. The
higher authorities have full power to refuse confirmation on any ground, and even without stating their
objections; but, on the whole, refusals are extremely
infrequent.

The term for which a Bürgermeister is selected is
usually twelve years; but in several of the large cities —
in Leipsic, Hanover, and Dresden, for example — the
appointment is made for life. When an official has
served his first term satisfactorily, a second term of
twelve years is almost certain to follow; and there are
Bürgermeisters who are now serving their third terms.[1]
The tendency of the whole system is to keep the chief
magistrate in office for a long period; hence vacancies
rarely occur save through the death of an official or because of his resignation to accept some higher position.
In the ten largest cities of Prussia taken together the
present Bürgermeisters have held their posts for an
average of slightly more than ten years, the individual
periods ranging from five to twenty years. Security and
length of tenure are, indeed, two of the most striking
features of the office.

The time actually spent in the chief magistracy, how-

*The Bürg-
ermeister's
term of
office.*

---

[1] Herr Oberbürgermeister Haken of Stettin has been in office since 1878, and
has now served more than half of his third term. Stande of Halle has held his
post since 1882, Becker of Cologne since 1886. Bender of Breslau, Adickes of
Frankfort-on-the-Main, and Tramm of Hanover have each been in office since
1891, and Beutler of Dresden since 1895.

ever, does not by any means usually represent the whole of the official's actual administrative experience; for election as Bürgermeister is almost invariably preceded by service in some subordinate municipal position. The Oberbürgermeister has usually served as Bürgermeister, and the latter, in turn, as a paid magistrate or chief of administration in some smaller city. The present Oberbürgermeister of Berlin, Herr Kirschner, served the cities of Bromberg and Breslau before coming to the capital as second Bürgermeister; Herr Tröndlin, who has been chief magistrate of Leipsic since 1899, was for no less than twenty-three years previously second Bürgermeister of the city; Dr. Bender of Breslau was formerly Bürgermeister of Thorn; and Dr. Adickes of Frankfort-on-the-Main served a term as Bürgermeister of Altona. Indeed, if one were to average the actual time spent by the chief magistrates of the larger cities in acquiring administrative experience, one would in all probability find that the mean term amounted to a score of years or more.[1]

As German salaries go, the Bürgermeisters are well-paid officials, the stipends ranging from thirty-six thousand marks per annum in cities like Berlin and Frankfort to three or four thousand marks in the smallest municipalities.[2] Ordinarily there is also a substantial allowance in lieu of an official residence; and the pension provisions are unusually liberal, an annual allowance of half the regular salary being given after twelve years' service, or an allotment of two-thirds after a service of twenty-four years.[3]

Post frequently filled by promotion.

Salary.

[1] Short sketches of the public life and services of each of the leading German Bürgermeisters may be found in Joseph Kürschner's *Staats-, Hof-, und Kommunales Handbuch* (Berlin, 1907), and in *Wer ist's?* (Berlin, 1908).

[2] In some other large cities the stipends (exclusive of allowances) are as follows : Leipsic, Magdeburg, and Cologne, each 25,000 marks; Dresden, 20,000 marks; Hanover, 17,000 marks.

[3] The municipal pension system is regulated by national law, and hence is uniform in all the municipalities. See Ledermann, *Die Städteordnung*, 418–447.

The remuneration of the chief Bürgermeister of Frankfort-on-the-Main (including allowances) is about the equivalent of the salary paid to the mayor of Boston, a city of nearly twice the size; indeed, if one compares the cities of the United States as a whole with those of the German Empire, one finds that the latter are the more liberal in the payment of their chief officials. It is to be remembered, furthermore, that the Bürgermeister has no political organization to support financially, that he has no expensive election campaigns to conduct, and that he is not expected to make heavy outlays for charitable and other purposes during his term of office. It is not considerations of salary alone, however, which attract men of ability to the municipal service and prevail upon them to select local administration as a career. It is rather the security of tenure, the liberal pension, the important public services which an incumbent may render, and the high social prestige attaching to the office, that cause the post of Bürgermeister to be ranked as a prize even by the ablest.

Remuneration compared with that of American chief executive.

According to the letter of the law the powers of the Bürgermeister are not extensive. In the act of 1853 they are enunciated very briefly, little jurisdiction being specified other than that of presiding at meetings of the administrative board and directing the general course of municipal administration; but in the letter of instructions which the national authorities issued some years previously and which is still in force, they are defined somewhat more explicitly.[1] From a study of the law alone, however, one cannot obtain an accurate idea of the official's duties, for much depends upon the character of the individual who may occupy the post. A Bürgermeister who so desires may leave almost every important matter to the administrative board, and may content himself

Powers of the Bürgermeister.

---

[1] Jebens, *Die Instruktion für die Stadt-Magisträte vom 25. Mai 1835*, § 20.

with following rather than leading its counsels. On the other hand, an official of pronounced individuality and vigor may even dominate the board, and thus make himself an influential factor in the direction of municipal policy. Such a one is Dr. Adickes of Frankfort, who for more than a decade has been a towering influence in the administration of that city, and who by his marked success in the field of local administration has acquired a reputation which extends far beyond the bounds of his own land. The office, in short, is one that possesses sufficient flexibility to make it capable of adaptation to the powers and tastes of different men.

Flexible nature of these powers.

First among the Bürgermeister's ordinary functions is that of presiding at all meetings of the Magistrat. He prepares the business which is to be considered, and sees to it that all matters come before the board in proper form. By the terms of the municipal code he is authorized to prevent the introduction of any proposal which is opposed to the general interest of the city or which contravenes the laws of the land; but this power, as has been seen, he uses very sparingly.[1] As presiding officer he determines all questions relating to "order, rank, and dignity" in the Magistrat, and interprets the board's own rules relating to procedure.[2] When the Magistrat reaches a decision upon any point, he must see that this decision is duly communicated, if communication be necessary, to the city council. When, on the other hand, the administrative body has exclusive jurisdiction in the matter, it is the task of the Bürgermeister to see that its resolutions are at once carried into effect. To this end he may issue ordinances, or "instructions," which fill in the necessary

Presides over Magistrat.

Powers as a presiding officer.

---

[1] Above, p. 183.

[2] *Die Instruktion für die Stadt-Magisträte vom 25. Mai 1835*, especially § 20, No. 3.

details, and may allot the work of executing the Magistrat's resolutions to the appropriate authorities.[1] In a word, he is the executive agent of the administrative board, preparing business for its consideration and supervising the execution of its orders. In the latter capacity he may have much or little discretion ; the actual amount will depend somewhat upon the degree of confidence which the members of the board put in the judgment and ability of their chief.

Besides guiding the deliberations and business of the Magistrat as a body, the Bürgermeister exercises supervisory jurisdiction over the work of its individual members, and indeed over that of all municipal officers. Unlike the chief executives in the cities of France and the United States, he makes no important appointments, for this function belongs either to the administrative board or to the council ; but he apportions the various departments of civic administration to the appropriate joint commissions, and he determines who shall be members of these commissions,[2] selecting some from the Magistrat, some from the council, and some from the citizen deputies. He may, furthermore, rearrange and reconstitute the commissions as he sees fit, a jurisdiction which gives him great influence in directing the civic departments if he chooses to make his own policy effective through these channels. Having organized the commissions and allotted their tasks, he is responsible for seeing that the various kinds of work are properly coördinated and that those in the pay of the city perform their duties properly. Complaints concerning all civic officials and employees are made to him directly, and he is vested with disciplinary power over the whole municipal service.[3] He may suspend, fine, or even imprison

Supervisory power.

Appoints members of various joint commissions.

Has disciplinary powers over civic officials.

---

[1] *Die Instrucktion für die Stadt-Magisträte vom 25. Mai 1835*, especially § 20, No. 4   [2] *Ibid.* No. 2.   [3] Städteordnung, § 58.

O

any official who has appeared remiss in his duties ; but his power to remove is closely circumscribed by the jurisdiction of the administrative courts, and from his local disciplinary measures appeal may be made to the higher administrative authorities. When the removal of any official seems to be urgently demanded by the best interests of the municipality, the Bürgermeister may displace him provided he forthwith notify the Magistrat. Indeed, with the assent of the district authorities he may even remove a member of the administrative board itself.[1]

Authority to inspect municipal departments. Another duty allotted to the Bürgermeister is that of inspecting from time to time the various municipal departments, in order to see, as the instructions express it, " that an active spirit prevails throughout the service." He receives the departmental reports, which in due course he lays before the administrative board ; and he is at liberty to call for further information from any civic department. One of his special duties is to supervise the affairs of the city treasury, and in particular to see that the Magistrat makes provision for the proper and regular auditing of accounts. If he thinks it desirable, he may cause a special audit or investigation to be undertaken in any department at any time. When difficulties or friction arise between departments, it is usually the function of the Bürgermeister to settle such misunderstandings. Under all circumstances, in short, he is expected to keep the machinery of civic administration in smooth working order at every point.

Police functions. Besides attending to all these duties, the Bürgermeister has a hand in the police administration of the city. In Prussian municipalities of over 100,000 population the police may be in charge of a national commissioner ap-

---

[1] For exact references to the various laws and decisions relating to the Bürgermeister's disciplinary powers, see Oertel's *Die Städteordnung*, 378.

pointed by and responsible to the Prussian government; but in all except the largest cities the control of the civic police service is given to the Bürgermeister, who in this sphere acts as the agent of the state authorities, with powers corresponding somewhat closely to those of the French maire.[1] He has general charge of all matters relating to police organization, discipline, and duties; but his discretionary power is somewhat closely circumscribed by the state regulations in regard to police administration and functions.[2] He issues the usual police ordinances; but before promulgating them he must usually consult with the Magistrat, whose assent is always required when the ordinance deals with matters pertaining to the public safety. The actual work of police administration is, of course, performed by the chief police commissioner, who in all cities which do not have state police control is appointed by the Bürgermeister, though from a range of choice that is rendered somewhat narrow by the strictness of the national laws relating to promotions in the police service. The power to remove this commissioner may be exercised only by the higher authorities, who also have the sole right to displace even the subordinate officers in the municipal police department. In the whole matter of police administration the Prussian national government has maintained an unyielding grip.

Scope of the Bürgermeister's powers in relation to local police.

The various functions included within the scope of the term "police administration" are much more numerous and more comprehensive in Prussia than in England or in

Broad extent of police functions in Germany.

[1] Städteordnung, § 62.

[2] The whole matter of local police administration and control (örtliche Polizei-Verwaltung) was dealt with by a comprehensive statute in 1850 (" Gesetz über die Polizei-Verwaltung vom 11. März 1850," in *Gesetz-Sammlung für 1850*, pp. 265 ff.); but this code has been considerably altered by subsequent legislation. The present state of the laws relating to local police control may be studied in Arnstedt's *Das Preussische Polizeirecht* (Berlin, 1905).

the United States.   In Prussia the phrase covers not alone the protection of life and property, but the maintenance of security, order, and ease of intercourse upon the public streets, squares, bridges, and rivers; the supervision of markets and the sale of provisions in general; the enforcement of rules relating to the opening and closing of places of business; the oversight of public assemblies; the supervision of hotels, lodging-houses, cafés, and places of amusement; the protection of the public health and the abatement of nuisances; and the supervision of all matters relating to the registration of strangers and aliens, as well as to the enrolment of citizens in the official records of the municipality.[1]   The exercise of this last-named function alone concentrates in the police-stations a large amount of clerical routine and engages the attention of a great many officials.   Every person, citizen or alien, who comes into a police district must promptly file his Anmeldung with the officers of the district station; and every person leaving the district must similarly file his Abmeldung.   These documents are prepared in triplicate, one copy being retained at the local station (Polizei-Revier), another sent to the city police headquarters, and a third to the national

The recording of personnel.

police headquarters in Berlin.   This recording of personnel (Meldewesen), which in many respects corresponds to the French system of maintaining the état civil, is of fundamental importance in several branches of Prussian civic administration; for the police records are used by several other municipal departments in their work, notably by the

---

[1] Von Hippel's *Handbuch der Polizeiverwaltung* (Berlin, 1905) is the best convenient manual to use in studying the organization and functions of the different branches of the service into which the Prussian police system is divided, particularly the local police (Ortspolizei).   A very serviceable chapter on the subject, with elaborate references to the various laws and to the administrative jurisprudence, may be found in Hue de Grais's *Handbuch der Verfassung und Verwaltung* (17th ed., Berlin, 1906), 313–400.

poor-relief administration and by the bureau which prepares the voters' lists.[1]

From the foregoing rather cursory sketch of the Bürger- The Bürg-
meister's powers it will be seen that his jurisdiction falls compared
considerably short of that usually exercised by the Ameri- with the
American
can mayor. He does not possess the appointing power, mayor.
he has no veto over the resolutions of the municipal legislature, and no important part in the preparation of the
municipal budget. Though he does, to be sure, enjoy some
special authority of distinct importance, he can hardly be
ranked as an independent factor in civic administration.
The real municipal executive is the Magistrat, of which the
Bürgermeister is simply the presiding officer and formal
head. As such he takes precedence over his colleagues on
all ceremonious occasions, and usually represents the municipality at state or imperial festivities; but these incidents
of his office do not necessarily indicate, any more than do
similar ones in the case of the English mayor, that he is a
dominating agent in the guidance of municipal policy.

Much of the efficiency of Prussian municipal administra- The Prus-
tion has doubtless been due to the fact that the city coun- pal "Ver-
cil has attained a high standard as a deliberative body, its waltungs-
Deputa-
decisions on important questions of municipal policy bear- tion."
ing almost invariably the marks of sound and careful
judgment. Still more of the efficiency, perhaps, may be
attributed to the unique capacity for prompt and effective
administrative action which the Magistrat, through its
peculiar composition, powers, and procedure, possesses as
an executive body. The carefully-weighed decisions of the
council, however, and the businesslike instructions of the
Magistrat would lose much of their high value were it not
for the work of the subordinate bodies which immediately

---

[1] On these functions, see F. Throl's *Das polizeiliche Meldewesen* (Berlin,1897),
and M. Koehne's *Polizei und Publikum* (Berlin, 1897).

supervise the various civic departments and seek to carry out, in spirit as well as in letter, the instructions that come to them from above. These efficient bodies are the joint commissions, or deputations.

Has charge of administrative departments. For purposes of actual administration the functions of the Prussian city are divided into departments, the division being arranged along much the same lines as in American cities. The number of such departments depends, of course, upon the size of the city and the complexity of its administrative problems, and accordingly varies from four or five departments in the smaller municipalities to a score or more in cities like Berlin and Frankfort. New departments are created as necessity arises, or two departments may be merged into one, the decision in each case resting with the Magistrat unless additional expenditures are involved, when the concurrence of the council must also be obtained. Each department is committed to the charge of a separate deputation, or joint commission, which, subject to the supervision and control of the Magistrat, performs the routine work of departmental administration.

Has no exact prototype in municipal systems of other countries. The Prussian municipal deputation does not correspond either in organization or in functions to the appointive civic board or commission which is a familiar factor in the American municipal system; nor is it in all respects the prototype of the council committee which, in the English borough, assumes immediate charge of some particular field of municipal activity. It rather embodies the principles at the basis of each of these types, and yet differs from each in some important features. Like the American civic board or commission, it contains in its membership men who do not belong to the municipal council and who have not gone before the people at the polls; but, unlike the American commission, it is directly responsible to a branch of the civic legislature, without the approval of which it can take no final action of importance. In this limitation it corresponds rather closely to the English borough committee, though in its organization it differs fundamentally from that body. The deputation is, indeed, a unique institution in the science of city government; it is German in origin and exclusively German in use.

In size the deputations vary considerably, the membership ranging from three or five to perhaps thirty or more, according to the importance and extent of the work to be performed. At the head of each deputation is a chairman (Vorsitzender), who is invariably a member of the Magistrat. The post is ordinarily held by one of the paid members of the board, especially when the department concerned is a legal, financial, or some technical branch of the city's service; but unpaid members are frequently utilized as chairmen of the less important deputations, and sometimes even of the more important ones. The chairman is designated by the Bürgermeister from among the members of the administrative board, and holds his post until the chief magistrate sees fit to make a change. In the most important deputations, however, changes in the chairmanships are very infrequent. The members of the deputation are also named by the Bürgermeister, who may draw them wholly from the Magistrat, or partly from the Magistrat and partly from the council, or may make up a commission of magistrates, councillors, officials, and citizen deputies. The last-named procedure is the one most commonly followed, the quota of each class being determined by agreement between the Magistrat and the council. The typical deputation contains members drawn from all four sources.

The presence of officials and of citizen deputies on the various deputations calls for some explanation. The officials, of whom each deputation contains one or two, are drawn from among the higher professional officers in the

Composition of the joint commissions.

Members of the Magistrat.

Councillors.

Officials.

departments interested. They are utilized as members in order that the deputation may at all times have the benefit of their expert advice in matters that may come before it, — advice which from the nature of things usually carries important weight in enabling the deputation to reach its conclusions. They are entitled to be present at all meetings and may speak on any question, but they do not vote. The citizen deputies, on the other hand, are laymen, who otherwise have no official connection with the city government. They are not employed by all the Prussian cities, and the number of them thus brought into direct relation with municipal administration varies greatly in the different municipalities. Berlin has ninety-three in all.[1] The citizen deputies are men of professional, business, or other influence, drawn from all parts of the municipality and from all ranks of its population. They are selected by the council for a six-year term, draw no remuneration, and do not constitute an organ of municipal administration. They do not meet as a body, and their membership is constantly shifting. They are simply posted to the different deputations, a few to each one; but as members of these bodies they have full voting rights on all questions. By thus enlisting private citizens in the direct work of civic government, and combining with the skill of the professional the enthusiasm of the amateur, the Prussian system has served to give to the departmental administrations an elasticity and responsiveness to popular opinion which they might not otherwise have had; and it has drawn to the service of the municipality the coöperation and sympathy of a considerable body of laymen representing important and influential interests.

The selection of the members of deputations rests with the Bürgermeister, who makes rearrangements from time

Citizen deputies.

Value of the deputies in city administration.

---

[1] *Bericht über die Gemeinde-Verwaltung der Stadt Berlin, 1901–1905,* I. 7.

to time, and always after a new council has been elected.[1] Ordinarily his choice does not require confirmation by any higher authority; but to this rule there are a few exceptions. His appointments to membership in the school deputation, for instance, must have higher approval; for the schools of Prussia are not regarded simply as local institutions, but are placed under strict supervision by the national Ministry of Public Instruction.[2]

Commissions are constituted by the Bürgermeister.

The various deputations meet frequently, often once a week, and handle a formidable amount of routine business, which is usually prepared in advance by the chairman. The work of the members consists in discussing, revising, and voting upon proposals thus laid before them. After finally passing upon a matter, the deputation transmits its decision in the form of a report to the Magistrat; for its powers are in no case final. It may simply recommend action, and its recommendations may be adopted or rejected by the Magistrat as that body thinks fit. As a matter of practice, however, the suggestions of the deputation so far as they concern matters of routine are invariably approved, and even in important affairs they carry almost decisive weight; they are rarely rejected except for very good reasons. Some deputations have more independence than others, — the school commission, for instance, has an almost entirely free hand in matters relating to the supervision of school buildings, the appointment and transfer of teachers, the hearing of complaints, and so on ; but in general the deputations are strictly subordinate to the administrative board, with no powers except such as may be delegated to them by that body. In this respect they find almost exact counterparts in the English council committees.

Work of the commissions.

[1] *Die Instruktion für die Stadt-Magisträte vom 25. Mai 835*, § 20, No. 2.
[2] Städteordnung, § 59.

Influence of the chairmen of deputations.

From every point of view the most important member of the deputation is its chairman, who, as has been said, is usually a paid member of the Magistrat. On behalf of the commission he supervises directly the work of the departmental staff, from the higher officials downward; he is intrusted with the task of enforcing the instructions of the deputation after they have been approved; and he attends to all such details as may not have been considered in the framing of the general proposals. When emergencies arise in his department, the chairman takes action upon his own responsibility, reporting to the deputation at its next meeting. He is the connecting link between the Magistrat and the departmental staff, and for the smooth working of his department is held strictly accountable by the Magistrat. At the council-meetings he may at any time be called upon for information relating to his department, and may be asked to explain or justify any action recommended by his deputation. In-

Compared with chairmen of council committees in England.

deed, in the general framework of administration the chairman of the Prussian deputation occupies a place which corresponds very closely to that held by the chairman of an English council committee, the chief difference being that the former is usually a paid expert and the latter an unpaid layman. In either case the efficiency of civic administration depends to a considerable degree upon the character and capabilities of the individual who happens to hold the office; for in all matters concerning his department each chairman exerts much influence over his colleagues.

Nature of work performed by deputations.

It is a rule in Prussian municipal administration that all important proposals must be considered by the appropriate deputation before they come up for consideration in the administrative board. If a matter is of consequence to more than a single department it must be submitted to all the deputations concerned, and if any additional expenditures are involved it must also go before the finance deputation. Though often productive of delay, this policy serves to secure careful consideration of almost every important matter from various points of view; for in every large city the administration is apportioned into so many departments that every question of any significance is very likely to be of concern to more than one division. Berlin, for example, has deputations in charge of poor relief, city buildings, fire protection, hospitals, industrial and workingmen's insurance, industrial and mercantile courts, finance, libraries and reading-rooms, civic art, markets, parks and gardens, municipal savings-banks, taxes, statistics, street cleaning and watering, traffic, gas, sewers, municipal stables, municipal slaughter-houses, and water, besides the commissions in control of the various grades of schools, and many others of minor importance. It is not often, therefore, that an important matter concerns a single department.

In order to get a clearer idea of the structure and functions of the deputation in general, it may be well to examine a typical commission, — that in charge of the sewers and sewer-farms of Berlin, for example. This body is at present made up of seventeen persons in all, — a paid member of the Magistrat as chairman, four other members of the same board (two paid and two unpaid), ten members of the city council, one city official, and one citizen deputy. It has charge of the construction and maintenance of the sewage tunnels, collectors, and pumping-stations, and of the city farms upon which the sewage is profitably utilized. It prepares the estimate of yearly expenditures in this department; and, besides providing for current expenses, it must plan for additions to a sinking fund for the ultimate repayment of the cost of the sewer-

A typical deputation described.

age plant.   After the budget has been passed, the deputation superintends the expenditure of the amounts allotted
to its use in the regular list and of any additional appropriations made to it during the year.   It determines,
subject to the Magistrat's approval, the amount of sewer
taxes to be paid by householders.   It recommends all
appointments within the department, makes contracts for
materials, arranges for the leasing of the sewage-farms
or for their direct management by its own officials, and
in general attends to every important incident of departmental administration.   Once a year it presents to the
Magistrat an elaborate report on the conduct of its service ; and this record, after consideration by the board, is
incorporated in the general report made yearly by the
latter body.

Internal organization of a typical commission.   For the more efficient administration of its affairs the
department is divided into three bureaus, all of which are
immediately under the deputation's control and supervision.   One of these bureaus deals with general questions
of administration, another with all matters connected with
the collection of the sewage and its transmission to the
farms, the third with the management of the farms and
the disposal of the farm products.   Each bureau has its
chairman, and under his control is ranged the staff of permanent officials, who, like the chairmen, hold their appointments from the Magistrat.   As a matter of practice, when
a vacancy occurs in any branch of the administrative service of the department, recommendations in regard to the
filling of the post are sent to the Magistrat by the appropriate deputation, but usually not until it has consulted
the chief of the subordinate bureau concerned.   Except
for technical positions no special requirements are exacted.
Those whose duties are of a clerical nature must, of course,
give proof of a general education ; but from ordinary

workmen no particular qualifications are demanded. In all save the lowest offices appointments are, as a rule, made only for probationary periods varying from six months to a year in length, at the end of which the nominations are declared permanent if the appointees have shown satisfactory efficiency. Promotions are likewise made on recommendation of the officials at the head of the bureaus or the department; and increases of remuneration come, in most cases, at specified intervals. In all the higher branches of the service municipal employees are entitled to liberal pensions on retirement after long terms. Except that those who openly profess allegiance to the doctrines of the Social Democracy are rather generally excluded from any place on the civic pay-roll, partisan predilections have little or no part in influencing appointments, promotions, or removals.

The German municipal bureaucracy secures, indeed, most of the advantages which some American cities have sought to gain for their municipal staffs through civil service reform regulations. Non-partisan appointments, probationary periods of service, promotion on the recommendation of superior officers with due regard to merit and experience, security of tenure and protection against arbitrary dismissal, exclusion of civic employees and officials from all part in election campaigns, — all these features find place in the German system, and to their presence may be attributed much of the integrity and efficiency which characterize the civic bureaucracy, particularly in Prussia but to an almost equal degree in the other German states. It may be suggested that the German civic official soon develops the methods or the views of a martinet, that he quickly loses any spirit of individual initiative which he may have possessed on entering the service, and becomes in due time little more than an instrument for performing mechanically the rigid routine committed to him by an immediate superior. It may also be true that the German official, whether in the state or in the municipal service, too often appears to forget, in his dealings with the ordinary citizen, that he is the servant and not the master of the public. The Prussian municipal bureaucracy may thus, perhaps, properly be termed a machine; but it is one of the most efficient administrative machines in the world. Its general esprit de corps, its impregnability to corrupt influences, and its persevering industry have rightly commanded the admiration of foreign students.

Extensive use of private citizens in municipal administration.

An interesting feature of the German municipal service is the practice of intrusting a good many minor administrative functions to private citizens, who give their assistance without any remuneration whatever even though the duties may make important demands upon their time and patience. An excellent example of this practice is seen in the administration of the poor-relief systems of the various cities. This branch of municipal service is, like the other departments, put in charge of a deputation, which, because of the comprehensive work under its supervision, is usually very large. The Armen-Deputation in Berlin, for instance, at the head of which is Dr. Emil Münsterberg, a prominent member of the Magistrat and an authority of international reputation on all questions concerning the care of the poor, has forty-five members, being made up of four members of the administrative board besides the chairman, seventeen councilmen, eleven citizen deputies, and twelve permanent civic officials. This deputation, subject to the general supervision and control of the Magistrat, determines the main policy to be followed in dealing with the problems of poverty; it guides and directs the work of the numerous district committees which perform the actual work of

The department of poor relief as an example.

relief, supervises all the city's charitable institutions, and prepares that section of the annual budget which relates to its own department. For the carrying out of the work of actual relief the city is divided into twenty-six poor-relief sections (Armenkreise), each with its chairman, who is in every case one of the members of the deputation. Each section, again, comprises a number of administrative districts (Stadtbezirke), of which there are in all over two hundred and fifty. Each district has its local poor commission (Armen-Kommission), made up of a chairman, a vice-chairman, and a dozen or more members all appointed by the city council, — one of them a physician, who receives a small annual stipend, the others private citizens who give their services gratuitously. Every commission, in its turn, divides its district into small sections and gives to each of its members immediate supervision of a section. In this way the administration is brought into the closest personal touch with those who need relief, hard and fast methods of inquiry are avoided, and local knowledge is made to do service as a safeguard against imposture. The most noteworthy point in connection with the administration of this department, however, is that it draws into the direct service of the municipality a very large number of voluntary workers, and thus relieves the civic treasury of what would in an American city be a formidable expense were it to undertake this branch of administration on a similar scale. In Berlin over forty-five hundred private citizens are drawn, in some capacity or other, into the service of this one department,[1] an arrangement which has served to give to the Berlin poor-relief administration a flexibility and a responsiveness to popular feeling that is not surpassed in any other city

Salutary results of the system.

----

[1] *Bericht über die Gemeinde-Verwaltung der Stadt Berlin, 1901 bis 1905,* I. 7.

in the world, and which should make one careful not to generalize too broadly concerning the " bureaucratic " methods of Prussian civic administration.

Berlin.   In outlining the framework of Prussian city government, it is unnecessary to give special consideration to Berlin; for, unlike the French, English, and American capitals, the Prussian metropolis is not under a special system of civic administration, but is in general governed like the other Prussian cities.   Its police department is, to be sure, in charge of a special police president, who performs functions roughly similar to those of the prefect of police in Paris, and it deals with the national government directly through a provincial president and not through subordinate authorities; but otherwise it presents no very important deviations from the general type.[1]

[1] The best short study of Berlin municipal organization is Heinrich Dove's "Berlin," in *Schriften des Vereins für Socialpolitik*, XVII. i. 95–152.   See also E. Loening's " Die Verwaltung der Stadt Berlin," in *Preussische Jahrbücher*, Vols. LV.–LVI. *passim;* and R. Eberstadt's " System und Princip in der Berliner Stadtverwaltung," *Ibid.* Vol. LXX.   Data relating to the organization and activities of the civic departments may be found in the *Statistisches Jahrbuch der Stadt Berlin*, published annually by the municipal authorities, as well as in the quinquennial *Bericht über die Gemeinde-Verwaltung der Stadt Berlin*, issued by the Magistrat.

CHAPTER III

THE GOVERNMENT OF ENGLISH CITIES

Of all the countries of Europe, England presents the most interesting field for the study of city government and administration, a preëminence that may be accounted for partly by the continuity of English municipal history, partly by the wide range of functions directly exercised by the civic authorities, and partly by the fact that the phenomenon of urban concentration has been more marked in England than in any other European state. Municipal government directly concerns a larger proportion of the national population in England than it does in any other country; indeed, the problem of governing the urban municipality may properly be said to be a problem of the whole English people.

It was not until the nineteenth century that England Growth felt the full force of the urban movement. Even in Saxon of English cities. and Norman times, it is true, the government of the " borough " was regarded as a problem to some extent, and throughout the mediæval period the boroughs of England, with their struggles for local autonomy and their successful clamors for political recognition, exercised a considerable influence in the politics of the nation; but these towns, which have since received so much attention from the constitutional historian, were then, for the most part, distinctly rural units whose inhabitants formed but an insignificant proportion of the total population. Even in 1500 London In the Middle Ages. did not have more than 40,000 inhabitants, and no other

English city or borough approached it in size. Bristol and York had populations running into five figures, and three or four other cities had perhaps passed the 5000 mark; but taken all together the urban population of England did not at this time exceed 150,000, or about five per cent of the English people as a whole.[1]

During the Tudor and Stuart periods the boroughs grew slowly, notwithstanding the constant set-backs which resulted from the frequent occurrence of epidemics and plagues. According to Macaulay's estimate, the population of London had by the middle of the seventeenth century reached a half-million, a figure which entitled the English metropolis to rank second only to Paris among the great cities of Europe. Such progress was, however, very exceptional; for few of the English cities did much more than keep pace with the growth of the national population until well into the eighteenth century, when, with the agricultural and industrial revolutions, the urban movement received a decided impetus, which gained in strength as the threshold of the nineteenth century was passed. The national population now mounted every decade by leaps and bounds, and of this increase the new manufacturing and commercial cities received the lion's share. It has been estimated that in 1800 the urban population of England formed not more than one-quarter of the whole, that by the middle of the nineteenth century it had risen to not less than one-half, and at the close of the century to more than three-quarters.[2] England has thus come to be the classic land of urban concentration. The bulk of her population has shifted from rural to civic

In modern times.

---

[1] The various sources for the study of early English municipal history and organization are indicated in Charles Gross's *Bibliography of British Municipal History* (New York, 1897).

[2] Statistical tables showing the growth of urban population in England during this period may be found in A. F. Weber's *Growth of Cities in the Nineteenth Century* (New York, 1901), 40–67.

environment, until in the twentieth century the problems
of the city have become the problems of substantially the
whole people.

The history of English municipal organization is indeed
a long and somewhat curious story; but throughout the
greater part of the development the external forms of
borough government have undergone but little change.[1]
The theory of municipal administration at the beginning
of the nineteenth century was not essentially different from
that which existed in Plantagenet times; for the chartered
borough of the Middle Ages possessed the right to select
its own executive officials without outside interference, to
collect taxes from its citizens through its own taxgatherers,
and to set up and maintain its own borough courts.   In
the earlier stages of its history it had, to be sure, maintained
a form of government which was, in comparison with contemporary systems on the continent, extremely democratic.
The burghers in general meeting elected their mayor,
coroners, bailiffs, and other local officials, every adult male
inhabitant having, in theory at any rate, a part in the
choice.   At the outset there were probably, in most of the
boroughs, no municipal councils; but as the municipalities
grew in population the burghers seem to have adopted
the practice of turning over the actual administration to an
elective committee of their own number, or a sort of local
council.   This change, however, appears to have paved the
way for an ultimate sacrifice of local democracy; for, although the councillors were at first chosen annually, the
habit of reëlecting them year after year served in due time
to render the election little more than a formality.   The

Evolution of English local government.

The ancient borough.

---

[1] On the development of borough organization, see H. A. Merewether and
A. J. Stephens's *History of the Boroughs and Municipal Corporations of the
United Kingdom* (3 vols., London, 1835) ; and Sidney and Beatrice Webb's
*English Local Government from the Revolution to the Municipal Corporations
Act* (3 vols., London, 1904–1908), especially Vol. III.

borough electorate continued to include all the "freemen
of the town"; but, with the growing importance of the
guilds in local administration and the steadily developing
exclusiveness of these organizations, the list of freemen
gradually narrowed, until by the close of the fifteenth century the freemen of the borough often formed but a small
proportion of its population.[1] With this growth of oligarchy
the perpetuation of the municipal councils by coöptation
became common, and the governing body of the borough
settled into a close corporation.

The framework of borough organization was at this
stage substantially the same as it is to-day. At the head
of the administration was a mayor elected by the council;
then there were a number of magistrates known as aldermen, similarly selected; and, finally, there was a council
chosen by the burgesses or freemen. The mayor, aldermen, councillors, and freemen made up the "corporation"
of the borough, and exercised the powers of the municipality, including the right to elect representatives to the
House of Commons. This last-named privilege is of high
significance; for it is not improbable that during the seventeenth and eighteenth centuries the oligarchic organization would have broken down if the crown had not been
so desirous of maintaining it as a means of securing supporters in Parliament. In so far as the list of freemen
could be kept within narrow limits the crown had a better
opportunity to control the election of borough representatives in the House of Commons; for it was obviously
easier to dominate a small self-perpetuating body than the
whole mass of borough inhabitants. No wonder, therefore, that whenever the crown amended borough charters
or gave new ones it stood ready to assist the movement to

[1] On this development, see C. W. Colby on "The Growth of Oligarchy in
English Towns," in *English Historical Review*, V. 633-653.

municipal oligarchy. Indeed, when some of the larger boroughs showed a disposition to oppose the royal policy, it was the practice of the Stuart sovereigns to secure, by quo warranto proceedings, an annulment of their charters, and then to grant new ones which were designed not to improve the efficiency of borough government but to afford means whereby the selection of borough representatives might be controlled.

The revolution of 1688 did not bring about any marked change in the structure of borough government: the close corporations still remained in power. Royal interference with the charters ceased for the most part, it is true;[1] but the new charters given by the Hanoverian sovereigns differed little from those granted by the Stuarts. Despite the sweeping changes made in the local government systems of France and Prussia during this period, the old municipal régime in England remained as firmly intrenched as ever, — a situation the more unfortunate from the fact that, with the rapid growth of the towns during the industrial revolution, the close corporations proved entirely unable to cope with the new problems of urban administration. From such exigencies the larger boroughs sought relief by applying directly to Parliament for special legislation, as a result of which many of them obtained the appointment of commissions or boards that were empowered to provide the more important municipal services. It was by such commissions that many English towns were provided with their first systems of water supply, sewerage, and public lighting. As this practice of relying upon commissions developed, the "corporations" came in time to do little more than elect the borough representatives in the House of Commons.

The borough under the Hanoverians.

---

[1] F. W. Maitland, *Township and Borough* (London, 1898), 95.

Borough government in the first three decades of the nineteenth century.

It may seem strange that England, a country which was in the earlier part of the nineteenth century serving as a model of successful representative government to the nations of the continent, should have continued to maintain in full force a system of local administration that was in reality far less representative in character than the municipal system of either France or Prussia. This perpetuation of oligarchy in English borough government may, however, be explained partly by the inherent conservatism of Englishmen in regard to their political institutions, partly by the spirit of political optimism which pervaded the land in the years following the victory at Waterloo, partly by the overpowering parliamentary strength of vested interests, and partly, no doubt, by the popular ignorance as to the exact condition of municipal affairs. The movement for reform in local government, though it gained some headway during the first quarter of the nineteenth century, was compelled, for a substantial impetus, to await the culmination of the more important and more aggressive agitation for the reform of Parliament.

The era of reform.

The great reform measure of 1832 first brought the question of municipal reorganization well within the sphere of practical politics,[1] and the reformed House of Commons lost little time in attempting to deal with the matter. By an act passed in 1833 the cities of Scotland were first attended to, and later in the same year a royal commission was appointed to investigate affairs in the boroughs of England and Wales. This body was instructed to collect information in regard to existing defects in the municipal system, to inquire into the methods of selecting borough officers, and in

The royal commission of 1833.

[1] 2–3 William IV. c. 45.

general to look into the administrative conditions of all the chartered municipalities.[1]

The royal commissioners performed their work promptly and thoroughly, visiting many of the boroughs, examining their accounts and records minutely, and taking a large amount of evidence. With this body of facts as a basis, they presently laid before Parliament their famous report, a state paper which is distinguished among documents of its kind for its comprehensiveness, clearness, and vigor of statement.[2] *Its investigation of borough affairs.*

After touching briefly upon the manner in which the municipal corporations had come into existence and upon the general nature of their charters, the report proceeded to lay bare the more important anomalies and abuses which had been disclosed by an examination of affairs in two hundred and eighty-five boroughs. It laid emphasis upon the unrepresentative character of the borough authorities, and upon the fact that these authorities had long since lost the confidence of the local public, as was evidenced by the strong popular feeling that the " corporation " could no longer be relied upon to perform any municipal functions of importance, and that public services could be properly provided only by the appointment of special commissions. In nearly all the boroughs, it was shown, the voters comprised but a very small percentage

---

[1] Much interesting data relating to the discussions preliminary to the appointment of the commission, as well as concerning its composition, its methods of investigation, and the obstacles which it had to surmount, may be found in S. and B. Webb's *English Local Government*, III. ch. xi.

[2] This main report, entitled *First Report of the Municipal Corporations Commission*, was published in April, 1835, in five volumes, the first of which contains the report itself and the other four the evidence gathered by the commissioners. Four years later the whole was indexed in the *Analytical Index to the First Report of the Municipal Corporations Commission* (London, 1839). The *Second Report of the Municipal Corporations Commission* (London, 1837) deals with the city of London only.

of the population, and admission to the ranks of burgesses was not regulated by any reasonable rules.[1]

In most of the boroughs, the commissioners reported, the governing authorities consisted of a mayor and a council, the latter being usually made up of both aldermen and councillors. These two classes of members ordinarily met together, but in a few instances the aldermen were accustomed to meet separately for the consideration of special matters. The council-meetings were almost invariably secret ; and as a rule no report of the proceedings was ever given to the public, — a practice of conducting municipal business to which the commissioners attributed many evils. They found, for instance, that local offices were distributed by the councillors among their relatives and friends with little or no regard to the qualifications which the appointees possessed ; that in many cases non-resident municipal officers drew their stipends and gave no services in return ; that sinecure posts, on which much public money was expended with no tangible return, abounded in all the larger boroughs; and that a single individual sometimes held several offices, drawing the full salaries attached to them, but being entirely unable to perform all the duties involved. In a word, the commissioners found borough administration characterized by extravagance, inefficiency, and even dishonesty.

The report further drew attention to the loose and irregular manner in which the accounts of the boroughs were kept, and to the frequent misapplication and even peculation

---

[1] In the 212 boroughs from which definite figures could be obtained the total population was 1,800,000. Of this number somewhat more than 88,000, or less than five per cent, were " freemen " ; Liverpool, with a population of 165,000, had about 5000 voters ; Portsmouth, with 46,000 inhabitants, had only 102 ; Plymouth, with 75,000, had only 437 freemen, of whom 145 were non-residents. This condition of affairs was more or less characteristic of all the other boroughs. See the *First Report*, I. 32–33.

of public funds which the system of accounting not only permitted but encouraged. The property and funds of the borough were in many cases, it was shown, openly regarded by the members of the governing body, not in the light of trusts held by them for the borough population as a whole, but as their own patrimony, — an idea which they frequently acted upon by converting borough property to their private use, and by spending for their own profit and pleasure moneys that were sorely needed for public purposes. So many specific instances of these evils were given by the commissioners as to show clearly that in most of the boroughs all the traditions of local administration had become unsound.

Taken as a whole, the report disclosed a state of affairs undoubtedly worse than that which has marked the administration of any American city even when things have been at their most critical stage. There are, to be sure, some good reasons for thinking that the commissioners portrayed the situation as somewhat worse than it really was;[1] but that it was bad enough the evidence which they gathered shows unmistakably. If students of municipal government find to-day much that is admirable both in the framework of government and in the actual administration of English cities, they should not forget that only two or three generations ago the conditions in English cities were about as bad as they could well be. The change, furthermore, has not been brought about by any sweeping reconstruction of the organs of municipal government; for these are now almost exactly the same in structure and in functions as they were before 1835. It was the spirit not the form of local administration that was profoundly altered during the epoch of reform; the real

Enormity of the change since 1835.

[1] These reasons are given in Webb's *English Local Government*, III. 718–737.

change was that the citizens came to have a genuine voice in the administration of their own local affairs, — that municipal oligarchy gave way to municipal democracy.

English experience and American problems.

From English municipal experience in the nineteenth century one may, indeed, draw two somewhat palpable generalizations. One is that, however corrupt and inefficient the administration of the cities in any country may become, the situation is never entirely hopeless. Those friends of municipal reform who have, perhaps, been too ready to confess their utter discouragement with the state of things in the United States may well find new inspiration by comparing present conditions in English cities with those which existed there three-quarters of a century ago. In the second place, the course of events in England has shown that no radical reconstruction of local organs of government is necessary in order to transform a corrupt and inefficient administration into one which reflects at every turn the qualities of honesty and power.

Results of the investigations of 1833.

In due time the report on municipal corporations was laid before Parliament; and presently Lord John Russell came forward with a measure, commonly called the Whig Bill, designed to effect a general reform of the abuses which the commissioners had brought to light.[1] By the terms of this bill all provisions in borough charters inconsistent with the new arrangements were to be annulled, in order that all municipal charters, though nominally remaining in force, might be brought into entire uniformity. The idea of a municipal corporation was to be restored to its original place as " the legal personification of the local community, elected by, acting for, and

The "Whig Bill" of 1835.

[1] *Hansard's Parliamentary Debates*, 3d series, XXVIII. 541–558 (June 5, 1835). On Russell's share in drafting and promoting the measure, see Sir Spencer Walpole's *Life of Lord John Russell* (2d ed., 2 vols., London, 1889), I. 243 ff.

responsible to the inhabitants "; and it was further provided that the governing organ of the corporation should
consist of a body of councillors elected for a three-year
term by the equal and direct votes of all the local taxpayers, and that any inhabitant of the borough who had
paid rates for three consecutive years should be entitled
to vote at local elections.

A distinguishing feature of the bill was the signal step Its chief pro-
which it proposed in the direction of strengthening the visions.
control and supervision of the central over the municipal
authorities, — a superintendence which had thus far been
almost entirely lacking.   It also provided that the borough magistrates, hitherto appointed by the municipal
corporation, should thenceforth be named by the crown.
The bill further sought to define more precisely the legal
sphere of municipal administration, and to set some fixed
limits to the authority of local officers.   In general it made
the field controlled by the municipal council somewhat
narrower than it had been ; but, on the other hand, it
added some new powers to the body by giving it defini-
tive jurisdiction in the collection and expenditure of
borough revenues, in the disposition of municipal property
and the care of municipal police, in the making of local
by-laws or ordinances and the appointing of all municipal
officers, and, finally, in the matter of granting liquor licenses.   It was anticipated by those who framed the measure that, if the new régime proved efficient in operation,
more powers might be intrusted to the council from time
to time by amending legislation.

The bill proposed that its provisions should be applied Its scope.
to the one hundred and seventy-eight boroughs named in an
attached schedule, — a number which did not, however,
include all the municipal boroughs of England and Wales,
for many of the small municipalities were not deemed of

sufficient importance to warrant their insertion in the list. London was likewise excluded from the application of the bill; for it was thought that the metropolis might, on account of its great size and its special problems of administration, later be dealt with in a separate measure. As will be seen, however, no reform was accomplished in London until several more decades had passed; but the government of practically all the other important boroughs was, by the provisions of the bill, rendered uniform, and it was further stipulated that, although municipal charters were still to be given by the crown, no new charter should be issued save in conformity with the uniform arrangements.

Opposition to the measure.

The bill met with some opposition from the Tories in the House of Commons; but, since its general principles were acceptable to men of moderate views like Sir Robert Peel and his followers, it went through the House without any important changes, — an evidence of the general discredit into which the old municipal system had fallen with all parties. In the House of Lords, however, the influence of opposing interests was more powerful, and here the measure encountered its chief obstacles.[1] Though deterred from rejecting it as a whole by thought of the distinct impression which the report of the commissioners had made throughout the country, the Lords nevertheless made a determined effort to destroy the effectiveness of the measure by proposing amendments to it, — one, for instance, depriving the municipal councils of all jurisdiction over the granting of liquor licenses, another stipulating that one-fourth of the councillors should be elected for life terms,

---

[1] On the attitude of the various parliamentary leaders toward the bill, see, in addition to Walpole's *Life of Lord John Russell*, Graham Wallas's *Life of Francis Place* (London, 1898), Parker's *Life of Sir Robert Peel* (London, 1899), and Stuart J. Reid's *Life and Letters of the First Lord Durham* (2 vols., London, 1906).

and still others making similar changes in the direction of conservatism. In spite of this action, which indicated a wide divergence in views between the two branches of Parliament, the two Houses ultimately arranged a compromise. In regard to the license question, they decided to drop the clause altogether and leave the jurisdiction, as heretofore, with the justices of the peace. On the life-membership proposition the Commons met the Lords halfway by agreeing that the councillors, themselves elected for three years, should elect one-third of their own number to bear the title of aldermen and to remain members of the council for twice the period, a device which would, it was thought, secure an element of stability in the council. With these and some other changes the bill was passed in September, 1835, going on the statute-books as the Municipal Corporations Act;[1] and for three-quarters of a century its main outlines have since remained unaltered.

Compromises made necessary by this opposition.

The act of 1835 may scarcely be regarded as having effected any important break in the continuity of English municipal development. It did not, like the French decrees of 1789 and 1800, or like the Prussian enactments of 1806–1808, make any sweeping changes either in the framework of borough organization or in the relation of the municipality to the state. It endeavored simply to put into active operation what had for many centuries been the theory of English borough administration but had long since become little more than a theory. It effected a change in the spirit rather than in the form of local government. Even by its most ardent supporters it does not appear to have been regarded as a code that would, like the Great Reform Act of 1832, effect a final solution of all the problems with which it undertook to

The Municipal Corporations Act of 1835.

Not regarded as inaugurating any new theory of local government.

[1] 5–6 William IV. c. 76.

deal.   The framers of the measure did not give the municipal councils any very wide range of powers at the outset,
transferring to them only those functions which had been
exercised by various local boards; but, as time went on
and the council showed its capabilities, Parliament was
found ready to respond with special statutes amending
the original act in such ways as to increase the scope of
the council's jurisdiction.   So many such statutes were
passed, indeed, during the half-century following 1835
that before the interval had elapsed the multiplication of
these amending enactments had created much confusion.

The recodi-
fication of
1882.

In 1882, therefore, it was arranged that the whole mass of
legislation affecting the government of boroughs should be
consolidated into one comprehensive statute, which took
the form of the Municipal Corporations Consolidation Act
of that year, a measure that now forms the chief legal
basis of English municipal government.[1]

The areas
of urban
government
in England.

Consideration of the development of English municipal
government has thus far been limited to one class of urban units, the borough.   It should be noted at this point,
however, that the borough is not the only unit of urban
administration in England, and that even the term
"borough" is not itself applied uniformly.   One speaks,
for instance, of "municipal boroughs," "county boroughs,"
"cities," and "urban districts," the first three differing
very slightly from one another in the nature of their administration, the last-named presenting a type of local
government quite different from the others.   Most of the

The munici-
pal borough.

English "boroughs" are municipal boroughs, subject in certain respects to supervision by the authorities of the administrative counties in which they happen to lie.   The

---

[1] 45–46 Victoria, c. 50.   This code, with the amending legislation, may be
conveniently found in Rawlinson and Johnston's *Municipal Corporations Acts
and other Enactments* (9th ed., London, 1903).

county boroughs, on the other hand, are not subject to *The county borough.* any supervision by the county authorities; they are not even represented in the county council, but through their own borough authorities exercise the powers which are ordinarily vested with the former body.[1] Since, however, the jurisdiction of the county authorities is in any case connected chiefly with questions of sanitation and the protection of the public health, the two classes of boroughs are not essentially different in status: their governing bodies, or councils, are substantially the same in structure and in functions.[2] Some boroughs, again, are called cities; but *The city.* it ought to be made clear that the distinction between an ordinary borough and a city is not in England one of relative population or of differences in the form or scope of the municipal charter. The title of " city " is in England borne by a comparatively small number of boroughs — some large and some small, some ancient and some modern — which are or have been the seats of bishops or archbishops (as York, Westminster, and Oxford), or have, on the other hand, received the title by special patent from the crown (as Leeds and Sheffield). In neither the form nor the functions of government is there any difference between the city and the ordinary borough.

The distinction between the borough and the urban *The urban district.* district is somewhat more important. An urban district is an area and group of population which has not received a borough charter, but which has by the provisions of the Local Government Act of 1894[3] been equipped with a

[1] There are at present seventy county boroughs, each with a population exceeding 50,000. Any borough with a population above this figure may be made a county borough by an order of the Local Government Board. See 51–52 Victoria, c. 41, § 52.

[2] On this point see R. S. Wright and H. Hobhouse's *Local Government and Local Taxation* (2d ed., London, 1894), 24–26.

[3] 56–57 Victoria, c. 73. See also R. H. Hadden's *Handbook to the Local Government Act of 1894* (London, 1895).

framework of government somewhat simpler than that of the borough.[1] At present there are more than 800 of these communities, with populations ranging from 1000 to 75,000; and new districts may be created from time to time by the joint action of the county council and the Local Government Board. Every borough, indeed, is ipso facto an urban district; for the borough council possesses any power which may be given to the authorities of any such district. In brief, then, any non-rural area which enjoys local self-government is an urban district; if it has at any time received a royal charter, it is a borough; if it has been removed from the jurisdiction of the administrative county in which it is situated, it is a county borough, otherwise it is termed a municipal borough; if it is or has been the head of a diocese, or if it has received the title by royal patent, it is a city.

Importance of the borough among areas of local government.

Of these different areas of urban government the most important, from the standpoint of the student of comparative local administration, is the borough. The act of 1835 enumerated one hundred and seventy-eight boroughs, to which its provisions were forthwith made applicable; and it arranged that the crown should charter new boroughs only in accordance with the terms of the enactment, a provision which was retained in the act of 1882. England has, therefore, neither the general nor the special charter system familiar in the United States. Each borough has its own

Borough charters.

particular charter, sometimes of very ancient date but always granted by and in the name of the crown. Furthermore, every application for a borough charter is considered on its individual merits. Though size is a circumstance naturally taken into account, there is no arrangement whereby an urban unit, however large its population hap-

[1] For a discussion of the urban district council, see J. Redlich and F. W. Hirst, *Local Government in England* (2 vols., London, 1903), II. 118 ff.

pens to be, may obtain a borough charter as a matter of course. On the other hand, all the charters, ancient and modern, are now substantially alike in all their impor- Their na-
tant provisions, and all the boroughs have exactly the same ture.
organs of local government. Despite this uniformity, how-
ever, the powers possessed by these organs in different boroughs show considerable variation, for the reason that Parliament grants, from time to time, special privileges to the authorities of one borough which it does not grant to those of another, — a practice upon which there are, of course, no constitutional restrictions in England, as there are in many American states.[1]

When any community desires a borough charter, the first How ob-
step toward securing it is the drawing up of a petition tained.
which, before it becomes of service, must be signed by at least a majority of the ratepayers of the locality. This petition, addressed to the crown, is referred to the Privy Council ; but as a matter of practice it really goes — as those who are at all familiar with the workings of the English system of national government need scarcely be told — not to the Privy Council but to the Cabinet, and the member of the Cabinet to whom it is invariably referred is the president of the Local Government Board. In any case the receipt of the petition must be notified to this officer, and also to the county council within those jurisdiction the petitioners reside. It is also published in the official gazette. If the county council and the authorities of adjoin- Opposed and
ing municipalities interpose no objection, and if not more unopposed
applications
than one-twentieth of the ratepayers present a counter-peti- for charters.

[1] Under the title of " Constitutional Limitations relating to Cities and their Affairs," one of my students, Mr. R. W. Skinner, Jr., has prepared and pub-
lished in the Annals of the American Academy of Political and Social Science (XXVII. 232) an elaborate table which clearly shows that in the United States the practice of granting special powers to particular cities is being more and more restricted by constitutional provisions.

Q

tion, the application for a charter may be granted by the
crown without reference to Parliament; and in such cases
the request is ordinarily so granted. If, however, the petition
be opposed in either of the ways above mentioned, the application is laid before Parliament, and is considered by a
joint committee of the two Houses constituted for the consideration of this and similar petitions. This committee
hears whatever facts and arguments are laid before it by
either supporters or opponents of the application, and reports its decision to Parliament. If it recommends that the
petition be granted, Parliament usually authorizes the giving of a charter, which is issued in the name of the crown;
in fact, even if the committee reports unfavorably, Parliament may and sometimes does grant the prayer of the
petition, but not often.

Applications frequently refused. In order that an application for incorporation as a
borough may receive favorable consideration, it does not
have to come from any definite number of ratepayers;
neither by law nor by custom is there any fixed minimum
which the population of a locality must exceed before it may
be admitted to the category of municipal boroughs. Still,
a reasonable showing in the matter of populousness is ordinarily insisted upon; and as a rule petitions for borough
charters come from the larger urban districts only. That
the scrutiny which the authorities apply to applications is
somewhat strict is shown by the fact that during the period
from 1882 to 1907 they refused nearly one-third of all the
requests received by them: out of the more than sixty
petitions presented to them (most of them opposed ones)
they denied about twenty-five. Nevertheless, the number
of chartered boroughs has almost doubled since 1835, present statistics showing about 350 in all. At the head of the
list is Liverpool with its population of about three-quarters
of a million, and at the foot is Hedon with slightly over a

single thousand; more than thirty boroughs are above the 100,000 mark, and nearly seventy have populations ranging below 5000.[1]

When the commission made its investigations prior to the legislation of 1835, it was able to report that the boundaries of most boroughs were defined with "tolerable accuracy." As a matter of fact, these bounds had in most cases been fixed in times so remote as to be beyond the range of legal memory; and it was not deemed advisable that any general readjustment should be undertaken, lest such a proposal should arouse in opposition a local sentiment that would put a new obstacle in the path of the general proposals for borough reorganization. After the act of 1835 had been safely steered through Parliament, however, a Municipal Boundaries Commission was appointed, with instructions to go from borough to borough setting the metes and bounds of each municipality, but adhering as closely as possible to the traditional borough limits.[2] Only when there was a clear case for alteration was any change to be made. In due time the commission presented its recommendations to Parliament;[3] but no legislation followed, and the ancient lines of demarcation remained intact. The importance of the report is, however, to be found in the fact that, through its influence upon the national authorities in their decisions concerning municipal boundaries, many of its recommendations have since 1835 gradually been brought into actual operation. From 1835 to 1888 borough boundaries were changed by acts of Parliament, a special act being required in each case. Since 1888 the matter of borough limits has been dealt

(margin notes) Borough boundaries.

The Boundaries Commission of 1835.

Boundaries of boroughs now changed by provisional orders.

---

[1] Reliable statistics of population may be found in the *Municipal Year Book of the United Kingdom*, published annually.

[2] These instructions are printed in Redlich and Hirst's *Local Government in England*, I. 230–231.

[3] *Report of the Boundary Commissioners* (3 vols., London, 1837).

with for the most part by the Local Government Board, which is authorized to issue "provisional orders" determining all such questions.[1]   Such orders must, however, in certain cases be confirmed by Parliament.

The "municipal corporation."   By the Municipal Corporations Consolidation Act of 1882 the municipal corporation is defined as "the body corporate constituted by the incorporation of the inhabitants of a borough." These inhabitants are known as burgesses, the contemporary prototypes of the ancient "freemen of the town," their chief attribute being the right to vote at municipal elections, — in other words, the right to be enrolled on the burgess roll, or voters' list, of the municipality.   To secure enrolment as a burgess a person must satisfy certain qualifications, which may be briefly summarized as follows: he must be (1) a British subject either by birth or by naturalization, of the age of twenty-one years;[2] (2) an occupant, during the year last past, of some house, warehouse, or other building within the municipality upon which rates are assessed;[3]   (3) one who has during the same period been resident within the limits of the municipality or within seven miles thereof,[4] and who (4) has paid all such rates as have become due upon the qualifying property.   There are also certain disqualifications, particularly of persons convicted of serious crimes, or of persons who have within the year been in receipt of

Its personnel.

The qualifications of a "burgess" as municipal voter.

Disqualifications.

---

[1] 62–63 Victoria, c. 14, § 54.

[2] Men, unmarried women, and widows are included ; but married women are not enrolled as voters, even though they fulfil the ordinary conditions.

[3] The occupancy may be individual, joint, or several ; but occupancy of premises by a joint-stock company does not qualify the stockholders, nor does occupancy by a society qualify its members.   No minimum assessment is fixed. In order to qualify as an occupant of land upon which there is no building, an assessment of at least £10 is required.

[4] This has been construed to be seven miles in a straight line from the outer limits of the borough.   When the assessment is £10 or more, only six months' residence is required.

public charity or whose near relatives have received such assistance.

An interesting difference between the English and the American principle of enrolment is seen in the fact that, whereas in America the qualifications for voting are usually the same at all elections, national, state, and municipal, in England the lists of qualified voters are entirely different at parliamentary and borough elections. The parliamentary franchise is in some respects the more comprehensive ; for it includes all " lodgers " who pay an annual rental of ten pounds or more, a class which is not recognized as fulfilling the condition of " occupancy " demanded in the municipalities. On the other hand, the municipal franchise includes a good many female ratepayers, a class which has not as yet been recognized in the parliamentary lists. Still, in general the totals on the two lists do not vary greatly, although the borough electorate is probably, on an average, somewhat the larger, for the number of women who vote in the boroughs is scarcely offset by the number of lodgers and others who vote in parliamentary elections.[1] Exact comparisons are difficult to make, however, for municipal and parliamentary electoral boundaries do not always coincide.

Voting qualifications in parliamentary and local elections differ.

Although the franchise requirements in English boroughs are on the whole so elementary that they would seem on their face to shut out nobody who has any real interest in the municipality, the fact remains that the ratio of voters to the total population is much smaller in the English boroughs than in the cities of the United States, where a régime of manhood suffrage prevails. Some are un-

Scope of the municipal suffrage in England and in the United States.

[1] In 1898 the London County Council published a statement showing the comparative strength of the local and parliamentary electorates in some sixty large boroughs. On an average the local ones were about twelve per cent stronger than the parliamentary.

doubtedly kept out by the residence requirement; a
larger quota, perhaps, are disqualified by the receipt of
aid from the poor fund; and in most of the boroughs
there are always a good many, especially among the
poorer element of the population, who are denied enrolment on the voters' list because they fail to pay their
rates on time. It has been estimated that, in the boroughs as a whole, from twenty-five to forty per cent of
the adult male population is excluded by some one or
other of the franchise limitations.[1] In London the
voters' list contains about twelve per cent of the total
population, in New York about sixteen per cent. If
manhood suffrage were in New York to be supplanted
by the English franchise system, the electorate in that
city would be reduced in numbers from about 660,000
to about 480,000; that is, one voter in every four would
be disfranchised.[2]

The non-vot-
ing class in
England.
It would not be fair to say that the English voting requirements serve to disqualify only those who would, if
they had the suffrage, use it with the least intelligence
and with the least steadfastness against venality. On the
contrary, considerable numbers of intelligent, reputable,
and well-paid workingmen are excluded because they live
in low-priced lodgings; and hundreds or even thousands
of young men are debarred because they reside with their
parents, and hence rank neither as householders nor as
lodgers.[3] It must further be borne in mind that in every
English municipality there are many persons legally qualified as voters who do not assert their right to go on the

[1] Professor F. J. Goodnow, in *Report to the National Civic Federation Commission on Public Ownership and Operation* (3 vols., New York, 1907), Pt. I.
Vol. I. 47.

[2] *Ibid.* 49.

[3] See Professor John R. Commons's report on " Labor and Politics," *Ibid.*
Pt. II. Vol. II. 6.

list because, as will be pointed out later, such insistence would involve some disclosure of their private affairs. There are said to be at least 160,000 legally qualified voters in London whose names are, for one reason or another, not on the voters' list.[1]

As students of comparative administration have frequently pointed out, the English idea of the suffrage in municipal elections is that votes should in general represent units of property rather than individuals. Hence, mere residence within the municipal limits does not of itself give an adult citizen any franchise rights, nor does residence outside the limits preclude him from qualifying as a voter. With the important exception of corporate holdings, practically every unit of rateable property — that is to say, every unit of property which is assessed for local taxes — is entitled to be represented; and, as a rule, the person who is recognized as having the right to represent it is the one who pays the taxes assessed upon it. This person is, in most cases, the occupier. To be recognized as an occupier, moreover, one need not reside on the premises; for a business man who leases an office, a warehouse, or a store thereby becomes its occupant, and as such is qualified to vote although he may live outside the municipal limits. In recent years, however, the practice of admitting to voting rights in municipal elections persons who are virtually lodgers has tended greatly to confuse matters. Till within two years persons occupying rooms, or even suites of rooms, in a house in which their landlord lived were deemed " lodgers," and hence were denied the right to be enrolled as municipal voters; but by a decision rendered in 1906 such persons may now in certain cases be ranked as " occupants," and so are entitled to the borough

English theory of the suffrage.

---

[1] *Ibid.* 5.

franchise.[1]   A way has thus been opened for a large increase in the municipal electorate, and in many boroughs
this expansion has already taken place.

The voters'
list; how
compiled.
The work of compiling the voters' list is in the hands
of certain officials known as overseers of the poor, whose
chief duty, however, is that of preparing the assessment
rolls which form the basis for levying the annual " poor
rate." Each year these overseers are instructed by the
town clerk to prepare a preliminary list of municipal voters;
and this they proceed to do by copying from their assessment rolls the names of all qualified persons entered
thereon, a table which includes all occupants who pay
rates and who otherwise satisfy the legal requirements.
When rates are paid not by the occupant but by the owner,
the latter is called upon to send in the name of his tenant
that it may be duly enrolled.[2] This, unfortunately, he
does not always do; indeed, the returns transmitted by
owners are said to be so notoriously inaccurate as to
justify the charge, sometimes made, that English landlords
make a point of omitting the names of those of their
tenants who happen to be politically opposed to them.
Nevertheless, an occupant whose name is not returned to
the overseers by the owner may obtain a place on the list
by application to the revising authorities, if he chooses to
make such request, or to have it made for him by one of
his party managers. The lodgers, too, are not listed from
the assessment rolls, but must present applications for enrol-

---

[1] In the case of Kent vs. Fittall (1906) it was ruled that, if a person has independent control over his room or rooms, — that is to say, is in effect as independent as he would be in a self-contained apartment, — he is not to be ranked as a
"lodger" but as an "occupant." For obvious reasons this ruling is popularly
known in England as " the latch-key decision."

[2] The practice of arranging to have the landlord pay the rates has become
much more common in recent years, particularly in the case of workingmen's
tenements.

ment. In other words, the occupant who is assessed for local taxes is put on the voters' list each year without any action on his own part, whereas the non-taxpaying occupant and the lodger have to look after their own interests.

When the overseers have prepared their preliminary list, they transmit it to the town clerk, who posts it, receives any objections which may be made as to improper inclusions or exclusions, and then, in September of each year, hands it, together with such objections as may have been filed with him, to an officer known as the revising barrister.[1] Such an official, who must be a barrister of at least seven years' standing, is chosen for each of the ninety-seven revising districts into which the country is divided, his appointment lying with the senior judge of assize for the county within which the district is situated. These revising barristers go about to the boroughs within their districts, and during the months of September and October hold what are termed "courts of revision," due notice being given in each municipality of the place and date at which such a court is to be held. At this court, or "hearing," all claims regarding the addition or deleting of names are heard and determined, the revising barrister having power to take sworn testimony as to the facts whenever he deems such action desirable. Claims are, as a rule, brought forward by agents representing the political parties concerned, such counsel not only setting forth the facts upon which they base their claims, but also offering briefs and arguments in support of their contentions when they think best. On questions of fact the decision of the revising barrister is final; but a ruling on any point which involves the interpretation of the law may be made the basis of an appeal to the court of King's Bench. In the

Revising the list.

The revising barristers.

Their functions.

Appeals against their decisions.

[1] For all details concerning the compilation of municipal voters' lists, see *Rogers on Elections* (17th ed., by S. H. Day, 3 vols., London, 1894), III. 31–81.

court of the revising barrister the usual rules of evidence are observed; but if a name has been put on the list by the overseers the presumption is in favor of leaving it there. If, on the other hand, the addition of a name is desired, the burden of proof rests on the applicant for enrolment. When the list has passed the revising barrister, it is returned to the town clerk, who has it put into printed form and made ready for the election. No further change may be made except by an order of the court of King's Bench.

Merits of the system.   The English system of compiling and revising the voters' list has, on the whole, been found highly satisfactory. For the great majority of municipal voters it obviates the need of any personal action in order to be assured of a place on the roll, probably four-fifths of the qualified voters having their names regularly carried on the lists as a matter of course. It is only the small householders and the lodgers who need look out for themselves. Not only must these make application each year, but, if their claims happen to be challenged before the revising barrister, they frequently have to disclose under oath the amounts of annual rental paid by them, and other matters which some of them seem to regard as their private affairs. That many of this class, therefore, do not, whether through neglect or through positive disinclination, apply for places on the list may be accounted one of the evil results of the system. At the same time, the English arrangement greatly reduces the liability of danger from sinister practices like "colonization" or the padding of the lists with names of persons who have no legal title to be enrolled. Every name must be related to a specific occupancy, and the essential facts must be established to the satisfaction of the revising officer. Furthermore, the revising barristers have almost invariably been men of high standing, who, having as a rule no local party interests to serve, have performed their functions in a judicial and impartial spirit. Most of them are continued in office for long terms of years, and for their short periods of work receive very substantial remuneration.[1] Their rulings on points of law are sometimes questioned, and are occasionally reversed by the court of King's Bench; but that they have as a class secured an approach to absolute fairness in the compilation and revision of the lists is scarcely to be questioned.

In October of each year the revision of the municipal voters' list is finished, and in November the voters are called to the polls. The sole governing organ of the borough is a borough council, which is made up of a mayor, a number of aldermen, and a number of councillors. Of these members only the councillors are elected by the voters, the mayor and aldermen being chosen by the council. For the election of councillors the borough may be divided into wards and a certain number of councilmen allotted to each; or the election may be by general ticket for the whole municipality. Division into wards may be effected by the borough authorities themselves, provided the consent of the Local Government Board be obtained, — a precaution which aims to prevent any local gerrymandering. Most of the larger boroughs are so divided,[2] but the smaller ones commonly remain undistricted. In either case the councillors are chosen for a three-year term, and one-third of them retire annually; hence an election must ordinarily be held every year. In the large boroughs three councilmen are usually allotted to each ward or district, one being elected each November.

Municipal elections.

Usually held by wards.

[1] The revising barrister's fee is 250 guineas ($1275), for work which seldom takes more than two or three weeks. Further information concerning the functions of these officials may be found in the *Encyclopædia of Local Government Law.*

[2] Liverpool is divided into thirty-five wards, Manchester into thirty, Birmingham into eighteen, and Leicester into sixteen.

Eligibility
of candi-
dates.
In general terms it is true that any voter may be elected to the council; but, as a matter of fact, some voters are not eligible and some persons are eligible who are not voters.   Clergymen, for instance, are permitted to vote but not to stand for election except in the London boroughs. Women voters were until 1907 also ineligible, but they may now be chosen; indeed, it is legally possible that a woman may be selected to fill the post of mayor in any English borough.[1]   Ineligibility further attaches to any person who holds a post of profit that lies within the gift of the council, and also to any one who has either directly or indirectly a share or interest in any contract made with the borough authorities.   This last rule is not, however, applied to disqualify shareholders in a joint-stock corporation which obtains a municipal contract; nor does it render ineligible the publisher of a newspaper which prints municipal advertisements, or persons who covenant with the municipal council for the sale or lease of land or for the loan of money.[2]

Non-resident
candidates.
Apart from the provision permitting the election of women to the council, perhaps the most interesting of the English regulations relating to eligibility is that which allows councillors to be chosen from outside the ranks of voters.   According to this regulation, persons owning property in the municipality, or paying rates above a certain minimum, may be elected to the council if they live within fifteen miles of the borough, although they may not vote if their residence happens to lie beyond the seven-mile limit.   This somewhat anomalous situation is apparently an outgrowth of the provision that a ratepayer may reside

---

[1] 7 Edward VII. c. 33.   In at least one case a woman has been so selected.
[2] Municipal Corporations Consolidation Act, §§ 11–12.   See also *Rogers on Elections*, III. 1–30 ; and Redlich and Hirst, *Local Government in England*, I. 249–252.

anywhere within seven miles of the outer limits of the
city and still be a voter, — a principle that enables large
numbers of business men to retain their franchises in
the municipalities where their chief interests lie, instead
of being enrolled, as in the United States they would be,
on the lists of the suburban towns in which they happen
to live but in the affairs of which they may have comparatively little real interest. As a logical outcome of this
system, there are in the larger English cities like Birmingham, Liverpool, and Manchester some wards in which the
majority of the voters are persons who do not live in the
wards at all, a circumstance which has, as will be seen
later, led to the selection of non-resident councillors. All
this seems natural enough; but in permitting candidacy
to persons who are not only non-residents but non-voters
the English system goes a decided step farther, and gives
to the electorate an unusually broad range of choice.[1] A
circle extending fifteen miles round the outer limits of any
large English city covers over one hundred square miles of
territory, and hence must include almost every one whose
interest in the affairs of the borough is of any importance.

Candidates who are not even voters.

The English municipal system makes no provision for
the holding of any primary or other gathering of partisans
on the eve of an election; indeed, party organizations as
such are not recognized by law as having any rôle in the
making of municipal nominations. A candidate for election to the council is in all cases brought forward by means
of a simple nomination paper. This document, which
must be deposited with the town clerk as least seven days
before the polling, must give the candidate's full name,
place of residence, and occupation, and must bear the names
of at least ten qualified voters of the borough or ward

Nomination of candidates.

---

[1] The influence of these provisions upon the character of the councils in English boroughs is discussed below, pp. 248–249.

within which the nominee seeks election. A voter may sign as many nomination papers as there are posts to be filled, and no more. If he should sign more, his signature becomes ineffective on those which are presented latest to the town clerk.

Mayor determines validity of nomination papers. When the time for receiving nomination papers has expired, the mayor is called upon by the clerk to pass upon the validity of such as have been deposited; and he must do this within three days. If he decides in favor of a paper, there is no appeal from his judgment; but if, on the other hand, he declares against any, an appeal may be taken to the courts. In either case the list of valid nominations is duly posted, and the election proceeds. The roll as announced contains no reference whatever to the political affiliations of any candidate.[1]

No multiplication of candidates. One might reasonably suppose that the facility of nomination would serve to bring a plethora of candidates into the field. On the contrary, however, the number of names eventually printed on the ballot is almost invariably small, rarely exceeding two or three. A dozen nomination papers may be handed in; but the chances are that before the ballots are sent to the printer nearly all the nominees will go to the town clerk and insist that their names shall be withdrawn. Municipal experience in England certainly does not seem to show that the plan of nomination by individual voters multiplies candidates; for the number of men who aspire to public office under this system is proportionately much smaller than in the cities of the United States, where it is far more difficult to get one's name upon the ballot. To a busy man, unless he be possessed of public

---

[1] The regulations relating to municipal nominations are set forth in the Municipal Corporations Act of 1882, §§ 55–56, and the accompanying schedules. A summary on their interpretation by the courts may be found in *Rogers on Elections*, III. 88–96.

spirit, the post of councillor offers so little attraction that he is apt to decline the proffered honor unless some influence is brought to bear upon him to secure his acceptance of a nomination.   In fact, one might almost say that the first qualification for membership in the council of an English borough is a strong reluctance to enter it.

The duty of preparing the announcements, fitting up the polling-booths, having the ballots printed, and making provision for all the incidents of an election rests upon the mayor, who thus becomes the "returning officer" of the municipality.   Though responsible for everything, he does not, however, have to attend to all the details; for the actual work of preparation is usually performed by the town clerk or, in the larger boroughs, by the latter's assistant.   If the number of candidates in nomination does Unopposed elections. not exceed the number of posts to be filled, the mayor declares such nominees to have been elected unopposed, and hence has to make no provisions at all for polling. Elections by acclamation are very common in English boroughs; indeed, it is rather unusual for a contest to occur in every ward of a large borough at one time, and it sometimes happens that candidates are returned by acclamation in all the wards.[1]

When a polling is necessary, the mayor, in addition to Polling procedure. providing the ballots and other necessary papers, must arrange for polling-places, and must see that at least four days before the election the various locations are duly

[1] "In one hundred and three boroughs and urban districts, large and small, taken at random at the elections of 1899, decidedly less than half the seats in the aggregate were contested, while in thirteen of these places there was not a single contest.   Nor does there appear to be any marked difference in this respect between large and small towns, or between places where the nomination is made on party lines and those where it is not." — LOWELL, *The Government of England*, II. 154–155.

published for the information of voters.[1] No official notice of the place and hour of polling is sent to the voters, as in French and German cities; such intimation, if made at all, must come from the candidates or their agents. The polling takes place in some public building if there happens to be one conveniently located for the purpose; otherwise rooms in private buildings are hired for the day and paid for out of the municipal funds. In no case may a polling-place be located in any building which is used for the sale of intoxicants.

Poll officials. When a borough is divided into wards, there must be at least one polling-place for each ward; and each poll must be in charge of an alderman designated for the purpose by the council and constituting, for the polling-day, a "deputy returning officer." If there are more polling-places than there are aldermen, they may be put in care of councillors; but no councillor may preside over a poll in his own district. The poll-clerks and other clerical officials connected with the poll are appointed by the council. All expenses except the cost of printing the ballots are paid by the municipality; the ballots are printed at the expense of the candidates.

How votes are polled. When a voter enters the polling-booth on election day he is provided with an official ballot paper, which he takes into the compartment provided for marking the ballots. His name is thereupon checked off the list. Before receiving the ballot, however, he may be challenged by any of the scrutineers, or polling-agents, present in the room; for every candidate is entitled to be represented at each of the polls by two of these agents, who, like the other persons in the polling-booths, are sworn to secrecy. Not that these scrutineers may question the right of a voter to his

---

[1] The polling procedure in English borough elections is regulated by the Municipal Corporations Act of 1882, § 58, which adopted, with some modifications, the provisions of the Ballot Act of 1872 (35–36 Victoria, c. 33). At present the procedure in borough and parliamentary elections is substantially the same.

place on the list. All they can do is to compel him to establish his identity, and to take oath that he has not already voted elsewhere in the same election. Under no circumstances may a ballot be given to any one whose name is not on the voters' list; there is in England no provision for the method commonly known in American elections as " swearing in " votes.

The ballot is printed on plain white paper and contains **The ballot.** simply the name, residence, and occupation of each candidate; no reference to his party allegiance is permitted. Ordinarily there are only two or three names on the ballot, especially in the larger boroughs, where the councilmen are elected by wards; and these names are printed in alphabetical order, so that no advantage is gained through priority in the filing of nomination papers. After each name is a blank space, in which the voter may indicate his choice by making a cross. He must thus specifically designate each candidate for whom he desires his vote to be recorded, for there is no possibility of voting a whole " slate," or " ticket," by marking a single cross at the head of a column. Indeed, one of the most important differences between the English and the American municipal ballot is to be found in the fact that the former throws the voter wholly upon his personal knowledge of the individual candidates, and in the absence of such knowledge affords him no designations or methods of grouping whereby he may be guided to a choice. If a voter declare himself to be, from blindness or other physical disability, unable to read, his ballots may be marked for him, in accordance with his oral instructions, by the officer in charge of the poll.[1]

[1] An interesting testimony to the regard which the framers of the Ballot Act had for religious scruples is afforded by the provision that, if an election is held on a Saturday, orthodox Hebrews who object, on religious grounds, to voting in the ordinary way may on request have their ballots marked for them by the presiding officer of the poll.

R

Having prepared his ballot, the voter deposits it in the ballot-box, the whole process being thus strictly secret except in the case of one who cannot mark his own paper.

Duration of polling. The polling lasts a single day, and the polls must ordinarily be kept open from eight in the morning till eight in the evening;[1] but if all the registered votes have been polled before eight o'clock, or if the space of an hour shall have passed without a single vote's being cast, the poll may be closed earlier. At the conclusion of the voting the ballots are taken from the box and counted by the officer in charge, assisted by the polling-agents. Any papers which may be objected to by the latter are put into an envelope to be dealt with later, being counted or not meantime, as the officer in charge may decide. The announcement of the result is duly certified to the mayor, to whom the boxes and ballots are likewise returned under seal. **Recounts.** A recount may be had only by application to the courts, but such requests are granted very readily. In all cases a plurality of votes is sufficient to elect a candidate. When two persons receive the same number the decision rests, in a ward contest, with the alderman in charge, but in an election that covers the borough as a whole, with the mayor.

Influence of political parties in municipal elections. To speak in any general terms of the rôle played by political parties in English municipal elections is of necessity to deal unsatisfactorily with an interesting phase of English municipal life; for the subject is not one which may be dealt with properly in a few paragraphs.[2] Party

---

[1] This requirement is fixed by the Election Act of 1885 (48 Victoria, c. 10). Prior to this date the polling continued from nine till four only.

[2] For further and more concrete information on this topic, reference may be made to J. S. Lloyd's *Municipal Elections and How to Fight them* (London, 1906); to the interesting chapter on " Municipal Electioneering and Municipal Politics " in Redlich and Hirst's *Local Government in England*, I. 264–279; to the comprehensive discussion of the relations of " Labor and Politics " in

machinery, party activities, and party methods vary so much in different municipalities, and even in the same borough at different times, that broad generalizations in this field are liable to be misleading. Roughly speaking, however, one may say that in the larger boroughs the local elections are fought out, in the great majority of cases, between candidates who represent the two leading political parties. In most cities this identity of national and local party lines is not openly avowed, — that it exists at all, indeed, would be denied by some representative citizens; but as a matter of fact there is scarcely a large city in England, with the exception of London, in which the municipal campaigns are not conducted along straight party lines, and almost always with some assistance from the national party organizations. It is true, nevertheless, that candidates who call themselves Conservatives sometimes conduct their municipal campaigns as if they were rampant Radicals, and that some of those who profess to be Liberals may stand for everything that is reactionary.

In some few cases these parties are local; that is to say, they are not directly connected with the great national parties. In London, for example, the voters have grouped themselves into two factions, known as the Moderates (or Reformers) and the Progressives; but, although the former group seems to be recruited mainly from those who are Conservatives in national politics, and the latter mainly from those who are Liberals,[1] the two London parties have no direct connection with the two national organi-

Identity of national and local parties.

English cities, by Professor J. R. Commons and Mr. J. W. Sullivan, in the *Report to the National Civic Federation Commission on Public Ownership and Operation*, Pt. II. Vol. II. 1–112; and to the evidence brought together in the *Report of the Royal Commission on the Amalgamation of London* (London, 1894).

[1] See below, pp. 346–347.

zations.   They are local factions, with programmes based
on local issues.   In many of the smaller boroughs, furthermore, party politics play little or no part at all in the local
election campaigns, the contest for office being determined
wholly by the relative personal strength of the candidates.
On the whole, however, the electorates in the larger municipalities divide themselves along pretty nearly the
same lines in local elections as in parliamentary ones.
This identity Just as in a city of the United States party lines may at
is often
lacking. times be broken down and some prominent local issue
thrust to the front, so it often happens that in a large
English borough there may at some election be an unusual display of independence on the part of the voters,
resulting for the time being in an entirely new alignment
of the electorate.   Englishmen, like Americans, readily
concede that party politics are altogether out of place in
municipal affairs; but as a matter of fact the voter who
calls himself a Conservative in parliamentary campaigns
is, in probably nine cases out of ten, true to his party
allegiance in municipal contests.   It is of course substantially the same with adherents of the Liberal party,
and it seems to be equally true of the Labor element,
which has recently risen into importance as a factor in
national politics.   This adherence to party principles in
municipal elections may be attributed mainly to the
fact that in most of the boroughs the only permanent and
effective electoral organizations are the local branches of
the national party machine.[1]

It is true that at English local elections the party whip
is not so readily applied, and when applied is perhaps not
so readily obeyed, as in the United States; for in England
political leaders do not, as they do in America, regard a

[1] Compare the discussion of this topic in Professor Lowell's *Government of
England*, II. 150-153, 231-232.

local defeat as a blow at the national party interests. If Municipal
the party nominee be lacking in personal strength, he can- party or-
ganization
not, as in the United States, count with reasonable certainty in England
and in the
upon party loyalty to carry him through ; on the other United
States.
hand, a strong candidate readily appeals for support outside the ranks of his own party. In England the leeway is
distinctly greater than in the United States. At the
same time, it would be entirely misleading to assert that
national and municipal party lines are not identified, or
even to suggest that this coincidence is not as distinctive
a feature of English municipal politics as it is of American. The candidates for election to the English borough
councils, taken as a whole, count upon their local party
associations to elect them, or at least to muster the major
part of the votes needed for their election. The candidate
who has the backing of neither association can reasonably
look for success only when the local situation is for the
time being abnormal.[1]

It sometimes happens, to be sure, that those who Non-parti-
san organi-
zations.
are in all respects party candidates carefully avoid the
partisan label, and appeal to the electors as non-partisan
aspirants. In many of the boroughs there are electoral
organizations, usually known as Ratepayers' Associations
or Citizens' Unions, which profess to contain members
drawn from both political parties and to eschew partisanship in their attitude toward all municipal affairs. These
associations have their own definite local programmes, and
frequently stand sponsor for candidates either independently
or in coöperation with other organizations ; or they sometimes throw their weight to the side of those party can-

---

[1] "The man who wins a victory under such conditions deserves all the ap-
plause — and every vote — he gets. There are exceptions, but usually the only
position open to the independent candidate is a place at the bottom of the poll."
— J. S. LLOYD, *Municipal Elections and How to Fight them*, 34.

Their influ-
ence.

didates whose election is thought to be desirable.[1] Occasionally candidates who are backed by such organizations succeed in the face of opposition from both political parties; but such success is apt to be exceptional, and is at best spasmodic. Casual spurts of non-partisanship are perhaps more frequent in English boroughs than in American cities; but they are probably no more effectual in diminishing permanently the rôle which party politics play in the affairs of the municipality.

Local party
organiza-
tions.

Local party organizations are, throughout England, cast pretty much in the same mould. There are some variations in different municipalities, it is true; but these divergences are not of much consequence. As all the larger boroughs are divided into wards, the ward serves as the unit of political organization. Each ward of the borough has its ward associations, which comprise within their membership any partisans who wish to join. Sometimes there is a nominal membership fee of a shilling or two; more often there is none at all. The Liberal association of the ward, for instance, is made up of those who profess adherence to the Liberal party and consequently have their names enrolled on the party register. On the eve of an election campaign, each association, which in no respect differs widely from the American ward caucus, meets to elect a ward committee, and by this committee the bulk of the

How con-
structed.

actual work of campaigning is performed. For the borough as a whole each party ordinarily has its central committee, which is usually made up of delegates from the various ward committees. This central committee has its chairman, its secretary, and its treasurer, and sometimes maintains permanent headquarters during the

---

[1] In the *Year Book of the Glasgow Citizens' Union for 1906* may be found a full account of the programme and activities by one of the best known among these organizations.

campaign. It is the custodian of the campaign fund, and is entrusted with the work of coördinating the efforts made to secure the election of party candidates in the various wards. In national election contests these local committees are in close touch with the national bodies that direct party interests throughout England as a whole, and this fact frequently gives the national organizations opportunity to exert direct influence upon the local parliamentary contest.[1] In the municipal campaigns, however, the national bodies almost never interfere at all. Those who are familiar with the mechanism and the activities of party organizations in the United States need not be reminded of the frequent interference in purely local election campaigns which characterizes the work of the state party machines. This intrusion is, of course, dictated by a feeling that the interests of the party in state and city are identical, and that party success or defeat in the municipalities has a direct influence upon the interests of the party in the larger field of political activity. Municipal candidatures in America are, therefore, often inspired and sometimes even dictated from the headquarters of the state organization, a practice which has not in the main contributed to the good governance of the cities, — which has, indeed, more often been very pernicious in its effects. From this sort of interference the local party organizations in England have been almost entirely free ; for the borough associations have virtual autonomy in all that relates to local candidacy and the conduct of local campaigns. In this very important respect the principle of municipal home rule has been carried to its logical conclusion, and the outcome has been of advantage to all concerned.

Relation of local to national party machinery.

In England and in the United States.

---

[1] A very comprehensive discussion of this feature may be found in Lowell's *Government of England*, I. chs. xxvii–xxviii.

A feature of English borough campaigns which impresses the American observer is the very large number of non-resident candidates.   Few principles are more solidly embedded in American minds than that which regards the non-resident aspirant for office as an unwelcome intruder; hence in the United States the candidate who contests a ward in which he does not reside finds himself under a handicap that in most cases utterly eliminates all reasonable hope of success.   In England, public opinion on this matter is very different; for, although the English voter, like the American, undoubtedly prefers his own neighbor to a stranger, he does not allow this preference to militate decisively against the outsider's prospects of election. Evidence of this political hospitality may be found in the fact that in most of the larger English cities the majority of the councilmen live outside the wards which they are elected to represent.   In Liverpool, for instance, only 25 out of 137 members of the council reside in the wards from which they are elected; in Birmingham the percentage of resident councillors is even smaller; in Manchester the non-residents are in the majority; and the same is true of the membership of the London County Council, of which no less than 68 of the 118 councillors live outside the districts which they represent.[1]   In many cases these non-resident councillors reside not only beyond the limits of their wards, but even beyond the limits of the city itself.   Many come from the residential suburbs; and it is not without significance that even the wards which are peopled largely by the laboring classes often choose as their representatives men who live in the fashionable suburban districts.   In fact, this readiness on the part of the people to vote for candidates who are neither of their own neighbor-

[1] *National Civic Federation Commission on Public Ownership and Operation*, Pt. I. Vol. I. 45.

hood nor of their own social class is psychologically one of the most interesting points of contrast between the English and American municipal electorates; and without doubt it affords at least a partial explanation of the marked differences in the general caliber of the municipal councils in the two countries.

The activities of the party leaders in municipal election campaigns are considerably circumscribed by the strictness of the legal regulations relating to campaign methods. These laws, which are substantially the same as those applying to parliamentary elections, are based on the Municipal Elections (Corrupt and Illegal Practices) Act of 1884.[1] By the terms of this important enactment a fundamental distinction is drawn between two classes of practices, which are respectively denominated as " corrupt " and " illegal. " Within the category of "corrupt practices" are comprised all election tactics that are morally reprehensible, such as bribery, intimidation, personation, and the like. Within the category of " illegal practices," on the other hand, are included those incidents of a campaign which, though not involving any moral turpitude, lend themselves to make an election contest unfair to some of the candidates, or undignified, or unnecessarily expensive. Such forbidden practices are, for instance, the hiring of conveyances to take voters to the polls, the providing of decorations, posters, or campaign buttons, and the making of subscriptions to any local enterprise during the period of the election campaign. In fact, the laws proscribe the expenditure of money, either by or on behalf of a candidate, for practically everything outside the strictly necessary expenses of a dignified contest.

Prevention of corrupt and illegal practices at municipal elections.

The machinery provided for the enforcement of these regulations has proved tolerably effective. Within twenty-

[1] 47–48 Victoria, c. 70.

eight days after a municipal election each candidate must transmit to the town clerk an itemized return of his election expenses, accompanied by the necessary vouchers and duly

Limitation of campaign expenses.

verified by affidavit. In a borough or a ward which contains 500 voters or less, a candidate may, for strictly legal expenses, disburse a sum not exceeding twenty-five pounds ($125); when the enrolment is above 500, he may expend not more than threepence for each additional voter. Thus, in a ward which contains 2000 voters the maximum legitimate expenditure would be $250. It is worth noting, moreover, that the restriction applies not only to expenditures made by the candidate himself, but to those made by any of his agents; and by an agent is meant not merely one who has received specific recognition as an election agent, but any supporter whose political relations to the candidate, and whose efforts in his behalf, are such as to

Other restrictions.

give rise to a presumption of agency. In addition to setting a maximum limit to the legitimate expenses of a candidate, the law puts restrictions on many other incidents of an election campaign, — prescribing, for example, the number of committee-rooms that may be maintained, the number of clerks and messengers that may be employed, and so on.

Penalties for violating laws relative to elections.

The penalties provided in the event of violation of the election laws are very severe. If a candidate has been personally guilty of any corrupt or illegal practice, or has himself disbursed more than the established maximum in expenses, he not only loses his election, but is also disqualified from ever holding public office again, and even from voting. If he is not personally guilty of any offence, but has profited by corrupt or illegal practices on the part of his agent, he is unseated, and the disfranchisement is visited upon the agent concerned. He may also be unseated if it is proved that forbidden methods have been extensively employed in his behalf even by persons who cannot in any way be regarded as his agents. The general purpose of the laws is to secure not only an honest election, but also one that will be dignified and absolutely fair to all candidates, no matter what their respective financial resources may be. Although the maximum amount of legitimate expenditure is not unreasonably low, it suffices to preclude any attempt to secure a seat in the council by those whose only important qualification is a readiness to contribute generously to party funds.

The right of a councillor-elect to retain his seat is decided not by the council, but by the courts. Either a defeated candidate or any four qualified voters may protest a municipal election by lodging a petition inside of a given time with the court of King's Bench, which straightway refers such petition to some barrister of not less than fifteen years' standing.[1] This officer proceeds to the borough, where he takes evidence under oath, hears counsel for the petitioner and for the defendant councillor, and determines whether the election laws have been violated. This decision he certifies to the court, which issues a decree confirming or voiding the election, the costs of the protest being apportioned as the trial barrister may deem equitable. By thus giving the work of investigation to a non-partisan and disinterested authority the system proves its wisdom, for there are obvious objections to the practice of permitting members of a borough council, who are very apt to be guided by personal or partisan motives, to pass upon questions relating to the election of their own colleagues. On the other hand, there are equally obvious objections to

Contested municipal elections.

[1] The various legal regulations concerning the trial of election petitions are incorporated in the Municipal Corporations Act of 1882, §§ 87 ff. Full details concerning the present-day administration of the law may be found in R. G. Ellis's article on " Elections and Electors " in the *Encyclopædia of Local Government Law*, III. 16–40.

the plan of thrusting the decision of such matters upon
the regular law courts of the land; for such a policy,
though it may secure the fair determination of matters
at issue, tends to draw the judiciary into the arena of party
politics, and hence, in the long run, is apt to be detrimental to the general prestige of the courts. Of this
we have had, in the United States, convincing proof.

Merits of the
English plan
of hearing
election
protests.

The English system has avoided both evils by committing
the decision of election protests to semi-judicial officers
whom the judges appoint but for whose adjudication the
courts are not responsible. Indeed, the ease with which a
protest may be lodged, the promptness with which the
contestation is heard and determined, and the fairness
which characterizes the verdicts of the deciding authorities
have served to make candidates and their party supporters
recognize that strict observance of the election laws is the
part of prudence in all municipal contests.[1] It is not to
be understood, of course, that corrupt and illegal practices
in English municipal elections have been wholly eliminated
either by the strictness of the laws or by the excellence
of the machinery provided for their enforcement. Candidates may, and sometimes do, while keeping well within
the letter of the law, use tactics which are unfair to their
opponents. At the same time, it is quite beyond question
that the influence of the act of 1884 and of similar enactments has been extremely salutary, and that the legislation
has contributed substantially to the marked improvement
in the general conduct of English elections, both parliamentary and municipal, during the last quarter-century.

Immediately after the annual election the council holds
its organization meeting, at which the successful candidates

[1] The evidence brought together a decade ago by a select parliamentary
committee on the subject of contested elections shows that petitions following
parliamentary elections are not by any means so satisfactorily handled. See
House of Commons Papers (1898), IX. 558.

appear in order to take their oaths of qualification. The Selection of the mayor. first duty of the new council is to elect a mayor, whose task it is to preside over the deliberations for the current year.[1] By the terms of the Municipal Corporations Act of 1835, the mayor was to be chosen from the ranks of the councillors themselves; but the code of 1882 widened the field of choice by permitting the council to select " any fit person from among the aldermen or council, or persons Qualifications for the office. qualified to be such." [2] At the present time it is therefore legally possible for the council to select as mayor of the borough one who is not even a voter in the municipality, provided, however, that he reside within fifteen miles of the borough and is otherwise qualified as a candidate for election to the council. But although the law permits a council to go outside its own membership, and even outside the limits of the electorate, in search of a mayor, this is, of course, not the practice usually followed. In most of the larger boroughs the mayor is selected from the ranks of the council itself, and particularly from among those members who have had one or more terms of service as aldermen. Departures from this policy are doubtless more common now than they were a decade or more ago, for in England the selection of a non-member is apparently not now regarded as unusual enough to attract any comment. At the same time, such a choice is the exception rather than the rule, and it is distinctly unusual in the smaller boroughs.

The selection of a mayor is seldom a difficult problem The council's range of choice. in English municipalities; for the post is not, as it is in the cities of the United States, one of any serious administrative importance. Executive ability and experience are

[1] The mayor's term is ordinarily one year only, but reëlections are common. In some boroughs tradition requires an annual change.

[2] Municipal Corporations Act (1882), § 15.

in no wise essential to the proper performance of mayoral duties; for these, being very largely of a social nature, make heavier demands upon the mayor's purse and personality than upon his skill as a governing authority. He must entertain distinguished visitors to the borough, must assume a prominent part in all civic ceremonies and festivities, and must, above all things, be a leader in local philanthropic enterprises, incidentally contributing with generosity to their exchequers. His only special administrative function is that of presiding at meetings of the council, and even this he need not perform if it be not to his liking. In short, to the end that he may fill his position capably and satisfactorily, the mayor of an English borough must ordinarily be a man of some wealth, preferably with leisure and social attainments.

English mayors usually unpaid. Ordinarily the English mayor receives no stipend. The council is empowered by law to grant him from the borough funds " such remuneration as it may think reasonable " ; but many boroughs pay nothing at all, and, save in the largest boroughs, those which grant remuneration rarely afford anything approaching his personal outlay in the performance of his civic functions. Tenure of the office even for a single year thus involves some financial sacrifice;[1] but as a rule the post is satisfactorily filled without much trouble, for wealth and social aspirations are likely to be more plentiful than administrative energy and experience. It has sometimes been said that a wealthy peer makes an ideal English mayor; at any rate, if any such happens to reside within the fifteen-mile limit he is pretty certain to be invited to the post, and, if necessary, cajoled or persuaded into accepting it. In default of

---

[1] Statements of the mayor's expenditures are, of course, not made public; but tenure of the office in a city like Liverpool or Manchester is estimated to involve an outlay of from $15,000 to $25,000 per year.

a peer, some opulent bourgeois who is willing to prove his liberality may have an opportunity to do so as the chief magistrate of the borough.   Sometimes, it is true, men of slender means are chosen to the mayoralty; but the post presents so little attraction to such men that it is apt to be avoided by them.   This condition of things is by some persons, especially by the labor leaders, regarded as unfortunate; for it practically excludes from the office many who might otherwise be installed for a year or two in fitting recognition of lengthy and faithful service at the council-board.[1]

In most cases the mayor takes an active interest in the affairs of the borough during his term, even if his actual part in local administration is not much more influential than that of the ordinary alderman or councillor.   He presides at the council-meetings, is ex officio a member of all council committees, usually performing actual service on one or more of them, and he may even be chairman of some committee; but he has no veto power over resolutions of the council, makes no important appointments, takes no special part in the preparation of the municipal budget, and exercises no direct control over any of the civic departments.   He is ex officio a justice of the peace, but he very rarely exercises any judicial functions whatever. Hence it is that some English mayors know comparatively little about the actual administration of their municipalities, and that not all of them acquire, while in office, any comprehensive grasp of municipal problems. All this is not meant to imply, however, that the mayor of an English borough is free from copious demands upon his time and attention.   Almost every charitable organization in the borough expects him to preside at its annual

Influence of the mayor in borough administration.

---

[1] See the evidence on this point in the *Report of the Royal Commission on the Amalgamation of London* (1894), especially pp. 313 ff.

meeting, to make a speech in eulogy of its accomplish-
ments, and to subscribe something to its funds. Indeed,
for most local gatherings of a non-political character the
mayor of the borough is, as a matter of course, requisitioned as chairman. In addition he must spend certain
hours of each day in his office at the town hall, where
his chief function is to act as a "repository for every-
body's grievances." So slight is his influence upon the
course of local administrative policy that very rarely can an
English mayor be adjudged, at the close of his term,
either a signal failure or a striking success, though it is
of course true that a man of marked individuality and
personal vigor may use the mayor's prerogatives in such
a way as to leave a distinct stamp upon the affairs of the
municipality. A notable example of such efficiency is

The case of Mr. Chamberlain. seen in the career of Mr. Joseph Chamberlain, M.P., mayor
of Birmingham from 1873 to 1876; but the very fact
that Mr. Chamberlain's administration drew to itself
such marked attention is sufficient proof of its unusual
character. Viewed as a whole, the office of mayor in
England approaches neither in power nor in influence its
prototype in the cities of France, Germany, or the United
States.

The alder-men, how selected. Having selected its mayor, the new borough council
proceeds to choose a certain number of aldermen, the
quota being fixed by law at one-third of the number
of councillors. Liverpool, for instance, has 136 members
in its council, of whom 34 are aldermen and 102 councillors; Birmingham has 72 members, of whom 18 are
aldermen and 54 councillors. The aldermen are chosen
for a six-year term, and one-half retire triennially. The
range of choice is as wide as that for the selection of the
mayor; for the council may either take aldermen from
the ranks of the councillors, or go outside its own mem-

bership and enlist the services of any one who is qualified for election to the council. Usually it advances some of the councillors to the rank of aldermen, and then forthwith holds by-elections in order to fill the vacancies created among the councilmen ; but the practice of choosing as aldermen persons who have not been elected councillors is so common that it cannot be regarded as in any sense unusual or exceptional. Candidates who have failed of election to the council frequently secure places at the council-board in this way ; indeed, the system makes it quite possible for the council to enlist the services of men who, though possessed of marked administrative abilities, may not have the qualities which serve to insure success at the polls. It is, however, not the practice of the council to choose as aldermen citizens who have had no experience in municipal affairs. It may, to be sure, do even this occasionally ; but as a rule it selects men who have at some time or other served one or more terms in the council, or who have in some other way acquired considerable familiarity with local administration. Reëlections, moreover, are common ; and it is not unusual to find aldermen who are serving their third or even their fourth terms. The alderman thus possesses, on the whole, a somewhat more extended experience in municipal management than the councilman does ; hence his presence in the council is supposed to add stability to the body, as well as a tendency to conservatism.

Who are chosen aldermen.

In the selection of aldermen the council is undoubtedly influenced to a large extent by partisan considerations. If a majority of the councillors in any large borough are Liberals in politics, one may rest assured that a majority of the aldermen selected will represent the same political faith. Not that a party majority among the councilmen

Partisan considerations in the selection of aldermen.

s

uses its power to select all the aldermen from among its
own political partisans; on the contrary, the minority
expects, and usually receives, its fair quota. In Birmingham, for example, five of the eighteen aldermen are
Liberals, though nearly four-fifths of the councillors are
Conservatives. In fact, there is in some boroughs a more
or less definite understanding between the leaders of the
two parties that the minority shall in all cases receive
fair consideration when the council proceeds to the selection of aldermen.[1] Another circumstance which helps to
check the force of the partisan motive at the aldermanic
elections is found in the somewhat strong tradition in favor
of reëlecting aldermen whose services have been valuable;
and in addition to this motive, which perhaps in most of
the larger cities continues to be more influential than any
other, considerations of experience and administrative
capabilities are almost always taken well into account.

The alder-
men do not
form a sepa-
rate body.
It should be made entirely clear that the English aldermen do not, like the American, constitute a separate organ of
municipal government. The English council is not a bicameral body: in it councillors and aldermen always sit together.
At the common council-board the votes of councillors and
aldermen have precisely equal weight; and, strictly speaking, the aldermen have no powers of any sort which do
not pertain to the ordinary councillors. They differ in the
methods by which they are elected to office, in length of
term, and in the amount of prestige which attaches to their
respective posts, but not in point of powers. In many
boroughs they hold by custom the chairmanships of some
important council committees; but they are not required
by law to do so. At the council elections they also serve

---

[1] In Leeds, for example, an agreement was made in 1904 that aldermen
should be chosen in exact proportion to the respective strength of the Conservative, Liberal, and Labor parties as shown at the municipal elections.

as deputy returning-officers for the various wards,[1] a practice that has created a somewhat vague relation between the alderman and the ward to which he is posted. Hence an alderman is sometimes spoken of as "representing" such and such a ward. The aldermen are, however, in no sense the representatives of wards; as a matter of fact, several of them may live in one ward and none at all in another, for in the selection of aldermen the council gives very little heed to the matter of geographical distribution. There is, in fact, so little to distinguish the aldermen from the regular councillors that they may be said to constitute hardly more than a special element or group in the council.

The English borough council, made up of the mayor, the aldermen, and the councillors, is the sole organ of borough government. It meets in the town hall at regular intervals, — monthly in the smaller boroughs and fortnightly or weekly in the larger. The date of the annual meeting at which the mayor and aldermen are elected (November 9) is fixed by law; the dates of all other meetings are fixed by the council in its Standing Orders. One-third of the total membership constitutes a quorum. The mayor ordinarily presides; in the event of his absence the council invites one of its own members, usually an alderman, to take the chair. In general the meetings are open to the public, but closed sessions may be decided upon by a majority vote. The rules of order and procedure are such as the council may choose to adopt; but they do not vary greatly in different boroughs, for in the main they follow the usual so-termed "parliamentary procedure." The records are kept by the town clerk, or, in the largest cities, by one of his assistants; and after the council-meetings they are usually printed in the local newspapers. It is of some significance that in most American cities the news-

Organization and procedure of the council.

[1] Municipal Corporations Act, §§ 53, 57, 58, 67.

papers will publish the council minutes only when they are substantially paid for so doing, whereas in the English boroughs they find it worth while to print them gratuitously, because their readers are sufficiently interested in what is taking place in the council-chamber.

The council's powers.

The council is both the legislative and the administrative organ of the English city. Unlike the French, the German, and especially the American plan of municipal government, the English system affords no recognition to the principle of division of powers between legislative and executive organs, and attempts to provide no arrangement of checks and balances. In order to set forth the jurisdiction of the English council, therefore, it is only necessary to discover what powers have been committed to the borough in its corporate capacity, — a task not altogether easy, however, for borough powers are not derived from a single source, nor are those of all the boroughs precisely the same. Of the prerogatives possessed by the French commune one may readily obtain an adequate idea by referring to the Municipal Code of 1884; but of the administrative functions which have been intrusted to the English borough councils one gets a very inadequate idea from an examination of the English Municipal Corporations Consolidation Act of 1882. One may, for instance, search in vain through the provisions of this act for any information concerning the powers of the borough council in such matters as street improvements, public lighting, sewerage, water supply, parks, housing, and various other departments of local administrative activity over which the borough authorities do, as a matter of fact, exercise jurisdiction. Borough

Whence derived:

powers do not, indeed, rest upon any one enactment; they are obtained from a variety of sources, of which the act of 1882 is but one, and perhaps not the most important one. Parliament has never been partial to the practice of conveying privileges to subordinate authorities in broad and general terms; it has rather dealt piecemeal with the various branches of local jurisdiction by conferring powers at different times, by different enactments, and frequently in different degrees.[1]

The first and oldest source of borough powers is, of course, the common law. For centuries before the passing of the Municipal Corporations Act of 1835 the boroughs had ranked as corporations aggregate, with all the common-law powers ordinarily attaching to such bodies,— as, for example, the right to sue and be sued in the regular law courts of the land, to hold property, to borrow money on the corporate credit, and to have corporate seals. These powers the act of 1835 did not take away; it merely rendered more effective and more nearly uniform the channels through which they should thenceforth be exercised. Hence, even at the present day, some few borough powers of importance have their real source in the common law and not in any statute or statutes; and when questions relating to the interpretation of these powers arise they must be referred to the municipal jurisprudence of the ante-reform period.

1. from the common law;

By the act of 1835, however, as amended and recast in that of 1882 and in subsequent amending enactments, the boroughs have gained some powers which at common law they did not possess, — as, for example, the right to establish and maintain local police systems. On the other hand, some of their ancient privileges — such as their authority in the matter of judicial administration — have been taken away from them. None of the general municipal statutes have, however, attempted either to extend or to narrow ma-

2. from the Municipal Corporations Act;

---

[1] The most convenient handbook of borough powers is A. E. Lauder's *Municipal Manual* (London, 1907); but there are many special treatises dealing with particular services.

terially the scope of municipal activities; they have in the main dealt with matters affecting the organization of the borough administration.

Most of the important powers now possessed by the English boroughs, especially those which have to do with the provision of public services, are derived not from either of the two foregoing sources, but from a multitude of special enactments made by Parliament from year to year, some of them giving special powers to all the boroughs, others to only a limited number. Some of these measures, like the Public Health Act of 1875,[1] are mandatory: they confer on all the boroughs powers of which they must avail themselves. Others, like the Light Railways Act of 1896,[2] are permissive or adoptive: they confer powers upon such boroughs as may choose to "adopt" their empowering provisions in the manner they prescribe. Still others, like the Housing of the Working Classes Act of 1890, are in part mandatory and in part permissive. The question whether the municipality will or will not assume permissive powers conferred upon the borough by statute is always decided by the council on a two-thirds vote; for the English authorities have thus far manifested no disposition to follow the practice, so common in American cities, of submitting such matters by referendum to the whole municipal electorate. Even with the two-thirds restriction, their policy of adoption has no doubt operated in the direction of conservatism; for English cities have not on the whole shown any unseemly haste in assuming the somewhat extensive privileges put at their disposal by the national legislature.[3]

---

[1] 38–39 Victoria, c. 55.   [2] 59–60 Victoria, c. 48.

[3] The procedure followed in "adopting" legislation is fully explained in the article on "Adoptive Acts" by Messrs. H. J. Comyns and W. V. Ball in the *Encyclopædia of Local Government Law*, I. 234-269.

A fourth and increasingly important source of English 4. from private acts of Parliament. municipal powers, especially in the larger boroughs, is the multitude of so-called " private " acts by means of which Parliament has, from time to time, been in the habit of granting special powers to designated cities. When the provisions of a general adoptive statute do not seem to suit the particular needs of any borough, the local authorities may apply to Parliament for a special enactment drafted in accordance with their own ideas. Applications of this sort are so extremely numerous, and are so readily granted by Parliament, that in the minds of many persons this feature of English legislative practice constitutes an important defect in the whole system of relations between the central and local governments. The number of private Importance of this source. bills that pass Parliament at every session is very great; indeed, there are some large English boroughs that let hardly a session go by without trying to obtain special powers or privileges of one sort or another. There seems to be no limit to the variety of concessions asked for: authority to regulate matters not ordinarily within the jurisdiction of the borough, powers to expropriate property for special purposes, wider latitude in the provision of public services, are among the things petitioned for almost every year. So universal, in fact, is the practice of applying to Parliament for special privileges, that the consideration of private bills presented not only by the boroughs, but by the other local authorities, lays a heavy burden upon the time and patience of the national legislative bodies.[1]

This ready resort to Parliament for special legislation Private-bill procedure. is no doubt due in part to the facilities which have been afforded for securing it. When a borough desires some

---

[1] An interesting discussion on " The Rise and Development of Legislation by Private Bill " may be found in the Royal Statistical Society's *Journal*, LXIX. 1–31 (March, 1906).

special privilege or power, the council takes the first step by passing a resolution authorizing the town clerk or some other solicitor to draft a bill embodying the authority desired. This bill, accompanied by a petition from the council asking for its enactment, is handed to some member of Parliament, — preferably the member who represents the borough in question, — and is by him brought forward in the regular way.[1] If it proposes to lay any new duties upon a government department, or if, on the other hand, its proposals seem to be of sufficient importance to entitle it to a place in the category of public bills, Parliament may refuse to permit its introduction as a private one. Once introduced, however, it is, in accordance with the standing rules of parliamentary procedure, submitted to a preliminary scrutiny by the lord chairman of committees of the House of Lords and the chairman of committees of the House of Commons, who in their examination are assisted by their legal advisers. At this point changes in the bill may be insisted upon. Meantime copies of the measure are sent to all the authorities concerned, that an opportunity may be afforded for the development of any local opposition to the bill. The "Standing Orders of Lords and Commons relative to Private Bills" are very stringent in their provisions, demanding especially that their requirements in the matter of notifying interested parties, of filing plans, and so on must be complied with strictly if the measure is to proceed any farther. When a measure is presented in due form and meets with no opposition, it is usually, after a little further scrutiny, put through its various readings without difficulty. When, on the other hand,

[1] For a more detailed discussion of private-bill procedure, see F. Clifford, *History of Private Bill Legislation* (2 vols., London, 1885–1887) ; L. Macassey, *Private Bills and Provisional Orders* (London, 1887) ; F. G. Wheeler, *The Practice of Private Bills* (London, 1900) ; and the voluminous *Report of the Select Committee on Private Business* (1902).

its passage is opposed by individuals, corporations, or other local authorities, it is referred, usually after its second reading, to a select committee of the House in which the measure was first introduced. This committee duly opens a hearing or inquiry at which petitioners or remonstrants are at liberty to present their respective arguments either personally or by counsel whom they may choose to employ. At this hearing the borough is represented either by a parliamentary agent or by some barrister employed to "promote" the measure.[1] If the promoting requires the making of payments out of the borough funds (as it almost always does), the action of the council in presenting the bill to Parliament must be submitted to the voters of the borough, and must be sanctioned by them. This referendum to secure the assent of the electorate to paid promotion of private bills constitutes almost the sole use of the plebiscite procedure in English boroughs; but as a rule pollings of this sort, although they occasionally develop a spirited opposition to the council's projects, arouse little or no interest among the voters. In addition to the assent of the people, the sanction of the Local Government Board must be had before any such expenditure may be incurred; but its consent is not often withheld. The opponents of a private bill, on the other hand, may spend what they please in employing counsel and other legal agencies to the advancement of their cause, an arrangement which attracts to London a considerable body of "parliamentary agents," who make a specialty of practice

Margin notes: Hearings on private bills.

Margin notes: Expenses of promoting private legislation.

[1] Many years ago the question arose as to whether parliamentary agents employed to promote private bills for a borough might legally be paid out of public funds. In an important case (Regina *vs.* Sheffield, *Law Reports*, 6 Queen's Bench, 652) it was decided by the higher court that such payments might not be made legally. As a result of this decision, Parliament in 1872 passed the Borough Funds Act (35-36 Victoria, c. 91), a statute which, as somewhat amended in 1903, now affords legal authority for such disbursements, provided various conditions have been fulfilled.

before select committees.   It may be noted, however, that
the select committee does not hold "hearings" in the
American sense; that is to say, it does not afford indis-
criminate opportunities of protest to all who happen to
regard the proposed bill with disfavor whether they be
directly interested in or affected by its provisions or not.
It gives audience to no one, either personally or by counsel, who has not some tangible interest in the bill.

Relation of the government departments to private-bill legislation.

When the committee has heard both sides, it awaits a
report on the merits of the proposed measure from the appropriate government department, — from the Local Government Board, for example, or the Board of Trade, or the Home
Secretary.   This examination of all private bills by the departments has in recent years become so thorough and
careful that an adverse report from this quarter is now
practically fatal to the success of any measure ; for, although the committee itself may favor a bill which is thus
opposed by a government department, it forwards the departmental report along with its own, and the former, of
course, carries due weight when the matter comes up in
either house of Parliament.   When the committee has
completed its consideration, it may either reject the measure in whole or in part, or report the bill to Parliament
with or without amendments.   If it pursues the latter
course, and if the government department has also indorsed
the measure, the passage is virtually assured; though it
occasionally happens that a private bill encounters serious
opposition down to the very time of its final enactment.

Objections to the system.

The whole system of private-bill legislation is not a
little open to criticism.   In the first place, it is costly to
all parties concerned; for, when a measure is opposed,
parliamentary agents and counsel must be employed at
high rates, and in many cases expert witnesses must be
brought before the committee at the expense of those in

whose behalf they testify. Then, too, the process is rather slow ; it often happens that a private measure does not receive its place on the statute-books until a year and a half after the petitioners make their first preparations. The system also lays a heavy tax upon the time and energies of the national legislators, who should be left free to devote themselves to the consideration of broader and more important matters. Indeed, in view of the inability of the committees to give to every measure the detailed inspection which it deserves, it may well be doubted whether many provisions would not slip through Parliament without attracting proper attention, were it not for the watchful eyes of the government departments. In this supervision by the national executive authorities, English legislative procedure has provided a feature which the American system very sadly lacks, — the securing of some approach to uniformity in the field of private legislation. On the other hand, the English method affords less publicity to private measures than do the legislative systems of the American states ; for in England none but the parties directly concerned are notified that a bill is before a committee, and only those directly interested are permitted to appear in support of it or in opposition to it, whereas in the United States the hearing on every measure is publicly advertised and may be supported or opposed before the committee by any citizen, no matter whether he be directly interested in it or not.

The fifth and last source of borough powers are the so-termed "provisional orders," issued either to boroughs as a class or to specified places by government departments acting under authority of Parliament. Thus the Local Government Board may, by provisional order, permit a borough to extend its water service, or construct additional sewers, or change its boundaries, or municipalize

5. Powers derived from "provisional orders."

the local gas service ; the Board of Trade may by provisional order empower a borough to establish a municipal
electric-lighting plant, to buy out a street-railway company, or to provide municipal docks; and the Board of
Education, or the Board of Agriculture, or any other
central department may, within its respective sphere, confer various powers.

Provisional orders are granted in response to requests
from the borough authorities ; but in each case an inquiry
must first be undertaken by some officer of the department, and at this inquiry the application may be opposed
by any one interested. If the request for a provisional
order be refused, the borough may try to secure the
desired authority by means of a private bill ; if it be
granted, the authority conferred upon the municipality
becomes practically effective at once, even though the order

Confirma-
tion of pro-
visional
orders by
Parliament.
must eventually be confirmed by Parliament. As a matter of practice, large numbers of these provisional orders
are commonly embodied in a single confirmation bill and
provided with parliamentary sanction together. Parliament may, of course, refuse approval. It occasionally happens, too, that members of one or other of the Houses may
oppose an individual order contained in one of the bills ;
but such opposition is rarely of any avail. The method of
acquiring special borough powers by means of provisional
orders has grown in favor during the last two decades ;
for the plan, involving as it does a skilled administrative
inquiry into the merits of an application rather than a
duel of paid agents before a committee of parliamen-
tarians, is more speedy, less costly, and in almost every other
way more satisfactory than the procedure by private bill.

From the foregoing summary one may obtain some idea
of the variety of sources from which the English borough
draws its corporate powers, and may understand how diffi-

cult it is to speak broadly of the "powers of English municipal councils." Besides the considerable range of common-law jurisdiction and the many statutory powers of a mandatory nature possessed by all borough councils alike, there is also the wide scope of authority conferred by general statutes in adoptive form, though whether or not this authority has been formally "adopted" by a borough one must learn in each case. Then there is the multitude of private acts which have given special powers to particular municipalities, and the still larger host of provisional orders, either confirmed or pending confirmation, which have done the same. If one wishes, therefore, to know the exact powers of the borough council of Liverpool or Birmingham or Manchester, one must explore all five sources, — a task so great as to preclude all but the legal experts of the municipality from really knowing what powers the council possesses at any given time. The ordinary citizen knows those powers only in a very general way.

This lack of uniformity in municipal powers is of course very confusing to the student of local government; and yet the English system of granting different privileges to different boroughs has much in its favor. Since the conditions and needs of a municipality vary with its size and situation, they cannot be so adequately provided for by general enactments as by specific laws and orders, a fact which the English practice recognizes by permitting the adaptation of local powers to local problems with a degree of precision unknown to the legislative systems of other states. It allows Parliament to give to certain boroughs privileges which, rather than give them to all municipalities, it would probably give to none. It permits every application for added local powers to be dealt with on its own merits ; for, though following general rules to

Merits and defects of the English system of granting local powers.

some extent, Parliament has been disposed to act on the
principle that a borough itself knows best what it wants
in the way of legislation, and that it should get exactly
what it asks for unless good reason for refusal can be shown.
One might almost say that with the growth in importance
of the system of giving authority by provisional orders,
the adaptation of borough powers to local conditions has
become about as effective as it can possibly be made.   In
this respect the English situation has come to differentiate
itself sharply from the condition of affairs which exists in
many of the American states, where constitutional provisions absolutely prohibit the giving to one city of any
privilege which is not accorded to all.

Variety and
unity of
powers en-
joyed by
boroughs.

Although the English system of granting local powers
leaves room for a wide departure from uniformity in
borough jurisdiction, as a matter of fact the variation is
not so great as might be expected; and it remains entirely
possible to summarize in general terms and with reasonable
accuracy the powers which usually appertain to the
borough council as the sole governing organ of the municipality, due allowance being made, of course, for important
differences here and there.   In dealing with this topic,
however, it appears advisable to repeat at the outset that
the English council is both the chief executive and the sole
legislative organ of the municipality, and that in English
municipal government there is no recognition of the principle of " division of powers " which has been so scrupulously respected in American city administration.   The
English system does not seek to embody any arrangement
of checks and balances; on the contrary, it concentrates
all local authority and responsibility, legislative as well
as administrative, in the hands of a single organ, and that
organ is the council.

As the legislative authority of the borough, the council

has power to make by-laws or local ordinances for the Legislative protection of the public health, for the security of life and powers of the borough property, for the regulation of traffic in the streets, for the council. abatement of nuisances, and for promoting in various other ways the well-being of the citizens, provided always that such ordinances are not repugnant to the general laws of the land.[1]   These by-laws are usually drafted, at the request of the council or of one of its members, by the town clerk ; they are introduced by some individual councillor or alderman, and must be submitted to the three regular readings required by the Standing Orders of the council. If the projected by-law is of any importance, it is usually considered by a committee of the whole council before it goes to its third and final reading.   It may be passed by a simple majority of votes in the council ; and, as a rule, it becomes effective at once, for the mayor of an English borough has no veto power, either absolute or qualified. In the case of by-laws relating to the protection of the public health and a few other matters, however, the action of the council may be overridden by the Local Government Board ; indeed, the power of disallowance possessed by the different government departments in relation to municipal by-laws has grown considerably in recent years.   Nevertheless, over a wide range of local matters the borough councils still have almost entire freedom of action.

Next in importance to the council's legislative authority Financial are its powers connected with the financial affairs of the powers. borough.   The council is the custodian of the " borough fund," which is the term used to include proceeds from property owned by the municipality, payments for public

---

[1] The scope of the council's powers in these various fields of local administration is dealt with at length in W. C. Glen's *Laws of Public Health* (12th ed., London, 1899), and in F. N. Keen's *Urban Police and Sanitary Legislation* (London, 1904).

franchises, profits of civic enterprises, together with fines, fees, and other incidental revenues. The English borough, it may be explained, is sometimes an extensive holder of real property, much of which it leases for long terms to private parties, and from which it frequently derives a large annual income.[1] Over the proceeds accruing from the use of this property the power of the council is complete, but its jurisdiction in regard to the selling, mortgaging, or leasing of the lands is restricted by the municipal code and other legislation.[2] Save in exceptional cases, for example, the council can grant no lease of municipal property for a period exceeding thirty-one years without the

The "borough fund."

permission of the Local Government Board. In addition to the revenues annually derived from municipal property, the "borough fund" is considerably augmented, in a large municipality, by the receipts from holders of public franchises (such as water, lighting, or tramway companies) or by the profits of direct municipal operation of these services.[3] Many of the boroughs, moreover, obtain substantial yearly additions to their funds from market tolls, port dues, and similar sources. In 1905 the borough of Birkenhead received more than $30,000 from the operation of its ferries alone, a sum which more than covered its total expenditures for sewerage and fire protection.[4]

Under the authority and at the discretion of the council,

---

[1] The city of Bristol, for example, receives about $125,000 per annum in rentals of leased property ; and the borough of Doncaster, with a population of less than 30,000, receives about the same amount. See *Municipal Year Book of the United Kingdom*, 1906, pp. 78, 105.

[2] For the detailed restrictions, see "The Acquisition, Sale, and Letting of Land by Local Authorities" in the *Encyclopædia of Local Government Law*, I. 114–155.

[3] Elaborate statistics relating to borough income from public services are compiled in the National Civic Federation's *Report on Public Ownership and Operation*, especially Part II. Vol. II. *passim*.

[4] *Municipal Year Book of the United Kingdom*, 1906, p. 62.

the borough fund is, so far as it goes, applied to the payment of annual municipal expenditures. If it suffices to pay these expenses, no borough rates or annual taxes are levied; but, since it is rarely found to be adequate, the council almost invariably has to levy a "rate" of so many shillings or pence per pound upon the rental value of all real property within the municipality. This rental value is obtained by estimating the amount of clear annual rent which any parcel of real estate yields to its owner; but the rate is levied upon the tenant, not upon the landlord, unless it happens that the latter is tenant as well. Unoccupied real property is thus not "rated" at all. The assessment of rateable values may be made for the council by its own assessors; but this procedure is rarely followed. As a rule, the council accepts the valuations that have already been fixed by the "overseers of the poor," officials who are required by the terms of the national Poor Law to assess rental values as a basis for the annual levy of a special "poor rate," which is determined and the proceeds of which are disbursed by a special local authority, the "guardians of the poor." Accepting the figures of the overseers, the council, after it has estimated the municipal expenditure for the ensuing year, and has likewise reckoned the amount of income which will be derived from sources other than taxation, proceeds to fix its "borough rate," in determining which it has entire discretion.[1]

In most English boroughs the proceeds of the borough rate form the chief source of municipal revenue. In some cases, as has been pointed out, the borough fund is of

The levying of "rates" or local taxes.

---

[1] For a discussion of the law and practice of borough rating, see the *First Report of the Royal Commission on Local Taxation* (1899); W. C. Ryde's *Law and Practice of Rating* (London, 1904); E. M. Konstam's *Rates and Taxes* (London, 1906); and the same writer's "Rates and Rating" in the *Encyclopædia of Local Government Law*, V. 311–468.

high importance; but it very rarely exceeds the income from rates.[1] English cities, like American, obtain most of their revenues by levying direct taxes upon real property. They have also, of course, their share, and in some cases a very important one, of the large sums which the English national government distributes each year among the local authorities; but in the determination of this branch of local income the councils obviously have no jurisdiction.

The council's control of expenditures.

Besides being the receiving agent of the municipality, the borough council is also its appropriating organ; for it determines, practically without interference from any outside authority, the annual expenditures of the borough. Early in every calendar year it is the duty of each of the council's various committees to determine the amount that will be needed to carry on the work of the department over which it has supervision. This estimate is prepared by the committee in consultation with the permanent expert officials of the department, the basis of computation being usually the expenditures for pre-

The municipal budget.

vious years. The committees' estimates are then commonly sent to the finance committee of the council, and by it are collated and arranged into a comprehensive municipal budget, which its chairman lays before the council at a regular meeting. The items in this budget are next taken up one by one by the council in committee of the whole, and during this consideration such changes may be made as a majority of the councillors agree upon. Items may be stricken out, increased, diminished, or allowed to stand, the council being particularly free from hesitation in paring down committee estimates which seem to be too high. When the budget has been finally

---

[1] Expenditures under the Public Health Act are provided for in the General District Rate.

agreed upon by the council, each committee is authorized to expend the amount credited to it in the appropriations, a task which it forthwith proceeds to do. If the initial appropriations prove to be inadequate, a supplementary budget is presented by the finance committee later in the year.

As compared with the budget procedure in the cities of France, Prussia, or the United States, the English system may seem to afford a minimum of assurance in the direction of economy. The members of the finance committee who present the list of proposed appropriations to the council, are in no way responsible for the items contained in it; indeed, they may stanchly oppose the adoption of some of them. Nor for changes made while the budget is under consideration by the council is there any responsibility except that which may be attached to a shifting majority of the councillors. The municipal budget does not, as in Prussia, require the concurrence of two separate organs of administration; it does not, as in France, need the approval of any national officer or board of officers; nor does it, as in the United States, encounter any check in the way of a mayoral veto authority. It goes into effect as soon as it passes the council by a simple majority vote; and, if the voter regards its appropriations as excessive, his only remedy is to record his vote, at the next election, against those councillors from his own ward who may have helped to put the budget through. This redress is not very satisfactory, however; for appropriations are passed by the council as a whole, and the councillors as a whole do not come before the voter on his ballot. Decentralization of power and diffusion of responsibility are, indeed, the most outstanding features of the English system of municipal appropriations.

But while the channels through which the council exer-

The English budget procedure compared with methods of cities in other countries.

cises its powers in regard to municipal expenditures may seem, on their face, to put a premium on extravagance, and while in American cities a similar system, generally in vogue a half-century ago, did actually encourage every councilman to raid the civic treasury for the advantage of his own ward whenever he had opportunity, the experience of English boroughs seems to justify the existing arrangements as entirely efficient and satisfactory in actual operation. English municipal administration has not been conducted in wasteful fashion; on the contrary, there are few English boroughs which cannot give lessons in civic thrift to even those few American cities that profess to be bending every energy in the direction of economy. The situation merely adds its testimony to the truth of the popular feeling that the personnel of the appropriating authority, and not the procedure under which the appropriations are made, is the vital factor in determining the financial policy of any municipality.

The local borrowing power.

A third financial power of the council is its right to borrow on the credit of the municipality.[1] In all proposals for incurring civic indebtedness the initiative belongs to the council, but no permanent debt may be incurred without the approval of the central authorities. This approval may be, and often is, had through the provisions of a general or a private act of Parliament; but more often permission to borrow is obtained from one or other of the various government departments. For borrowing funds to erect public buildings the approval of the national Treasury must be secured; for raising loans to provide for sewer construction, the erection of hospitals, and other works which the boroughs are by statute compelled to

[1] The best short summary of borough borrowing powers is W. J. Jeeves's article on "Loans" in the *Encyclopædia of Local Government Law*, IV. 187–245.

supply, the consent of the Local Government Board is required. If a borough proposes to municipalize its tramways and to get the necessary capital by the issue of municipal bonds, it must have the approval both of the foregoing board and of the Board of Trade. In no case may the borough council authorize borrowing of its own sole authority; it must always have the countenance of some designated national officer or body. This approval, moreover, is given or withheld on the merits of the individual application; for there is no rigid rule as to the proportion which the gross debt of the borough may bear to the municipality's annual income, or to its assessed valuation, or to any other gauge of its financial resources. In a word, English cities, unlike those of the United States, have no fixed "debt limits." A borough may not borrow a single shilling as a permanent charge upon the municipality without the prior consent of some national authority; but with this permission it may incur indebtedness without any legal limit. Central supervision of all local loans.

In granting approval to projects for municipal borrowing, the central authorities carefully circumscribe the discretion of the borough councils as to the form of bonds to be issued, the rate of interest to be paid, and the provisions to be made in the way of sinking funds or other arrangements for the repayment of the loan on the expiry of the term for which it was contracted. The provisions in regard to sinking funds are usually of the strictest sort, — a reason, it may be, why many of the larger boroughs prefer to obtain their borrowing powers by applying to Parliament for private acts rather than by asking the appropriate boards for provisional orders. Strictness of this supervision.

Both Parliament and the government boards have been so liberal in approving projects of municipal borrowing that during the last few decades many of the boroughs have increased their funded indebtedness at a rapid rate, much more rapidly, indeed, than they have increased their population or the value of their rateable property. This development has created some misgivings in various quarters, and in many of the boroughs it has resulted in a marked increase in the annual tax rate; but the national government, far from giving any sign of subjecting the councils to a tighter rein in the matter, has for many years actually loaned funds to the municipalities, and this policy it still continues to pursue. All this is not meant to imply that the borough councils have been reckless in their applications for power to borrow, or that funds obtained by the issue of borough bonds have not, in the great majority of cases, been really needed for advancing the material interests of the municipalities. On the contrary, a large part of the total borough debt of England is offset by the civic ownership of productive enterprises — gas plants, water services, tramways, workingmen's dwellings, and so forth — which yield good returns upon the moneys invested. Notwithstanding these advantages, however, it is evident that the necessity of having the central authorities pass upon every loan project does not of itself serve to prevent a rapid expansion of local liabilities, or to afford any adequate protection against the usual consequence — an increase in local taxes.

Central control not wholly effective in checking local extravagance.

Administrative powers of the council.

Important as are the legislative and financial powers of the council, they are fully matched in scope and in significance by its administrative jurisdiction, which, with only two exceptions, covers everything that may properly be regarded as a branch of municipal activity, and is exercised by the council directly and entirely, without participation by any other local authority whatsoever. One of the two exceptions to this rule relates to the dispensation of public charity, a matter which by the act of 1834 and amending statutes is put in charge of local boards of guardians elected for the poor-law unions.[1] Every large borough forms at least one of these unions, and some of the largest form two or three; hence borough and union boundaries do not always coincide. A special poor rate is levied in each union, the amount being fixed by the Board of Guardians and the levy being made upon rateable values assessed by officials known as overseers of the poor. The custody and disbursement of the funds thus raised lie with the guardians, who have full charge of both in-door and out-door relief, including the administration of workhouses and other local institutions of public charity.[2]

Council does not administer system of poor relief.

The other exception to the council's absolute power of administration has to do with the granting of licenses for the sale of intoxicating liquors. Those who framed the Municipal Corporations Act of 1835 proposed to intrust this authority to the council; but the objections in the House of Lords were so strongly urged that the provision was finally eliminated and this branch of local jurisdiction was left with the justices of the peace. At the present time applications for licenses are made to the justices of the administrative county in which the borough is situated, and are granted or denied by them on a majority vote in special session; but the enforcement of all regulations governing the sale of intoxicating liquors is in the hands

Does not control licensing.

---

[1] 4–5 William IV. c. 76. The provisions of the Unemployed Workmen Act are, however, in municipalities of over 50,000, administered by the council.

[2] A short but comprehensive survey of local poor-relief administration may be found in Redlich and Hirst's *Local Government in England*, II. 203–223. For further information, see T. W. Fowle's *Poor Law* (2d ed., London, 1893), P. F. Aschrott's *The English Poor-Law System* (London, 1902), S. Lonsdale's *English Poor Laws* (London, 1897), and the *Fabian Society Tracts*, Nos. 44 and 54. The annual reports of the Local Government Board contain a great deal of material, and so do the general orders issued by this body and collected in W. C. Glen's *Poor-Law Orders* (11th ed., London, 1898).

of the local police, who are under the supervision of a committee of the council.

Until 1902 local education was another department over which the council had no jurisdiction; but by the Education Act of that year the administrative authority hitherto exercised by the elective school board of the borough was transferred to the council,[1] and is now exerted by one of its committees, the members of which may be taken wholly from within the ranks of the councillors or in part from outside.

Wide scope of the council's administrative jurisdiction. With respect to two important local matters, therefore, — poor relief and licensing, — the council has no jurisdiction; but in all other departments of municipal activity it is the sole directing organ. It has charge of all matters relating to the building and maintenance of streets, pavements, parks, and public buildings. As the local sanitary authority, it is charged with the administration of the Public Health Act and other mandatory legislation relating to the construction of sewers, the maintenance of isolation hospitals, and so on. It is intrusted with the task of providing, either directly or through an enfranchised company, a system of water supply. By a series of adoptive acts of Parliament it has been invested with wide powers in respect to the establishment and control of lighting and tramway services, utilities which it may, subject to the approval of the appropriate government departments,[2] provide either directly or through grants of franchises to private entrepreneurs, in the former case the council directly controlling all matters relating to the service and carrying on the work of

---

[1] 2 Edward VII. c. 42. Control of elementary education in boroughs of less than 10,000 was not transferred. See Graham Balfour's *Educational Systems of Great Britain and Ireland* (2d ed., London, 1904).

[2] See below, pp. 330–332.

detailed administration through its own committees.[1]
The borough council has further been empowered to
embark upon schemes for the better housing of the
working classes, and to provide public baths and wash-
houses, not to speak of museums, art galleries, and places
of recreation, markets, cemeteries, ferries over rivers,
and a multitude of minor public utilities.[2] Having provided all these services, it must also regulate them, and
provide also police and fire protection, two important
municipal departments over which it has entire control.
In short, the council is (with the two exceptions above
noted) the sole local authority exercising administrative
powers within the limits of the borough; hence, to name
its powers is merely to name the powers which may be
exercised by the borough as a public corporation. There
has in England been no apportionment of administrative
jurisdiction among independent boards or commissions
such as one commonly finds in the cities of the United
States; and there has, furthermore, been little or no
assumption of municipal functions by authorities who
owe their appointment to the state. The work of the
central authorities, as will be seen more clearly later on,
is that of supervision only; it is never that of direct
adminstration of civic departments. To the American
student, indeed, the dominating place of the council in
the affairs of the borough is perhaps the most salient
feature of the English municipal system.[3]

Notwithstanding the full and undivided control exer-

Other public utilities.

Preëminence of the council in administration.

---

[1] Much data concerning the manner in which this administration by council
committees is carried on may be found in the *Report of the Select Committee
on Municipal Trading* (1903) ; and in the National Civic Federation, *Report on
Public Ownership and Operation*, Pt. II. Vol. II.

[2] The scope and limitations of these powers may be found, in summarized
form, in Lauder's *Municipal Manual.*

[3] *Cf.* Frederick Howe, *The British City* (New York, 1907), especially ch. ii
(" The Town Council ").

The council's committees. cised by the council over the various civic departments, it is obvious that so large an assembly cannot well attend directly to the host of administrative details which in every great city must receive attention from some official organ. Most of these duties the council therefore thrusts upon its standing committees, of which in every large city there are a good many, usually selected by the borough council at its November session in each year. The national laws require that every borough council shall have at least two committees — the watch committee and the education committee, which are known as "statutory committees";[1] but it may have as many others as seem desirable, and a large borough usually has a dozen or "Standing" committees. more. Some of them, known as "standing committees," retain their organization throughout the year, dealing with all matters that arise from time to time within their allotted spheres of jurisdiction. Liverpool, for example, has "Special" committees. fourteen standing committees,[2] Birmingham eighteen,[3] and York twelve.[4] Other committees, commonly known as "special" ones, are organized as occasion may require, and are assigned such duties as the council may determine, notably the promoting of private bills before Parliament. The standing committees have regular meetings, but the special ones convene only when necessity arises. Most of the standing committees each have one or more sub-committees, to which they depute some of the routine work which they Sub-committees. would otherwise have to perform themselves. These sub-committees report, of course, to the main committee, and not directly to the whole council. Every councillor and alderman finds himself appointed to at least one of the

[1] The former is rendered obligatory by the Municipal Corporations Act of 1882, the latter by the Education Act of 1902.

[2] City of Liverpool, *Municipal Year Book*, 1906, pp. 70–95.

[3] City of Birmingham, *Municipal Diary*, 1905–1906, pp. 18–45.

[4] City of York, *Year Book*, 1905–1906, pp. 33–40.

foregoing committees; some serve on two or three; and by custom the mayor is ex officio a member of them all, though he rarely takes any active part in their deliberations. In addition the council annually delegates some of its members to sit as representatives of the borough upon joint committees with members of the county council. These joint committees are intrusted with the supervision of enterprises that are of common interest to county and borough alike, — such, for instance, as the protection of riverways from obstruction and pollution.[1] Finally, the council, in order to facilitate its business, frequently resolves itself into a "committee of the whole," a form of organization which it uniformly adopts when it has the local budget under consideration item by item.

Joint committees.

"Committee of the whole."

In the selection of its committees the English municipal council pursues methods very different from those common in the cities of the United States. In America, as is well known, the naming of committees, whether in national, state, or municipal legislatures, is almost invariably the prerogative of the presiding officer; in England this privilege is jealously reserved by the council itself. It is the custom of the English council to appoint at its November session a "committee of selection," which reports to the council a "slate" of standing and special committees for the year. These lists may, when laid before the council, be changed at pleasure by a simple majority vote of that body; but as a rule no important alterations are made. Of course, if a member asks to be relieved from service on a certain committee, or to be transferred from one committee to another, his request is usually granted.

Methods of constituting committees.

The "committee of selection."

The committee of selection is almost certain to be com-

---

[1] Much serviceable information concerning the inner organization of the councils may be found in the Minutes of Evidence contained in the *Report of the Royal Commission on the Amalgamation of London* (1894); see also Redlich and Hirst, *Local Government in England*, II. ch. vi.

Its composi-
tion.
posed, for the most part, of members who owe allegiance
to the same political party as the majority of the council;
likewise this committee may ordinarily be trusted to see
that a majority of the members of each important standing committee belong to the dominant political party. It
would be idle as well as misleading to give the impression
that in the selection of its committees the English borough
council considers nothing but the efficiency of its members in relation to the work to be performed. Not infrequently, indeed, the slate of committees is drawn up at
a caucus of those councillors and aldermen who represent
the majority party, and the report of the committee of
selection thus becomes a mere formality. The charge has
been made that in the larger boroughs councillors who are
directly or indirectly interested in the liquor traffic sometimes manœuvre to obtain places upon the watch committee in order that they may thereby influence the police
administration to the advantage of their friends, an object
in which they are now and then successful. In fact, any
one who is at all familiar with the actual on-goings in
connection with the selection of committees knows very
well that in England, as elsewhere, partisan and personal
motives have a place, and sometimes a very important one,
in the apportionment of committeeships among members
of the municipal council. This is not to say, however,
that such considerations are the only ones which weigh,
or indeed that they outweigh more wholesome motives.
As a matter of fact, it is very rarely that committees are
reconstructed bodily. On the contrary, most of the members hold over from one year to another,[1] some councillors serving on the same committee for a dozen years

Influences which oper- ate in the construction of commit- tees.

Permanence of commit- tee member- ships.

---

[1] The National Civic Federation Commission found one councillor who had
been on the gas committee in Birmingham for twenty-eight years. Other members of the same committee had served for sixteen, fifteen, thirteen, and ten
years respectively. See *Report of the Commission on Public Ownership and
Operation*, Pt. I. Vol. I. 52.

or more. An alderman or a councillor who shows an interest in the work of his committee and develops any degree of familiarity with the affairs under its supervision is reasonably sure to be left on it as long as he remains a member of the council, unless he should personally request a change. Party or personal opposition is not usually brought to bear in order to remove a member who has shown interest and energy in his work. Hence it is that the more important standing committees are quasi-permanent in composition, a circumstance which permits them to attain a high grade of efficiency in the despatch of business.

The number of members assigned to the standing committees shows marked variation, in the larger boroughs important committees sometimes including as many as twenty aldermen and councillors, and rarely fewer than eight or ten. The number is in each case fixed by the standing rules of the council, whose discretion in the matter is subject to no statutory limitation except the provision in the municipal code that the watch committee shall not include more than one-third of the council's entire membership.[1] A committee usually includes both aldermen and councillors, and neither by law nor by custom is any fixed proportion maintained between the two classes of members ; but, since the councillors are thrice as numerous as the aldermen in the council as a whole, it naturally follows that they are, as a rule, in the majority on all committees. This fact is, however, of little or no significance ; for the powers of all committeemen, whether aldermen or councillors, are exactly the same. *Size of committees.*

Each standing and each special committee has its own chairman, who is almost always chosen by the committee at its first meeting in the new fiscal year. In the selection of a chairman considerable care is taken by the com- *The chairmen of committees.*

[1] Municipal Corporations Act, § 190.

mittee, and partisan or personal considerations exert very little influence. In theory any member of the committee may be appointed to the post; but in practice the choice is almost always made from among those members who have had long service on the committee. In a few boroughs the Standing Orders of the council make provision that no chairman shall continue in his position for more than two successive years; but limitations of this sort are not at all common. On the contrary, it is the custom in most of the large boroughs to keep chairmen in office as long as they will stay there; and pressure is sometimes put upon them to retain their posts when they would gladly free themselves from the considerable responsibilities which the tenure frequently imposes. It often happens, therefore, that the chairmanship of a committee is held by the same person for a dozen years or more.[1] The chairman of a council committee presides at its meetings, calls special sessions when they appear desirable, and is the regular medium of communication between the committee and the council on the one hand, and the committee and the municipal employees on the other.

Importance of committees in English municipal administration. No feature of English municipal administration has received more meagre attention at the hands of foreign students than the work of the standing committees; yet none is so deserving of careful study, for none has contributed so effectually to the smoothness and precision with which the task of actual administration is performed. Strictly speaking, no standing or special committee (except the statutory watch committee[2]) has any final powers whatsoever; its decision upon every matter, great or small, requires the approval or ratification of the council. The

[1] Lowell, *The Government of England*, II. 167.

[2] As this committee has been given definite jurisdiction and functions by the Municipal Corporations Act (§§ 190–200), its proceedings are not open to review by the council.

influence of the committees upon the course of routine administration arises simply from the fact that, when a committee considers any matter within its sphere and reports its recommendation to the council, this recommendation almost invariably meets with acceptance.[1] Not that the council is under any definite obligation to adopt the report of a committee, or that its approval of recommendations has become a mere formality. On the contrary, the borough councils frequently refer matters back to committees with instructions that they reconsider their suggestions; and it occasionally happens that the council amends a committee's report without even the courtesy of referring it back. It is not easy to make any accurate assertion as to the extent to which the borough councils disregard, either in whole or in part, the advice of their committees; but " a cursory examination of local newspaper reports of the meetings of fifty-three borough and district councils, large and small, taken a few years ago, would seem to show that on an average there were in a council not more than three cases a year where anything in the reports of committees, of sufficient importance to attract the attention of the press, was amended or referred back." [2] Traditions on this point vary, of course, in the different cities, some councils handling their committees more considerately than others; but it may in general be said without any hesitation that in the vast majority of matters that come before a committee its decision is practically final. So far, indeed, do the committees act upon this assumption that they actually put many of their decisions into operation before reporting them to the

Subordination of committees to the will of the council.

The council is guided by the recommendations of its committees.

[1] The Standing Orders of the council frequently provide that copies of all reports and recommendations of committees must be sent to every councillor and alderman a number of days in advance of the council's meeting. See, for example, City of Birmingham, *Municipal Diary*, 1906, p. 80.

[2] Lowell, *The Government of England*, II. 169.

council at all, simply taking it for granted that approval will follow their action. This procedure is, of course, discouraged by the council, but it is frequently followed nevertheless.[1]

Nature of the work performed by committees. Almost everything that comes up for determination by the council has passed through the hands of some committee. Much new business goes directly to the appropriate committee for consideration before it is presented to the council at all; but more often, perhaps, a matter comes first to the attention of the council through the motion of some individual member, or through a petition presented by ratepayers, or through a communication (usually addressed to the town clerk) from some other official body, corporation, or individual. In the latter case the first step is almost invariably to refer the business to what seems to be the appropriate committee, the determination of this point resting with the council as a whole, and not, as in the cities of the United States, with the presiding officer. If the matter be one of minor consequence, the committee may and sometimes does report upon it at once; but questions of importance it ordinarily holds over till the next meeting of the council.

Division of work among them. The jurisdiction of each standing committee is usually defined with more or less precision in the Standing Orders of the council; and in cases of disagreement between committees as to the scope of their respective powers the point is decided by the council as a whole. It is the duty **The finance committee.** of the finance committee, for example, to prepare the annual budget for presentation to the council, to direct and superintend the keeping of all municipal accounts, to negotiate all loans of money which may from time to time be

[1] *Report of the Royal Commission on the Amalgamation of London*, I. 302, 326.

authorized by the council with the assent of the higher
authorities, and to see that no moneys are paid out of the
borough treasury save by order of the committee or of its
representative. These are portentous tasks, which give
the finance committee rank as the most important of all the
standing committees.[1] Of the other principal committees,   The estates
the estates committee has general charge of the public   committee.
buildings of the borough, as well as the superintendence
of all workingmen's dwellings, all tenements, lands, and
other real property owned by the municipality. The health,
or sanitary, committee superintends all provisions made by
the borough for the care of the public health and the abatement of nuisances, its jurisdiction including such matters
as the inspection of lodging-houses and the enforcement
of factory laws. The public-works, or buildings, committee   The public-
deals with the construction and maintenance of sewers and   works committee.
drains, streets and pavements, public lavatories, and various
other services. The watch committee has full charge of
the police force, and frequently of the fire-protection service
as well. The highways committee looks after the city's
streets; the water-works committee cares for the municipal
water supply; and the parliamentary committee guards the
city's interests at the hands of the national legislature.
The education committee, which now performs the func-   Other committees of
tions that were, prior to 1902, intrusted to the local school   importance.
boards, supervises all matters connected with the educational system of the borough, having full control over the
buildings and the personnel of the borough schools, though
subject, of course, to the general regulations provided by
the national Board of Education. Other prominent committees — such as the water committee, the gas committee,
the electric-supply committee, and the tramways com-

---

[1] For a full statement of the duties of a typical committee, see the *Municipal
Diary* of Birmingham for 1905–1906, p. 91.

U

mittee — are, as their names imply, intrusted with the
duty of caring for the so-termed public utilities of the
municipality.   When such a utility is provided by an enfranchised company, the appropriate committee looks after
the interests of the borough in all its relations with the
private corporation ; when the service is provided by the
borough itself, the committee controls all the incidents of
public operation, such as the purchase of materials, the
employment of labor, and the fixing of all charges for
use.

Growth in the administrative functions of committees.

The considerable progress which the English municipalities have made along the path of municipal socialism —
or municipal trade, as it is more commonly termed in
Great Britain — has served to put upon the council committees a large amount of work and an even larger
amount of responsibility.[1] Every question, whether of
general policy or of detailed administration, connected
with the operation of a municipal plant must be considered and passed upon by the standing committee in
charge ; all contracts for the purchase of materials are
virtually awarded by it ; and it has practically absolute
control over all appointments and removals of officials
connected with the particular service.   When it is borne
in mind that some municipal utilities represent the investment of millions of pounds and number their employees
by the hundreds, it can readily be seen that the powers
and responsibilities of these committees are very great,
and that upon the care and intelligence with which they
are exercised the success or the failure of public operation
entirely depends.   It is not within the scope of this
volume, however, to discuss the merits and defects of the
policy of municipal operation of public utilities as shown

[1] It is not easy to afford any exact data on this point, for a councillor may be
a member of several committees at the same time.

by the experience of English cities.[1] It is enough to say
that the outcome has been to add very much to the work
which the borough council is, through its committees,
called upon to perform; that the policy has in consequence greatly increased the amount of time and energy which many of the councillors must give to their
public duties; and that it has probably operated to foster
the tendency of the council to put almost entire reliance
upon the recommendation of its committees. There are
some who believe that much of the work which now has
to be done by certain committees is pure drudgery, and
that this fact is tending more and more to deter from
candidacy the class of citizens whose presence in the
council is most to be desired. "The man who has retired from business, or from whom business has retired,
may be willing to offer his services in spite of the possibility of considerable calls being made upon his time;
whereas the younger, more successful, or more able traders
or professional men may well be deterred from joining a
municipal council on account of any increase in the work
thrown on that body."[2] Hitherto Englishmen have, on

---

[1] The most recent, as well as the most comprehensive, compilation of data to
which one may refer for information on this phase of English borough administration is the *Report to the National Civic Federation Commission on Public
Ownership and Operation* (3 vols., New York, 1907). The second volume of this
exhaustive report is wholly devoted to a presentation of material relating to
private and public operation of lighting and tramway services in Great Britain.
The reports of the Select Committees on Municipal Trading (London, 1900
and 1902) contain much serviceable data, both historical and statistical. Useful
monographs on various aspects of the question are Major Leonard Darwin's
Municipal Trade (New York, 1903), and his *Municipal Ownership* (London,
1907); H. R. Meyer's *Municipal Ownership in Great Britain* (New York, 1906);
George Bernard Shaw's *The Common Sense of Municipal Trading* (London,
1904); Frederick Howe's *British City* (New York, 1907); Lord Avebury's
Municipal Trading (London, 1907); and R. P. Porter's *The Dangers of Municipal Ownership* (New York, 1907). A fair and conservative summary of the
situation may be found in Lowell's *Government of England*, II. ch. xliv.

[2] Leonard Darwin, *Municipal Trade* (New York, 1903), 102.

the whole, given very liberally of their time and energies
to the public service ; but there is a limit to such generosity,
and the steady increase in the amount of work to be performed by the municipal councils of the larger boroughs
may very soon cause this limit to be reached.

The rôle of the committees in actual government.

The rôle which the council committees play in the administration of an English city is extremely important,
and entirely justifies the strongest emphasis. It would be
safe to say that nine out of every ten matters of routine
are virtually settled in committee and come before the
council only for formal ratification.[1] Now, in view of
the fact that the members of the committees are after all
only laymen, it might readily be assumed that the committees would be likely to cope very ineffectually with the
large number of technical problems which they have to
solve ; and this would probably be the case were it not
that behind the committees there stand as steadying factors the permanent, professional, paid officials of the municipality. To every important committee-meeting one or
more of these officials are almost invariably summoned.
They have no right to vote, it is true; but their counsel
carries strong weight with members of the committee,
particularly when the matter in hand is of a technical
nature. The borough engineer, for instance, attends all
important meetings of the committee on highways; and
his judgment on plans, specifications, methods of construction and repair, hiring of employees, and a host of
other matters is in many cases practically decisive. It is
true enough that a committee may and often does disregard the advice of the permanent officials after it has asked
for and received their opinion ; but it would be entirely
out of consonance with the spirit and traditions of English

The amateur and professional factors.

Influence of permanent officials upon the work of committees.

[1] As a rule, the committee-meetings are not open to the public. See the
Report of the Royal Commission on the Amalgamation of London, I. 321.

borough government for any committee to make a practice
of disregarding such advice.   Much depends, naturally, on
the caliber and experience of the official; for an expert
who has held his post with success for a long term of
years has an obvious advantage in dealing with a shifting
body of laymen.   Hence it comes to pass that an efficient
and tactful head of a city department usually finds it
possible to carry out his plans about as he pleases, provided always that he has the confidence of the committee
in charge.   When the official and the chairman of the
committee work in harmony, their influence in determining
matters of routine administration is usually conclusive.
There is consequently very little basis for the distinction   German and
English
frequently drawn between English and German city ad-   committees
ministration, to the effect that in England the government   compared.
of cities is in the hands of amateurs, whereas in Germany
it is confided to paid experts.   A study of the municipal
codes of England and Prussia would certainly leave one
with just this impression; but an examination of the
actual practice in the cities of the two countries will prove
very conclusively that the distinction has little or no real
foundation.   German cities have both the form and the
fact of administration by paid experts; the cities of England and France have the fact but not the form.   Indeed,
it may very well be doubted whether the German expert
has a whit more of actual influence in the determination of
civic policy than have his prototypes in the other two
countries.   In all three lands the most potent factor in
securing efficient and economical administration for the
municipalities is the plain fact that, whatever the external
forms of local government may be, the actual conduct of
affairs is intrusted very largely to professional officials
who hold office for long terms.   It is the existence of
this policy throughout Europe and the absence of it in

America that chiefly distinguishes the municipal systems
of the two continents.

The act of 1882 required that every borough should engage the services of at least two officials, a town clerk
and a treasurer; but it empowered the council to appoint
such other officers as it might deem necessary, a permission of which practically all the cities have availed themselves.[1] Besides the two officials named, a borough
ordinarily has an engineer or surveyor, a medical officer, a
chief constable or head of the local police establishment,
a clerk of works, a public analyst, and various other officials, the number being, of course, considerably larger in a
city which has municipalized its public utilities, for in
that case each service has its own permanent head or
manager. All these higher officers are appointed by the
council; with the single exception of one auditor, the English
city chooses none of its regular officials by popular vote.
In making its selection, moreover, the council is guided
very largely by the recommendations of the committee
within whose sphere of influence the matter happens to
lie : in its choice of a chief constable, it would be guided

by the recommendation made to it by the watch committee, in the choice of a treasurer by the advice of the
finance committee, and so on. Whenever one of these
higher posts becomes vacant, the council usually authorizes
the town clerk to announce, either through the local newspaper or otherwise, that applications for appointment to
the position will be entertained. These applications may
be filed by non-residents as well as by residents of the
borough, and as a rule no limitations in the way of
specific qualifications are imposed. No examinations,
either competitive or of any other kind, are ever held as a
preliminary to municipal appointments; the council has

[1] Municipal Corporations Act, §§ 17–20.

absolute discretion in selecting whomsoever it desires. It is undoubtedly true, however, that an applicant who does not possess such general qualifications as seem to fit him to perform the duties of the office would have little or no chance of favorable consideration. Thus, it is expected that an applicant for the post of town clerk shall have qualified himself as a solicitor, or legal practitioner; for the duties of this office are of such a nature as to make it almost absolutely necessary that its incumbent shall have a knowledge of the law. Again, no one but a trained engineer may with any chance of success apply for the position of borough surveyor; and no one but a qualified physician is ever considered as eligible to the post of health officer. The qualifications demanded are, however, general rather than specific. *Qualifications for appointment.*

When the time for receiving applications has expired, those which have come to hand are turned over to the appropriate committee for consideration. The committee carefully examines the testimonials that have been submitted with the applications, obtains such outside information regarding the candidates as it desires, occasionally calls before it some of the stronger applicants, and finally makes its selection, very commonly designating to the council not only its first choice from among the candidates but its second and third ones as well. This recommendation the council usually indorses as a matter of course, although cases in which it has for some special reason declined to accept the committee's advice are by no means unknown. In general, however, it is safe enough to say that, when a committee decides in favor of an applicant, the appointment is practically settled. *Influence of committees in the selection of officials.*

Since members of the council are, for the most part, chosen at elections in which party lines are closely drawn, and since the various committees are constituted with *Party influence almost wholly absent.*

party motives well in the foreground, it may very well
be asked what there is to prevent partisan considerations
from determining municipal appointments in England as
they do in most cities of the United States. As a matter
of fact, there is absolutely nothing between English cities
and the spoils system but sound municipal traditions
and the good sense of the councilmen ; save for these two
barriers there is nothing to prevent each new borough
council from turning out every borough official, from highest to lowest, and installing a hierarchy of its own party
henchmen. Any such policy is, however, entirely incon-
ceivable ; for any borough council that should take an
open step in that direction would bring down upon itself
a torrent of condemnation, not only from the voters of its
own city, but from Englishmen throughout the land.[1] This
is not to say, however, that partisan considerations play
no part whatever in determining appointments to municipal office. Those who have followed closely the proceedings of council committees in the larger English cities
know very well that such considerations have an influence,
and that this influence is often very important. When a
lucrative post like that of town clerk or town treasurer is to
be filled, it is unusual to find that the appointee comes
from a party other than that represented by a majority
of the committeemen who make the recommendation. If
a borough council contains a majority of Liberals when such
a post becomes vacant, it may be pretty definitely counted
upon that, whatever else happens, a Liberal will get the
office. It does not at all follow, however, that the appointee
will be selected merely because he has rendered yeoman
service to his party, or that he will be unfit to perform

[1] An interesting example of this was afforded in the borough of West Ham,
where, in 1899, the Socialist party obtained control of the council and dismissed
the borough surveyor. See Lowell, *The Government of England*, II. 173.

efficiently the duties of his position. It simply means that, as between applicants whose general qualifications are approximately equal, a co-partisan is preferred. To be successful a candidate for municipal office must first of all show that he is thoroughly qualified for the post which he seeks; having done this, he finds that a record for having served his party well is a useful supplement to his claims.

Without resorting to any intricate legislative safeguards, therefore, the English cities have maintained practically all the advantages which American municipalities seek to secure for themselves through civil service regulations. Appointments dictated by the qualifications of the aspirants and not by the record of their party services, security of tenure on the part of all the higher officials, and the entire absence of removals without valid cause, — all these features characterize the English municipal service, though no one of them is in the least degree maintained or protected by any legal enactment. Officials are put into office without any fixed limit of term. This means in theory that they are removable at the pleasure or even at the caprice of a majority of the council; it means in practice that they remain in office during good behavior and efficiency. There is no spoils system, therefore, because there are no spoils, or rather because the spoils are distributed so infrequently. This security of tenure has in England, as elsewhere in Europe, contributed very greatly to elevate the plane of municipal politics; for it has saved the cities from the activities of the professional office-seeker, whose influence is scarcely ever other than debasing. *Absence of civil service restrictions is not felt.*

In order that the actual part taken by the higher paid officials in the administration of the boroughs may be adequately emphasized, it may be well to note in a general *The duties and powers of city officials.*

way just what these officers are expected to do.[1]   The
The town
clerk. town clerk, to begin with, has the custody of all the charters, deeds, leases, and other legal documents of the municipality ; he must see that these are kept safe, and that
they are produced before the council when desired.   He is in
all ordinary matters the legal counsel of the borough ; to
him the council turns for advice upon any matter concerning the rights and responsibilities of the municipality.
He is the one man in the city who must profess familiarity
with the mass of legislative enactments, provisional orders,
and judicial decisions relating to the boroughs in general
and to his own municipality in particular.   In a word, he
performs practically all the functions that in an American
city are intrusted to a special officer — to the city solic-
Legal duties. itor, or municipal counsel.   When important litigation
arises, the town clerk is always authorized by the council to
employ one or more barristers to represent the city before
the courts ; but he is expected to prepare all the preliminary papers himself, and indeed to work up the entire case.
When the municipality desires to promote any private bill
before Parliament, it is the town clerk who frames the first
draft of the bill, marshals the evidence in its behalf, employs parliamentary agents to support it before the legislative committee, and in most cases goes personally to London to see the matter through.[2]   All the correspondence
of the city with individuals, with other municipalities,
and with the government departments passes through his
hands ; and to his office belongs the task of preparing and
transmitting all the accounts and reports which the Local
Government Board, the Board of Trade, and the other central authorities may require from time to time.   When

[1] This enumeration of duties has been compiled after an examination of the
Standing Orders, By-laws, and other rules of various boroughs as set forth in
their annual year-books.

[2] Cf. above, pp. 263–267.

provisional orders are desired from one or another of these central authorities, the town clerk makes the application and prepares the data to be sent in support of the request.

In addition to the foregoing duties, which are largely of a legal nature, the clerk has many important secretarial functions. He is expected, for example, to attend all meetings of the council and all meetings of the various council committees ; since, however, this task would in a large city be a virtual impossibility for any one man, he is usually provided with one or more assistant clerks, who attend the committee-meetings for him. It is expected that either the town clerk or his assistant shall take the minutes of all council or committee meetings, shall prepare all committee reports in proper form for presentation to the council, shall draft all resolutions, memorials, and by-laws that come before the council for its consideration, and shall act as the factotum of the municipal authorities in all their clerical work. To his shoulders, also, are virtually transferred many functions that are by law assigned to the mayor, — as, for example, the entire work of getting ready for the annual municipal nominations and elections. Not infrequently, too, he is ex officio clerk of the peace for the city, and performs various minor duties as registrar of the local court, such as giving certificates of admission to citizenship, authenticating legal documents, and so on. As if these tasks were not sufficient, it is sometimes provided in the standing regulations of the borough council that the town clerk shall "perform and carry out all other duties which may be required of him by the council or which may hereafter be imposed upon him." [1]

The English town clerk is the highest paid official in the municipality; his duties are the most comprehensive and the most important, and upon him more than upon

Secretarial functions.

Miscellaneous tasks.

Importance of this post.

[1] City of York, *Year Book*, 1905-1906, p. 78.

any other officer depends the general efficiency of municipal administration. In the larger boroughs he is almost invariably a man of long experience in his particular branch of administration; for a large municipality does not, when the post becomes vacant, ordinarily appoint some one from private life, but selects its man from among the clerks of smaller cities, who, having usually entered the municipal service at an early age and in a subordinate capacity, have grown up in the work. The town clerk of a large city commonly finds places in his office for several "articled clerks," or young men who go to him to learn the duties of the post. These young men serve without pay, — indeed, they sometimes actually pay the town clerk for the privilege of working with him ; and, when they have served their terms and have passed their examinations as solicitors, they seek posts as clerks in the smaller boroughs, expecting in time to gain promotion to the larger ones. This branch of the municipal service has therefore become a career, for the town clerk of a large city usually comes to be an authority on every matter connected with municipal administration. If the evidence taken by the Royal Commission on the Amalgamation of London some years ago be examined, it will appear very conclusively that the clerks of the larger boroughs stand out clearly as the men from whom the commissioners invariably derived the most accurate information and the most profitable suggestions. Their testimony shows some of them to have been complete masters of their craft.[1] Under such circumstances, therefore, the influence of the town clerk with the local authorities is always large and occasionally dominating, for in dealing with laymen his professional

---

[1] See, for example, the testimony of Sir Samuel Johnson, town clerk of Nottingham, and of Mr. Clare, town clerk of Liverpool, in the *Minutes of Evidence* appended to the commission's *Report*.

skill and his long experience give him a great advantage. It is he and not the mayor who is the helmsman of the municipal craft, a fact that is recognized by none more readily than by the councillors themselves, for it is with him that the chairmen of committees constantly confer when any difficulties arise. In return for such important services the clerk receives an annual stipend which is usually quite in keeping with the importance of his position. In some cases he gets as much as ten thousand dollars a year, with additional allowances for travelling expenses ; but, except in a very few cities, he is not provided with a pension on retirement.

A second permanent borough official, whose duties are of nearly equal scope and consequence, is the city surveyor, or municipal engineer.[1]   This officer superintends all the work of construction and repair carried on by the municipality.   He is required to examine and report to the council all sites for proposed new buildings, and all projects for the construction of new streets, sewers, parks, or squares ; to prepare the plans and specifications for any work which the city proposes to undertake ; and to inspect and superintend the laying of pavements, the building of sewers, and all similar undertakings.   No moneys are paid for any work done for the municipality by contractors except on production of a certificate from the surveyor vouching that the work has been satisfactorily completed. This official also arranges for the purchase, by tender or otherwise, of all materials needed by the borough ; but for such purchases he must have the prior authorization of the appropriate council committee.   He superintends the inspection of the materials when delivered, and is responsible for seeing that the municipality obtains, both in quantity

The city surveyor.

---

[1] The appointment of this officer is made mandatory in all boroughs by the Public Health Act of 1875 (38–39 Victoria, c. 55, § 189).

His duties. and in quality, what it has bargained for. All the labor required on municipal works is hired under his supervision, and all pay-sheets must bear his signature before any wages are disbursed by the treasurer. Subject to the direction and control of the council through its committee on public works or other appropriate committee, the surveyor concentrates in himself full responsibility in all matters relating to the construction and repair of city property. In the approval of plans, the award of contracts, and the general determination of construction policy, both the public-works committee and the council are guided very largely by his advice.[1] At all meetings of this committee the surveyor is present, and on all important matters his counsel is in demand. Sometimes, it is true, the committee sets aside his opinion in favor of its own judgment; but such rejection is uncommon. Indeed, a committee which regularly disregarded the advice of its expert would very soon find itself advertising for a new surveyor.

Special aptitude required. As the borough surveyor is invariably a trained engineer, he, like the town clerk, has during the last few decades found his branch of the municipal service tending more and more to become a definite career. The larger boroughs now frequently select their surveyors from among the smaller municipalities; it is becoming less common for engineers in private practice to transfer to the municipal service, and less common for municipal engineers to transfer to private practice. The borough surveyor receives a salary which compares very favorably with that of an engineer in an unofficial enterprise; and, if he performs his duties efficiently, he need have no fear of removal from office, a consideration which enables him to look far ahead

---

[1] In English cities contracts are always approved by the council, — never, as in most American cities, by the mayor.

in mapping out his plans. When he enjoys the confidence of the committee he virtually holds the larger part of the municipal patronage, which he exercises with a sole eye to getting full value for the moneys that his department is allowed to spend. Thus it comes about that, although the awarding of municipal contracts and the employment of the city's labor force are legally vested with a large elective council, the actual exercise of these prerogatives of patronage is almost wholly in the hands of a man who holds office virtually for life, and who has no reason to develop a following among the electors since he never seeks their suffrages at the polls.

Another important post is that of city treasurer, the *The city treasurer.* official who keeps the accounts of the municipality, receives all moneys paid to the corporation, and disburses funds when authorized by proper vouchers. The law demands that the treasurer shall make up the accounts of the municipality at least twice annually, and the councils ordinarily require this to be done in September and March of each year. These accounts go at once to the borough auditors. Although the treasurer plays no large part in determining the financial policy of the borough, he is frequently called upon by the finance committee of the council to give expert advice regarding advantageous times, places, and methods of borrowing money, and about many other such matters. In the larger boroughs the occupant of the post is usually one who has had some considerable financial experience; he gives all his time to the duties of his office, and receives in return a substantial salary.

Hardly less influential is the chief constable, who is *The chief constable.* at the head of the local police establishment, but subject, of course, to the supervision of the watch committee of the council. Over the working of the police system this committee maintains in all the boroughs rather close inspection, but the advice of the chief constable always carries considerable weight with its members. All appointments to positions on the police force are made by the council on the recommendation of the watch committee; and all questions relating to pay, equipment, and discipline are within the jurisdiction of the same authority. Part of the cost of maintaining the police in the English boroughs is, as will be seen later on, borne by the national government, provided always that after due inspection the system is found to be up to the proper standard.[1] For the maintenance of this standard the chief constable is held primarily responsible.

The auditors.

Of somewhat less importance among the officers of the borough are the auditors, of whom every borough has three. Two of them are chosen at the annual elections of the municipality, only such persons as are qualified for election to the borough council being eligible. Nominally these two auditors hold office for a single year only; but as a matter of practice they are in the larger cities regularly reëlected. The third auditor is appointed by the mayor from among the members of the borough council. There is no legal requirement that the auditors shall be men of any training or skill in the work which they are supposed to perform; indeed, all three of them are usually mere laymen, who, even though they might strive earnestly to do their work efficiently, would be very likely to overlook financial irregularities. The larger cities have therefore, for the most part, made provision that the three regular auditors shall be assisted in their work by a professional accountant, appointed by the council and paid a substantial remuneration from the municipal treasury. In some cases the cities have obtained special parliamentary powers to

[1] See below, pp. 333-337.

enable them to do this without laying the validity of their action open to question.

The Municipal Corporations Act requires that the finan- Methods of auditing. cial accounts of each borough shall be made up semi-annually, and that within one month after they have been balanced they shall be submitted, with the usual vouchers and papers, to the three auditors.[1]   These officials, either by themselves or with the help of the professional accountant employed by the council, go over the bills and make a report to the council.   They have no power to disallow any payment which the treasurer may have made under the warrant of the council or other proper authority, but they may make public any disbursement which they deem to have been illegal.   Occasionally they embody in their report to the council various suggestions designed to secure improvements in the methods of municipal financing and accounting; but much more often the auditors' report is a purely formal and perfunctory affair.   When the audit has been concluded, an abstract of the treasurer's account is prepared and printed, and is distributed to such ratepayers as may desire copies of it.[2]   In addition, the town clerk is required to transmit once a year to the Local Government Board a statement of the borough's receipts and expenditures; and the latter body must annually lay before Parliament an abstract of these returns from all the boroughs.[3]   By providing special forms upon which these annual tables of borough revenues and expenditures must be made, the board has not only been enabled to lay before Parliament a digest of borough finances in comprehensive and comparable form, but has

[1] Municipal Corporations Act, §§ 25–28.

[2] There is no legal requirement that this abstract shall be published in the local newspapers; but it is, in the larger boroughs, usually printed in the annual year-book of the municipality.

[3] See also below, p. 328.

x

also secured a greater approach to uniformity in the methods of accounting pursued by the borough treasurers and auditors. It should be clearly understood, however, that borough accounts are not, like those of urban districts, counties, and other local units, audited by the officials of the Local Government Board or by any other central authority. Each borough is wholly responsible for the final auditing of its own accounts.[1]

Other officials. In addition to the various local officers already named, each municipal council appoints such others as it is from time to time required by statute to choose, or such as it may deem desirable for the carrying on of the various administrative functions of the municipality. Every large borough has many such officials, some paid and some unpaid, some professional experts and some amateurs, some who give all their time and attention to civic duties, others who give but a small part of it. In every case the council is the appointing authority; in every case, also, it prescribes the duties of the officer and supervises his work. In no instance are such officials either named by the mayor or elected by popular vote, as they are in American cities.

The municipal employees. In addition to these higher, permanent officials of administration, every large borough has its hierarchy of lower officers and employees, ranging from the assistants of the chief officials down to the ranks of the unskilled day-laborers of the street and sewer-construction departments. The number of such employees depends not only upon the size of the municipality, but to an even greater degree upon the extent to which the borough has embarked upon the policy of directly owning and operating various public services. Strictly speaking, all these employees —

[1] An exception is made in the case of Education accounts, which are subject to central audit.

and in the largest cities they number well up into the thousands — are appointed by the municipal council; but, as a matter of practice, employment in the lower walks of the city's service is given either by the higher permanent officials in charge or by the appropriate council committees. Since, however, these subordinates exercise nothing but a delegated power, they may be overruled by the council at any time.

A system which vests such an enormous amount of patronage in the hands of a large council, allowing this body to exercise its appointing power either directly or through its committees, with no restrictions in the way of civil service regulations, and with apparently no adequate means of centralizing responsibility for appointments good or bad, would seem on its face to render easy the debauchment of the city's entire working force for partisan ends. Nothing of the sort has taken place, however; for, although personal and partisan considerations occasionally assist men to places on the borough's pay-roll, public opinion has consistently held the local authorities to a general observance of the principle of non-partisanship in the exercise of their patronage. The simple fact is that here again healthy local traditions have secured what American cities have failed to obtain even by the application of the most stringent legislative safeguards. In this circumstance lies the explanation of the paradox that, although all municipal employees are removable at any time by a bare majority vote of the council, without any statement of cause and even without the formality of a hearing, yet removals for any reason other than gross inefficiency are practically unknown.[1]

How the system of patronage works in practice.

---

[1] The whole matter of the relation of labor to English municipal administration is fully discussed in the article on " Labor and Politics," in National Civic Federation, *Report on Public Ownership and Operation*, Pt. II. Vol. II. 1–112.

The larger English boroughs, especially those which have embarked in municipal trading, are extensive employers of labor, and hence are brought into close relations with various labor organizations. With two exceptions, however, no large city has adopted the policy of agreeing to employ union men exclusively in any municipal department:[1] the principle of the "open shop" is almost everywhere followed. A careful investigation of the labor situation in English cities, made a year or two ago under impartial auspices, showed that in general the boroughs paid no more for their "skilled or partly skilled labor" than did private employers. With respect to "common, unorganized labor," however, it was found that the English cities had in most cases a minimum rate of wages which appeared to be distinctly higher than the minimum in private employment; but it was also discovered that the municipalities usually secured a better grade of unskilled labor, and were accordingly warranted in affording it better remuneration. There seems, indeed, to be no doubt whatever that the English cities, taken together, have succeeded in obtaining for their labor expenditures returns which are fairly comparable with those secured by well-conducted business corporations, a statement which cannot truthfully be made concerning the cities of the United States. This difference is manifestly one of very great importance; for upon the capabilities that cities are able to show in this direction hinges in a very large measure the whole argument for or against the policy of direct operation of municipal services.[2]

When the city becomes a large employer of labor, and

---

[1] These exceptions are Birmingham in its gas department and Manchester in its tramway service. National Civic Federation's *Report*, Pt. I. Vol. I. 103–104.

[2] "The words 'municipal ownership' do not suggest the real points at issue. When should labor be directly employed by municipalities is the vital question." — LEONARD DARWIN, *Municipal Ownership* (New York, 1907), p. ix.

when its employees are also voters, the danger that the municipal authorities will be subjected to strong pressure in the interests of higher pay, shorter hours, and so on, is obvious and real. An excellent illustration of the means by which this pressure may be made effective is afforded by the tactics of the Municipal Employees Association of Great Britain, an organization whose members are united to influence municipal elections in favor of those candidates who are ready to promise a betterment in the conditions of civic employment. This body already claims a membership of about twelve thousand, and, according to its officers, is growing steadily every year. " We have never been defeated by a municipal body yet," truculently declares an official circular of the association ; " if they decline a request to-day, we are up and at them again to-morrow." It is not at all difficult to see that pressure put upon the municipal authorities by an organization of this sort might well become prejudicial to the interests of economy and labor discipline; in fact, in one of the larger English cities the situation has given rise to the proposal that all municipal employees shall be precluded from voting at local elections. This proposal, it is fair to say, did not receive much support ; and, on the whole, the English borough councils have shown themselves able to stand firm against the pressure of this and other organizations. They have rigorously insisted upon the principle of a fair day's work for a fair day's pay, and in this attitude have received from public opinion a support which has thus far proved entirely adequate.

Municipal labor and municipal politics.

Having thus outlined the composition and functions of that organ which in English cities combines all local legislative and executive powers, and having mentioned the methods of appointment and the respective tasks of those municipal officers who, under the supervision of the council, carry on

The organization of municipal justice.

the work of local government, one may pass to a very brief consideration of the organization of judicial administration in the boroughs; for from a very early period local government and the local administration of justice have been closely associated. Even in the England of the Normans and Plantagenets the borough was a recognized unit of jurisdiction; and, as the judicial system of the country developed, this peculiar position of the boroughs was recognized definitely in the fact that the larger cities were exempted from the jurisdiction of the county courts and allowed to have their own justices. For several centuries these borough justices formed an integral part of the municipal organizations.[1] Their powers and functions varied considerably, to be sure, from borough to borough; but in most cases they possessed, in addition to their local office of dispensing justice, various administrative duties which were from time to time laid upon them by the national government.[2]

The arrangements of 1835.

In 1835 the Municipal Corporations Act strove to make a clear distinction between judicial and administrative functions, and to this end transferred to the borough councils most of the administrative tasks hitherto laid upon the borough justices. To the latter it left only one important administrative power, — that of deciding upon applications for liquor licenses; and even this concession was not intended by those who framed the act. Although the provisions of the statute thus secured substantial uniformity throughout England in the matter of restricting the work of borough justices to the administration of borough justice, they did not attempt to secure uniformity in the amount of judicial jurisdiction which the

---

[1] Further information concerning the history of borough courts before 1835 may be readily found in F. W. Maitland's *Justice and Police* (London, 1885).

[2] C. A. Beard, *The Office of Justice of the Peace in England* (New York, 1904).

justices should possess; nor has subsequent legislation served to bring about such conformity. At the present time, therefore, there is great variation between the powers possessed by the local tribunals in different classes of boroughs.[1] In some of them, chiefly the larger ones, the administration of justice is entirely divorced from that of the county in which the borough is situated, in such cases the boroughs having their own justices and their own courts of quarter sessions, from which appeals go directly to the national high courts of justice. In such a city the court of quarter sessions is presided over by a recorder, who is appointed by the crown and who must, at the time of his appointment, be a barrister of at least five years' standing. This officer is paid from the funds of the borough, holds office during good behavior, and exercises a jurisdiction corresponding to that possessed by the county courts of quarter sessions.[2] He is assisted by a clerk of the peace (or court clerk), who is appointed by the borough council and paid either by fees or by stipend, as that body may determine. Some of the boroughs have also, in accordance with permissive legal provisions, replaced the unpaid justices of the peace with stipendiary magistrates, who are appointed by the crown, but whose stipends are paid out of the borough treasuries.

Diversity of local courts in organization and powers.

On the other hand, many boroughs — most of them, indeed — have no autonomy in the matter of judicial administration, but are regarded, in this respect, as parts of the administrative county in which they happen to be situated. These cities have no separate courts of quarter sessions; but some of them have received "commissions of the

---

[1] An excellent chapter on "The Organization of Justice in Municipal Boroughs" is included in Redlich and Hirst's *Local Government in England*, Vol. I. ch. x.

[2] Municipal Corporations Act, §§ 159–165 *passim*.

peace," by which their justices are invested with a considerable range of summary authority that includes much of the petty sessional jurisdiction which would otherwise be exercised by the county bench. In the boroughs that have no such "commissions" the unpaid justices enjoy only a very limited power. In all the boroughs, it may be added, the justices of the peace are appointed by the crown, never by the local authority and never by popular vote.

As a rule, borough courts possess criminal jurisdiction only; but a few boroughs have retained courts in which minor civil suits may be conducted. Liverpool, for instance, has its ancient Court of Passage, which is presided over by an assessor appointed by the city council and paid out of the city's funds, and which possesses jurisdiction in admiralty cases chiefly. A few of the boroughs still have sheriffs, and a few have lord-lieutenants; but these posts are now wholly honorary. Their incumbents perform no judicial or administrative functions whatever; neither of them is paid; and both are expected to give liberally from their private purses to local philanthropic and social enterprises.

Efficiency of municipal justice. Despite its lack of uniformity, the administration of local justice in England is prompt, efficient, and economical. Since no one either directly or indirectly connected with it is chosen by popular vote, no one need under any circumstances trim his official conduct to local political exigencies. Criminal justice is a branch of English administration which has consistently held itself free from the blight of partisanship; its promptness and impartiality have long been the pride of Englishmen and the admiration of others.[1] From the local courts the borough

---

[1] See, for example, the tribute to English administration of criminal justice in Hon. Andrew D. White's *Autobiography* (2 vols., New York, 1905), II. 226.

police authorities have always received stanch and vigorous support, a backing which has contributed greatly to the effectiveness of police administration ; for these two branches of local government are so intimately related that any weakness in one quickly recoils upon the other.

Englishmen have for a long period plumed themselves upon the degree of local autonomy which their cities enjoy as compared with the cities of Continental states. This attitude has for the most part, moreover, been entirely justified by the existing facts; for throughout the major part of modern English history the central government has left the local authorities to regulate their own affairs in their own way. In the time of the Stuarts, it is true, the rapid growth into prominence of the court of Star Chamber seemed to promise that the régime of local autonomy would speedily become a thing of the past; but the fall of this administrative court assured, for the time being at any rate, the continuance of a thoroughly decentralized system of local administration.[1] Throughout the eighteenth century, and well down into the nineteenth, the internal administration of the country was subordinated to the dictates of no central body whatsoever. The borough councils and the justices of the peace were allowed to exercise a free hand in the management, and more often in the mismanagement, of the affairs of the municipalities, subject only to the possibility that the courts of law might at any time be invoked to curb their activities if these should exceed the powers conferred upon them by the rules of common law or by the vast accumulation of uncoördinated statutes. The control of local police, the making of local provision for the protection of the public health, the care of the local poor, the building and

Central control of local government.

Its slow development.

[1] A. V. Dicey, *The Privy Council* (London, 1887), 130.

repair of local streets and bridges, together with many other matters of like character, were intrusted to the slothful and inefficient hands of local justices of the peace ; and other municipal services were, when provided at all, controlled and supervised by the borough councils. The first quarter of the nineteenth century, therefore, found England almost absolutely devoid of any administrative machinery whereby the central government might exercise a controlling hand in the conduct of municipal affairs. Only by parliamentary legislation might any such control or supervision be applied.[1]

Evil effects of administrative decentralization. The great economic and social changes that came over the land during the period intervening between 1775 and 1825 served to render a continuance of this decentralized policy a public evil. Most of the services left to be locally managed were locally mismanaged. The apathy, inefficiency, and even dishonesty of the local justices and corporation authorities became so great a public scandal as to render the spur of central control necessary in order to secure an improvement. This, of course, meant a departure from administrative traditions which many Englishmen regarded as sacred ; but the change seemed to be imperatively demanded by the existence of a situation that could be bettered in no other way. Particularly in connection with the administration of the poor-law system was the breakdown apparent ; for in this sphere the " era of old Toryism " had been productive of much inefficiency and extravagance. It was here that reform was most pressing, and here naturally that it was first applied.[2]

---

[1] See above, pp. 212–213 ; and, for further information, Merewether and Stephens's *History of the Boroughs;* Webb's *English Local Government*, Vol. III ; and Edward Porritt's *History of the Unreformed House of Commons* (2 vols., Cambridge, 1903), Vol. I.

[2] The change in English popular feeling that rendered possible the abandonment of the old policy of complete administrative decentralization and the intro-

The passing of the great Poor Law of 1834 was accompanied by the establishment of a central commission whose duty it was to oversee the enforcement of the statute.[1]   Although in the prosecution of this work the body became highly unpopular, it performed its duties so well that in 1847, when the desirability of having central control had come to be generally recognized, the commission was turned into a poor-law board,[2] with its president a member of the national cabinet.   A quarter-century later, in 1871, the body was reorganized, and under the title of Local Government Board assumed supervision over a broad range of municipal affairs.[3]   Its president became president of the new body, and, like his predecessor in office, had a seat in the national ministry.   By subsequent legislation the scope of its powers as originally set forth in 1871 has been still farther widened, until it is now the most powerful of the several central organs exercising supervisory jurisdiction over the affairs of the municipalities.

The Poor Law of 1834.

The establishment of the Local Government Board in 1871.

The movement which brought into existence the Local Government Board did not stop with the establishment of this body alone.   Central committees for the supervision and control of local education were created, and these in time were united into a single central board under the name of Board of Education.   Likewise a merger of two central commissions created during the first half of the nineteenth century resulted in the establishment of the Board of Agriculture, which nowadays supervises the work of the local authorities in several important matters.   To some of the existing central organs, furthermore, were allotted new items of jurisdiction over

Other central authorities.

duction of the new organs of central control is discussed at length in Professor A. V. Dicey's *Law and Public Opinion in England* (London, 1905).

[1] 4–5 William IV. c. 76.   [2] 10–11 Victoria, c. 109.   [3] 34–35 Victoria, c. 70.

local affairs. The Home Office, for example, which had all but ceased to be an active department in the opening years of the nineteenth century, was brought into renewed prominence by the transfer to it of supervision over local police administration, — to use the term in its broadest sense. The old Council for Trade and Plantations, also, having been duly shorn of its original functions, was invested with fresh fields of jurisdiction which brought it, under its new title of Board of Trade, constantly into touch with the local authorities wherever the latter undertook to provide public utilities. All these branches of central control have within the last three-quarters of a century undergone a development that constitutes one of the most thoroughgoing of all the changes which the nineteenth century brought about in the realm of English local government.[1] It is therefore proper that the structure and functions of each of these organs should be made clear.

The Local Government Board; its organization.

The Local Government Board consists, strictly speaking, of a president, who is a member of the ministry, and of several other members of the ministry ex officio.[2] As these other ministers, however, never take any part whatever in the work of the board, its jurisdiction is exercised wholly by the president. This officer, who receives a salary of £2000 per annum, devotes his whole time to the work of his office, in which he is assisted by a perma-

---

[1] The history of this development is set forth in Redlich and Hirst's *Local Government in England*, II. 237 ff.; and in M. R. Maltbie's *English Local Government of To-day* (New York, 1897).

[2] The organization and functions of the Local Government Board may be studied most satisfactorily in its published annual reports, and in W. A. Casson's *Decisions of the Local Government Board* (published annually) ; but a general discussion of the topic may be found in M. R. Maltbie's paper on "The Local Government Board," in the *Political Science Quarterly*, XIII. 232 ff.; and in J. Lithiby's article on "The Local Government Board," in the *Encyclopædia of Local Government Law*, IV. 246–263.

nent secretary and a large staff. There is in addition a
parliamentary secretary, who must be a member of Parliament and has usually belonged to the House of Commons.
All the officers on the regular staff of the board are appointed by the crown, usually on recommendation of the
president of the board ; and all are members of the national
civil service.

The powers of the Local Government Board, though *Its powers.*
fundamentally based on the law of 1871, which created the
body, have been extended, altered, and rearranged by at
least one hundred different statutes during the last thirty-five years, — a mass of legislation which would, if any
attempt were made to summarize its varied provisions, bewilder the reader as effectually as Glanvil was upset by the
confusa multitudo of the customary laws of the twelfth
century. It is, indeed, a rare session of Parliament that
does not see the passage of some new measure conferring
some new power upon the Local Government Board, or
imposing some new duty upon it, or amending its procedure in some way. The task, therefore, of presenting in
comprehensive yet concise form any adequate survey of its
powers and functions, one that will convey to the student
of institutions something more than a mere elementary
notion of the rôle which this central organ has assumed in
the field of local administration, is not devoid of serious
difficulties. Of such infinite variety and complexity is its
work, in short, that only the higher officers of the board
itself seem accurately to know the scope and the limitations of its authority. It may serve the interests of clearness, however, if its various powers are roughly grouped
under the three main heads of legislative, administrative,
and financial control.

The Local Government Board has important sub-legisla- *1. Legislative powers.*
tive powers, particularly with reference to the system of

public poor relief.[1]   It may issue to the local poor authorities a general regulation which is binding throughout the
whole country, or an order which affects a single union
only.   Already it has published an enormous number of
such orders, and each year marks a further addition to the
The issuing
of "orders." list.[2]   These regulations deal with all sorts of matters,
from general questions relating to the methods of raising
the poor rates or taxes, to petty details in regard to the
internal economy of individual poorhouses.   An order
prescribing the manner in which guardians of the poor
shall be elected rubs shoulders with a rule fixing the
allowance of snuff to aged paupers.   Nothing in the
domain of public charity seems either too large or too
small to engage the watchful care of the board's higher
officials.

This supervision of the local poor authorities is, however, not the only field in which the legislative activities
of the Local Government Board are exercised.   It is the
central supervising authority in all matters relating to
local sanitation and care of the public health.   It issues
orders designed to carry into actual effect the provisions
of the Public Health Acts,[3] including rules for the prevention of epidemics, the inspection of local milk supplies,
and a variety of like matters.   It may even, in some cases,
compel the borough council to provide a public water
supply, or appoint medical officers, or establish a public
cemetery, or improve its drainage system.   As general

[1] For the history of poor-relief supervision prior to the establishment of the
Local Government Board, see Thomas Mackay (editor), *History of the English
Poor Laws* (3 vols., London, 1899) ; and P. F. Aschrott, *The English Poor-
Law System, Past and Present* (London, 1902).

[2] These regulations are brought together in W. C. Glen's *Poor-Law Orders*
(London, 1898).

[3] Particularly the act of 1875 (38-39 Victoria, c. 55). See W. C. Glen's
Laws of Public Health (London, 1899); and Sir John Simon's *English Sanitary Institutions* (2d ed., London, 1897).

guardian of the public health, however, it should be added, the board's power to issue orders is by no means so great as in the domain of public poor relief ; nor has it in the former sphere sought to exercise its functions by the regulation of minute details.

A third important legislative power of the Local Government Board concerns itself with municipal boundaries. With reference to the poor-law unions or districts its power to divide or unite areas, to alter boundaries, and to create new administrative units is of the most extensive nature ; but with reference to the areas and boundaries of boroughs its authority is much more restricted and its action must in most cases have parliamentary confirmation.[1]

Local boundaries.

These legislative powers are so comprehensive as to give the board a wide range of jurisdiction ; but, it must be borne in mind, they are not exercised with entire discretion. They are, on the contrary, closely circumscribed in several ways. In the first place, the Local Government Board may issue orders only upon the express authority of a parliamentary statute. Its legislative powers are delegated to it by Parliament solely for the purpose of making sure that the statutes of the realm shall be accurately interpreted and applied in the local jurisdictions. The board acts merely as the creature of Parliament ; hence its legislative authority may at any moment be contracted or rescinded. In the second place, it must lay before Parliament, as soon as practicable after promulgation, a copy of every general rule, order, or regulation that it makes ; and its measure must, if it comes within the category of " provisional orders," receive specific confirmation by statute. Thirdly, the sovereign may, theoretically at any rate, disallow any order issued by the board ; and, finally, any citizen may apply to

Importance of the board's legislative functions.

Safeguards against abuses of its power.

[1] See above, pp. 227–228.

the High Court of Justice for a writ of *certiorari*, which will bring before this tribunal the question whether the board has exceeded its statutory powers.   On this ground any ordinance of the board may be quashed and nullified by the court.   These various safeguards have proved entirely sufficient to keep the activities of the board within their proper sphere; but even if they were not adequate there would still remain the most effectual safeguard of all, — the responsibility of the president of the board to the elected representatives of the people.   A member of the ministry, this officer is accountable to the House of Commons for all his official acts, and at the proper time may be compelled to find justification for them in the support of a majority among the members of that body.

Its right of veto.

In addition to the foregoing direct and positive powers in the issuing of orders and regulations, the Local Government Board has important jurisdiction in the matter of vetoing or amending ordinances and by-laws made by the municipalities.   Its approval must be sought for all regulations framed by the local poor authorities, and for all by-laws made by a borough council if they relate to any matter of sanitation or public health or to any other field within the supervisory jurisdiction of the board.   Such by-laws the board may disallow or amend either in whole or in part, if it finds them contrary to the provisions of any statute, — a very salutary function, it may be noted, for the local authorities frequently take strange views as to their statutory powers.   This important prerogative has further operated to secure a closer approach to uniformity in municipal rules relating to the public health; for the board has adopted the practice of publishing model by-laws, which the local authorities find it safe to follow without danger of disallowance.   It has thus come about that a large proportion of the by-laws of English boroughs have in reality been drafted by the paid experts of the national government in London, a fact that serves to reduce to a minimum the possibility of their being successfully attacked before the courts.

This power of disallowance and amendment might seem, on its face, to constitute a gross infringement of the principle of municipal home rule, and to afford an opportunity for captious and meddlesome interference with the acts of local authorities. Such, however, is not the case; for the right of disallowance may be exercised only upon the ground that the municipal ordinance is unlawful, never because it appears to be unwise or inexpedient. So long as the borough councils keep within their legal powers they are free from central interference; and when they unconsciously exceed their authority the uplifted hand of the Local Government Board ought to be welcomed, not resented, for not only has this body uniformly done its work with judgment, but through its unremitting watchfulness it has undoubtedly spared the boroughs much troublesome and costly litigation that would otherwise have followed their attempts to enforce regulations which their local authorities possessed no power to provide. Notwithstanding all this, the borough authorities are, on the whole, unfriendly to the board.

More important than the legislative authority of the Local Government Board are its administrative powers, which, though considerably restricted in some fields of local government, are over the poor-law areas direct and comprehensive, extending even to the removal of local officers. Save in this field, however, and in matters relating to sanitation and public health, it has no very important administrative powers with respect to the boroughs or cities except when the borough councils desire to raise

Scope of the board's veto power.

2. Administrative powers.

Y

funds by loan.   Here its influence is at once apparent;
for, as will be seen a little later, the boroughs are required
to secure its approval of their borrowing projects, and the
board, in granting approval, may impose various conditions as to the manner in which the borrowed funds may
be applied.   If, for example, a borough council decides to
adopt the permissive provisions of the acts relating to the
housing of the working classes, and to undertake the expropriation of lands for the erection of municipal tenements, it must get the sanction of the Local Government
Board before it may borrow any money for the undertaking.   Before granting this permission the board will,
through one or more of its officers, conduct an inquiry into
the merits of the project, and, if it gives its consent, will
usually require the scheme to be carried out subject, in
many important respects, to its further approval.   It will
undertake to see, for example, that the new dwellings
erected by the council provide for the housing of as many
persons as have been displaced, that the buildings are
of proper character, and that the various other ends
contemplated by the statutes are duly secured.   Many
other so-termed "adoptive acts" have given broad powers
to the boroughs, to be exercised by them subject to the
supervision of the Local Government Board; indeed, the
existence of this board as a suitable supervising authority
has prompted Parliament to intrust borough councils with
much authority which it would probably never have
granted them to be used without supervision.   If the
boroughs ask for powers which seem in general to be
desirable but which might easily be abused, the usual parliamentary practice has been to grant the privileges asked
for but to make the Local Government Board responsible
for seeing that they are not misused.   It should be em-
phatically declared, however, that this body is the balance-

wheel, and not the engine, of local administration. It does not drive the machinery of borough government, for this function rests with the borough council;[1] but it does see that the machinery is driven smoothly and with due regard to the principles underlying the legislative mechanism. The initiative, the elaboration of projects, and the immediate supervision of all undertakings must be supplied locally; it is for the board to keep the wheels in their proper grooves.

Where the Local Government Board has no right of interference, and where its approval is not asked by local authorities, it may tender its advice for what it is worth; and this it frequently does. On the other hand, any local authority is entitled to seek counsel from the board and its expert staff, a privilege of which the officials of the boroughs freely avail themselves, not infrequently in order to find a means of extricating themselves from serious legal or administrative dilemmas. John Stuart Mill has somewhere remarked with great truth that "power may be localized, but knowledge to be most useful must be centralized." At the headquarters of the Local Government Board is accumulated a vast fund of the most useful knowledge concerning every phase of municipal administration; a wealth of statistical and other data is there on file, and some of the best legal, financial, and technical skill in England is at hand to interpret it. When the wording of a new statute is not clear to a town clerk, when a borough treasurer gets his accounts tangled or fails to agree with his auditors on any point, when a committee of the borough council is at a loss to know how it should proceed with any project, — in a word, when any local authority wishes to get expert and reliable advice without having to pay for it, the first and

Advice to local authorities.

[1] See above, pp. 270–281.

logical recourse is to Whitehall. Whether the question relates to the extension of a water service, or to the purchase of supplies for a local hospital, or to the distribution of duties among officials, or to the wrangles of councillors over some rule of procedure, it is the duty of the Local Government Board to give its counsel or advice whenever it is asked for. Not infrequently, indeed, the matter at issue is so complicated that the board finds it necessary to send one of its experts to make a personal inquiry before it feels justified in giving its opinion.

Advice to Parliament.

Not only does the board give advice to the local authorities concerning the motives and the spirit of parliamentary legislation, but it advises Parliament itself in regard to all the important proposals that are laid before that body by or on behalf of the local powers. As has already been pointed out in connection with the subject of "private bill" procedure, the opinion of the Local Government Board must be had by Parliament before this body can give final consideration to any private measure relating to local administration.[1] It is particularly the duty of the board to call the attention of Parliament to any features of such measure that may seem to be objectionable or out of accord with established practice. Parliament may, to be sure, pass a bill to which the board has registered its strong objections; but this is not the course which it usually pursues. On the contrary, the national legislature has come to lay more and more stress upon the board's reports concerning matters within its special field; and it is becoming increasingly difficult to procure the passage of any such measure in the face of an adverse report. This function of the Local Government Board, though it has not always received the emphasis which it deserves, is extremely im-

[1] Above, p. 266.

portant ; for not only does it serve as a restraining influence upon those local authorities who are too ready to seek special powers and privileges by private bill, but it enforces greater care and circumspection upon those who present private measures, and it relieves the parliamentary committees of the imperative necessity of giving a thorough examination to every such measure that may come before them.

In addition to its legislative and administrative jurisdiction, the Local Government Board possesses, in the third place, important functions in the particular field of supervision over local finances. So far as the boroughs are concerned, its chief duty is, as we have seen, that of examining applications for permission to borrow money on the credit of the municipalities. Parliament has granted wide borrowing powers to the English boroughs, — much wider, indeed, than those which the various state legislatures in America have seen fit to give to their civic authorities.[1] Without the special permission of the central government, it is true, the English boroughs are practically powerless to borrow at all ; but with this permission there is no obstacle in their way. To the authorities of a borough that wishes to raise funds for any public improvement two courses are open. One method is to make application for a private act of Parliament which will confer the power ; the other is to ask the Local Government Board for permission to borrow under the provisions of some general statute that Parliament has already passed. When the borrowing is to take place on a large scale, the "private bill" method is the one more commonly followed ; but for ordinary loans the boroughs usually take their proj-

3. Financial powers.

Municipal loans.

---

[1] See, for example, the Public Health Act of 1875, § 233 ; the Municipal Corporations Act of 1882, § 107 ; the Public Libraries Act of 1892, § 19 ; and the Local Government Act of 1894, § 12.

ects to the board. This body is asked almost every year to sanction loans for the laying out and paving of streets, for the erection of borough buildings, for the construction or the improvement of the water service, the municipal gas plant, the local markets, hospitals, public baths, and so on. In every case the application for borrowing powers must be accompanied by full data as to the purposes for which the money is required, the estimates of cost, the probable increases in borough revenue that will result from the expenditure, the financial situation of the municipality, and by any other information that may be called for. All such returns are scrutinized carefully by the board's financial experts before the application is either granted or refused. If the request be granted, the board will usually prescribe the terms under which the loan may be effected, including such items as the rate of interest to be paid, the periods for which the bonds may run, the nature of the sinking fund to be provided for the repayment of the loan on expiry, and every other important incident connected with the consummation of the borrowing project.[1]

Relation of the board to municipal trading.   It is through its power to grant or to refuse permission to borrow money that the Local Government Board exerts a potent influence in the field of municipal trading. No borough can embark to any extent upon the policy of direct ownership and operation of its public services without a large initial expenditure, and this money must invariably be raised by the issue of municipal bonds. Upon the readiness or reluctance, therefore, which the board displays in granting permission to borrow for such purposes depends in considerable degree the progress which the movement to municipal socialism is able to make ; for,

[1] Many of these matters are regulated by the Local Loans Act of 1875 (38–39 Victoria, c. 83) and amending acts. See also the article on "Loans" by W. J. Jeeves in the *Encyclopædia of Local Government Law*, IV. 187–245.

though a borough may go behind the board and seek the desired borrowing powers by private act, it finds this procedure expensive, tedious, and uncertain. On the whole, the board has dealt generously with applications of this sort, a fact which may in part account for the rapid extension of municipal trade in English cities.

Another very important aspect of the board's financial powers is that connected with the auditing of the accounts of local authorities. Through its permanent officials the books of nearly every local administrative body are subjected to a thorough and independent examination at least once a year. The only important area of local government (outside of London) to which this auditing jurisdiction does not apply is the municipal borough, the books of which are examined by local auditors whose work is not subject to revision by the experts of the Local Government Board.[1] The extension of this body's auditing authority to all the accounts of the boroughs has, however, frequently been urged, and there is little doubt that such an extension would prove advantageous in many ways; for, although the present system of borough auditing is tolerable, the books of the local treasurers receive no such careful scrutiny as is given to the accounts of county treasurers by the district auditors of the Local Government Board. These officers are well-paid, professional accountants, with large experience in the examination of public ledgers and with no local interests to favor or to fear; hence the extension of their jurisdiction to the boroughs would improve municipal administration at a very vital point.

Audits of local accounts.

But if the Local Government Board has not been authorized to examine thoroughly the accounts of borough

Returns from local authorities.

---

[1] Municipal Corporations Act of 1882, §§ 25–28. See also above, pp. 304–306. For further details relating to this system, see the article on " Accounts and Audit," by A. O. Hobbs, in the *Encyclopædia of Local Government Law*, I. 1–111.

treasurers, it has been empowered to exact from them full
and accurate returns of all borough expenditures.   Every
year the town clerk of each borough is required, on liability to a fine of $100, to transmit to the board a detailed
statement of municipal revenues and disbursements; and
this statement he must render in accordance with a form
prescribed by the board, which is thus enabled to compare
items in the accounts of different boroughs.   These data
are of great value to the board ; for, though it may not
disallow any expenditure made by the borough authorities,
it may call attention to items which it deems to be illegal,
or it may notify any borough that it is, as compared with
other places, paying excessively for some branch of the
service which it receives.   In a word, it has forced the
cities to keep their accounts in comparable form, and to
important discrepancies between the expenditures of different boroughs it has given a degree of publicity which
such disparities rarely receive in American cities.   The
board may also at any time call for a special statement
or return on any matter, and may insist that this report be
made to it in proper form.   Since requests for returns of
this sort are often inspired by some inquisitive ratepayer
who writes to the board for information, they are liable to
come suddenly and without warning, affording no time or
opportunity for juggling accounts back into favorable
shape.   The existence of this contingency thus compels
the treasurers and finance committees of the various municipalities to be circumspect at all times, and not to rely
upon whipping everything into shape in time for the
annual audit.   From the data gathered during the year
the board prepares an annual abstract of local revenues
and expenditures, which, after it has been laid before
Parliament, is printed for public distribution.   This return is so concise, comprehensive, and intelligible that it

renders the study of English municipal money matters one of the simplest tasks ; whereas, as many have found to their discomfiture, the comparative study of municipal finances in any one of the United States is a very difficult undertaking.[1]

In the performance of these varied functions it is, of course, only natural that the Local Government Board should find it necessary to employ a large staff of officials. The total number of these now runs well up into the hundreds, including sanitary engineers, medical officers, inspectors of poorhouses and workhouses, auditors, legal experts, and many similar officers embodying a high grade of specialized skill. All these officials are appointed by the crown on recommendation of the president of the board ; they hold office during good behavior and efficiency ; they are members of the national civil service ; and they receive liberal remuneration. Secure in the tenure of their posts, responsible to the central government alone and hence having no local interests to serve, these officers are able to go about their work in an unbiassed frame of mind, and hence have earned a general reputation for impartiality and fearlessness in their recommendations. There is, on the other hand, no doubt that the Local Government Board is not popular with the local authorities, and that many of these latter would welcome a diminution of the board's supervisory jurisdiction. Were the officials of the board susceptible to partisan influences, the whole system of central supervision would lose its chief prop, which lies

The board's staff.

---

[1] It is only just to recognize, however, that the Bureau of the Census, in its carefully prepared *Statistics of Cities*, issued annually, has performed signal service in the matter of rendering the finances of the various American municipalities more readily comparable. In this connection, mention should also be made of the admirable compilation entitled *The Cost of Municipal Government in Massachusetts* (Boston, 1908), recently prepared by Charles F. Gettemy, chief of the Massachusetts Bureau of Statistics of Labor.

primarily in the efficiency and integrity of the officers
who exercise the guiding authority. Englishmen would
scarcely tolerate the supervision of their local government
by any officer who, like the French prefect, attempted to
combine the duties of an administrative official with the
activities of a party agent.

The Board of Trade. A second organ of central control is the Board of Trade,
which, like the body just described, consists of a president
(who is a member of the national ministry) and the usual
secretaries.[1] Strictly speaking, the Board of Trade has no
supervisory jurisdiction over any of the municipal authorities; but as a matter of fact it is constantly brought into
contact with them through the exercise of its powers over
public services. In general it may be said that this body
has been authorized by a number of different statutes to
grant provisional orders empowering the borough councils
to undertake the direct ownership or operation of public

Its powers. utilities. If the council of an English city should decide
to enter the field of municipal trading, or to extend its existing operations in this field, it must obtain authority
either by private act of Parliament or by application to
the Board of Trade for permission to use powers that have
been conferred by general statutes. If the project is large
and comprehensive, involving the taking over of large gas
plants or of extensive water services owned and operated
by private interests, the council usually seeks its powers
by applying to Parliament for special legislation; but before Parliament will grant such legislation it must have
the opinion of the Board of Trade, and this opinion carries
considerable weight for or against the success of the meas-

---

[1] Most of the statutory provisions relating to this body may be found in the
Board of Trade Acts of 1861 and 1867 (24–25 Victoria, c. 47 ; and 30–31 Victoria, c. 72). A summary of its functions is given in Sir W. R. Anson's *Law
and Custom of the Constitution* (2 vols., Oxford, 1896), II. 188–193. Only a
few of these functions relate to municipal matters.

ure.[1] If, on the other hand, the project is not comprehensive, — if, for example, it relates only to the extension of a gas, tramways, or electric service that is already owned and operated by the municipal authorities, — the city council commonly applies to the Board of Trade for a provisional order enabling the municipality to proceed with its project. Before granting this permission the Board of Trade will examine carefully the local conditions, including such matters as the need for the proposed extension, the practicability of the council's plans, the private interests to be affected, the financial situation of the borough, and so on, the inquiry ordinarily involving an investigation on the ground by one or more engineers or other expert officials. If, upon examination, the board proves to be favorably disposed toward the council's application, it issues a provisional order, which, like the orders of the Local Government Board, is subsequently confirmed by an act of Parliament.

Having an efficient supervising organ in the Board of Trade, Parliament has been disposed to grant larger powers to the local authorities in the matter of municipal trading than it would otherwise have been willing to bestow. By the Tramways Act of 1870 and the Light Railways Act of 1896,[2] for example, it gave them large and comprehensive freedom in the matter of constructing new lines of street railways and of expropriating lines owned by private companies; but it also stipulated that the municipal councils might not avail themselves of the powers thus conferred except with the consent of the Board of Trade, and then only in accordance with such terms as this board, in issuing its permission, might see fit to prescribe. Under

Its relation to general grants of power.

---

[1] *Cf.* above, p. 266.

[2] Useful commentaries on this later law are S. W. Brice's *Law relating to Tramways and Light Railways* (London, 1898), and Evans Austin's *Light Railways Act of 1896* (London, 1899).

the provisions of these two statutes the various local authorities of the United Kingdom now own somewhat
fewer than two hundred tramway systems, and directly
operate considerably more than half of this number.[1]   In
some cases they have obtained their privileges by private
act of Parliament; but in the great majority of instances
they have secured them from the Board of Trade under
the terms of the general statutes named.   Not only, therefore, does the system permit Parliament to grant comprehensive powers with little danger that they will be abused
by the local authorities, but it serves to establish a relation between the powers of the municipal councils and the
merits and urgency of their respective projects; and it
gives to the English boroughs a reasonable and even a
liberal degree of freedom in determining what public
services they will own and operate directly.   On the other
hand, it provides a restraining hand upon those local authorities who, without due consideration of the financial
and physical problems involved, sometimes show themselves over-zealous in the cause of municipal exploitation.

The board's staff.   The Board of Trade, like the Local Government Board,
has its staff of expert officers, engineers, accountants, and
legal advisers.   These officers conduct the local inquiries
into the merits of applications, whether the requests come
from municipal authorities or from private operating companies; and upon the reports made by them the board
usually bases its decisions.   A high grade of technical
skill, sound judgment, and of thorough impartiality as
between the interests involved are essential factors in the
proper performance of their duties; and these qualities
most of them possess.   With the increasing demand for
more elaborate and more complicated public utilities, the

---

[1] *Municipal Year Book of the United Kingdom*, 1906. The board issues
each year a *Return of Street and Road Tramways authorized by Parliament*, etc.

work of the board has grown rapidly in recent years. Its annual reports bear testimony not only to the important rôle which it has come to assume on the economic side of municipal administration, but also to the care and thoroughness with which its staff performs the tasks allotted to it.

A third important organ of central supervision is that commonly known as the Home Office, the chief officer of which is the home secretary, likewise a member of the cabinet.[1] The Home Office is brought into contact with the borough authorities of England chiefly through its power of supervising, in a general way, the exercise of police functions by the local administrations of the land. With respect to London the authority of the Home Office in police matters is direct, for the metropolitan police system is, as will be seen later, immediately under the home secretary's control;[2] but with respect to the police administration of the ordinary boroughs the jurisdiction of the Home Office is supervisory only, the direct control being here vested in a local authority, the watch committee of the borough council. Save within the limits of the Metropolitan Police District of London, police power in English cities is regarded as distinctly a branch of municipal administration over which the central government has a very limited right of inspection and supervision; and, in obedience to the well-known feelings of Englishmen on this point, the power of the central authorities to interfere in matters affecting the management of the local police has been consistently kept at a minimum.

Direct control and conduct of borough police administration is, then, in the hands of the borough watch com-

The Home Office.

Relation of the Home Office to municipal police.

---

[1] The general duties of this office are set forth in Anson's *Law and Custom of the Constitution*, II. 227–240.

[2] Below, p. 377.

mittee, a body selected by the borough council from among the ranks of its own members.[1] This committee determines the size of the local police force, appoints the chief constable, elaborates the necessary rules for the governance and discipline of the force, and exercises every other incident of immediate administration. Somewhat more than a half-century ago, however, it was provided by law that a share in the cost of maintaining borough police should be borne by the national government wherever it should appear that the police establishment had been "maintained in a state of efficiency in point of numbers and discipline";[2] and to this provision the central authorities owe their powers of police inspection and supervision. They have the right to insist that borough police establishments shall be "maintained in a state of efficiency" upon pain of having the national subvention withheld; but they have no positive authority in relation to either the organization or the discipline of local police.

The "inspectors of constabulary." For performing the work of inspection the Home Office maintains a corps of officials known as "inspectors of constabulary," whose duty it is to make periodic visits to the various boroughs and other police areas of the country, in each of them to prosecute a more or less careful inquiry into the efficiency of the local police establishment, and in each case to make a report to the Home Office. If this report is satisfactory, the local authorities receive from the national government a subvention or allowance that amounts in round figures to one-half of the local police expenditure for the year.[3] If the report is unfavorable,

---

[1] See above, p. 289.

[2] The County and Borough Police Act of 1856 (19-20 Victoria, c. 69), § 16.

[3] The subvention covers one-half the cost of police salaries and clothing, and makes an allowance for police pensions. Further details concerning it may be conveniently found in Redlich and Hirst's *Local Government in England*, II. 310-312.

this subvention is withheld, or is suspended until the local authorities bring their police system up to the required standard. The inspectors have no right to order any changes to be made or to remove any local police official; their sole task is to inspect and to report the results of their inspection.[1] Usually, however, if one may believe the local police officials, the scrutiny is not very thorough: unless a police system falls very plainly below a reasonable standard, it is likely to pass muster. At any rate, no borough has lost its annual subvention in recent years, although on one or two occasions the Home Office has given warning to a municipality that the grant would be withheld unless certain shortcomings were promptly remedied.

This system of central police inspection is a compromise that has resulted on the one hand from the English passion for local autonomy, and on the other from the well-established fact that complete decentralization of borough police administration is liable to bring inefficiency and even corruption in its train. Central domination over local police as it exists in Prussia would not be brooked in England; on the other hand, the majority of Englishmen seem to have no desire to allow local liberty to develop into local license, as it has done in many municipalities of the United States. The national government of England desires that borough police administration shall be reasonably uniform and reasonably efficient, and for this it is willing to pay liberally; but if the local authorities prefer to content themselves with a police system that is below the Home Office standard, and incidentally to forego the government subvention, there

Results of the English system.

[1] These reports are printed annually under the title " Reports of Inspectors of Constabulary, — Counties and Boroughs." An interesting discussion of the subject may be had in the article on " Police," by H. B. Simpson, in the *Encyclopædia of Local Government Law,* V. 146–177.

is nothing, so far as the powers of the central office are
concerned, to prevent their doing so.   There is, however,
an effective check upon anything of this sort in the absolute certainty that any watch committee which permitted
local police conditions to become such as to cause the
subvention to be withheld would bring down upon itself
a storm of condemnation from the ratepayers of the
borough.   In other words, it is much more economical to
maintain an efficient police system with the national
treasury bearing half the cost than to maintain an inferior service with the cost falling entirely on the local ratepayers.   The Home Office has therefore only to insist
upon any reasonable improvement that it desires; the
local response is usually ready enough.

National
subven-
tion to
municipal
police.

This system of national subvention is obviously a
source of heavy expense to the central government, for
the total allowance paid to all the local authorities
amounts to many millions of dollars per annum.   Every
year, moreover, with the steady growth of large cities and
the increase in size and expensiveness of local police
forces, the amount looms larger, and this in the face of
ever increasing demands upon the national exchequer for
other and perhaps more distinctly national purposes.   As
a result of these payments the police systems of English
cities have undoubtedly maintained a fair standard, as
European standards of police efficiency go, but not so
high a one as might be expected in view of the enormous leverage which the Home Office exerts in raising
the general plane ; for there is no disguising the truth
that the powers of this office, though amply sugar-coated
for the benefit of local autonomists, constitute a very
effectual form of direct administrative compulsion.   The
fact is, however, that the Home Office inspectors have
not set themselves to screw up the standard year by

year, but have merely satisfied themselves that all things
connected with the civic police administrations were satisfactory enough to pass muster. The system gives the
citizens an assurance that their management of the local
police is not clearly inefficient; it does not afford them
any further guarantee. The periodical inspection has
become a safeguard rather than a spur ; though it may
scarcely be termed cursory, it has by no means exhausted
its possibilities.

Two other organs of central government that come
into contact with local authorities in a supervisory way
are the Board of Agriculture[1] and the Board of Education.[2] The former body exercises sundry powers of
supervision over the work of municipal officials, so far as
this work concerns itself with the prevention of epidemics
among animals, the destruction of insects, the preservation of local fisheries, and so forth.   It has power to enforce the provisions of various acts of Parliament relating
to such matters, and to this end it may issue orders to local
authorities.   It maintains its staff of expert officials, and
in all matters that come within its particular sphere its
counsel and advice are at the disposal of the borough
authorities.   The Board of Education has charge of the
whole matter of school inspection, and of the distribution of those sums of money which the national government annually pays to the municipalities for the support
of secondary education.   Through its officials it inspects
all schools that receive public funds, approves plans for
school buildings, and prescribes the general curriculum; but
it has no right to interfere directly in the work of immediate
school administration.   All that it can do in this direction

Other organs of central supervision.

---

[1] Board of Agriculture Act of 1888 (52–53 Victoria, c. 30).
[2] Board of Education Act of 1899 (62–63 Victoria, c. 33), and Education Act
of 1902 (2 Edward VII. c. 42).

z

is to come into general supervisory contact with the Education Committee of the council, which in every borough has immediate control of the local school system.

English and continental methods of central control.   If the activities and influence of all these various central boards be considered together, it will be apparent that England has during the last century made considerable progress along the paths that lead logically to administrative centralization as seen in various continental states. Yet the system of national supervision as it now exists falls far short of the stage reached by the contemporary administrative arrangements of either France or Prussia. To the various central organs Parliament has doled out authority very grudgingly, giving but a little at a time and usually only a tithe of what is asked for. It will have been noticed, furthermore, that there is in England no concentration of supervisory jurisdiction in the hands of a single officer or in a single department of the national government. In the English system of administration there is no branch that in any way corresponds either in power or in influence to the French Ministère de l'Intérieur or to the Prussian Ministerium des Innern. Much of the authority which these departments possess is doubtless exercised in England as truly as on the continent; but instead of being concentrated in any one place it is scattered about in various hands. One finds in England, therefore, not only decentralization of local administrative authority, but diffusion of central supervisory jurisdiction as well. It may also be noted that the English system provides no official whose task it is to serve as a link between the local and the central authorities. It has no officer corresponding to the French préfet or the Prussian Regierungspräsident. If the state deals with the municipality, it does so directly and without assistance from any intermediate authority. All this has naturally served to give the English system great flexibility, as well as to render much less facile the development of bureaucratic methods. The effect of the whole procedure has been to stimulate the local authorities to the proper discharge of their functions, without at the same time involving any radical departure from the traditional policy of municipal autonomy.[1]

In any discussion of English city government, however elementary, some special consideration must be given to one very important urban area, the metropolis, which has a system of local government quite unlike that of the ordinary borough. In several countries besides England, indeed, it has seemed desirable, for some reason or other, to provide the national capital with a framework of local administration quite different from that in vogue in the rest of the cities of the land. Thus the administration of Paris differs from that of the ordinary French commune, and the government of Washington is wholly unlike that of the other cities of the United States. Of this individuality in point of local management London furnishes a conspicuous example; for, being by far the largest of English cities, as well as the national capital, it has local problems that are peculiarly comprehensive and complicated, and hence its administration departs widely from the regular English type. This is not, however, because the national government of England, like that of the republic across the channel, regards as axiomatic the principle that the metropolis should be held with a tighter rein than the other municipalities. Unlike Paris, London has assumed no place in history as the cradle of national discord; and although its rôle in the contemporary political life of the nation is highly important, it is very far from being domi-

The government of the metropolis.

Why London has a special system of administration.

---

[1] See the interesting chapter entitled " A Fundamental Antithesis," in Redlich and Hirst's *Local Government in England,* I. 10–43.

nant. The peculiar system of local government which has been applied to London is not, therefore, the outcome of any direct policy of strict control ; it is rather a result of the nation's disinclination to deal with a huge problem at the appropriate time and in a comprehensive way. When the Municipal Corporations Act of 1835 was framed, the question of reorganizing the administration of London was regarded as a separate matter, not to be dealt with in a general enactment relating to the boroughs as a whole. London was therefore left outside the pale of reform, on the understanding that her case would receive due attention from Parliament in the form of special legislation. This special legislation was long delayed, however ; for not until a full half-century had passed did any substantial measures for the reform of metropolitan administration make their appearance on the statute-books.

The areas of London government.

Before one can speak intelligently of contemporary London government one should try to make clear just what "London" is ; for the conglomeration of population to which this term applies is not, like Paris, Berlin, or New York, a single unit or area of local administration. First of all, there is the "City of London," the ancient municipality and the core of the modern metropolis. This unit comprises an extent of about one square mile, and has a permanent population of about thirty thousand persons. Constituting, as it does, the financial centre of the whole metropolitan area, the "city" is the daily resort of many hundreds of thousands whose residences are in the suburban boroughs. Then there is the "County of London," an administrative municipality, with an area of about one hundred and twenty square miles and a population of somewhat less than five millions. This tract ranges itself in a somewhat circular form round the old city, and for most purposes may be looked upon as

the real municipal London.   Besides these two units there
are more comprehensive London areas, chief among which
is the London Metropolitan Police District, which includes
all the parishes within fifteen miles of Charing Cross.
This district comprises slightly less than seven hundred
square miles, and contains a population that does not fall
far below the seven million mark.   It does not, however,
include the old city, which in the matter of police administration has been left with its ancient autonomy.   In form
of administration these three areas are separate and independent ; but all three systems taken together make up
the government of London, the metropolis.

The City of London presents the only important survival of the " unreformed corporation."   From the time of
Alfred the Great down to the present day this municipal
unit has been especially favored by the national authorities ; and even through the political storm and stress of
the nineteenth century the organization and privileges of
the city corporation passed almost entirely unscathed.[1]
For almost all administrative purposes the " corporation of the City of London " is the sole local authority
within the rather narrow civic limits; except in one or
two matters, neither the authorities of the county nor
the officers of the Metropolitan Police District have any
jurisdiction within the confines of the city.   The " corporation " is made up of the freemen of the city, —
that is to say, of those who have been regularly admitted
to the freedom of the city and enrolled as citizens.
There was a time when the category of freemen was
strictly limited; but now any ratepayer within the city
may obtain enrolment as a freeman on payment of a

The City of London.

---

[1] On the early administrative history of London, material may be had in J.
F. B. Firth's *Municipal London* (London, 1876), and G. L. Gomme's *Governance of London* (London, 1907).

one-guinea fee, and the same privilege extends to such persons as are qualified to vote at parliamentary elections within the city. The freemen no longer, therefore, form a close corporation in the proper sense of the term.

The city authorities. The corporation exercises its administrative powers through the lord mayor and three councils, which are called respectively the Court of Aldermen, the Court of Common Council, and the Court of Common Hall.[1] The first of the three, the Court of Aldermen, consists of twenty-seven members, — the lord mayor, and twenty-six aldermen representing the twenty-six wards into which the city is divided. These aldermen are elected by the freemen, and hold office for life; but as a body they have but one or two powers, and these are of little consequence. The Court of Common Council is the chief legislative and executive body of the city. It is made up of twenty-six aldermen and two hundred and six common councillors, who are elected annually from the different wards of the city in unequal proportions, some wards having a much larger representation than others. The body has all the powers that ordinarily appertain to a borough council: it frames the usual city ordinances, appoints nearly all the city officials, and manages such services as street paving and repairing, sewerage (except main drainage), lighting, police, and so on. It does not elect the lord mayor, however. This prerogative belongs jointly to the aldermen and the Court of Common Hall, which is made up of the members of all the "livery companies" of London, its nominal membership being therefore about nine thousand. It meets only twice a year, and its only important func-

[1] The best account of the composition and powers of these bodies is that given in the *Report of the Royal Commission on the Amalgamation of London* (1894), Appendix iii. See also the earlier *Report of the Commissioners appointed to inquire into the Existing State of the Corporation of the City of London* (1854).

tion is to elect the lord mayor, the city sheriffs, and the chamberlain or city treasurer.

The lord mayor of London is chosen annually from among the aldermen who have served in the office of sheriff. From this list the Court of Common Hall selects two names and presents them to the Court of Aldermen, which as a matter of custom invariably selects the senior of the two for its confirmation. Election to this position is thus little more than a form; for only on the rarest occasions is there any departure from the rule of taking the qualified aldermen in order of their seniority. The post of lord mayor is almost purely honorary; for the incumbent has no special administrative powers, the real work of administration being performed by the various committees of the common council. The lord mayor is, however, expected to take a prominent part in the dispensing of official hospitality, to provide the lord mayor's annual banquet and annual pageant, and to entertain all distinguished visitors to the city. Out of the large revenues of the corporation he receives a salary of $50,000 per annum, together with the use of the Mansion House as an official residence. A lord mayor who performs what is generally expected of him in the way of entertainment finds it necessary to spend perhaps double his stipend.

The office of lord mayor.

The administration of the city is thus an interesting survival from the days of borough government by close corporations. It is cumbrous and complicated, affording no concentration of powers and so giving the ratepayers little or no opportunity to fix responsibility upon any one in public office. Nevertheless, the city has been well governed. Its officials are competent; its public services are efficiently managed; its revenues are large; its debt is small; and its ratepayers seem, in the main, to be entirely satisfied that the system shall remain as it stands without

An antiquated but efficient system.

any important changes.   So long, therefore, as the administration is satisfactory to those within there seems to be little probability that any reorganization will be dictated from without.

The County of London. The government of the "city" is but a small factor in the administration of metropolitan London as a whole. Very much more important as an area of local rule is the County of London, of which the dominating organ is the London County Council.   As the old city grew in population beyond its ancient confines many extra-mural parishes were **Origins.** organized, and from time to time a few of these were annexed to the original municipality.   More of them, however, remained autonomous; and in course of time there were dozens of such parishes, each governed by its own local vestry, but with no central authority to coördinate the interests of the district as a whole or to deal with matters that affected more than a single parish.   This administrative decentralization was productive of so many marked evils that, when Parliament undertook the reform of municipal government in 1835, there was urgent need for reorganization under the very shadow of Westminster. For the time being, however, no steps were taken in this direction; but twenty years later, when it became clear that public services which were seriously needed could not possibly be undertaken except by some central authority, Parliament bestirred itself, and in 1855 established **The metropolitan Board of Works.** the Metropolitan Board of Works.[1]   This body was composed of forty-six members, selected not by the ratepayers directly, but by the various parish vestries and other local authorities; and to it was intrusted the task of providing a system of main drainage, of constructing and maintaining new streets and bridges across the Thames, and of con-

[1] An elaborate and accurate study of this board's activities is presented in Ludwig Sinzheimer's *Der Londoner Grafschaftsrat* (Stuttgart, 1900), Vol. I.

trolling the fire-protection service, all within an extensive
area which may be said to have comprised the whole metropolis of that date.

The Metropolitan Board of Works performed very valuable functions in its time. At its hands metropolitan London obtained its first modern sanitary system, extensive public works like the Thames Embankment were constructed,
many new streets were opened, and an adequate fire-protection service was installed. Still, its work was neither
popular nor satisfactory to the citizens, a circumstance
that may be laid chiefly to the manner in which the body
was organized; for not only was it too large to be effective as an administrative board, but the system of indirect
election resulted in the choice of men whose interests
were chiefly local in scope. Moreover, some of its members were proved to have profited corruptly in certain
undertakings of the board, and hence as a body it never
managed to anchor itself in the public confidence. Some
of its doings were ultimately investigated by a parliamentary commission, which reported very unfavorably ; whereupon it was legislated out of existence, and its place was
taken by a new organization.

Functions of the board.

In this change, made in 1888, the area which had
hitherto been comprised within the jurisdiction of the
Metropolitan Board of Works was organized into an administrative county and put under the authority of a
county council.[1] This body, known as the London County
Council, is composed, in accordance with the act of 1888,
of one hundred and eighteen councillors, elected two each
from fifty-seven " parliamentary boroughs," or election dis-

Creation of the county and county council.

[1] 51–52 Victoria, c. 41, commonly known as the Local Government Act of 1888.
Sections 40–45, 88–90, and 113–117 deal particularly with the new organization.
See also G. L. Gomme, *The London County Council : its Duties and Powers,
according to the Local Government Act of 1888* (London, 1888) ; and McMorran
and Dill, *The Local Government Act of 1888* (3d ed., London, 1898).

Organiza-
tion of the
London
County
Council.
tricts, and four from the old city. These councillors are
chosen for a three-year term ; and the method of nomination, the procedure in election, and the qualifications for
voting are all much the same as in the ordinary municipalities. The councillors select and add to the membership
of the council nineteen aldermen, who serve for a six-year
term, approximately one-half of them retiring triennially.
The aldermen may be elected by the councillors from
within their own ranks, or they may be chosen from outside, a procedure which is sometimes followed. The one
hundred and thirty-seven councillors and aldermen select
each year a chairman of the council, and to fill this post the
council is entirely free to go outside of its own membership.
A chairman may be reëlected, but of late the custom has
been to choose a different one each year. The council
further elects, from within its own ranks, a vice-chairman
and a deputy-chairman, who each serve for an annual term ;
it also appoints a clerk and various minor officials, who
are chosen during the pleasure of the council, but whose
tenure is really permanent.

County
Council
elections.
In the council elections party considerations have from
the outset played a dominating rôle. In the initial contest
for membership the ratepayers ranged themselves into two
leading political divisions under the names of Moderates and Progressives ; and this cleavage has remained
down to the present time, although at the last elections the
Moderates forsook their older appellation for that of Reformers. In a general way the two groups coincide with
the two leading national parties, the Moderates (Reformers)
drawing their main strength from among those who in
national politics owe allegiance to the Conservatives, while
the Progressives derive their support chiefly from the Liberals. Not that the lines of cleavage in local and national
politics run precisely parallel, by any means. On the con-

trary, there are thousands of Conservatives who rank as Progressives in local politics, and thousands of Liberals who seem to have no compunction in supporting the London Moderates or Reformers. It is to be remembered, moreover, that the suffrage requirements are not at all the same in council as in parliamentary elections, and hence that the body of voters, though in the main identical, must necessarily differ somewhat in the two branches. Different voters' lists are used at the two elections, and the polling of course takes place at different times.[1] Strictly speaking, therefore, the London parties are local parties, each of them declaring allegiance to a party platform which professes to deal solely with municipal issues. The Progressives, for instance, have stood consistently for the policy of direct ownership and operation of all the important public services by the County Council ; and, as they controlled the council for almost twenty years, they were able to put many of their principles into practice. The Moderates or Reformers, on the other hand, have about as steadily opposed the lavish expenditures and the heavy borrowing which the pursuance of the Progressives' policy necessarily involves, and have in many other lines striven to put obstacles in the way of radical changes. At the last elections this question of municipal ownership and operation, with its merits and its limitations, was the chief issue upon which the contests were conducted. It may fairly be said, therefore, that, although there is a general tendency on the part of the voters to follow the lines on which they divide in matters of national politics, yet the issues at the council elections are chiefly, if not exclusively, local ones, and in meeting them the local parties are almost entirely free from any control or interference on the part of the national organizations. It is an inter-

London parties.

The issue at the last London elections.

[1] See also above, p. 229.

·esting fact that, in the period of nearly twenty years during which the Progressives held control of the County
Council, a majority of the members sent to the House
of Commons from the same election districts were
Conservatives.

The Fabian Society.

In speaking of partisan activities in the County of
London, one should not fail to mention two local factors
that have had considerable to do with the course of recent
London government. One of these is the Fabian Society,
an organization which, though not relatively powerful in
point of numbers,[1] has exerted a striking influence upon
London politics during the past two decades. Founded in
1885, the society at once set itself to champion the cause
of municipal socialism ; and it soon secured the assistance
of several influential writers who gave vigor and quality to
its work of educational propaganda.[2] It adopted a pro-

Its pro-
gramme.

gramme which embodied many radical reforms in the
administration of metropolitan affairs, and at the various
County Council elections has used its whole influence in
behalf of those candidates who promised their support to
this programme.[3] Its numerous publications, issued in the
form of tracts or short discussions on specific reforms, have
had unquestionable weight in moulding London political
opinion in general and the political attitude of the employed classes in particular ; for these tracts, besides being
subtle in the arguments which they put forth, usually present a convincing array of pertinent facts, and they are
written by men who appear to have mastered the art of

---

[1] Its present membership numbers less than 1000 in a municipality of nearly
5,000,000.

[2] Perhaps the most prominent of these are Messrs. Sidney Webb, Graham
Wallas, and George Bernard Shaw.

[3] *Fabian Society Tracts*, Nos. 30–37, 90–97. See also Sidney Webb's
London Program (London, 1891) ; and George Bernard Shaw's *Fabian Essays
in Socialism* (London, 1889).

catching the popular ear. In many other ways the work
of the society has proved of high service, particularly in
ameliorating class prejudices; but there appears to be
reason for believing that during the last few years its
influence has been on the decline.

The other factor that is potent in London local politics The Labor
party in
London poli-
tics.
has been interjected into them by the recent rise to prominence of a party organized to represent the interests of
labor. During almost the whole of the nineteenth century neither the national nor the local political situation
was complicated by the activities of any influential party
specifically committed to the labor interests; hence it
came about that both the regular political parties sought
and obtained a share of the workingmen's suffrages by
warping their party programmes into such grooves as
policy seemed for the time being to dictate. In London
the Progressives were, until a few years ago, somewhat
the more successful in the exploitation of this element;
but in the local election campaign of 1907 the labor
organizations, encouraged no doubt by the showing which
the Independent Labor party had been able to make in
the parliamentary elections of the preceding year, manifested some disposition to shake themselves free from the
regular party trammels. The present London County
Council contains eleven Labor representatives, and there
seems to be considerable likelihood that at subsequent
elections this delegation will be increased. It is doubt-
ful, however, whether such an outcome would very materially alter the general course of municipal policy; for two
decades of Progressive domination in London government
have served to send the municipality an alarming distance
along the lines of concession to labor demands. As a
result of this cumulative liberality to the interests of labor,
the County Council was some years ago compelled to

admit, through a committee of inquiry, that work undertaken by it directly cost much more than work of a similar
nature performed for private concerns.[1]

The per-
sonnel of the
County
Council.

County Council elections are fought out on partisan
lines, and often, as was clearly shown in the last campaign, with considerable bitterness.   This fact does not,
however, involve as a corollary any abstention from
candidacy on the part of the best element among the
citizens of the metropolis.   On the contrary, the personnel
of the council set a high standard at the outset; and, although it may have lapsed somewhat from its initial
plane, the general caliber of its membership still continues
high enough to compare very favorably with that of any
municipal council in any other country.   The laws permit
a citizen to be at one and the same time a member of the
London County Council and of the House of Commons;
and of this dual membership there are numerous ex-

Its chair-
men.

amples.   The first chairman of the council was Lord Rose-
bery, afterwards prime minister of England; the second
was Sir John Lubbock (now Lord Avebury); and upon
the roll of past and present members are many names of
almost equal prominence.[2]   At the time of its establishment the council attracted a great deal of attention not
only in England but in other countries; and the privilege
of membership was from the outset counted a distinct
honor, for it was evident that the new body possessed
great possibilities in the way of effective action.   It is,
indeed, without doubt this promised opportunity for ser-

[1] See the *Report of the Council's Committee on the Works Department*
(1896–1897), a quotation from which is given in Lowell's *Government of England*, II. 219–220.

[2] Among subsequent chairmen of the London County Council may be men-
tioned the names of Sir John Hutton, Sir Arthur Arnold, Sir W. J. Collins,
Lord Welby, Sir John McDougall, Lord Monkswell, Sir E. A. Cornwall, Mr. J.
W. Benn, M.P., Mr. T. Mackinnon Wood, M.P., and Mr. Evan Spicer.

vice that has since drawn to its membership so many men of progressive administrative ideas. When one bears in mind the fact that the councillors, despite the large demands made upon them by committee work, receive no salaries or allowances, one feels that the success with which Londoners have been able to maintain the quality of the council is worth more than a passing word of admiration.[1]

The powers given to the London County Council are comprehensive, and in their exercise are of the most direct interest to the citizen. In the first place, the body inherited the jurisdiction of the former Metropolitan Board of Works, which, as has been noticed, had extensive authority in sanitary matters.[2] Through this administrative legacy the council became the sole controlling authority with respect to main drainage and general sewage disposal, all the trunk sewers of the county being constructed and kept in repair by those who work under its direct supervision. Subsidiary drains, however, and everything affecting them are left to the control of the authorities in the different boroughs into which the county is divided. In all matters pertaining to the protection of property against fire the council is the sole authority; its powers in all that relates to the organization and discipline of the London fire brigade are without any limitation whatever. In this respect the London system distinguishes itself somewhat sharply from that of either Paris or Berlin; for in each of these cities the fire-protection service is, like the police administration, directly under the control of the state authorities. As

Powers of the London County Council.

---

[1] The present council contains 21 merchants, 15 manufacturers, 18 lawyers, 11 workmen (of whom 7 are trades-union officials), 10 retired civil servants, and 26 " gentlemen," or persons whose independent means exempt them from the necessity of pursuing any regular occupations.

[2] Above, p. 345.

for streets, all new projects and improvements that may
properly be termed metropolitan in character are carried
out by the County Council; those that are not distinctly
of this nature are conducted sometimes by the joint

Public
works.

action of the council and the authorities of the local
boroughs affected, and sometimes, if the project be purely
local in character, by the borough authorities alone. The
cleansing, scavenging, and watering of all streets, however
constructed, are matters within the purview of the
boroughs; but jurisdiction with reference to the naming
or the renaming of streets is reserved by the County
Council. Traffic regulations for all streets within the
Metropolitan Police District (and this includes the County
of London) are made by the metropolitan police authorities. The bridges that cross the Thames (except those
within the limits of the old city) are constructed and
maintained by the County Council, which also has charge
of the Thames Embankment.[1]

Housing and
sanitation.

To the care of the council is further committed the
administration of the building laws, a jurisdiction that
includes the enforcement of the rules relating to the construction and maintenance of tenement-houses. By the
act of 1890, commonly known as the Housing of the
Working Classes Act,[2] the council is empowered to order
the clearance of unsanitary and congested areas whenever
these are large enough to be considered more than local
nuisances, and the boroughs are authorized to deal with
areas of minor extent. When there is any dispute between the two authorities as to whether an undertaking
is metropolitan or local in character, the Home Office is

[1] This brief outline of the council's powers has been condensed from the
" Statement of the Powers and Duties of the London County Council," which
is printed in the *Report of the Royal Commission on the Amalgamation of
London*, Appendix vii. Such changes as have been made since 1894 have been
duly noted.   [2] 53–54 Victoria, c. 70.

empowered to act as final arbiter. After a congested area has been razed, the council may erect and maintain improved dwellings or lodging-houses, which it may rent to private occupants; or the County Council and the councils of individual boroughs may jointly undertake projects of this sort, contributing to the cost in such proportions as may be agreed upon.

With respect to the provision of the major public utilities, such as water, lighting, and transportation, the powers of the County Council are not so broad. The whole question of London's water supply, for instance, was settled by Parliament in the Metropolitan Water Act of 1902, which mapped out a metropolitan water district including the whole of the County of London and a large circle of territory outside, comprising in all about six hundred and twenty square miles.[1] For the control of the water supply within this new district the act provided a Metropolitan Water Board of sixty-six members, selected by various authorities within the district, county, borough, and parishes, and including fourteen members of the County Council. This board forthwith took over, by purchase, the plants of all the private water companies operating within the district, and now has direct supervision[2] over all matters pertaining to this particular form of public service.

Major public utilities.

London's water supply.

With respect to lighting by electricity the County Council likewise has almost no powers. All the streets are lighted, either with electricity or with gas, by the boroughs; and electricity for private use is supplied either by the boroughs directly through plants which they own

Electric lighting.

---

[1] On the conditions prior to this time, see Arthur Shadwell's *London Water Supply* (London, 1899), and the *Report of the Royal Commission on the London Water Supply* (1900).

[2] *Fifth Annual Report of the Metropolitan Water Board, for the Year ending March 31, 1908* (London, 1908).

2 A

and operate, or by private companies that provide the service for them under borough franchises. The County Council has eagerly sought powers to deal with the problem of electric lighting, but Parliament has steadfastly refused to confer this authority. At the present time, therefore, the county authorities may neither own nor operate this service directly, nor may they grant any franchises for the provision of electricity. They have, however, some powers with regard to determining the location of cables and wires in the streets, and they may provide testing-stations.

London's gas.
The gas-lighting service of London is wholly in the hands of private companies, which carry on their operations under parliamentary franchises, and subject to such regulations as have been provided by statute, notably the various " sliding-scale " laws.[1] The County Council may neither own nor operate gas plants, nor may it exercise any effectual supervision over private gas companies operating within its territory. It has, however, secured the right to make regulations for the testing of gas, and in the exercise of this power has frequently come into conflict with the companies. The municipalization of this service has long been an important plank in the Fabian platform, and there is little doubt that the County Council would have assumed direct charge of the utility many years ago if the laws of the land had permitted it to do so.

London's tramways.
In the matter of transportation services the powers of the County Council are much more liberal than they are with respect to the provision of water and light. It has now acquired practically all the tramway lines within the

---

[1] A great deal of material relating to the working of these laws is embodied in the *National Civic Federation: Report on Public Ownership and Operation*, Pt. II. Vol. II. 113–247.

county ; and in addition it has authority to construct and
operate new lines, provided always that it obtains from
the borough councils, who are in all cases the local road
authorities, permission to use streets in which the lines
are to run, — an exceedingly important restriction, as will
appear later on. The jurisdiction of the County Council
is confined to surface transportation ; underground transit
is in the hands of private companies operating under parliamentary franchises. Supervision of transportation by
water is intrusted to a special authority, the Thames Conservancy ; but the County Council has been empowered
to engage directly in this service, and has for some years
operated a fleet of river steamboats for the transportation
of passengers from one part of the county to another.

Various other powers have at different times been given
to the London County Council. It has charge of parks and
places of recreation, except the royal parks and certain
local spaces that are left to the borough authorities ; and
in these parks it provides band concerts and other entertainments for the public. It licenses music halls and
theatres, except certain theatres that are under a royal officer, the lord chamberlain. It has power to establish technical schools ; and through its Education Committee,
which was invested by the London Education Act (1903)
with practically the same powers that appertain to
similar committees in the provincial cities, it exercises
supervision over other schools. Many functions of a minor
nature also come within its jurisdiction, — as, for example,
the appointment of coroners, the inspection of weights and
measures, the licensing of abattoirs, the enforcement of
regulations relating to hours of labor in shops, and so
on.

Minor public services.

For carrying on its work the County Council has
authority to levy annual rates, which are assessed and

The County Council's revenues.

collected substantially as in the other municipalities. It levies two rates each year, one for general and one for special county purposes, — the former for the maintenance of those services that extend throughout the county, the latter for the support of those that do not include the old city. These rates amount to so many shillings in the pound on the rental value of real property. With the per-

mission of the Local Government Board, or, alternatively, through authority obtained by private act of Parliament, the council is further empowered to borrow money, a privilege of which it has availed itself very extensively during the past decade or more. Some sweeping reform in the methods of assessment has long been sought by the Progressive majority in the council, on the ground that the means by which the annual revenues are now raised are not sufficiently broad and inclusive; for under the present system unimproved land, no matter how valuable on account of its location, pays no rates. The "dead hand of the land," it is claimed, has been one of the most formidable obstacles encountered by the council in the practical exercise of its powers.[1]   The council has also sought earnestly the privilege of assessing upon the owners of abutting property a part at least of the cost of public improvements,[2] a system that prevails very widely in American cities.[3]   This concession Parliament has occasionally granted, but always somewhat grudgingly and under

strict limitation.

Taken as a whole, the powers of the London County Council, despite the important restrictions set upon them,

[1] The chief arguments against the present system are given in Frederick Howe's *British City*, ch. xvi.

[2] In support of its claims the council issued in 1893 a publication entitled *Precedents of Assessment according to Benefits*.

[3] Victor Rosewater, *Special Assessments : a Study in Municipal Finance* (New York, 1893).

are extensive in scope and portentous in character. At the outset the new organization was endowed with prerogatives that made it the most powerful municipal council in the world ; but the vigorous and somewhat radical use which it at once began to make of its powers seems to have shocked parliamentary conservatism, till the feeling that no further functions should be intrusted to it soon came to be dominant, especially in the House of Lords. Thenceforth, when the council asked for new powers or for an extension of its old ones, it usually encountered refusal, even when its requests were to all appearances entirely logical.   Thus, Parliament effectually sidetracked its aspirations to control London's water supply by creating the Metropolitan Board, and frustrated its plans to secure charge of electric lighting by committing this function to the borough councils.   It has come to pass, therefore, that the powers possessed by the County Council are very far from displaying any logic or symmetry.   On the one hand, some functions that appear to be of little more than local interest or importance have been given to it ; and, on the other hand, some powers of a distinctly metropolitan character have been withheld from it and apportioned among the local authorities.   Indeed, the apportionment of administrative powers among the various London authorities, metropolitan, county, borough, and parish, not to speak of the special boards and commissions, is likely to appall by its very complexity and lack of reasonableness any one who seeks an elementary grasp of the situation.   It is only fair to add, however, that, needlessly complicated as this contemporary division of powers may appear, it is a vast improvement over the condition that existed prior to 1888, when the chaos of overlapping and conflicting jurisdictions served to render the government of London an excellent model

of what an effective municipal system ought not to
be.[1]

The council's method of work. It is, of course, obvious that a council of nearly one
hundred and forty members cannot efficiently perform
work of detailed administration. The London County
Council has not attempted to do so directly, but has
accomplished most of its labors through its standing and
special committees.[2] It meets, however, very frequently,
— once a week except during the summer months, — and
on these occasions determines the general course of municipal policy.[3] The chairman, who presides at the meetings, has nothing more than the usual powers of a
presiding officer; he is in no sense the executive head of
the county. The real work of administration is performed by the council committees, and the chairmen of
the more important of these committees are the dominat-
Its committees. ing personalities. Of the standing committees there are
about a score, among the more important being the
General Purposes Committee (which is made up of the
chairmen of all other standing committees), the Finance Committee, the Highways Committee, the Education
Committee, the Works Committee, and the Fire Brigade
Committee.[4] These committees are appointed, not by
the chairmen, but by the council itself; and, though some
rearrangement is made necessary after each election, it is

[1] See, for example, the description of London government given in J.
Toulmin Smith's *The Metropolis and its Municipal Administration* (London,
1852).

[2] The " Standing Orders " of the council, last revised in March, 1907, and
published the year following, regulate all important matters relating to procedure.

[3] The *Minutes of the Proceedings of the London County Council* are printed
weekly after each meeting.

[4] One of the clearest discussions of the London County Council's procedure,
and particularly of its committee system, is that presented in F. W. Hirst's
"London," in the *Schriften des Vereins für Sozialpolitik*, Vol. 123, pt. vii,
especially pp. 109–123.

regarded as desirable that the personnel of important committees be varied as little as is practicable. In the selection of its committees the London County Council shows to a somewhat greater extent than do the ordinary city councils the influence of partisan considerations. This is particularly true in the choice of committees that have to do immediately with the operation of the public utilities; for, if a majority of the members of any such committee were not in full sympathy with the majority of the council, there would in all probability be no end of difficulties in putting the council's policy into satisfactory operation. When the Progressives were in control of the council, they saw to it that a majority of the men on all the more important committees came from their own ranks; and when the Reformers got the upper hand a year or two ago they took the same precaution in their own behalf. The minority party is, however, invariably treated with consideration both in the selection of the nineteen aldermen whom the councillors add to their number, and in the organization of all the committees. In all cases, furthermore, individual capacity plays an important part in the work of selection.

Party influences in the selection of committees.

Each standing committee has its chairman, its vice-chairman, and from seven to thirty-five members. The chairmen are selected by the council, and in all the work of the committees exercise an important if not a dominating influence. They are the connecting links between the committees and the whole council, preparing for committee consideration such matters as the council may refer to it, and presenting to the council the committees' reports and recommendations. The committees meet either fortnightly or weekly as the pressure of business seems to require, and often for several hours at a time. In general operation and influence the council committees in

Organization and work of committees.

London do not differ greatly from those in the other cities of the kingdom : their sessions are attended, when necessary, by the paid officials of the municipality; they have no final powers, but may simply report to the council with advice as to action; and their influence rests wholly upon the fact that the council usually accepts their recommendations. No committee has authority, for example, to make an appointment to any office in the service of the county; but as a matter of practice the council is accustomed, whenever an appointment is to be made, to seek and to accept the advice of the particular committee within whose special sphere the appointee's work is to be performed. In all matters relating to public construction also, to the maintenance of public services, the awarding of contracts, and the purchase of supplies, the deciding power, though technically vested in the hands of the whole council, is in the vast majority of instances really exercised by the appropriate committee. It is, of course, entirely true that the council may upon occasion set aside a committee's recommendation, or accept its minority report, and this without creating any impression that it lacks confidence in the committee's general judgment or efficiency; but instances of this sort are not sufficiently frequent to disprove the rule concerning the practical finality of committee action. They come just often enough to impress upon the committees the necessity that their recommendations be prudent and carefully considered. From this point of view, indeed, the council's occasional recalcitrancy is a very salutary feature of its procedure.[1]

It has been pointed out that, in most of the English

Sources of their influence.

---

[1] For an outsider's opinions regarding the efficient manner in which the council performs its work, see G. L. Fox's article on "The London County Council," in the *Yale Review*, May, 1895.

cities, the council committees are disposed to lean more or less heavily upon the permanent officials whenever they have difficult administrative problems to solve, and especially when they have technical questions to deal with. The same is broadly true of everyday administration in London, particularly in recent years. In the first decade of the County Council's existence not so much dependence was put upon these officials, a circumstance probably due to the fact that, prior to 1888, the permanent officers of the Metropolitan Board of Works (to whose jurisdiction the County Council succeeded) were generally regarded as having been too influential and as having used their influence in pernicious ways. The practice of depending more and more upon the counsel of the paid officials has, however, been steadily increasing, a growth that has unquestionably been promoted by the fact that the chairmen of committees of the London County Council are not usually left in their posts for long terms of years, and hence do not have much opportunity to become skilled in the work of their respective departments. It seems to be fortunate that this line of development is being followed; for the English system of departmental administration by council committees appears to owe much of its general excellence to the substantial influence which it actually vests in the hands of municipal experts.[1]

Relation of committees to paid officials.

The permanent officials of the administrative County of London form, of course, a very large company and embody almost every imaginable form of skill, — legal, medical, educational, technical, and so on. From highest to lowest, all are appointed on the authority of the County Council to serve during its pleasure; and any one of them may at any time be removed by a majority vote of its

The paid officials of London.

---

[1] On this point, see Professor Lowell's paper on " The Need for Municipal Experts," in *Proceedings of the National Municipal League,* 1908.

members. In making its selections the council is subject to no civil service regulations imposed upon it by any higher authority, and in the exercise of its power of removal it is hampered by no external jurisdiction whatsoever. As in the other cities of the land, all appointments of any importance, though technically during the pleasure of the appointing authority, are virtually for life, or for so long as anything approaching satisfactory service is rendered. In the period of nearly twenty years during which the Progressives controlled the making of London appointments, they must in many cases have been more or less influenced by party considerations in determining their choices; yet the advent of the Reformers to power a year or two ago was not followed by a single removal of any consequence. As posts become vacant in the natural course of events, the Reformers will doubtless fill them with men of their own political creed; but that they will force vacancies in order to provide avaricious followers with due rewards for party services there is apparently no danger whatever. In London, as in the provincial cities, the only real barrier to the adoption of the spoils system with all its demoralizing concomitants is the existence of a public opinion which clings with steadfastness and loyalty to the idea that public office is a public trust. As a safeguard this has, however, proved entirely adequate.

In the exercise of its appointing power the London County Council proceeds along lines similar to those followed by the councils of the ordinary English boroughs. The higher posts it fills directly by calling for applications, referring these to the appropriate committee, and, as a rule, accepting the committee's recommendation. As party lines are perhaps more closely drawn in the metropolis than in most of the boroughs, the recommendations which these committees make are apt to have a distinctly partisan flavor; but this does not mean that the gloss of party prominence is made to cloak obvious lack of qualification. Although a majority of the committeemen will almost invariably prefer a candidate of their own political faith, they must have entirely other grounds upon which to justify their recommendation; and these grounds are usually to be found only in the personal fitness of the applicant.

The minor posts in the County of London are ordinarily filled, not by the council, but by the heads of the various departments in consultation with the appropriate committees, or more often with the chairmen of such committees. Sometimes, of course, individual councillors may, in order to secure favors for their constituents, bring pressure to bear upon heads of department or upon chairmen; but most councillors refuse to do this. Such pressure can, moreover, be effectually resisted. Thus, the Tramways Department, which employs thousands of car-drivers and conductors, is always glad to consider the claims of applicants who bear recommendations from members of the County Council; but it may be doubted whether such testimonials have any greater weight than those presented by citizens of equal prominence outside the ranks of the council. In the choice of his employees the general manager of the London tramway system has about as much freedom as that enjoyed by the corresponding executive head of any similar private enterprise. The council has, it is true, provided various general regulations relating to the minimum wages of employees in this department, the length of a day's labor, the provision of uniforms, and so on; but it has not attempted to interfere in the actual routine of appointments and promotions or in any other matter of detailed management. The same may be said of all the other departments;

The absence of patronage.

in each of them the permanent head has generous latitude.

The clerk of the council.

Among the permanent officials of the county may be mentioned, first of all, the clerk of the council. The act of 1888 made no provision for such an officer, but arranged instead that a deputy-chairman, selected by the council from its own ranks, should have charge of the clerical work. It soon became apparent, however, that there was serious need of an official who would do for the County Council what the town clerk does for the council of a borough, — in other words, an official who would do much more than keep the minute-book. Accordingly, in 1896 a change was made whereby the council was provided with a permanent clerk. In the hands of its present occupant the post has risen to one of high service and importance in London government, contributing in considerable degree to the smoothness with which the council has been able to carry on its work.[1] The clerk now has a staff of assistants who attend the various committee-meetings and perform the large amount of clerical labor which the system of committee administration involves.

The comptroller.

Then there is the comptroller, an officer who has general supervision of the county's financial affairs, with functions similar in the main to those of the borough treasurers, but with much greater responsibilities and vastly more work.[2] The complicated financial relations that exist between the County of London and the twenty-eight boroughs into which it is apportioned make the comp-

---

[1] The present clerk is G. L. Gomme, Esq., well known to American students of government through his volume on *The Governance of London*, and other works.

[2] These summaries concerning the duties of officials are compiled from the *By-laws and Regulations of the London County Council, revised to March, 1906* (London, 1906) ; the *Handbook of the Work of the London County Council* (issued annually since 1900) ; and the *London Manual*.

troller's office no sinecure; and the enormous indebtedness of the county provides an unusually large amount of routine labor. In addition, there is the task of financing the huge services (such as tramways) that are operated directly by the County Council, a burden which falls to some extent upon the Finance Committee of the council, but is by this body shifted more or less upon the comptroller's office. With all its other duties this office also has charge of all disbursements. A deputy-comptroller, two assistant comptrollers, and a staff of clerks aid the chief.

A third permanent official with large tasks and responsibilities is the chief engineer of the county, whose supervision of the system of main drainage is perhaps the most important of his multifarious duties, for in this particular branch of administration his department employs over a thousand persons. The construction of new main highways, the maintenance of the county bridges, and several other like matters of importance also come within the scope of the engineer's jurisdiction. The post commands a high stipend, and gives the incumbent charge of a corps of high-grade assistant engineers. It is now filled by one of the best-known construction engineers in Europe.[1] *The chief engineer.*

Other permanent officials are the solicitor, the superintending architect, the medical officer, the chief officer of the park department, the manager of works, and the chief officer of the fire brigade, each of whom has charge of the department indicated by his title.[2] There is also the general manager of tramways, with his two chief assistants (the electrical engineer and the traffic manager); and, finally, the housing manager, who has general care of the work which the council has undertaken in the way of *Other heads of departments.*

---

[1] Maurice Fitzmaurice, Esq., C. M. G., is the present incumbent.

[2] For details concerning the duties of these officials, see the *London Manual* (1907).

providing municipal dwellings. All these officials receive annual salaries varying from six hundred to two thousand pounds. The general staff of each department is ranged into seven classes, which pay different rates of remuneration. Men ordinarily enter the service as fourth-class assistants and work their way up to the highest order, where they are known as principal assistants.[1] From this class the heads of departments are usually chosen, but sometimes they come from outside the regular service altogether.

Summary of the council's work.

Since the London County Council has just rounded out two decades of existence, it may be opportune to note briefly just what it has accomplished during this period. To attempt this in even the most general fashion is, however, to enter the realm of controversy; for, although the new organization has unquestionably accomplished much for the metropolis, opinions do not agree as to just how far its work has been crowned with success. There are, indeed, very many who think that by profitless ventures into the domain of municipal trading the council has offset many of the achievements that stand to its credit.[2] It is admitted by all, however, that its work has been conducted honestly and with almost entire freedom from corruption or scandal, and that in every way it has marked a decided improvement over the achievements of its predecessors.

---

[1] The organization of the staff is as follows: (1) Heads of Departments, £600 to £2000; (2) Principal Assistants, £400 to £500; (3) Senior Assistants, £300 to £400; (4) First-class Assistants, £200 with increases of £15 per annum to £245; (5) Second-class Assistants, £150 with stated increases to £200; (6) Third-class Assistants, £100 with increases of £10 per year to £150; (7) Fourth-class Assistants, £80 with annual increases of £5 to £100.

[2] The annual reports of the council will repay study. Each contains a review of the year's work by the chairman, and these reviews are in many cases extremely interesting. Statistical data relating to every branch of the council's work may be found in the annual publication entitled *London Statistics.*

Since the council took hold of affairs it has greatly Marked im-
extended and improved the sewerage system of the me- provements in public
tropolis as regards both the collection and the ultimate services.
disposal of sewage.   It has now under its immediate control more than three hundred miles of trunk sewers, which
discharge over two hundred and fifty million gallons of
sewage per day.   It has constructed many new and important arteries of metropolitan traffic, notably the Black-
wall Tunnel, the Tower Bridge Approaches and Tunnel,
the new King's Way, the Thames Embankment Extension,
and the new Vauxhall Bridge.[1] It has provided a number
of new parks and places of recreation, besides greatly improving those which existed before the date of its organization.   Most of these tasks it has undertaken directly
through its Works Department, which was established in
1892 in order that the authorities might be rendered less
dependent upon private contractors.   Through this branch
the council has during the past fifteen years constructed
most of its artisans' dwellings, fire stations, streets, sewers,
and other works; for, though work done in this way seems
to cost somewhat more than when performed by private
contractors, it appears to be of higher quality and more
satisfactory in ultimate results.   Large improvements have
also been made in the fire-protection service.   Since 1889
the brigade has been doubled in numbers and the general
efficiency of the system greatly increased.   A small part
of the cost of maintaining this utility is borne by the national government, and the insurance companies are also
contributors to some extent; but the bulk of the expense
falls on the ratepayers, who contribute about a quarter of
a million pounds per annum for the support of the service,[2]

---

[1] The cost of these improvements from 1889 to 1907 amounted to upward of
£10,000,000.

[2] *London Manual* (1906), 42.

a sum, it may be added, less than the amount which the fire-protection service of the city of Boston costs its citizens.[1]

Tramways operated by the council. In providing major public utilities the council has shown unusual activity. The county now owns about one hundred and thirty miles of tramway lines, some of them acquired by purchase from private companies and some constructed by the council. Much more would have been undertaken in this direction but for the fact that the County Council cannot lay lines upon any street without the permission of the councils of the various metropolitan boroughs,[2] who, as the local road authorities, have time and again refused the desired license. Hence it is that the county is ill served as regards tramways, having only about one mile of lines to every 30,000 population, whereas more than half the cities of the United States have a mile or more for every 2000.[3] As a manager of tramways, however, the council has had tolerable success. The net profits accruing to the public treasury have not been very large, it is true; but this circumstance has been due, in part at least, to the policy of running workingmen's cars with reduced fares, to the increases that have been granted in the wages of drivers and conductors, to the institution of a ten-hour day for employees, to the inauguration of all-night car services, and to other like innovations of a costly nature. Moreover, the council has shown itself able to keep the management fairly clear of local politics, and, so far as its lines extend, to provide a satisfactory service. It is per-**Underground transit.** haps unfortunate that it did not exert more zeal in an endeavor to get hold of the underground transit facilities,

[1] Bureau of the Census, *Statistics of Cities* (1906), 136–137.

[2] 33–34 Victoria, c. 78, § 4.

[3] An interesting table, showing the ratio between street-railway trackage and population in the United Kingdom and the United States, may be found in H. R. Meyer's *Municipal Ownership in Great Britain* (New York, 1906), 89.

for it is here that the greatest developments of the future are likely to occur. At any rate, private companies have had their own way in this field thus far, and are likely to have it for many years to come.

In its attempt to cope with one other factor of the transportation problem of the metropolis, the council seems to have met with little success. There has always been an idea among Londoners that the congestion of passenger traffic in the streets might be greatly relieved by a more extensive use of the Thames; and for a time a steamboat service was maintained by a private company. The patronage proving too small, however, to warrant any extension of the service, the enterprise was in 1905 about to be given up altogether, when the County Council, despite the company's unprofitable experience, at once took over the investment, expanding and improving it at heavy cost. One of the Progressive leaders estimated that it could be made to yield a net profit of about £100,000 per annum;[1] but three years of operation have shown that the council cannot even make both ends meet, and must ask the ratepayers to shoulder an annual deficit as the outcome of the venture. This unfortunate experiment has laid the Progressives open to much criticism, and doubtless contributed somewhat to their defeat in the elections of 1907.

The Thames steamboats.

An important branch of the council's work is connected with the erection and maintenance of dwellings and lodging-houses for the working classes. The statutes require that, wherever the council displaces any population in order to make way for public improvements, it shall provide for the rehousing, in the immediate neighborhood, of an equal number of persons. In addition to these mandatory statutes a number of permissive acts have

The council's housing policy.

---

[1] Sir E. Cornwall, in the London *Times*, May 9, 1903.

2 B

empowered the council, as well as other local authorities, to demolish insanitary buildings and replace them by modern structures, due compensation being of course awarded to the owners of the expropriated property. Under both the above classes of powers the County Council has embarked extensively upon housing schemes. In one case it laid waste a tract of nearly fifteen acres and immediately rebuilt it with model tenements that now accommodate upward of 5000 persons.[1] Many less extensive undertakings of the same nature have been put through by the council, till at the present time the dwellings and lodging-houses which it has provided accommodate about 35,000 persons, a small-sized city of themselves. As to the success of these housing enterprises opinions differ widely; for one's judgment of the matter will depend largely upon whether one emphasizes the financial or the social aspects of the question. At any rate, the municipal tenements have managed to pay their way, which is all that has been expected of them.

The relation of the council to the system of education. By the London Education Act of 1903 the County Council took the place of the old London school board as the local authority for elementary education, its powers in this capacity being exercised through an Education Committee of forty-three members, which at the present time has charge of both elementary and higher education, including the management of the technical schools. In facilities of the latter sort London was, until very recently, singularly deficient; but during the last twenty years the council has achieved much in the direction of technical education, both by grants of money to institutions founded by private patronage and by direct undertakings of its own. The story of what it has accomplished

---

[1] This was the Boundary Street area in Bethnal Green. The experiment is described in Owen Fleming's *Working-Class Dwellings* (London, 1900).

in this field would, indeed, form one of the most creditable chapters in any narration of its work.

Besides all these main lines of service, there are various other fields of metropolitan administration in which the London County Council has displayed its activity. It has provided additional asylum accommodation for imbeciles and inebriates; although the general supervision of public charity is not within its jurisdiction, it has undertaken sundry measures for the relief of the unemployed; it has taken various steps to insure the proper preservation of historic places and buildings; it has provided a multitude of public entertainments, as well as unique facilities for athletic sports; and it has sought in many other ways to ameliorate the conditions of life in a congested area. If one will refer to the *Handbook of the Work of the London County Council*, which has been issued yearly since 1900, one will find that this list of minor or subsidiary activities is very extensive, touching almost every walk of everyday life in the metropolis. It has been the particular aim of the council to improve the conditions and environment of the employed classes; hence certain of its enterprises have been justified in the minds of some persons not so much for their intrinsic merit as for their "beneficent social reactions."[1] It has, for example, striven to take rank as a model employer of labor, in the hope that its example might be followed by private contractors; it has professed a "temperance policy," the chief principle of which is that, wherever the council acquires by expropriation any property which includes licensed premises, the licenses are thereby abandoned; and in many other ways it has shown that, however opinions may differ as to its soundness of judgment, it has at least been enterprising, versatile, and aggressive.

Other achievements of the council.

---

[1] George Bernard Shaw, *The Common Sense of Municipal Trading* (London, 1904).

Costly na-
ture of its
work.
All these undertakings have, of course, cost money. Most of them have been so broad in scope and expensive in character that they could not be paid for out of the annual rates; and the laws have not permitted, on any large scale, the practice of assessing a part of the cost upon the owners of private properties that may have been directly benefited by the enterprises. In some instances (as, for example, in the construction of the new King's Way) the council has taken over more land than was needed for the improvement, and then, to offset part of the expense, has sold back at greatly enchanced prices such portions as were not utilized. In the main, however, the county authorities have found it necessary to raise funds by borrowing on the credit of the munici-

The
county's
heavy debt.
pality. Year by year the county debt has mounted steadily, until at the present time the liabilities for which the County Council is directly responsible stand well above quarter of a billion dollars; and if to this be added the enormous consolidated indebtedness of the Metropolitan Water Board, which is for the most part an obligation upon the ratepayers of the county, the debt of London passes the half-billion mark. It must be remembered, moreover, that each of the twenty-eight London boroughs has its own local debt. If all these obligations be put together, it will appear that the English metropolis is bearing a grievous financial burden, most of which has been accumulated during the past two decades. Much of this debt is offset, it is true, by substantial assets in the form of a water system, several tramway lines, hundreds of workingmen's dwellings, and so forth, — a showing, it is fair to add, which could hardly be made by some American cities that have larger per capita debts than that of metropolitan London. Still, there is a feeling among a large element of Londoners that the County Council has

been too prodigal of the county's credit, that it has earned only too well its title of "the world's greatest spendthrift." [1] It is, indeed, to the strength which this idea has gained during the last few years that the accession of the Reformers to power at the last council elections may, in part at least, be attributed.   Nevertheless, there is no question that the efficiency of London's local administration has been improved almost beyond recognition during the past twenty years, and that for this betterment the London County Council should have its due share of credit.

When the administrative County of London was organ- *Local administration within the metropolis.*
ized in 1888, no serious attempt was made to reorganize
the structure and powers of the multitude of local author-
ities, such as parish vestries and district boards, that had been exercising all sorts of local functions within the limits of the new county.   For the time being these local authorities continued to exert such powers as had not been taken over by the County Council; but their work was entirely unsatisfactory, for there were so many of them that each exercised its functions within a very limited area. Within the limits of the old city there were no fewer than one hundred and thirteen parishes, each with its own vestry; and outside the city proper, but within the administrative county, there were seventy-eight parishes, of which thirty administered their local affairs through vestries selected by the parochial voters, the remainder being grouped into twelve districts with a board for each district. As the parochial voters had very little interest in the parish elections, and as the vestries and boards were composed for the most part of men who took little initiative in any local matter, the result was a hopeless decentralization of powers and responsibilities that ren-

[1] R. P. Porter, *The Dangers of Municipal Ownership* (New York, 1907), ch. ix.

dered almost impossible any considerable improvement in the local services which these authorities controlled.[1]

After spending considerable time in the discussion of various aspects of the problem, Parliament passed the London Government Act of 1899, which went into operation in the autumn of 1900.[2] The terms of this enactment left the parishes and parish organizations within the old city just as they were ; but the act abolished all vestries and district boards that had been exercising jurisdiction within the outer area, and then provided for the division of the administrative county (outside the city) into twenty-eight metropolitan boroughs. These boroughs are very unequal in area and population, but they show that an attempt was made to weld together units which had some

community of interest and tradition.[3] Each borough has a local government consisting of a mayor, not more than ten aldermen, and not more than sixty councillors, all sitting together to form a borough council. The councillors are elected by the borough voters, the aldermen and the mayor by the council. The qualifications for voting, the procedure in nominations and elections, and the other incidents of organization are almost identical with those in vogue in the ordinary boroughs of the country.[4] Borough elections are fought out upon party lines which coincide

[1] John Hunt, *London Local Government* (2 vols., London, 1897).

[2] 62–63 Victoria, c. 14. There are several commentaries on this enactment, including A. MacMorran's *London Government Act* (London, 1899), Terry and Morle's *London Government Act* (London, 1899), A. Bassett Hopkins's *Boroughs of the Metropolis* (London, 1900), and J. Renwick Seager's *Government of London under the London Government Act* (London, 1904).

[3] These boroughs are Battersea, Bermondsey, Bethnal Green, Camberwell, Chelsea, Deptford, Finsbury, Fulham, Greenwich, Hackney, Hammersmith, Hampstead, Holborn, Islington, Kensington, Lambeth, Lewisham, Paddington, Poplar, St. Marylebone, St. Pancras, Shoreditch, Southwark, Stepney, Stoke-Newington, Wandsworth, Woolich, and the City of Westminster.

[4] For further information, see John Hunt's *Metropolitan Borough Council's Elections* (London, 1900).

with those of county elections, the chief ground of division
in the borough as in the county being the issue of municipal socialism.   At the elections of 1900 and 1903, despite
the fact that the Progressives controlled the County Council, the Moderates carried most of the boroughs, and at the
elections of 1906 they made sweeping gains, — facts that
bear striking evidence to the volatile nature of London politics.   Party considerations are also influential in the organization of the committees through which the borough
councils perform the work of detailed administration; but
in all other important incidents the procedure of these councils conforms closely to that of the regular English type.

In scope of jurisdiction, however, the metropolitan borough councils are somewhat more limited than the councils
of ordinary cities.   Their main powers, given to them in
1900, are those which had previously been exercised by the
local vestries and boards, together with some minor functions that had hitherto been held by the County Council.[1]
In general the borough council is the local highway authority.   The county constructs all main highways; but
the borough attends to all purely local enterprises in the
way of street improvements, including maintenance, paving, lighting, cleansing, and watering.   It may also undertake the construction and maintenance of subsidiary sewers,
and the enforcement of most of the provisions in the Public Health Act.   It may provide workingmen's dwellings
and lodging-houses; it has charge of public baths and
wash-houses; it looks after the public libraries; and it
controls the local cemeteries.   The borough councils likewise enjoy wide powers in connection with the electric-
lighting service; at the present time about half of them
have municipal plants in operation, and the rest have

*Powers of
the
boroughs.*

[1] For an exact statement of these powers, see the special works cited above,
p. 374, note 2.

arranged with private concerns for the supply. For either direct operation or the grant of a franchise the authority of the Board of Trade is required; and this is had by means of a provisional order.[1] By similar orders of the Local Government Board further powers may be transferred to the borough councils from the County Council, or vice versa, whenever it appears that the County Council and a majority of the borough councils are in agreement upon the point of transfer. Matters which in the ordinary English city come within the control of the council, but which in the metropolitan boroughs are not exercised by the corresponding bodies, are main drainage, fire protection, police, transportation, water supply, and education.

On the whole, the system of borough government within the administrative county has worked well.[2] Local administration during the past eight or nine years shows a very marked improvement over the old régime of parish vestries and district boards, as any one who knows London, old and new, can readily testify. There are complaints, however, that the authorities of the boroughs, like those of the county, have been extravagant and have too often made their appearance in the loan market. Each borough council has, of course, power to levy its own local rate or municipal tax, and its action in this matter is not subject to the approval of any higher authority. If it wishes to borrow money, however, it must, save in exceptional cases covered by special statute, obtain the assent of the London County Council; and if that body refuse permission, it may appeal to the Local Government Board, which has authority to override the county's veto. Stringent as are these limitations upon the borrowing powers

Borough revenues.

---

[1] *Cf.* above, p. 268.
[2] A summary of the work performed by each borough is given annually in the *London Manual.*

of the metropolitan boroughs, they seem not to have proved a very effectual check; for all the boroughs have funded debts, and in some cases the indebtedness is very heavy.[1] Since, however, much of it has been incurred in the establishment of electric-lighting plants and the erection of workingmen's dwellings, there are in some boroughs marketable assets to nearly the entire amount of the liabilities.

With two functions that are ordinarily intrusted to local authorities neither the County Council nor the metropolitan borough councils have anything to do, — namely, with the control of police and of poor relief.   So far as the old city is concerned, the policing of London is in the hands of a committee of the Court of Common Council. Beyond the old limits it is in the care of a metropolitan police commissioner, who has jurisdiction over what is called the Metropolitan Police District, an area of nearly seven hundred square miles comprising the whole of the County of London and a considerable territory outside. This district was established by Peel's Act of 1829, which gave London its first body of professional, uniformed police.   By this legislation the new metropolitan police were kept directly under the control of the Home Office; but by the act of 1856, which changed the system in some respects, they were put in charge of a commissioner appointed by the home secretary and responsible to that official.[2]   This commissioner is not chosen for any definite term, but holds office during the pleasure of the Home Office.   Nor is the appointment political; for the incumbent is almost invariably a man of extensive administrative experience, and usually one who has been in either the

The Metropolitan Police District.

---

[1] The borough of St. Marylebone, for example, has an indebtedness that exceeds the total rateable value of all property within the borough limits.

[2] 19–20 Victoria, c. 69.

military or the civil service of the nation. The office commands a salary of £2000 per annum, and employs a corps of three assistant commissioners (appointed like the principal one) and five chief constables. The metropolitan police force now consists of over 17,000 men of all ranks, a membership that gives it place as the largest body of its kind. The cost of maintaining this huge establishment is considerably less than $10,000,000 per year, a sum that is exceeded by New York City in the maintenance of a force not half so large. Four-ninths of the total cost is assumed by the national government. The commissioner has entire charge of organization and discipline; but the financial administration of the force is intrusted to a receiver, appointed by the crown, who is responsible for the erection and management of all police stations, the awarding of contracts, the purchase of supplies, and for all other matters outside the actual work of preserving law and order.[1] The high standard of efficiency that is maintained by the metropolitan police force is a matter of world-wide knowledge.

The administration of London's poor relief is in the hands of more than thirty boards of guardians, which have jurisdiction over as many poor-law unions or local districts. These guardians are elective boards, each levying and expending its own special poor rate; but they are subject to very close supervision by the Local Government Board. The Metropolitan Poor Act of 1867 provided also for the establishment of an Asylums Board, which supplies and maintains public hospitals for the poor.

Organization of the metropolitan police.

Poor relief.

---

[1] There is, so far as I am aware, no monograph on the metropolitan police system. Only in the Home Office reports and the annual reports of the metropolitan commissioner can one find much information about its detailed organization, though mention may be made of the *Report of the Royal Commission on the Duties of the Metropolitan Police* (1908), and the long series of articles which appeared in the London *Times* during January, 1909.

These, then, are the various authorities, more than two hundred in all, that exercise jurisdiction within the confines of the metropolis.   More than half the number, including the vestries of one hundred and thirteen parishes with no powers of importance, operate within the limits of the old city.   In the outer area the present authorities are the County Council, the councils of the twenty-eight boroughs, the metropolitan police commissioner, the thirty-one boards of poor-law guardians, the Asylums Board, the Metropolitan Water Board, and the Thames Conservancy. There seems, in truth, to be considerable room for simplification in the machinery of metropolitan government.

CHAPTER IV

SOURCES AND LITERATURE

PART I

FRENCH CITIES

BIBLIOGRAPHIES. The best general bibliography of the literature relating to French and other European cities is R. C. Brooks, *Bibliography of Municipal Problems and City Conditions* (New York, 1901). This compilation is admirably arranged, and at the time of its issue was as comprehensive in scope as one could desire. In the field of French municipal administration much has been written during the past half-dozen years, however, and record of this has not been compiled in any single publication. The *Catalogue de la bibliothèque administrative du département de la Seine* (2 vols. Paris, 1898) affords useful lists of the older books; and the *Catalogue des livres composant la bibliothèque du conseil municipal de Paris* (Paris, 1904) contains a less extensive but more modern list.

OFFICIAL AND SEMI-OFFICIAL PUBLICATIONS. The national laws relating to French city government may be found in the *Bulletin des lois de la République Française* (issued annually), and the more important enactments, such as the municipal code of 1884, are also printed separately for distribution. Attention may be called particularly to Léon Morgand's commentary on this enactment (see below, p. 386). The discussions, which in the Senate or Chamber of Deputies precede the passing of laws, are embodied in the *Journal officiel* of each of these bodies, and printed annually under official auspices. The *Circulaires ministérielles*, issued by the Ministère de l'Intérieur, are printed at the time of issue for distribution to the local authorities. Copies of these are kept on file at the mairie of each commune. Statistical material relating to French cities in general may be drawn from the *Annuaire statistique*, and all matters relating to municipal finance are fully set forth in the annual publication known as the *Situation financière des communes*.

For the study of Paris government the chief official sources are the *Rapports et documents du conseil municipal de Paris* (printed annually since 1871); the *Bulletin municipal officiel de la ville de Paris* (issued from the Imprimerie municipale at monthly intervals since July 1, 1882); the *Annuaire statistique de la ville de Paris* (giving each year the figures for the second year preceding); and the *Encyclopédie municipale de la ville de Paris* (2 vols. Paris, 1904). The last-named publication contains a formidable amount of the most useful data, conveniently arranged for use. Paul Massat's *Manuel de législation administrative spéciale à la ville de Paris et au département de la Seine* (Paris, 1901) embodies the nearest approach which Parisians have to a city charter.

Some of the larger communes issue *Annuaires* and *Bulletins* dealing with their own local activities; but these are not of much service to the general student, as they usually require, for any intelligent interpretation, considerable knowledge of local conditions.

JURISPRUDENCE. The decisions of the administrative courts relating to the rights and responsibilities of French municipalities and their officials may be found in the *Recueil des arrêts du Conseil d'État statuant au contentieux, des décisions du Tribunal des Conflits, et de la Cour des Comptes* (2d series. Ed. Panhard. 78 vols. Paris, 1831–1908); but only a few of the largest American law libraries have this compilation. Léon Béquet's *Répertoire du droit administratif* (25 vols. Paris, 1882–1908) is more often available for consultation, and will be found nearly as serviceable. Additional volumes in both of the foregoing sets are published annually.

The civil code of France touches local administration at many points, as, for example, in connection with the care of the local *état civil*. On such matters accurate information may be had from any of the various commentaries on the code. Of these, Gabriel Baudry-Lacantinerie's *Traité théorique et pratique de droit civil* (26 vols. Paris, 1899–1907) has been found to be the most useful so far as it goes, but it is not yet complete.

PERIODICALS. France is well supplied with periodical literature devoted to the consideration of municipal affairs. The *Journal des conseillers municipaux* and the *Journal des maires* are monthly publications designed to be of service to persons directly connected with communal administration, and are devoted mainly to explanations of new laws, reports of decisions made by the administrative courts, and so on. The *Revue communale* (published monthly) and the *Revue municipale* (published semi-monthly) are somewhat broader in their scope, and usually contain some short articles, as well as administrative notes and news. In addition to those specialized periodicals, the regular political reviews devote considerable attention to municipal matters. The *Revue générale d'administration* is the most serviceable of these, and its regular numbers should be followed carefully by any one who desires to keep in touch with any branch of French administration. The *Revue politique et parlementaire* and the *Revue du droit public* frequently contain contributions bearing on French city government; and occasionally one may find informing articles of the same sort in the more popular publications, like the *Revue des Deux-Mondes*.

MISCELLANEOUS BOOKS (arranged alphabetically).

ADAMS, ALPHONSE. Guide pratique du percepteur-receveur municipal. Paris, 1897.

ANDERSON, F. M. Constitutions and other Select Documents illustrative of the History of France. Minneapolis, 1904.

> Contains English versions of the more important enactments relating to local administration, but not the Municipal Code.

ARNAT, G.   Les pouvoirs et rôles des maires au point de vue de la protection de la santé publique.   Paris, 1905.

ARTIGUES, G.   Le régime municipal de la ville de Paris.   Paris, 1898.
One of the best short works on contemporary Paris government.

ASHLEY, PERCY W. L.   Local and Central Government.   London, 1906.
A consideration of the structure and functions of the local authorities in France, Germany, and Great Britain, with special emphasis upon the relations of local to central government.

BABEAU, ALBERT.   La ville sous l'ancien régime.   Paris, 1880.
Somewhat obsolete, but contains much interesting and useful material.

BAUER, LÉON.   Les devoirs des maires et des municipalités en ce qui concerne l'armée.   Paris, 1894.
A lengthy discussion of the mayor's military functions.

BÉQUET, L.   Le conseil d'État.   Paris, 1891.
The powers and procedure of that court to which all contested matters relating to the powers of municipal officials are finally referred.

BERTHÉLEMY, H.   Traité de droit administratif.   5th ed.   Paris, 1908.
A very serviceable volume on contemporary French administration, concise, well arranged, accurate, and readable.

BERTHÉLEMY, H.   "Les institutions municipales de la France," in Schriften des Vereins für Sozialpolitik, Vol. 123, Part vii.

BERTHÉLEMY, J.   "De l'exercice de la souveraineté par l'autorité administrative," in Revue du droit public, 1904.

BLOCK, M.   L'administration de la ville de Paris et du département de la Seine.   Paris, 1898.
A comprehensive description of Parisian administration.

BODLEY, J. E. C.   France.   2 vols.   London, 1898.
An interesting work on the government of the French Republic, discussing in readable fashion many phases of French political life.

BOURDEAU, E.   "Le socialisme municipal," in Revue des Deux-Mondes, July, 1900.

BOURGUEIL, E.   Le vade-mecum de l'instituteur secretaire de mairie. Paris, 1892.

BRÈS, EUGÈNE.   De la municipalisation des services d'interêt public. Paris, 1904.

CÉNAC, ERNEST.   La liste électorale, sa composition et sa révision annuelle.   Paris, 1890.

CHARDENET, PANHARD, ET GÉRARD.   Les élections municipales.   Paris, 1896.
A commentary on the laws relating to municipal elections and electoral procedure.

CHASSAGNE, DR. Dix-neuf ans du conseil municipal élu de la ville de Paris, 1871–1890. 3 vols. Paris, 1893.

Contains much interesting matter concerning the personnel and work of the Paris council.

CHRÉTIEN, H. De l'organisation du conseil municipal de Paris. Paris, 1906.

A thesis. Somewhat superficial, but containing useful data concerning council procedure.

CLÉRAY, EDMOND. De la mise en valeur des biens communaux. Paris, 1900.

COLSON, C. Abrégé de la législation des chemins de fer et tramways. 2d ed. Paris, 1904.

COMBARIEU, A. "La mairie centrale de Paris," in Revue politique et parlementaire, July 10, 1897.

COURCELLE, L. Traité de la voirie. Paris, 1900

A standard work.

CROISSY, T. DE. Dictionnaire municipal. 2 vols. Paris, 1903.

An extremely useful work for general reference. It is almost indispensable to students of local administration in France.

DALEM, LUCIEN. Des voies de recours contre les délibérations des conseils municipaux. Paris, 1904.

DAURE, J. Manuel pratique de la révision des listes électorales. Paris, 1898.

DELAÎTRE, J. La municipalité parisienne et les projets de réforme. Paris, 1902.

A useful thesis.

DÉLEST, ANDRÉ. Nomination et révocation des fonctionnaires. Paris, 1899.

A doctoral thesis on the power of appointment and removal.

DESBATS, A. G. Le budget municipal. Paris, 1885.

DESTRUELS, E. Manuel de l'officier de l'état civil. Paris, 1903.

DISLÈRE, PAUL. Les devoirs des maires en cas de mobilisation générale. Paris, 1893.

A short discussion of the mayor's duties on the outbreak of war.

DODANTHUM, ALFRED. Des affiches électorales. Paris, 1903.

A discussion of the regulations relating to campaign posters.

DORLHAC, JOSEPH. De l'électorat politique: étude sur la capacité électorale et les conditions d'exercice du droit de vote. Paris, 1890.

DREYFUS, F. Manuel populaire du conseiller municipal. Paris, 1904.

DROUILLE, J.   Le pouvoir disciplinaire sur les fonctionnaires publics. Toulouse, 1900.

Thesis.

DUBARRY, G.   Le secrétaire de mairie.   Paris, 1892.

DUBOIS, PAUL.   Essai sur les finances communales.   Paris, 1888.

DUVERGIER, J. B.   Collection complète des lois, décrets, ordonnances, réglements, avis du conseil d'état.   107 vols.   Paris, 1834–1907.

The most comprehensive work of its kind.

ESMEIN, ADHÉMAR.   "La délégation du pouvoir législatif," in *Revue politique et parlementaire*, August, 1894.

ESMEIN, ADHÉMAR.   Histoire du droit français.   8th ed.   Paris, 1908.

The best elementary treatise on the development of local government law.

FAIRLIE, J. A.   "Municipal Accounts and Statistics in Continental Europe," in National Municipal League *Proceedings*, 1901.

FRANCESCHI, G.   Manuel des maires.   2 vols.   Paris, 1903.

An elaborate digest of mayor's powers and duties.

FRANCESCHI, G.   Dictionnaire des formules ou mairie pratique.   2 vols. Paris, 1903.

GASQUET, AMÉDEE.   Précis des institutions politiques et sociales de l'ancienne France.   2 vols.   Paris, 1885.

Includes much valuable data concerning the government of communes during the old régime.

GAUCHERON, MAURICE.   Études sur l'œuvre économique des municipalités.   Paris, 1906.

A thesis.   Somewhat general in scope.

GENNEN, RENÉ.   Organisation municipale de Paris.   Paris, 1904.

A doctoral thesis dealing mainly with projects of reform.

GOODNOW, F. J.   Comparative Administrative Law.   2d ed.   New York, 1903.

Originally issued in two volumes, but now to be had in a single book. It is much the best work of its kind in English.

GOURGEOIS, H.   Code manuel des conseillers municipaux.   Paris, 1890.

GUERLIN DE GUER, ALBERT.   La protection de la santé publique; les pouvoirs des maires et la loi du 15 février, 1902.   Caen, 1903.

HANOTAUX, GABRIEL.   Contemporary France.   3 vols.   London, 1903–1907.

An illuminating political history of France since 1870.   Not yet completed.

HÉLIE, F. A.   Les constitutions de la France.   Paris, 1880.

A convenient compendium containing all the more important enactments relating to local government.

JEANVROT, VICTOR. Manuel des élections municipales. Paris, 1892.

A useful work, but inferior to Saint-Lager's volume on the same topic.

JOUARRE, L. Des pouvoirs de l'autorité municipale en matière d'hygiene et de salubrité. Paris, 1899.

JOUET, ALPHONSE. Les clubs, leur histoire et leur rôle. Paris, 1891.

An interesting survey of the part which the "clubs" have played in the political history of France during the nineteenth century.

JOURDAIN, GUSTAVE. Les pouvoirs des maires en matière de salubrité des habitations. 3d ed. Paris, 1900.

LA CHAPELLE, SEVERIN DE. Le principe proportionnel dans les élections municipales françaises en 1904. Paris, 1904.

In support of the principle of proportional representation.

LACROIX, S. Rapport sur l'organisation municipale de la ville de Paris. Paris, 1880.

A plan for the reorganization of Paris government.

LAGARDE, M. La police municipale. Alençon, 1895.

LANFANT, H. Le conseil général de la Seine, ses origines et attributions. Paris, 1903.

LA SIZERANNE, ROBERT DE LA. Le referendum communal. Paris, 1893.

LAVALÉE, A. "Le régime administratif du département de la Seine et de la ville de Paris," in *Revue générale d'administration*, 1900–1901, *passim*.

An excellent outline.

LAVERGNE, P. "Du pouvoir central et des conseils municipaux," in *Revue générale d'administration*, 1900.

LAVISSE, E., and RAMBAUD, A. Histoire générale du IVᵉ· siècle à nos jours. 12 vols. Paris, 1896–1908.

A monumental history on the coöperative plan, but not yet completed.

LE BRETON, G. Du pouvoir réglementaire des préfets. Caen, 1900.

LECARON, F. Les origines de la municipalité parisienne. 2 vols. Paris, 1881–1882.

The earlier municipal history of Paris with special reference to the development of administrative institutions.

LEFOURNIER, J. "Les battues communales," in *Revue générale d'administration*, 1888.

LÉONARD, LÉONARD. L'élection du maire de la commune par le nouveau conseil municipal, — farce électorale. Paris, 1902.

Pamphlet in advocacy of popular election of mayors.

LESAGE, H. Souvenirs d'un maire-adjoint de Paris, 1880–1895. Paris, [1898].

2 c

LOWELL, A. L.   Governments and Parties in Continental Europe.   2 vols. Boston, 1897.

LUCHAIRE, ACHILLE.   Les communes françaises.   Paris, 1890.

A standard work on communal history.

MAGNÉ DE LA LONDE, EUGÈNE.   Les attributions du préfet de la Seine. Paris, 1902.

A discussion of the position and powers of the chief administrative officer of Paris.

MAITHOL, D. DE.   Code des conseillers municipaux.   Paris, 1885.

MARIE, J.   Le droit positif et la juridiction administrative.   2 vols. Paris, 1903.

MARTINEAU, R.   Les secrétaires de mairie.   Paris, 1906.

A thoroughly good short study.

MASSAT, PAUL.   Manuel de législation administrative spéciale à la ville de Paris et au département de la Seine.   Paris, 1901.

A most useful compilation of all the national laws relating to the administration of the French capital.

MERCIER, PIERRE.   Les exploitations municipales, commerciales, et industrielles en France.   Paris, 1905.

MÉTERIE-LARREY, L. F.   Les emplois publics.   Paris, 1888.

A treatise on the French administrative service, including appointments to public office and removals.

MEURIOT, M. P.   Des agglomérations urbaines dans l'Europe contemporaine.   Paris, 1898.

A statistical study of the causes and results of city growth in European countries.

MICHOUD, M.   "La responsabilité des communes," in *Revue du droit public*, 1897.

MIRIEL, ÉMILE.   Des rapports des municipalités et du pouvoir central en matière de police.   Paris, 1897.

MORGAND, LÉON.   La loi municipale.   7th ed.   2 vols.   Paris, 1907.

Of all works on French municipal government, this is the most useful to the general student.   It is a clause by clause commentary on the Municipal Code of 1884, avoiding needless detail, but covering in a comprehensive way every aspect of municipal organization.

MOSNY, M.   La protection de la santé publique.   Paris, 1904.

MOUNEYRAT, E.   La préfecture de police.   Paris, 1906.

A doctoral thesis presenting a serviceable, though not exhaustive, study of the office of police prefect in Paris.

NANCY, DURAND DE. Nouveau guide pratique des maires, des adjoints, des secrétaires de mairies, et des conseillers municipaux. Paris, 1905.

> A handbook of municipal duties.

PARKER, E. M. "State and Official Liability," in *Harvard Law Review*, March, 1906.

PELETANT, M. De l'organisation de la police. Dijon, 1899.

PÉNARD, D. Le problème du mode d'élection des conseillers municipaux de Paris. Paris, 1905.

> A plea for radical changes in the system of electing members of the Paris municipal council.

PERRIER, E. G. De la révocation des fonctionnaires. Paris, 1903.

PERRIN, EDOUARD. De la compétence réglementaire des maires, et des voies de recours contre leurs arrêtés. Paris, 1904.

PERRINJAQUET, JEAN. De la responsabilité des communes en matière de police. Paris, 1905.

> An excellent discussion of the subject in short compass and from a lawyer's point of view.

PILON, EUSTACHE. Monopoles communaux. Paris, 1899.

> A general summary of achievements in the sphere of municipal socialism.

PINDRAY, M. DE. De l'abstentionisme en matière électorale et des moyens propres à y remédier. Paris, 1902.

> A plea for the system of voting by proxy.

PORCHE, ALFRED. La question des grandes et des petites communes. Paris, 1900.

> A doctoral thesis on the question of uniformity in local administration.

POUDRA, A., and PIERRE, E. Traité pratique de droit parlementaire. 8 vols. Versailles, 1878–1880.

> The standard work on French parliamentary procedure. These parliamentary rules are usually followed by local councils.

PRÉVOISIN, ROBERT DE. Guide pratique d'électeur. Paris, 1906.

> A voter's handbook of municipal administration.

RAGEL, CHARLES. Manuel formulaire des actes de l'état civil à l'usage des maires. Paris, 1898.

RAMALHO, ALBERT. "Des changements de nom des communes," in *Revue générale d'administration*, 1896.

REISSER, E., et RIDEL, G. Guide électoral pratique. Paris, 1901.

> A voter's handbook of municipal law.

RENDU, AMBROISE. "La représentation proportionelle dans les conseils municipaux," in *Revue municipale*, March 3, 1900.

RENDU, AMBROISE. Rapport sur le service des eaux. Paris, 1905.

REY, A. Théorie du budget communal. Paris, 1897.

ROGER, LOUIS. Le domaine industriel des municipalités. Paris, 1901.

SAINT-LAGER, M. J. Élections municipales. 6th ed. Ed. C. Vuille-mot. Paris, 1904.

> A full presentation of the law and practice relating to municipal elections.

ST. PREUIL, L. DE. L'impuissance des partis politiques actuels en France. Paris, 1898.

> An attempt to explain the decentralization of political parties in France and to set forth some of the direct consequences of this feature.

SAUSSON, A. Des monopoles communaux. Paris, 1902.

SPIRE, ANDRÉ. Étude historique et juridique de la responsabilité des communes en cas d'attroupements. Paris, 1895.

STEHLIN, L. Essais de socialisme municipal. Paris, 1901.

TAILLANDIER, A. DE. Manuel formulaire de la révision de la liste électorale. Paris, 1893.

> A manual of forms and instructions for the use of the listing authorities.

TAUDIÈRE, H. " Restrictions apportées aux libertés locales depuis un quart de siècle," in *La réforme sociale*, November, 1904.

TCHERNOFF, M. Du pouvoir réglementaire des maires. Paris, 1899.

> Thesis for the doctorate at the University of Paris.

THORLET, LÉON. Traité des travaux communaux. Paris, 1894.

> A useful small treatise on the relation of the French municipality to its public services.

THORLET, LÉON. Traité de police à l'usage des maires. Paris, 1891.

TOUCHE, P. DE. Quatre ans de nationalisme à l'Hôtel de Ville, 1900–1904. Paris, 1904.

UZE, CHARLES. De la nullité en matière d'élections municipales. Paris, 1896.

> The law and precedents relating to the annulment of municipal elections.

VEL-DURAND, MAURICE. De la responsabilité des communes en cas de dommages par des attroupements ou rassemblements. Paris, 1902.

VERDALLE, ROMAIN. Traité pratique des emprunts des communes. Paris, 1881.

VILLAIN, G. Paris et la mairie centrale ; étude de centralisation administrative. Paris, 1884.

> Arguments in favor of Parisian administrative autonomy.

WEBER, A. F. The Growth of Cities in the Nineteenth Century. New York, 1899.

Much the best work, in English, on the phenomenon of urban concentration, its causes and its results.

PART II

PRUSSIAN CITIES

BIBLIOGRAPHY. The best collection of books and other publications relating to German city government is that contained in the *Magistratsbibliothek* at the Rathaus in Berlin. But there is, unfortunately, no recent catalogue of this collection. Brooks's *Bibliography* (see above, p. 380) includes extensive lists of publications on German municipal administration prior to 1901: for the special literature since this date one must trust the general bibliographical aids, of which the most convenient for this purpose is the *Uebersicht der gesammten staats- und rechtswissenschaftlichen Litteratur* (ed. Otto Mühlbrecht), published annually in Berlin. One may keep closely in touch with new publications relating to German municipal administration by following the book reviews in the *Centralblatt für Rechtswissenschaft* (ed. von Kirchenheim), published at Stuttgart.

OFFICIAL AND SEMI-OFFICIAL PUBLICATIONS. Imperial laws are printed in the *Reichs-Gesetz-Blatt*, and in the *Centralblatt für das deutsche Reich*. Sometimes new functions are intrusted to cities by these enactments. The Prussian laws relating to municipal and all other matters are published annually in the *Preussische Gesetz-Sammlung*: there is no compilation, so far as I am aware, which makes accessible in convenient form the various laws relating to city administration alone. The City Government Act of 1853 (*Die Städteordnung für die sechs östlichen Provinzen der preussischen Monarchie*) is printed separately, however, and particular attention should be called to the two excellent commentaries on this code by Ledermann and Oertel respectively (see below, pp. 393, 394). The ministerial instructions relating to the manner in which local authorities should perform their functions, as, for example, the *Instruktion für die Stadt-Magisträte vom 25. Mai* 1835, are also printed separately and may be found at any administrative library.

In the matter of statistical data relating to the cities of the empire, the *Statistisches Jahrbuch deutscher Städte* (ed. Neefe), which has been published at Breslau each year since 1890, is of the highest service. This is the most comprehensive and the most accurate compilation of its kind in any country. For data relating to Berlin, the *Statistisches Jahrbuch der Stadt Berlin* is of similarly high value. It is issued each year and is in every way a model publication.

Each large German city issues every year official returns of various sorts. Berlin, for example, publishes annually the *Verwaltungsbericht des Magistrats zu Berlin*, which contains full accounts, both statistical and descriptive, of the work of every municipal department. In addition the city publishes quinquennially a *Bericht über die Gemeinde-Verwaltung der Stadt Berlin.* The latest publication under this title covers the years 1900-1905 and has appeared in three volumes during 1907-1908. It contains almost everything that the ordinary student would be apt to look for concerning the actual working of Berlin administration. Publications of a more special nature are the *Vorlagen für die Stadtverordneten-Versammlung zu Berlin* (published before every meeting of the municipal council) ; the *Amtlicher stenographischer Bericht für die Sitzung der Stadtverordneten-Versammlung zu Berlin* (published after each council meeting) ; and the *Gemeinde-Blatt*, or municipal gazette, which contains all official announcements. Information concerning the personnel of Berlin government may be drawn from the *Personal-Nachweisung der Berliner Gemeinde-Verwaltung* (published annually).

JURISPRUDENCE. The chief Prussian administrative court renders each year a considerable number of decisions relating to the powers and responsibilities of city authorities, and these may be found in the annual reports of the court's decisions entitled *Entscheidungen des Oberverwaltungsgerichts.* The gist of these decisions is, however, usually to be found in the standard commentaries on the City Government Act.

PERIODICALS. Two well-known publications devote their attention exclusively to city government. These are *Die deutsche Gemeinde-Zeitung*, a weekly, which contains announcements, notes, and news of special interest to those actually engaged in local administration ; and *Die Städte-Zeitung*, a somewhat more pretentious periodical published fortnightly, and containing occasionally contributed articles. A third periodical, not so well known, is *Die deutsche Stadt*, published fortnightly at Dresden. Discussions of city problems are frequently to be found, furthermore, in the more general publications, such as the *Annalen des deutschen Reiches*, the *Preussische Jahrbücher*, the various "Jahrbücher" which cover the whole field of political science, and particularly in that admirable series the *Schriften des Vereins für Sozialpolitik.*

MISCELLANEOUS BOOKS (arranged alphabetically).

ANSCHÜTZ, G. Die Organisationsgesetze der innern Verwaltung in Preussen. Berlin, 1897.

A monograph on the laws relating to the Prussian administrative service.

ARNSTEDT, H. Das preussische Polizeirecht. Berlin, 1905.

A manual of police jurisdiction.

BELOW, GEORG VON. Das ältere deutsche Städtewesen. Bielefeld, 1898.

BERGHEIM, M. Der Wohnsitz in bürgerlichen Recht. Rostock, 1907.

A study of the principle of domicile in relation to voting and other civil rights.

BISHOP, J. T. "The Bürgermeister, Germany's Chief Municipal Magistrate," in *American Political Science Review*, May, 1908.

BORNHAK, CONRAD. Preussisches Staatsrecht. 3 vols. Freiburg in Baden, 1888–1890.

An exhaustive work on Prussian administration, including the administration of cities.

BROOKS, R. C. "Berlin's Tax Problem," in *Political Science Quarterly*, Vol. xx.

BROOKS, R. C. "The Three-Class System in Prussian Cities," in *Municipal Affairs*. Vol. ii.

The best discussion of the topic in English.

BROOKS, R. C. "Berlin without an Oberbürgermeister," in *Annals of the American Academy of Political and Social Science*, July, 1899.

DOVE, HEINRICH. "Berlin," in *Schriften des Vereins für Sozialpolitik*, Vol. 117.

The best short survey of contemporary Berlin administration.

DRYANDER, G. "Der § 16 der preussischen Städteordnung und die Hausbesitzer unserer Grosstädte," in *Annalen des deutschen Reiches*, 1903.

A criticism of the legal requirement that, in Prussian city councils, one-half the members shall be house-owners.

EBERT, L. Der Stadtverordnete im Geltungsbereiche der Städteordnung vom 30 Mai 1853. Berlin, 1883.

EHERSTADT, R. "System und Princip in der Berliner Stadtverwaltung," in *Preussische Jahrbücher*. Vol. lxx.

EVERT, GEORG. Die Dreiklassenwahl in den preussischen Stadt- und Landgemeinden. Berlin, 1901.

A small handbook devoted to explanations of the changes made in the three-class system by the Law of 1900.

GNEIST, RUDOLPH VON. Die nationale Rechtsidee von den Ständen und das preussische Dreiklassensystem. Berlin, 1894.

GRAIS, HUE DE, COUNT. Handbuch der Verfassung und Verwaltung in Preussen, etc. 17th ed. Berlin, 1906.

A very useful handbook of German government in general, covering the imperial, state, and municipal administrations.

GRASSMAN, R. Das Wahlrecht der Städteordnung. Stettin, 1876.

HABERLAND, G. Gross-Berlin, ein Beitrag zur Eingemeindungsfrage. Berlin, 1904.

HATTON, A. R. Digest of City Charters. Chicago, 1906.

Devoted mainly to American cities, but contains useful summaries relating to organization, procedure, and powers of city governments in the various other countries of Europe.

HEGEL, KARL. Die Entstehung des deutschen Städtewesens. Leipsic, 1898.

HEUSLER, A.   Der Ursprung der deutschen Stadtverfassung.   Weimar, 1872.

Studies in the origins of contemporary municipal institutions.

HILL, J. A.   "The Prussian Income Tax," in *Quarterly Journal of Economics*, Vol. vi.

HIPPEL, R. VON.   Handbuch der Polizeiverwaltung.   Berlin, 1905.

An inclusive and well-written work on police administration.

HULLMAN, K. D.   Das Stadtwesen des Mittelalters.   4 vols.   Bonn, 1826–1829.

An elaborate and trustworthy work on the organization and activities of German cities during the mediæval period.

JAMES, E. J.   "The Government of a Typical Prussian City," in *Annals of the American Academy of Political and Social Science*, May, 1900.

JASTROW, I.   Das Dreiklassensystem.   Berlin, 1894.

A description of the workings of the three-class system of voting.

JEBENS, A. W.   Die Instruktion für die Stadt-Magisträte vom 25. Mai. 1835 nach neusten Recht.   Berlin, 1901.

JEBENS, A. W.   Die Stadtverordneten.   Berlin, 1905.

A small manual designed for use by councillors and other active officers of Prussian city government.   It is informing and well put together.

KAPPLEMAN, H.   "Die Verfassung und Verwaltungsorganisation der preussischen Städte," in *Schriften des Vereins für Sozialpolitik*, Vol. 117.

Quite the best short survey of contemporary Prussian city government.

KAUTZ, G., and APPELIUS, F.   Preussisches Kommunalbeamtenrecht. Berlin, 1900.

The rights and responsibilities of municipal officials.

KLOSE, W.   Die Finanzpolitik der preussischen Gross-Städte.   Halle, 1907.

A doctoral dissertation.

KOEHNE, M.   Polizei und Publikum.   Berlin, 1897.

KOSLIK, P.   Das Bürgerrecht in den preussischen Provinzen.   Berlin, 1888.

A treatise on the law of citizenship.

KREMSKI, F.   Preussische Kommunalbeamtengesetzgebung.   Berlin, 1901.

A commentary on the laws relating to local office-holding.

KUNTZE, J. E.   Untersuchungen über den Ursprung des deutschen Städtewesens.   Leipsic, 1895.

KÜRSCHNER, JOSEPH. Das Staats-, Hof- und Kommunales Handbuch. Berlin, 1907.

An annual publication containing much useful data of a personal nature concerning all those who are prominent either in national, state, or local administration.

LEDERMANN, WALTER. Die Anstellung und Versorgung der Kommunalbeamten. Berlin, 1899.

A treatise on the installation, tenure, and rights of municipal officials.

LEDERMANN, WALTER. Die Städteordnung von 1853 nebst ihren gesetzlichen Ergänzungen. Berlin, 1902.

An inexpensive but exhaustive and trustworthy commentary on the City Government Act of 1853, with the subsequent amendments and several useful appendices. For the ordinary student it is the most serviceable handbook of its kind.

LEHMANN, MAX. Freiherr von Stein. 3 vols. Berlin, 1902–1905.

The best German biography of Stein so far as his administrative work is concerned.

LEIDIG, EUGEN. Preussisches Stadtrecht. Berlin, 1891.

A standard monograph on the subject, still frequently referred to, but now too old to be of high service.

LINDEMANN, H. Arbeiterpolitik und Wirthschaftspflege in der deutschen Städteverwaltung. Stuttgart, 1904.

A study of the relation of the city to public utilities, and particularly of municipal policy toward labor.

LINDEMANN, H. Die deutsche Städteverwaltung. Stuttgart, 1906.

A very useful and up-to-date survey of the whole field of Prussian city administration.

LOENING, E. "Die Verwaltung der Stadt Berlin," in *Preussische Jahrbücher*. Vols. lv.–lvi. *passim*.

MAATZ, R. Das preussische Einkommensteuergesetz, systematisch dargestellt. Berlin, 1902.

McNEILL, W. S. Eine Studie über die Aufgaben der Stadtgemeinden in der Wohnungsfrage. Berlin, 1902.

MAURER, G. L. VON. Geschichte der Stadtverfassung in Deutschland. 4 vols. Erlangen, 1869–1871.

An authoritative history of German municipal organization.

MAYER, D. E. Rapport sur les institutions municipales de Berlin. Paris, 1886.

MEIER, ERNST. Die Reform der Verwaltungsorganisation unter Stein und Hardenberg. Leipsic, 1881.

NÉZARD, H. L'evolution du suffrage universel en Prusse et dans l'empire allemand. Paris, 1905.

An outsider's view of the Prussian suffrage problem.

OERTEL, O.   Die Städteordnung vom 30. Mai 1853 mit Ergänzungen und Erläuterungen.   4th ed.   Liegnitz, 1905.

> The standard commentary on the City Government Act of 1853 and subsequent amendments thereto, by a writer who has had service as the Oberbürgermeister of a large Prussian city.

POLLARD, J.   A Study in Municipal Government: The Corporation of Berlin.   2d ed.   London, 1894.

> An elementary study, of service mainly because there is little else in English on the subject.

PREUSS, HUGO.   Das städtische Amtsrecht in Preussen.   Berlin, 1902.

> Studies in the jurisprudence relating to municipal office-holding in Prussia.

PREUSS, HUGO.   Das Recht der städtischen Schulverwaltung in Preussen. Berlin, 1905.

> A study of the relation of the city to its schools.

PREUSS, HUGO.   Die Entwickelung des deutschen Städtewesens.   Leipsic, 1906.

> This work is planned to occupy two volumes, of which only one has as yet appeared.   This volume presents a lucid and readable outline of German municipal development from the standpoint of an advanced Liberal.

REIMANN, A.   Der preussische Stadtverordnete, seine Rechte und Pflichten. Danzig, 1900.

> A guide to the rights and duties of municipal councillors.

ROWE, L. S.   Problems of City Government.   New York, 1908.

> Contains a chapter on municipal ownership of street railways in Germany.

SCHÖN, PAUL.   "Die Organisation der städtischen Verwaltung in Preussen," in *Annalen des deutschen Reiches*, 1891.

> An essay on the Prussian municipal system, concise and comprehensive.

SCHULZE, BRUNO.   Editor.   Die Städteordnung vom 30. Mai 1853 zum praktischen Gebrauch ausführlich erläutert.   Berlin, 1901.

> A convenient, small handbook containing a commentary on the City Government Act of 1853.

SEELEY, SIR J. R.   The Life and Times of Stein.   2 vols.   Cambridge, 1878.

> Contains a summary of the municipal reorganization of 1808.

SHAW, ALBERT.   Municipal Government in Continental Europe.   New York, 1897.

> Chapters V. and VI. deal in a popular way with German municipal government and administration.

STEFFENHAGEN, H.   Handbuch der städtischen Verfassung und Verwaltung in Preussen.   2 vols.   Berlin, 1887.

> An exhaustive and systematic discussion, clearly written.

STENGEL, KARL. Die Organisation der preussischen Verwaltung. 2 vols. Berlin, 1884.

An older work on Prussian administration, still frequently referred to by writers.

TAUSSIG, F. W. "Love of Wealth and the Public Service," in *Atlantic Monthly*, March, 1906.

THROL, F. Das polizeiliche Meldewesen. Berlin, 1897.

Describes in detail the system of police registration.

WAITZ, G. Deutsche Verfassungsgeschichte. 8 vols. Kiel, 1844–1861.

The second volume contains much relating to the development of German city government in earlier times.

"*Wer ist's?*" Berlin, 1908.

The German "*Who's Who*," published yearly.

ZELLE, R. Die Städteordnung von 1853 in ihrer heutigen Gestalt. 3d ed. Berlin, 1893.

A useful commentary in some respects, but quite inferior to those of Ledermann and Oertel.

PART III

ENGLISH CITIES

BIBLIOGRAPHY. On all matters pertaining to the history of English cities and the development of municipal institutions, Professor Charles Gross's *Bibliography of British Municipal History* (New York, 1897) is invaluable. In addition to extensive lists of books on general and municipal history this work contains useful selected bibliographies on such topics as municipal reform, the government of the City of London, the London County Council, and so forth. Brooks's *Bibliography of Municipal Problems* (see above, p. 380) contains a great deal of information concerning materials for the study of English city government, and on this topic is for all practical purposes a complete record down to the date of its issue in 1901. The unofficial publications since this date have not been listed completely in any single place, but one may conveniently follow the recent book literature in G. K. Fortescue's *Subject Index of the Modern Works added to the Library of the British Museum in the Years 1901–1905* (London, 1906); and the periodical literature in Poole's *Index to Periodicals*. Less comprehensive lists which may serve bibliographical purposes are the *Catalogue of the Contents of the Library of the London County Council,* published in 1902; the *Catalogue of Books in the Library of the Local Government Board*, printed a year later; and Sidney Webb's *Select Bibliography of Municipal Socialism* (London, 1900).

OFFICIAL AND SEMI-OFFICIAL PUBLICATIONS. All the laws relating to local government may be found, of course, in the Statutes of the Realm;

but the more important of them are printed separately and may be had from His Majesty's Stationery Office. Rawlinson's Municipal Corporations Acts (9th ed., London, 1903) contains all the more important enactments. Much material of the most useful character has been brought together in the reports of the various Royal Commissions and Select Committees which have from time to time inquired into some phase of municipal administration. Reports of character are listed in the *Catalogue of Parliamentary Papers published during the XIX Century* (London, 1901). Since 1900 there have been some important inquiries, notably that of the *Select Committees on Municipal Trading* (1903), and these are enumerated in the *Numerical List and Index to the Parliamentary Papers,* printed after each session. Of the earlier reports, two should be singled out as being invaluable to every student of English municipal affairs, namely, the *Report of the Royal Commission on Municipal Corporations* (1835), and the *Report of the Royal Commission on the Amalgamation of London* (1894). The last-named report, with its voluminous minutes of evidence, forms a veritable storehouse of data relating to every branch of actual borough administration.

Other official publications to which direct reference should be made when occasion requires are the annual *Report of the Local Government Board* and the blue books which each year contain the *Returns of the Board of Trade.* The latter body issues each year its *Annual Returns of Tramway and Gas Undertakings* as well as various other statements. All publications of this sort may be had at a nominal price on application to the King's Printers (Messrs. Eyre and Spottiswoode).

For statistical information a very handy volume (which though not official is compiled from the official returns) is Robert Donald's *Municipal Year Book of the United Kingdom,* issued annually in the early months of the year. This compilation contains statistical and other matter relating to every borough of Great Britain and Ireland, all conveniently arranged for use even by the untrained. It is to this volume that one should first turn for information concerning the administrative activities of any English city. A. E. Lauder's *Municipal Manual* is a useful yearly handbook of municipal powers; and for any information relative to the personnel of English local government, reference may be made to the *Local Government Manual,* which has made its appearance each year with unfailing regularity for over half a century.

Official publications relating to London there are in plenty. The *Minutes of the Proceedings of the London County Council* are printed weekly, and although intended primarily for members, may be had by any outsider who cares to pay the subscription of thirty shillings per year. Each year the Council issues its *Annual Report,* a feature of this publication being a review of the Council's work for the year written by its chairman. The *Handbook of the Work of the London County Council,* a one-shilling publication issued each year since 1900, gives the same data in more condensed form. The Council has also published many interesting documents embodying the results of inquiries made by its committees on different occasions and the reports of its various chief officials. A full list of these may be found in the catalogue of Messrs. P. S. King & Son, publishers to the London County Council.

London Statistics is the title of the publication to which reference should be made for accurate figures relating to any department of metropolitan administration. Volume XVII., recently issued, gives the figures for the fiscal year 1907–1908. Those who are loth to enter this wilderness of statistics may be referred to the *Statistical Abstract for London*, an annual digest of the larger compilation. The *London Manual*, an unofficial handbook based upon official returns, is printed yearly, and includes within its covers about all the information the general student of local government is apt to seek.

PERIODICALS. The *Municipal Journal*, published weekly in London, is the only important periodical publication devoting its pages exclusively to the affairs of British municipalities. There are, however, several technical journals like *The Tramway and Railway World*, *The Electric Engineer*, the *Journal of Gas Lighting*, and *The Surveyor*, which deal in almost every issue with matters of municipal trading. Mention may also be made of the year-books or municipal diaries which most of the large cities issue annually or oftener, and which doubtless serve a useful purpose in making the citizens familiar with the personnel and powers of their local authorities. The *Fabian Tracts* issued from time to time by the Fabian Society are usually both interesting and informing.

MISCELLANEOUS BOOKS (arranged alphabetically).

ARMINJON, PIERRE. L'administration locale en Angleterre. Paris, 1895.

Contains some interesting comparison of English with French methods in local government and central supervision.

ASCHROTT, P. F. The English Poor Law System. London, 1902.

The relation of the local authorities to the problem of public charity.

ASHLEY, PERCY. English Local Government. London, 1905.

A small one-shilling manual which in less than two hundred pages gives an admirable résumé of the whole field.

AUSTIN, E. The Light Railways Act of 1896. 2d ed. London, 1899.

A manual of the law relating to street railways.

AVEBURY, LORD (Sir John Lubbock). Municipal and National Trading. London, 1907.

In opposition to the policy of municipal ownership and operation.

BALFOUR, GRAHAM. The Educational Systems of Great Britain and Ireland. 2d ed. London, 1904.

The best short treatise on English school administration and the powers of the Education Committee of the municipal council.

BEARD, C. A.   The Office of Justice of the Peace in England.   New York, 1904.

BRICE, S. W.   The Law relating to Tramways and Light Railways. London, 1898.

The best commentary on the legal powers of the city with reference to street railways.

CANAAN, E.   History of Local Rates in England.   London, 1896.

CASSON, W. A.   Decisions of the Local Government Board.   Issued annually.

CHANCE, W.   Our Treatment of the Poor.   London, 1899.

A readable discussion of the English poor-relief system.

CLIFFORD, F.   History of Private Bill Legislation.   2 vols.   London, 1885–1887.

The chief authority on the subject.

COLBY, C. W.   "The Growth of Oligarchy in English Towns," in *English Historical Review*, Vol. v.

DARWIN, LEONARD.   Municipal Trade.   New York, 1903.

The best presentation of the case against municipal operation of public services.

DARWIN, LEONARD.   Municipal Ownership.   London, 1907.

A restatement in condensed form of the main arguments set forth in the same author's larger work.

DAVIES, D. H.   The Cost of Municipal Trading.   Westminster, 1903.

A pamphlet.

DAY, S. H.   Editor.   Rogers on Elections.   3 vols.   London, 1894.

Vol. iii. is devoted entirely to municipal elections, covering this subject in the most thorough fashion.

DEWSNUP, E. R.   The Housing Problem in England.   Manchester, 1907.

DICEY, A. V.   Law and Public Opinion in England.   London, 1905.

DICEY, A. V.   The Privy Council.   London, 1887.

DILLON, J. F.   The Law of Municipal Corporations.   2 vols.   Boston, 1890.

The most elaborate work of its kind, it still remains in many respects the best. A new edition is now in preparation.

DOLMAN, F.   Municipalities at Work.   London, 1895.

A summary of English municipal activities.   Now somewhat out of date.

EATON, DORMAN B.   The Civil Service in Great Britain.   New York, 1880.

Encyclopædia of Local Government Law. Ed. J. Scholefield. 6 vols. London, 1905–1908.

Contains a great many informing but concisely-written articles on matters of borough administration.

FAIRLIE, J. A. Essays in Municipal Administration. New York, 1908.

Chapter xv. deals with municipal activities in Great Britain.

FOWLE, T. W. The Poor Law. 2d ed. London, 1893.

FOWLER, H. H. Municipal Finance and Municipal Enterprise. London, 1900.

A pamphlet.

FOX, G. L. "The London County Council," in Yale Review, 1895.

GLEN, W. C. The Laws of Public Health. 12th ed. London, 1899.

GLEN, W. C. Poor Law Orders. 11th ed. London, 1898.

A compilation of the orders issued by the Local Government Board as central poor-law authority.

GOMME, G. L. Lectures on the Principles of Local Government. London, 1897.

GOMME, G. L. The Governance of London. London, 1907.

An elaborate treatise on the earlier municipal history of London by a scholarly historian, now clerk of the London County Council.

GREEN, MRS. J. R. Town Life in the Fifteenth Century. 2 vols. London, 1895.

HADDEN, R. H. Handbook to the Local Government Act of 1894. London, 1895.

HIRST, F. W. "Municipalities in England," in Schriften des Vereins für Sozialpolitik, Vol. 123, Part vii.

HOPKINS, A. BASSETT. The Boroughs of the Metropolis. London, 1900.

HOWE, FREDERICK. The British City. New York, 1907.

A highly eulogistic description of British municipal administration, and especially of British achievements in the domain of public ownership and operation.

HUGO, C. Städteverwaltung und Munizipal-Sozialismus in England. Stuttgart, 1897.

English experience in municipal trading from a German standpoint.

HUNT, J. London Local Government. 2 vols. London, 1897.

Discusses the powers and duties of parish authorities prior to the reorganization of 1899. Is still valuable as an exposition of parish administration within the limits of the old city.

HUNT, J. The London Government Act. London, 1899.

A commentary on the law which created the London boroughs. Contains useful notes.

Hunt, J.   The Metropolitan Borough Council Elections.   London, 1900.

Jenks, E.   The Outlines of English Local Government.   London, 1894.
A useful little book in its time, but now somewhat out of date.

Keen, F. N.   Urban Police and Sanitary Legislation.   London, 1904.

Konstam, E. M.   Rates and Taxes.   London, 1906.
The law and practice of local taxation.

Lee, Melville.   A Short History of Police in England.   2d ed.   London, 1905.
Contains useful information concerning earlier police organization and the conditions which led to the passing of the Metropolitan Police Act of 1829.

Lloyd, J. S.   Municipal Elections and How to fight Them.   London, 1906.
A popular manual for the use of local politicians, containing much shrewd advice to candidates and their agents.

Lonsdale, S.   The English Poor Laws.   London, 1897.

Lowell, A. L.   The Government of England.   2 vols.   New York, 1908.
An authoritative work on the structure and functions of English government in general, containing several masterly chapters on local administration.

Macassey, L.   Private Bills and Provisional Orders.   London, 1887.

Maitland, F. W.   Justice and Police.   London, 1885.
Some matter relating to the local administration of justice.

Maitland, F. W.   Township and Borough.   London, 1898.

Maltbie, M. R.   "The Local Government Board," in *Political Science Quarterly*, June, 1898.

Maltbie, M. R.   English Local Government of To-day.   London, 1897.

Merewether, H. A., and Stephens, A. J.   History of the Boroughs and Municipal Corporations of the United Kingdom.   3 vols.   London, 1835.
The most elaborate of all the older treatises on English municipal history, and commonly regarded as the best among them.   It was written to influence public opinion in favor of municipal reform.

Meyer, H. R.   Municipal Ownership in Great Britain.   New York, 1906.
An able but obviously biassed discussion of the subject.

National Civic Federation: Commission on Public Ownership and Operation.   Report on Municipal and Private Operation of Public Utilities.   3 vols.   New York and London, 1907.
Contains a great deal of statistical and descriptive data relating to English municipal administration, all carefully arranged and indexed.

Odgers, W. B.   Local Government.   London, 1899.
A convenient small volume giving a general survey of the whole field of English local government.

OSTROGORSKI, M. Democracy and the Organization of Political Parties. 2 vols. London, 1902.

The standard work on political parties in England and elsewhere.

PORTER, R. P. The Dangers of Municipal Ownership. New York, 1907.

Mainly a criticism of the financial results of municipal trade.

PROBYN, J. W. Editor. Local Government and Taxation. Cobden Club Essays. London, 1875.

A collection of essays on different subjects connected with local administration in England and abroad. Now somewhat obsolete, but useful on matters of historical development.

RAWLINSON, SIR C. Municipal Corporations Acts, and Other Enactments. 9th ed. London, 1903.

A useful compendium of the laws relating to city government in England.

REDLICH, J., and HIRST, F. W. Local Government in England. 2 vols. London, 1903.

Much the best work on the general field of English local government. Vol. ii. contains several valuable chapters relating to different phases of borough administration.

RICARDS, A. G., and PEMBER, F. W. The Metropolis Water Act of 1902. London, 1903.

Explains fully the organization and powers of the Metropolitan Water Board.

RYDE, W. C. The Law and Practice of Rating. London, 1904.

Explains in detail the methods by which boroughs raise the larger part of their annual revenues.

SEAGER, J. RENWICK. The Government of London under the London Government Act. London, 1902.

A very useful volume on the organization and powers of the metropolitan boroughs.

SHADWELL, ARTHUR. The London Water Supply. London, 1899.

An analysis of conditions prior to the passing of the Metropolis Water Act.

SHAW, ALBERT. Municipal Government in Great Britain. New York, 1898.

A very sympathetic study of the subject by a distinguished American journalist. It is an unusually readable book.

SHAW, GEORGE BERNARD. The Common Sense of Municipal Trading. London, 1904.

A cleverly-executed argument in support of municipal socialism.

SIMON, J. English Sanitary Institutions. London, 1897.

SINZHEIMER, LUDWIG. Der Londoner Grafschaftsrat. Stuttgart, 1900.

Originally planned to present, in two volumes, a narrative of the achievements of the London County Council. The first volume (which alone has yet appeared) deals in detail with the activities of the Metropolitan Board of Works, whose functions the Council took over in 1888.

2 D

SMITH, J. TOULMIN. The Metropolis and its Municipal Administration. London, 1852.

> A study of the administration of unreformed London.

SMITH, W. R. Municipal Trading in Great Britain. Toronto, 1904.

SYKES, J. F. Public Health and Housing. London, 1901.

THOMPSON, W. The Powers of Local Authorities. *Fabian Tract No. 101.* London, 1900.

> Makes clear a complicated subject.

VAUTHIER, MAURICE. Le gouvernement local d'Angleterre. Brussels, 1895.

VINE, J. R. SOMERS. English Municipal Institutions. London, 1879.

> An older work which will still be found useful on matters relating to the development of institutions.

WALPOLE, SIR SPENCER. Life of Lord John Russell. 2 vols. London, 1889.

> Contains interesting matter relating to the passage of the Municipal Corporations Act of 1835.

WEBB, SIDNEY. London Education. London, 1904.

> Discusses the new régime in London Education following the Act of 1902.

WEBB, SIDNEY. The London Programme. London, 1891.

WEBB, SIDNEY. Socialism in England. London, 1893.

WEBB, SIDNEY and BEATRICE. English Local Government from the Revolution to the Municipal Corporations Act. 3 vols. London, 1904–1908.

> The most exhaustive modern work. To the student of borough government vol. iii. is of the highest service.

WHALE, GEORGE. Greater London and its Government. London, 1888.

WHELEN, F. London Government. London, 1898.

WHEELER, F. G. The Practice of Private Bills. London, 1900.

WHITMORE, C. A. Municipal London. London, 1900.

WRIGHT, R. S., and HOBHOUSE, H. Local Government and Local Taxation. 2d ed. London, 1894.

> Of special service to the student of the financial powers of the boroughs.

INDEX

By JOHN FAIRLIE, Ph.D., Professor of Administrative Law in
the University of Michigan

Municipal Administration

Cloth, 8vo, xiii + 448 pages, $3.00 net; by mail, $3.18

The work begins with a historical survey of cities and municipal government. In the second part there is a general survey of the active functions of municipal administration. The third part deals with the problems
of municipal finance. In the fourth part the various methods and problems of municipal organization are discussed with special reference to the
recent tendencies of reform in American cities.

The book aims to give a general knowledge of the whole field of municipal administration for those interested in public affairs, and at the same
time to form the groundwork for more detailed investigation by those
who make this a special field for either academic study or practical work.

Essays in Municipal Administration

Cloth, 8vo, viii + 374 pages, $2.50 net; by mail, $2.70

" In the United States students of municipal government have come to
regard Professor Fairlie as one of our most trustworthy writers on their
subject. His work has been distinguished by a broad and accurate
knowledge of the facts and sanity of view. . . . All together the volume
forms a useful commentary on many phases of municipal government
here and abroad." — *American Journal of Sociology.*

By LORD AVEBURY (Sir John Lubbock)

On Municipal and National Trading

Limp cloth, 8vo, 178 pages, $1.00 net; by mail, $1.08

" It has been generally agreed that it sums up more conclusively than any
other work the arguments against the municipal ownership of public
utilities." — *Chicago Evening Post.*

PUBLISHED BY

THE MACMILLAN COMPANY
64–66 FIFTH AVENUE, NEW YORK

By FRANK J. GOODNOW, A.M., LL.D., Professor of Administrative Law in Columbia University

Municipal Problems

Columbia University Press, cloth, 12mo, 321 pp., $1.50 net

A discussion of municipal organization in the United States, and of the problems concerned, which the *London Liberal* describes as : "One that all those interested in municipal matters should read. . . . We question if any book before has achieved quite its important service to what may be termed theoretic municipalism."

Municipal Home Rule

A Study in Administration

Columbia University Press, cloth, 12mo, $1.50 net

An attempt to ascertain what have been the effects of the various constitutional provisions adopted in the United States for the purpose of securing municipal home rule ; what according to the decision of our courts was the content of the sphere of municipal as distinguished from state activity ; and what had been the success of the methods adopted in foreign countries to insure municipal self-government.

By HUGO RICHARD MEYER, Author of " Government Regulation of Railway Rates "

Municipal Ownership in Great Britain

Cloth, 12mo, $1.50 net; by mail, $1.62

"It is of value in laying emphasis on aspects of the question which the advocates of municipal ownership are prone to forget, and should, consequently, make for more careful and intelligent discussion of the subject." — *Outlook.*

By SAMUEL WHINERY, New York City Engineer

Municipal Public Works

Their Inception, Construction, and Management

Cloth, 8vo, $1.50 net; by mail, $1.63

The book aims to present clearly, concisely, and impartially what is needed to enable public boards of administration to judge wisely of the work they are committing to public officers ; and more, to make possible the comparison of methods in force for some time with those latest adopted elsewhere, with a view to the improvement of public service.

PUBLISHED BY

THE MACMILLAN COMPANY
64-66 FIFTH AVENUE, NEW YORK

The Government of England

By A. LAWRENCE LOWELL

President of Harvard University

Formerly Professor of the Science of Government
Author of " Colonial Civil Service," etc.

*In two volumes.   Bound in the style of Bryce's
"American Commonwealth."   Cloth, 8vo, $4 net*

PUBLISHED BY

THE MACMILLAN COMPANY
64-66 FIFTH AVENUE, NEW YORK